Always *at the* Frontier

SAINT LOUIS UNIVERSITY 1818-2018

BY DOLORES M. BYRNES
WITH JOHN W. PADBERG, S.J. AND JOHN WAIDE

SAINT LOUIS
UNIVERSITY™

— EST. 1818 —

The fonts in this book are Crimson and Brandon Grotesque.
The book was printed on 100# Endurance silk book.

Printed by The Printing Source: St. Louis, Missouri
ISBN: 978-0-692-90251-6

Cover: Saint Louis University's north campus at Grand
and Lindell boulevards, photograph by Justin Barr

Lead Author and Editor: Dolores Byrnes, Ph.D.,
with John W. Padberg, S.J., and John Waide
Graphic Design and Layout: Dana Hinterleitner
Contributing authors and researchers: Alicia Detelich, Christy Finsel,
Gregory Pass, Ph.D., Maureen Wangard, Ph.D.

TABLE OF CONTENTS

5   Introduction

CHAPTER 1
6   "It will require a miracle to give us a college at St. Louis" 1818-1832
Bishop DuBourg, page 10
Osage and Jesuits, page 12
Slavery, page 21
A Visitor from Rome, page 26

CHAPTER 2
30   A true university 1833-1867
Father Peter John De Smet, S.J., page 33
Meteorology, page 40

CHAPTER 3
56   "A feast of reason and spirit" 1868-1913
Father Rudolph Meyer, S.J., page 64
Rerum Novarum, page 67
Father William Banks Rogers, S.J., page 78

CHAPTER 4
86   "Beyond the possibility of disaster or retrogression" 1914-1948
"Our poor, war-torn world," page 92
Father Alphonse Schwitalla, S.J., page 106
Integration, page 108

CHAPTER 5
116   "A civic jewel" 1949-1979
A Soccer Hotbed, page 119
Father Paul Reinert, S.J., page 125
Dr. Edward A. Doisy, page 129
Vatican Film Library, page 132
Saint Louis University in Spain, page 137
Father Walter Ong, S.J., page 139

CHAPTER 6
146   "Our campus is the community" 1979-2018
Father Thomas Fitzgerald, S.J., page 152
Father Lawrence Biondi, S.J., page 156
Dr. Fred Pestello, page 175

APPENDICES

182   PRESIDENTS of Saint Louis University

188   HONORARY DEGREE RECIPIENTS and COMMENCEMENT SPEAKERS

204   NOTES

211   SOURCES CONSULTED

214   ACKNOWLEDGMENTS

215   CREDITS

219   INDEX

A Message from President Fred P. Pestello

The Society of Jesus was formed in 1540 by ten men; principal among them was Ignatius of Loyola. They undertook a particular vow of obedience to Pope Paul III and to all of his successors, to go to "whatever provinces he shall wish to send us." A teaching order, their spark was soon kindled in North America, and in time, Jesuits shared their unique form of discipline and brilliance in the Middle West of the United States of America. Saint Louis University was at the base of the Missouri Mission, elevated to the status of a Province in 1863. In the American West, the Province and its university served as a crucible for an educational transformation that has no parallel.

Established in 1818 by Bishop Louis DuBourg, Saint Louis University and Saint Louis University High School are the oldest St. Louis-founded institutions in the city. We gained this honor in 2001, when Teutenberg's Bakery (founded 1812) closed.[1] Saint Louis University is proud of our role in this city, our identity within the Society of Jesus, and our position in American Catholic higher education.

We are especially proud of the achievements of the people who work and study at this university—today and over the last two hundred years. Furthermore, we are thankful for the organizations and people who have partnered with the university, nudging us to be a better neighbor and institution. Having spent a large part of my life studying and working at Jesuit institutions, I am deeply grateful for the Society of Jesus who saw Saint Louis University's potential early on, and who continue to believe in and support SLU today. Many thousands of people have contributed to this, our collective story, and while their names may not be listed in this book, their impact is certainly not forgotten.

Reflecting upon two hundred years of institutional history, we renew our commitment and remain humbled by our mission: the pursuit of truth for the greater glory of God and for the service of humanity.

What you hold in your hands is more than just a book. I hope that each time you return to these pages, you experience feelings of fondness for our heritage, a resurgence of intellectual inquiry, and an appreciation of our past that is faithful to our future.

Sincerely,

Dr. Fred P. Pestello, President
Saint Louis University

Seeking truth.
Transforming lives.

INTRODUCTION

In 1826, his dreams for Missouri dashed, Bishop Louis W.V. DuBourg wrote a letter noting with some relief that he had closed St. Louis College, after only eight years of operation.[2]

And yet, somehow, classes continued to be offered … and the school survived.

In 1840, the Missouri Mission of the Society of Jesus was elevated to the status of a Vice Province. Father Peter J. Verhaegen, S.J. wrote at the time: "thus far we have but a faint prospect of seeing the adjunct *vice* erased. The number of professed fathers here is so small, that, if we be compelled to wait, until we shall have completed the number usually required for a Province before the little word can be struck out, we old folks, shall be all dead and forgotten. This circumstance, however, does not disturb my own mind. We try to go ahead as fast as we prudently can without exposing ourselves to the danger of breaking down, and what more can be required of us?"

Despite his own prediction, Verhaegen lived to see the "little word" removed in 1863. And as the province flourished, so did its university in the city of St. Louis. Of American Jesuit schools, Father Claude H. Heithaus, S.J. in 1940 asserted: "Saint Louis University was the first to establish the various schools and faculties which constitute a true university."[3]

Over two centuries, this remarkable institution has weathered constant challenge. Its leaders have braved great risk, while maintaining the university's integrity and independence in balance with service to the region and loyalty to the Society of Jesus.

In 1995, Jesuits from around the world crafted an important document called "Jesuits and University Life." Drawing upon more than four centuries of research, teaching and scholarship, the 34th General Congregation wrote that the university is: "a place of serene and open search for and discussion of the truth," for discovering and promoting wisdom. Moreover, it is a place where Jesuits "must regularly ask, 'Knowledge for what?'"[4] A sustained effort to carve out the space and time for this relationship to truth: that is one possible summary of Saint Louis University.

Today, world-renowned Saint Louis University has over 6,000 faculty, staff, and clinicians, and enrolls nearly 13,000 graduate and undergraduate students, with an endowment of over $1 billion, while also operating a prestigious campus in Madrid, Spain. Many excellent, highly detailed histories of the Missouri Mission and this university exist, among them works by Jesuits: Gilbert Garraghan, Walter Hill, and William Faherty. The present book can only attempt to supplement these wonderful antecedents, aiming to illustrate some of the many people who, together over time, took an idea about education and the salvation of souls from a few rented rooms to a powerful, wide-ranging institution.

Improbable twists? Quirky characters? There are plenty. The university's history is one of doggedness, audacity, shrewdness, errors, brilliance. There are stern aescetics, more than a few strong-willed individuals, some true heroes, maybe even a miracle or two. Their legacy guides us as we shape meaning through our own lives. Relish the stories, and keep them in your heart as you create new ones.

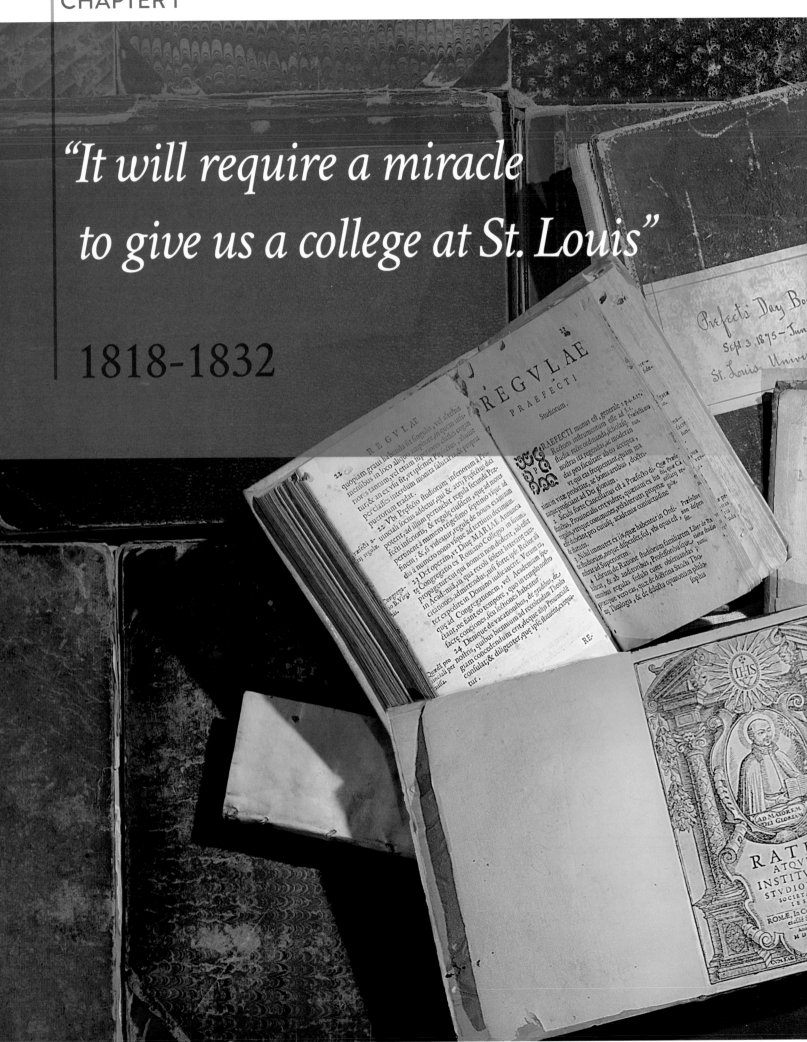

CHAPTER I

"It will require a miracle to give us a college at St. Louis"

1818-1832

The origins of Saint Louis University are profoundly contingent. In 1780, the greatly outnumbered, primarily French-speaking inhabitants of a village on the Mississippi River had somehow staved off an attack by English settlers and Native tribes. Just over three decades later, largely due to personal danger, a bishop chose to relocate from New Orleans to that village: St. Louis. He celebrated his first Mass there on Epiphany in 1818, and a few months later, as a banking crisis was engulfing the United States, established an "Academy for young Gentlemen." Bishop Louis W. V. DuBourg rented rooms for this school in a house on Church Street, and a few years later he managed to recruit a small band of Jesuit novices to trek from Maryland to Missouri and teach Indian boys at another school he planned to start in the region, which closed after seven years. In 1826, DuBourg took actions that he thought had resulted in the closing of his original College. Or so it seemed to him at the time.

The uncertainty of Saint Louis University's early years is not so unusual; not all of the schools, seminaries, and missions attempted by religious orders in North America survived. In the case of St. Louis, one of DuBourg's unlikely schemes became a reality. To some extent without clear approval from their superiors, the Missouri Jesuits took over DuBourg's failing, downtown St. Louis College and carried it forward to a state charter in 1832: the first university in the American West. The novice recruits went on to become central figures in Saint Louis University history.

"ESTABLISHING A COLLEGE ON THE SPOT"

It takes a certain audacity to declare that a few classes in rented rooms constitute an "Academy for young Gentlemen." This was especially true in the unsettling months leading up to the Panic of 1819.[1] Yet, an October 23, 1818 advertisement in the *Missouri Gazette* made this claim.

Under the heading "Education," readers learned that classes in Latin, English, and French languages, as well as "Arithmetic, the Elements of Mathematics and Geography," would be offered in a house on Church Street for $12 per quarter. This announcement marks the humble origin of Saint Louis University. Careful attention to pedagogy is evinced in the reference to: "the ability of the pupil and the intention of the parents." This phrase anticipates the debate which was still occurring a century later: whether school curricula should be adapted to student needs.[2] There is respect for order: for making "proper" assignments, avoiding "confusion and loss of time." One hears the guarded sternness that neither books nor the bags to carry them are the responsibility of the teachers. This tone is balanced with an awareness of the limits in the local environment. Students must "read at least tolerably well."

With this advertisement, the highly persuasive, peripatetic and visionary Bishop Louis W. V. DuBourg quietly set in motion a new era in St. Louis, at that time a muddy, bustling settlement.

First classes were held on November 16, taught by three diocesan priests under the direction of Father François Niel, of France, curate of the Cathedral. Father Edmund Saulnier was later placed in charge of the school, called at various times the "Latin Academy" or "St. Louis Academy." From his studies in Bordeaux and his administrative experience at Georgetown College in Washington and St. Mary's College in Baltimore, DuBourg had a clear vision in mind: "It would be a true Classical College, infused with Catholic religious formation, but open to all comers, whatever their religious persuasion."[3]

The house used for the first classes was registered to Eugenie Alvarez and shown as Block 60 on an 1804 map, listed as "a house of posts on wall since 1770."[4] In the contemporary style, the wooden logs of the walls stood vertically rather than horizontally.

In 1820, the school's name was changed to St. Louis College, as it moved from rented rooms to a two-story edifice of brick erected on the property of the Cathedral block, on the south side toward Walnut Street. The townsfolk contributed funds: "subscribing" to pay the costs of constructing[5] on donated land

The 1818 advertisement for Bishop DuBourg's "Academy for young Gentlemen"

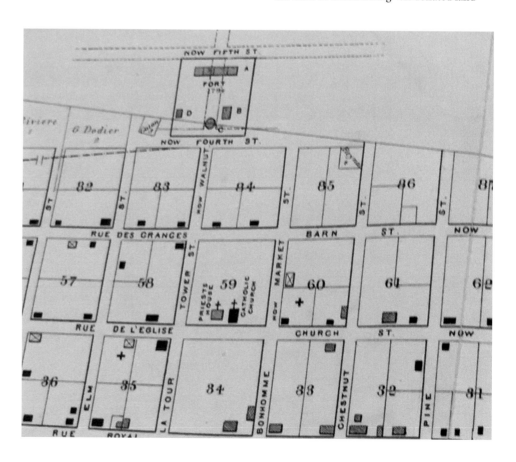

The Alvarez house was the site of first classes, and is shown on Block 60 of this map, reproduced in Thomas J. Scharf's 1883 publication, *History of Saint Louis City and County.*

The 1820 college was part of a complex of buildings including the cathedral and priest residence.

First classes were held in rented rooms in a house of this style, typical of colonial St. Louis.

between Second, Third, Walnut and Market streets. The 1820 teachers included: Father Aristides Anduzi, Father Leon Deys, François Guyot, John Martin, Niel, Father Saulnier, Samuel Smith, and Patrick Sullivan; by 1823, Elihu Shepard and City Engineer Colonel Rene Paul joined the teaching staff.

The intellectual atmosphere of the school benefited from its association with visiting seminarians. Vincentian novices were in St. Louis from "the Barrens," while their own building in Perryville, Missouri was under construction. They received theological training in St. Louis under Father Felix De Andreis, who was the first superior of the Lazarists in the United States. Part of Bishop DuBourg's house was given up as a seminary for the Vincentians. University historian Richard Roberts notes: "Saint Louis University thus began as a "one-room schoolhouse," where the curriculum stretched from the 'three R's' (reading, writing and arithmetic) all the way to college-level theology."[6]

An 1821 city directory states that, connected with DuBourg's cathedral and library is: "the St. Louis College, under the direction of Bishop Du Bourg. It is a two-story brick building and has about sixty-five students, who are taught the Greek, Latin, French, English, Spanish and Italian languages, mathematics, elementary and transcendent, drawing, &cc. There are several teachers. Connected with the college is an ecclesiastical seminary, at the Barrens, in Ste. Genevieve county, where divinity, the oriental languages and philosophy are taught."[7] Leo-Raymond de Neckére, later Bishop of New Orleans, wrote in November 1819 that "M. De Andreis began today the teaching of the Sacred Scriptures."

Bishop DuBourg had travelled a long, complex route to be in St. Louis in the first place. To understand his founding role at the university, some context is helpful.

Bishop DuBourg

Bishop Louis William DuBourg lived a life of constant travel, planning, and what we today would call "networking." With few resources, high hopes, and ongoing opposition, Bishop DuBourg helped to establish Catholic education in the United States. President of Georgetown College from 1796 to 1798, he founded both Saint Louis College, the forerunner to Saint Louis University, and St. Mary's College in Baltimore. He assisted Mother Elizabeth Ann Seton, a foundress of the Sisters of Charity and the first native-born American to be canonized in the United States, as well as Mother Philippine Duchesne, an important early member of the Sisters of the Sacred Heart.

In 1815, DuBourg was consecrated as Bishop of Upper and Lower Louisiana, and assigned his apostolic see in New Orleans. But when he attempted to take up a position of religious authority in that city, he was rebuffed, and physically threatened. In contrast to the "den of iniquity" with its dancing, theaters, and priests living with concubines and their illegitimate children, "St. Louis may offer me a residence where I may settle with greater profit to religion," he wrote. He worked in New Orleans through intermediaries, directing more of his personal efforts to the Middle West.

Enduring the arduous trip to St. Louis via stagecoach, steamboat, and horseback, he settled in to his "muddy, dilapidated" cathedral and celebrated Mass as cold winds blew through the cracks in the walls. He arranged for a new "fine cathedral" to be built on the spot of the original log church, and collected an impressive library, numerous paintings, and an organ sent by a European baroness. DuBourg's extensive correspondence shows that no detail was too small for his attention. Steady themes were concerns over money, and constant negotiations for Jesuits to come to St. Louis and begin a mission amongst the Native Americans. He makes colorful references to riding on "one of those boats propelled with steam," and provides highly detailed advice, for example telling a sea-faring colleague to "come back by way of New York, for fear of pirates." He was involved in every care: issuing instructions on planting trees in the Jesuit seminary that he began in Florissant, Missouri, noting troubles with the "shingles" at "the Barrens" in Perryville, and even sending buffalo robes for the Indian boys' beds at the St. Regis school.

Regarding the region under his spiritual care, DuBourg was especially concerned with the conversion of Native Americans. In 1821, he wrote that "for this paramount work of charity," Jesuits were best suited. He met with the Osages and other tribes, paving the way for the legendary Father Peter John De Smet. While he did not physically spend much time in St. Louis, his efforts on behalf of the school and his insistence on having Jesuits run it demonstrate his persistence and vision. DuBourg visited St. Louis for the last time in spring 1826, then left for France, never to return. Jovial and personable, he was also very private, according to his biographer Annabelle Melville. He had a strong aversion to uncertainty. For these and other reasons, he did not tell others of his plan to resign as Bishop, not knowing if his decision would be accepted by Church authorities. Later appointed Archbishop of Besançon, in France, DuBourg died in 1833, pressing humble tokens upon those who were at his bedside.

10

"YOU NEED JESUITS" — FROM SAINT DOMINGUE TO "THE VILLAGE OF THE CHOUTEAU"

Even before his first meeting with Pope Pius VII in 1815, DuBourg had Jesuits in mind to run missions and schools in the territory under his spiritual care.[8] He later wrote that the Pope told him: "You need Jesuits," but it is likely that the resourceful new bishop initiated the idea with Pius. Certainly for DuBourg, the sight of eighty Jesuit novices in Rome must have been a wondrous one, after forty-one years of the suppression of the Society of Jesus.[9]

DuBourg was in Rome in 1815 to be consecrated as Bishop of Upper and Lower Louisiana, the 828,000 square mile tract of land acquired by the United States in 1803 from France in the Louisiana Purchase. He had experienced the disruptions of political change: having joined the Sulpician order in 1786, he was among the thousands of priests expelled from France and exiled to Spain. Born to French parents living in Saint Domingue (now Cap-Haïtien, Haiti), he and his siblings had experienced loss, trying for years to resolve family finances affected by both natural and political disasters. He knew that the Society had been restored in 1814, after decades of suppression; indeed, as a youth he attended the Collège de Guyenne, which had merged with a Jesuit school suppressed in 1772, the Collège

Father Charles Nerinckx recruited the Belgian men who established the Missouri Mission of the Society of Jesus.

de la Madeleine. The imperative to advance and preserve Christianity, as a constantly endangered faith, strengthened DuBourg's resolve to save souls in the territory which Europeans imagined as a New World inhabited by "primitives."

To serve in a place that historian Gilbert Garraghan, S.J. termed his "destitute diocese," it was particularly urgent to find Jesuits, renowned for their erudition, self-discipline, and willingness to take on risk and even danger.

The persuasive bishop requested the pontiff's help; the Pope accordingly appealed to Father General Thaddeus Brzozowski of the Society of Jesus. The Pope's letter, enclosed with one from DuBourg, never reached Father Brzozowski. The latter was still living in Russia, as the suppression of the Jesuits was ending. Catherine the Great had provided a refuge for members of the Society during the suppression. When he finally learned of the existence of the letter, Brzozowksi requested and later received details about its contents, but it was eight years before Jesuits were found for the Louisiana territory. When DuBourg did find them, it was through an interesting coincidence: a Belgian-born priest living in Kentucky, Father Charles Nerinckx, had refused the offer of a position as

"Administrator-Apostolic" of New Orleans, an early form of DuBourg's 1812 appointment. Nerinckx begged his superiors instead to allow him to continue assisting Kentucky's only other priest, Father Stephen Badin. An extraordinarily humble man and one of the "iron race of pioneers,"[10] Nerinckx guided Mary Rhodes, Ann Havern, and Christina Stuart in 1812, as they founded a group that came to be known as the Sisters of Loretto at the Foot of the Cross. In September 1815, he gave a speech in Belgium titled: *A Glance at the Present Condition of the Roman Catholic Religion in North America,* also issued in pamphlet form. In 1821, in the city of Mechlin, Belgium, he used this same pamphlet to recruit young men for the Society of Jesus; he even accompanied them on their journey to North America. This action proved critical to the future of the St. Louis College, for these were the very men who were later invited to Missouri by DuBourg.

Father Nerinckx used this 1815 pamphlet to recruit men for the Native American missions in the United States.

EENEN OOGSLAG
OP DEN TEGENWOORDIGEN STAET
DER
ROOMSCH-CATHOLYKE RELIGIE
IN NOORD-AMERICA,

Doór eenen Priester van het Aertsbisdom van Mechelen, tot Amsterdam uyt Baltimore aengekomen den 18 November 1815.

Rev. Charles Nerinckx.

DE bedriegeryen en boosheyd van onze verwaende renegaeten, geloofsverzaekers of sophisten, en de trouweloosheyd der geéne van ons in geloofs-belydenis verschillen, hebben my beweégt om myne vaderlanders en medelidmaeten van het H. Roomsch-Catholyk Geloof een relaes te geéven van de tegenwoórdige gesteltenis onzer H. Religie in de vereenigde staeten van America, doch geen wydloopig, mits daer eene voldoende beschryvinge beloófd is, die in alle bezonderheden zal treéden.

Wanneer wy, elf jaeren geleden, tot Amsterdam den oogenblik afwagtten om naer America te zeylen, hadden wy dikwils de pynelykheyd van te hooren uyt den mond van deéze ontrouwe en eerlooze spotters ende in hunne schriften te leézen, dat die algemeyne, zoo oude, zoo agtbaere en noyt verwonne Religie niet in weézen was waer wy henen gingen, en eerlang verdwynen zoude uyt het land, dat wy verlieten. Waernen lyk den stigter van deéze H. Religie scheén alsdan voór eenen tyd als te slaepen, terwyl het schipken geslingerd wierd tusschen de gevaerlykste stormen, die oyt de magten der helle en des zelfs aenhang hebben t' saemen gebruykt oft konnen te wege brengen; maer de onfaelbaere belofte van den almagtigen stigter van deéze H. Religie on-

Osage and Jesuits: A Continuity of Relationship from the 1600s to Present

by Christy Finsel, Osage Tribal Member and Saint Louis University Graduate (1998, 2001)

Note: The author wishes to thank Eddy Red Eagle Jr. (Osage Tribal Member and Elder), and Felix and Margaret Diskin (Volunteers, Osage Mission Neosho County Museum, Saint Paul, Kansas) for their time and contributions.

The Osage are descended from those who built the Cahokia Mounds, in present day Illinois. From about 700 to 1200, A.D., the Late Woodland Indians and later, members of the Mississippian culture lived east of the Mississippi river from present-day St. Louis. Their abandoned city was eventually named for the Cahokia tribe of the Illiniwek (Illinois) confederacy, who arrived in the 1600s. French Trappist monks lived nearby from 1809 to 1813; the largest mound, "Monks Mound," is named for them. Osage, as sovereign people, were stewards of the land that later became the city of St. Louis. Saint Louis University is situated on Osage homeland.

The first documented connection between the Osage and the Jesuits is found on a map produced by Father Jacques Marquette, S.J. during his explorations in 1673. The map shows an Osage village. Since then, the Osage and the Jesuits have built a covenant relationship marked by trust. The Jesuits developed their missionary approach with the Osage, as they sought to spread Christianity to Natives.[1] Father Gilbert J. Garraghan, S.J. writes: "at about the end of the 17th century, the Osage requested that Father Gravier (a Jesuit) visit their villages on the Osage River."[2] By 1823, Father Charles Van Quickenborne, S.J. met Indians who still remembered Jesuits from before the Suppression. Garraghan notes: "Father Odin, the future first Bishop of Galveston, tells in a letter of 1823 of an Indian woman, more than a centenarian in years, who remembered being present at services conducted by eighteenth-century Jesuits."[3]

In 1808, the Osage signed the Fort Osage Treaty with the federal government, initiating the loss of their land base and eventual removal toward western Missouri.[4] In 1820, Osage leaders met with Bishop DuBourg in St. Louis to request mission schools.[5] DuBourg sent Father Charles De La Croix, who, in 1822, arrived in an Osage village near Papinville, in Missouri, along the Osage River.[6] In 1825, the Osage signed another treaty that moved them out of Missouri and into an Osage reserve in Kansas. Father Van Quickenborne visited them in 1827, 1828,

and 1830;" he also visited the village near Papinville,[7] and "found the Mass vestments left by Father de La Croix five years before, carefully guarded by the Indians."[8]

In 1823, Van Quickenborne opened an Indian school in Saint Ferdinand (now Florissant, Missouri), connected with a seminary Bishop DuBourg envisioned: "I propose to receive in the seminary a half dozen Indian children from the different tribes in order to familiarize my young missionaries with their habits and language." The Indian school was also connected to Saint Louis College, as Bishop Joseph Rosati wrote: "It would, moreover, be necessary to establish a college of the Society in St. Louis. There is already property there to be used for this purpose ... [it] could be of great help to the establishment at St. Ferdinand for the Indian agents reside there, and there, also, are held the councils of deputies from the various Indian nations who come to treat with the American Government."[9]

In 1827 and 1828, Van Quickenborne recruited Osage boys and girls for the Indian School, including the sons of Osage Chief White Hair (Pawhuska), Gratamantze and Clermont. The boys experienced a mixture of care and harshness from Father Van Quickenborne.[10] In 1830, Van Quickenborne accompanied Osage students back to their families. The Indian school was closed, and a new phase of missionary activity began.

In 1847, Father John Schoenmakers, S.J., came to work with the Osage in Kansas, and other Jesuits: Fathers Felix Verreydt, Christian Hoecken, Herman Aelen, and Francis Xavier De Coen, all visited the Osage. An Osage Mission was established at Saint Francis de Hieronymo in Kansas for Osage boys, and Father Schoenmakers recruited the Sisters of Loretto to establish the Osage School for Girls nearby.[11] Eddy Red Eagle, Jr. believes: "the Jesuits, through their mission work with the Osage people, generally extended them a gentle hand. They recognized Osage ways and did not try to stop the Osage from dancing, speaking their language, or performing certain cultural activities, such as a naming ceremony for infants."[12]

The Osage understand that God guided us to believe, similar to the Jesuits, in the depths of God's creative power. Therefore, the Osage did not fear Catholic sacraments or Jesuits' education of their children. Eddy Red Eagle, Jr. notes, "as protective as the Osage were of their children, this understanding of Osage worldviews and Catholicism allowed for the Osage clan leaders to overall trust that the Jesuits could educate the Osage children in ways that would not hurt them or be antithetical to their views." The Osage sent children to the Jesuits for schooling and safety into the 1890s, and Jesuits also continued to perform marriages, baptisms, and funerals.[13] They accompanied the Osage on their move to Oklahoma in 1871-1872, and the beloved Father Paul Mary Ponziglione, S.J. and Father Schoenmakers visited them in Oklahoma. They ministered at a time of extreme cultural transition: huge population losses of clan leaders and family members, and staggering changes to their ways of life. Within seventy years of the Lewis and Clark Expedition, (1804 to 1806), the Osage lost 90% of their population due to disease, relocation, and related food shortages.[15]

The high regard felt by Osage for Jesuits is clear. They asked Father Schoenmakers to advise on negotiations of the Sturgis Treaty of 1865 at Drum Creek.[16] The Osage word for Catholic, in the Osage language, is Sho Mein Key, a derivative of Father Schoenmakers' name.[17] They built Catholic churches in Oklahoma, including one at the Immaculate Conception Parish in Pawhuska with a stained glass window depicting Osage youth, elders and Father Schoenmakers. None are saints, so the Osage sought permission from Rome for the window. When Father Schoenmakers fell ill during a visit, the Osage stayed with him, round the clock, while he recovered.[18] In 1871, Father Ponziglione conducted the baptism for Mary Euphrasia Roy, the great-great grandmother of this essay's author (Christy Finsel).[19] On December 1885, Osage leaders signed a letter that Father Ponziglione wrote to Pope Leo XIII requesting canonization for Kateri Tekakwitha.[20]

The Osage remain connected to the Jesuits and the Catholic Church, also navigating membership in the Native American Church. As Eddy Red Eagle, Jr., a leader of the Native American Church in Pawhuska, notes: "the fact I am Catholic makes me a better part of the Native American Church, and being a part of the Native American Church makes me a better Catholic."[21] The Osage Nation is a Federally Recognized Indian Tribe with nearly 20,200 members.[22] Their relationship with the Jesuits continues, through study and employment at the university; marriages and baptisms at College Church; and participation in celebrations. The Osage look forward to many more years of collaboration with the Society of Jesus and Saint Louis University.

Stained glass window depicting Osage elders and youth with Father Schoenmakers in the Immaculate Conception Church in Pawhuska, Oklahoma (by Cody Hammer, Osage Nation Communications Department)

George Catlin's "Beautiful grassy bluffs, 110 miles above St. Louis" (1832), of which he wrote: "We landed our canoe at the base of a beautiful series of grass-covered bluffs, which, like thousands and thousands of others on the banks of this river, are designated by no name, that I know of and I therefore introduce them as fair specimens of the *grassy bluffs* of the Missouri . . . I took my easel, and canvas and brushes, to the top of the bluff, and painted the two views from the same spot; the one looking up, and the other down the river."

ST. LOUIS, 1818

Bishop DuBourg arrived in St. Louis on the Vigil of the Epiphany: January 5, 1818. For the cosmopolitan prelate, the village and its humble "cathedral"— a "muddy dilapidated" church built of logs— was a safe haven compared to the dangerous "den of iniquity" of his episcopal see: New Orleans. DuBourg's authority in New Orleans had been rejected by the powerful Father Antonio de Sedella, and he had been physically threatened there. In 1816, he wrote, after summarizing his troubles: "From this I might be led to conclude that God does not wish me in my Diocese... St. Louis may offer me a residence where I may settle with greater profit to religion."

In St. Louis, however, residents eagerly awaited his arrival: "the whole town is in an uproar about it," wrote one resident.[11] As early as 1817, the bishop was a focus of many hopes, as noted in another letter: "if he be not fairly teased into it by you Gentlemen he will be for putting it off for other Schemes; but how easily may you convince him that the establishing a College on the spot will be a sure means of gaining him the affection of all..."[12]

THE VILLAGE OF THE CHOUTEAU

Memories of the pre-Suppression Jesuits remained among Native tribes in the area around St. Louis. In 1823, writing from the Jesuit seminary in Florissant, Missouri, Father Charles Felix Van Quickenborne, S.J. noted: "We find as yet persons that were with our old Fathers here before the Suppression."[13] Father Jacques Marquette, S.J. had sought to establish a mission among Illinois Indians, but died in 1675 before completing that task.[14]

French traders had been in the region as early as the 17th century, in contact with the numerous Native tribes who traveled on the waterways and hunted on the land. In 1764, trader and merchant Pierre Laclède Liguest left New Orleans to travel up the Mississippi River, marking a place along the river for a future trading post. In 1762, France ceded its claims to Spain; in effect Laclède was a "trespasser" on Spanish territory.[15] Lacléde and his family remained, and prospered. Father Sébastian Louis Meurin, S.J. was the first priest to officiate in the settlement, probably performing the first baptism in St. Louis in 1766.[16]

Local Native American tribes tolerated the French-speaking immigrants who settled in the area now called St. Louis. In exchange for gifts from Laclède and others, such as blankets and gunpowder, they let the French live in peace. A partnership between Laclède and a French military officer in charge of the settlement, Captain Louis Groston de Saint-Ange de Bellerive, maintained this stability. The village was visited by the Missouria, Kickapoo, Potawotami, Chippewa, Ottawa, Sac, and Fox, and later: Panis, Otos, Big and Little Osages, and Kansas tribes.

This "uneasy détente" prevailed between natives and the French, as long as the French were in charge.[17] The little enclave was called "the village of the Chouteau" by Native tribes, in reference to Laclède's family: his common-law wife Marie-Thérèse Bourgeois Chouteau, and her sons Pierre and Auguste.

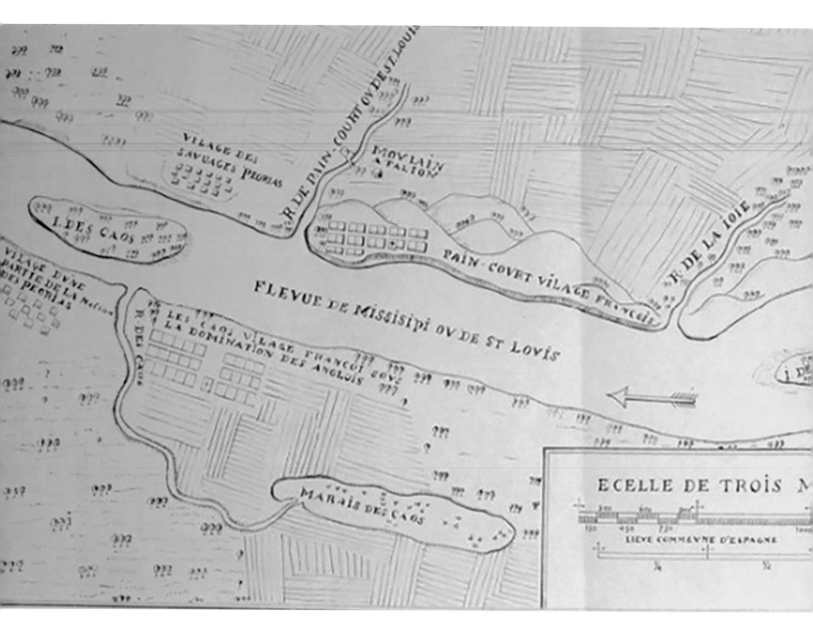

A map from 1767 shows the streets that Laclède established, running parallel to the river. He laid out communal fields in the long strip pattern he knew from French, medieval village life.[18] Corn and wheat were the primary crops; the timbered areas were used to gather firewood. The design made it difficult to keep animals from eating the crops, however.

Lafayette Park in St. Louis is now the only trace left of the large, original commons, which in 1812 had been granted to the French inhabitants of the town. The rest of the parcel was sold by the city in 1836.

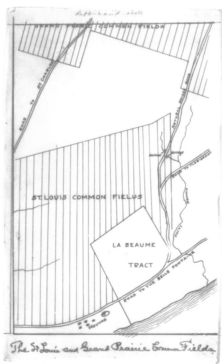

The fields were arranged in long strips, in a pattern dating from medieval France.

A thin slice of riverfront land in a remote, northwestern territory inhabited by numerous Native American tribes and then claimed by Europeans: France, then Spain, then secretly retroceded to France again in 1801, finally claimed by the American colonists — the place now called St. Louis was marked by cultural and linguistic variety. Inhabitants were known for their love of brandy, dueling, billiards, and hunting. At first they imported flour, although the soil was rich; villagers were reputed to be more interested in commerce than agriculture, hence the town's teasing nickname: *Paincourt,* French for "short of bread" or possibly "shortage of

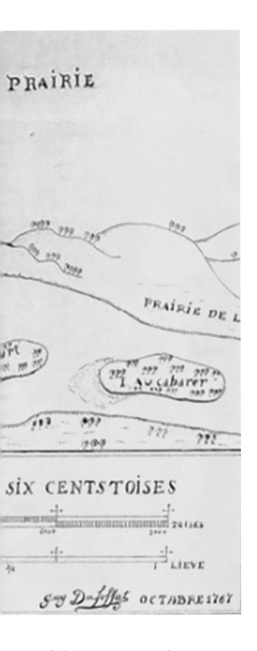

The village was constructed close along the banks of the river, as shown in the 1780 map by Auguste Chouteau. The French style of housing is clear in the sketch.

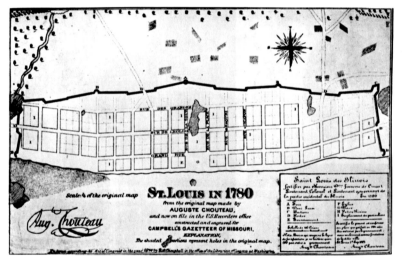

bread." There are numerous other instances of tongue-in-cheek place-names in Missouri, often referring to hunger. It may have meant: "suspected of selling bread that was short of weight."[19] If there was a lack of interest in farming, it could also be attributed to the fact that working out in the fields, relatively far from the town and beyond its fences, left one exposed to attack by both natives and animals.

A Catholic church was built by 1770, and by 1774, a Catholic elementary school was operating, with classes taught by Jean Baptiste Trudeau.[20]

Town rules were read out to the population in front of the church after services. Chronicles tell of a wide variety of sexual liaisons and "tolerance of questionable behavior." In 1780, an attack on St. Louis was mounted by British and Native American tribes, with some loss of life. Fernando de Leyba, the Spanish lieutenant governor of St. Louis, bravely led the defense; he was not credited until many years later.[21] These early days of the city are evoked in a quote from the 1821 city directory, cited in 1875: "It is but about forty years since the now flourishing but yet more promising State of Missouri was but a vast wilderness, many of the inhabitants of this country yet remembering the time when they met togeth-er to kill the buffalo at the same place where Mr. Phillipson's ox saw and flour mill is now erected, and on Mill creek, near to where Mr. Chouteau's mill now stands."[22]

Prior to the arrival of Bishop DuBourg and Mother Rose Philippine Duchesne of the Sisters of the Sacred Heart, there seems to have been "religious disinterest" among the free-thinking French elites of St. Louis.[23] In addition, many Osages may have resisted conversion.[24] Enslaved African-Americans in North America during this time rejected Christianity as the "religion of the masters," yet some slave-holders feared Christianity for its threat to their power; sentiments varied widely over time and place.[25]

Amidst this complex culture, DuBourg set in motion several important developments. He raised funds for the construction of a new cathedral in St. Louis. He launched two educational schemes that soon combined to become Saint Louis University. Fondly characterized by historian Father John W. Padberg, S.J. as "the greatest snake oil salesman of all time," he recruited, among others, Bishop Joseph Rosati, Father Felix De Andreis, and Rose Philippine Duchesne, R.S.C.J.

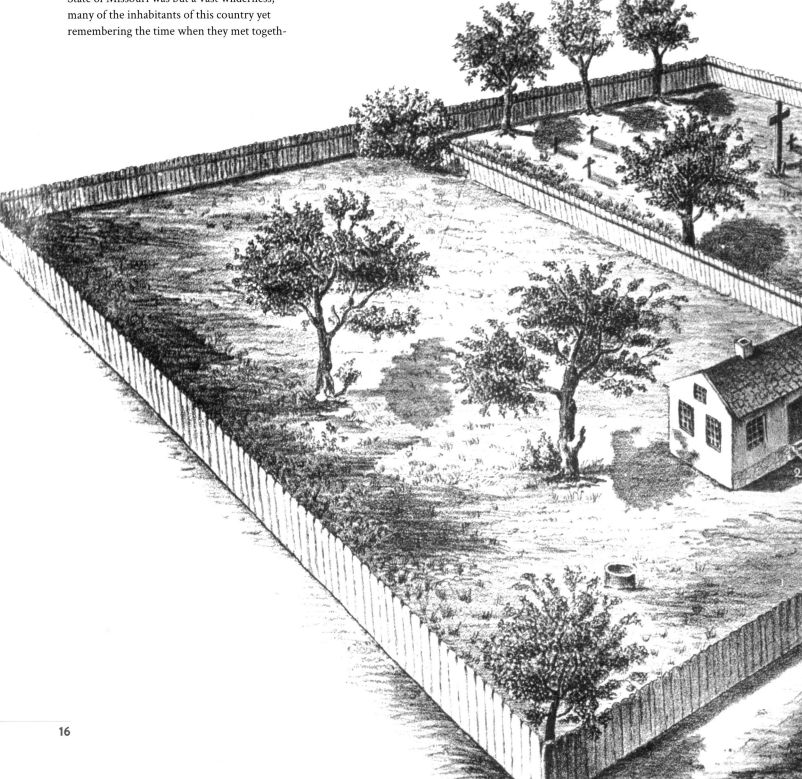

"SAILING ALMOST AT RANDOM…"

FATHER JAMES VAN DE VELDE, S.J.[26]

Across the Atlantic Ocean, nine young Belgian men snuck aboard a ship called the *Columbia.* They set sail for America from Amsterdam on Assumption Day: August 15, 1821, eluding authorities and their own families in order to become missionaries. Traveling with Father Nerinckx, they came on the strength of a letter from Father James Van de Velde, S.J. to his former pupil, Judocus Van Assche. Van de Velde was already in the United States. He traveled from Belgium with Nerinckx in 1817, joined the Society of Jesus at Nerinckx's suggestion, and by 1821 was a librarian at Georgetown. He was later to be a president of Saint Louis University, a Vice Provincial, bishop of Chicago, and bishop of Natchez, Mississippi.

The group of young recruits travelling with Nerinckx in 1821 included: Peter John De Smet; John Anthony Elet; Francis de Maillet; John Baptist Smedts; Van Assche; Joseph Van Horsigh; Peter John Verhaegen; and Felix Levinus Verreydt. After landing in Philadelphia, the group went to live at a seminary run by the Maryland Province of the Society of Jesus in White Marsh, Maryland.[27] The seminary farm did not yield sufficient food or income to sustain the men and their slaves. The rector begged flour and meat from neighbors; coffee and sugar were too expensive and thereby not provided. Father Verreydt later wrote: "our Colored people were working at our farm, which could scarcely support them."[28]

By 1823, amidst constant travel, fund-raising and letter-writing, DuBourg was convinced that he could fund his vision of a school for Indian boys through a federal government program. He believed that a sufficient number of boarders could be recruited to qualify for a grant of $800 per year; he also believed he had clear title to some farmland in Florissant, Missouri, near St. Louis. Accounts differ, but it seems that when DuBourg learned that Belgian Jesuit novices were barely eking out an existence on potatoes and water in White Marsh, he saw his dream within reach at last: an Indian school and seminary that would also prepare Jesuit novices for future mission work.

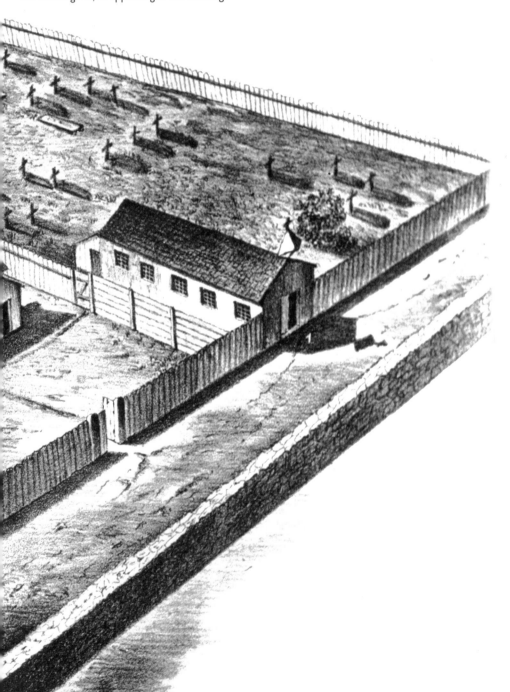

The first Catholic church of St. Louis, built 1770, with the "priest house" to the left of the church. Records note that Bishops DuBourg and Benedict Joseph Flaget "found the lot and the buildings so, as appearing in the drawing."

DuBourg crafted a lofty "Concordat" with the Society of Jesus, which was signed March 19, 1823. It was never fully honored by any of the parties, but it enshrined an ambitious arrangement. In the document, the Society of Jesus accepted responsibility for the spiritual direction of "the white population" and "various Indian tribes" inhabiting the region. The Concordat's only mention of African Americans is a promise to send "at least four or five negroes to be employed in preparing and providing additional buildings that may be found necessary, and in cultivating the land of the above mentioned farm."

While their original goal of serving Native Americans was realized only in part, the Belgian novices went on to serve important roles at the first university in the American West.

"SEIZES WITH JOY A PROPOSAL MADE TO HIM BY THE SUPERIOR OF THE SOCIETY IN THE U. STATES TO COOPERATE WITH HIM ... BY FURNISHING HIM WITH A NUMBER OF ABLE AND ZEALOUS MISSIONARIES."

BISHOP WILLIAM DUBOURG, 1823

by the Rt. Rev.d W.m [...]

Rev.d Charles Neale Superior

[...] on the other part; respecting

[...] Society in his Diocess. —

[...] animated by the desire of propaga- [...] of two years, counting from

[...] Diocess, and anxious to promote as [...] qualified shall proceed

[...] al welfare of the numerous savage [...] the vicinity of Council Bluffs,

[...] tributary streams, by conferring [...] specified above, for the

[...] & at the same time instructing

[...] to the truths of his holy religion as [...] as much as he is able, the

[...] his Church, seizes with joy a Pro- [...] and until it shall be

[...] Society in the U. States into a separate [...] upon some other site,

[...] by furnishing him with a number of [...] in this mission, to re-

[...] proceed to the work. — And in order [...] Fathers, whose chief

[...] subsist between the Bishop of New - [...] fying the youth, who

[...] of the Society of Jesus & his Successors, [...] with the approbation

[...] into, & has been signed by each of

[...] ratified by his Holiness as well as by the [...] the establishment a-

[...] shall be perpetually binding upon them [...] obligates himself

[...] whatever [...] on

[...] of to apply tow[...]

[...] cedes & surrenders to the Society of Jesus [...] shall hereafter app[...]

[...] increase of members enables it to undertake [...] towards the further:

[...] of all the Missions already established, and

[...] the Missouri River & its tributary streams;

[...] cession, the spiritual direction agreeably to

[...] white population as of the various Indian [...] is signed by both

[...] District of country, together with all the Churches.

[...] March 19. A. D. 1823.

+ L. W.m DuBourg Bp of N. Orleans

[...]les Neale Superior of the Mission

[...] Society of Jesus in the United States

THE JOURNEY TO MISSOURI

This map shows the route travelled by the group, from Maryland to St. Louis, in 1823. They walked for most of the journey; for part of the trip, they navigated the Ohio River on two rafts tied together.

DuBourg could not fund the group's journey to Missouri, but he presented their leader: Father Charles Felix Van Quickenborne, S.J. with a letter to take on a tour, appealing for money in various Northeastern cities. Van Quickenborne raised $900 to fund the trek. The religious men: Van Quickenborne, S.J. as master of novices and his assistant Father Peter Joseph Timmermans, S.J., were accompanied by the six Belgians recruited by Nerinckx: De Smet, Elet, Smedts, Van Assche, Verhaegen, and Verreydt. Also making the journey were: Belgian novice, Francis de Maillet, and three coadjutor-brothers: Peter De Meyer, Henry Reiselman, and Charles Strahan, as well as six enslaved persons from the White Marsh farm. They were three married couples: Isaac and Succy, whose son Peter was born into slavery; Nancy and Moses; and Tom and Polly. In this period, many enslaved persons lacked surnames, although records suggest their full names were: Isaac, Succy (Susan), and Peter Queen/Hawkins; Moses and Nancy Queen; and Tom and Molly/Polly/Mary Brown. Verreydt includes brief descriptions of these enslaved people, noting their piety and their work in paddling the makeshift vessel (two rafts tied together) at night on the Ohio River.[29]

"A FEW LINES ABOUT OLD TIMES..."

FATHER JUDOCUS VAN ASSCHE, S.J., 1874[30]

The group left Maryland for "the wilds of Missouri"[31] undertaking a journey that lasted from April 11 to May 31, 1823. They walked for most of the trip. Along the turnpike between Baltimore and Wheeling, they were able to stay with Irish families. They baptized children, said Mass, and heard confessions as they proceeded. The next stage of the journey was an expedition down the Ohio River, which they maneuvered with the help of a manual. De Meyer called it a "floating monastery" because of the ringing of the "little bell" for all of their religious exercises. Father Walter J. Hill, S.J. writes: "Very often also, toward evening some unexpected voice would speak from the shore and warning them of the dangers near them, would entreat so earnestly to stop that it they would obey. Nor did they ever regret to have obeyed, for in the morning when they resumed their course, they would find all kinds of impediments on their way, which made them conclude that it was the Merciful God had spoken that seasonable warning for the safety of the little band."[32]

Brother Pete

Born on. Florissant premises as a slave

"As they were good people, I do not doubt, they were saying their beads in a corner of the boat."

FATHER FELIX VERREYDT, S.J., 1874

The United States remains scarred by the terrible legacy of its long history of legal slavery. At his inaugural address in January 1865, Governor Thomas C. Fletcher of Missouri called slavery a "curse" that had "poisoned" the state. After the Civil War, a brutal, lucrative system of involuntary servitude developed in the eleven states of the Confederacy, ensnaring tens of thousands of African Americans in a condition Douglas Blackmon terms "neo-slavery." Reports of involuntary servitude in the Deep South continued *into the 1950s.*

Dr. Martin Luther King, Jr. often used the word "sin" to describe slavery. Saidiya Hartman writes: "I am the relic of an experience most prefer not to remember, as if the sheer will to forget could settle or decide the matter of history. I am a reminder that twelve million crossed the Atlantic and the past is not yet over. I am the progeny of captives. I am the vestige of the dead. And history is how the secular world attends to the dead."[1]

Prior to colonization in North America, Native tribes enslaved people captured from their enemies. James Dickey writes: "The arrival of the French soon altered the concept of captives among the Indian nations. The French needed laborers to work their farms and plantations in lower Louisiana and the West Indies." Indians became a source of slavery; "by 1700, Frenchmen were trading brandy and merchandise to the Missouria, Osage, Kansa and Illini for captives taken in war. The Jesuits decried this situation and complained that the traders were constantly inciting the Indians to make war in order to buy their captives and then sell them as slaves."[2]

Although Thomas Jefferson praised the Louisiana Purchase as creating an 'empire of liberty,' Ira Berlin writes that, on the contrary it created "an empire for slavery." Between 1787 and 1861, nearly one million slaves in the United States were forcibly relocated from the upper South to the lower South in the Second Middle Passage. An estimated two thirds of these relocations were through the domestic slave trade.[3] Their lives and labor fed the massive growth of cotton plantations, as even free blacks were caught and re-enslaved, while those already in slavery were "sold down the river." Thousands walked in coffles to the south. This period was devastating for all slaves and for family life, as marriage, parenthood, indeed all kin relationships were disrupted. Due to the demands of Deep South slave-

Tax receipts and other records for the Missouri Province show:

1848- Received of Peter Verhaegen and others = $75.33 for 21 slaves, 10 horses, and 35 cattle, as well as tax on land

1850- Received of Peter Verhaegen and others = $60.50 for 21 slaves, 10 horses, and 20 cattle, as well as tax on land

1854- Received of St. Louis University = $178.10 pd. $6980 "valuation" for slaves, but no number of people given.

The university's "Personal Property" in 1863 was recorded inside the cover of a financial journal, and included: "One Negro family to whom we have offered the Liberty."

holders, there was an absolute decline in slaves in Missouri during 1820-1860.

The early years of Saint Louis University are entangled in this tragedy. SLU's "Slavery, History and Memory Project" researches slavery at the Missouri Mission (later Province), and at the university. In 1810, there were 740 slaves in the District of St. Louis; the number of slaves increased to 1,800 out of a population of 10,000 in St. Louis County by 1820.[4] SLU's founder, Bishop W.V. DuBourg, resided in St. Louis periodically; in an 1823 letter, he wrote that he "leaves" Rachel and Charles to St. Louis, presumably a reference to slaves. In 1823, six Belgian Jesuit novices traveled from Maryland to Missouri to begin an Indian school at the request of DuBourg. Their first seminary, connected with Georgetown College and located in White Marsh, Maryland, had hundreds of slaves. The novices brought six enslaved persons (three married couples) on the journey to Florissant: Isaac and Succy; Nancy and Moses, and Tom and Polly. Father Felix Verreydt, S.J. was one of the Belgian novices in the group that trekked from Maryland in 1823. Years later, he wrote a memoir of the journey. He described the piety of the six slaves, and the prowess of the men steering the two rafts down the Ohio River at night.

The six original slaves of the Missouri Mission were followed a few weeks later by sixteen more slaves sent by the Maryland Province. They lived and worked at the farm associated with the St. Stanislaus Seminary in Florissant, Missouri. Some of the slaves worked at the university when the Jesuits took over its administration (see page 25). Tax receipts and other records for the Missouri Province suggest that twenty-one persons were owned as slaves in 1848 and 1850, and as many as thirty-nine persons were owned in 1863.

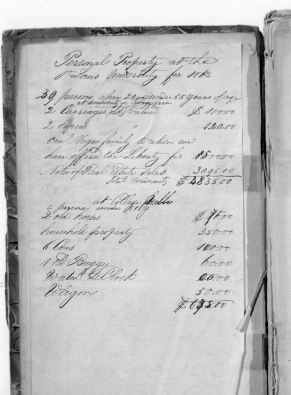

Sleeping on the ground within earshot of growling wolves, or on the floors of kind peoples' homes and barns, they slowly progressed. During the last stage, their trail went from dust to swamp, and they were beset by gnats and mosquitos. A violent storm had struck, turning all to mud; at times they were forced to build bridges to replace those which had been washed away. For the final miles, they waded barefoot through knee-deep rivulets. They kept their "courage and spirit" by singing sacred hymns and telling stories of deeds of the Apostles. The sight of the city of St. Louis rising up over the river was a beautiful "spectacle," writes Hill.

"WE CAN ONLY COMMENCE THE WORK."
BISHOP DUBOURG

The group arrived in St. Louis. De Meyer recalled: "St. Louis was small … there were only 2 streets tolerably well built up, about 8 or 10 Squares long; but a good many houses scattered about in the hazel bushes." He rode in an open horse cart to Florissant, about sixteen miles west. The group slept for one night in the house of the workman at the convent where the Sacred Heart of Jesus community lived. In the morning, they journeyed to the farm given to them by DuBourg. There was a one-story log house with one room where the family lived who had rented a part of the farm to the bishop, and "Two old cabins where colored people used to live." The owner of the farm "took pity on them," writes De Meyer, and moved his family to the village so that the Jesuits could use the house. They divided the room in two with a curtain and used one side as a chapel, and one side for

Van Quickenborne. They began felling trees and dragging logs to the farm to construct a place to live. The Jesuit novices studied philosophy and theology, while also teaching boys they had recruited from Native tribes. (See sidebar on Osage). The novitiate was called St. Stanislaus, and the Indian school was called St. Regis.[33]

Around this time, enrollment at St. Louis College, DuBourg's school, had gone from thirty-seven to fifty thanks to a popular teacher named Elihu Shepard. However, the bishop was discouraged about its prospects. Its alumni in subsequent years occupied positions of power and influence in the city, but the college struggled, in part due to the teachers' ecclesiastical duties. When DuBourg returned to St. Louis in 1826, he decided to close it.

This was not to be. First, Father Saulnier refused to let the school die. While Bishop Joseph Rosati of the St. Louis Diocese negotiated with the Jesuits to take over DuBourg's college, Saulnier, by then quite ill, was able to offer classes in 1827 assisted by John Servary and Peter Walsh. There were about a dozen students.[34] Second, when the school was unable to reopen after 1826-27, the families asked the Jesuits to teach their sons at Florissant. Fifteen of the St. Louis students attended St. Regis in 1828, later enrolling at the resuscitated college when it opened in its new building at Ninth and Washington in 1829. Significantly, it was *the students themselves*, in making the tran-

St. Stanislaus Novitiate near Florissant, Missouri, in an image from 1847

sition from the old to the new school, who helped to maintain the college's continuity. As the primary chronicler of the Jesuits of the Middle West, Father Gilbert J. Garraghan, S.J. notes: "As early as June 24, 1824, Bishop Du Bourg wrote concerning the western Jesuits to his brother at Bourdeaux in France 'They will take over the College of St Louis, this is the means to assure its stability.'" DuBourg's hopes began to be realized even before the new building was ready.

However, the bishop's dreams and assumptions about the Indian School were not borne out: the land he had counted on was owned by someone else, and families did not want to relinquish their young boys, so the school never attained the level of enrollment it needed to receive full government support let alone cover costs. Even the nearby Sisters of the Sacred Heart contributed their labor: sewing and repairing clothes, while teachers, students and slaves alike planted and harvested. The pupils scorned the agricul-

tural labor that was part of the educational regime, and often tried to run away. DuBourg closed the Indian school at Florissant in 1830. However, the seminary in Florissant remained in operation until 1971, the longest continuously operating Jesuit novitiate in the world at that time.

The Jesuits took over the bishop's St. Louis College; in effect, it never really closed. From his two educational enterprises: the Indian School and Saint Louis College— emerged a potent combination of people, ideas and materials. The six men who had come from Belgium to Maryland and thence to Missouri, who studied and taught at Florissant, now formed the teaching and leadership core. Some were administrators, guiding St. Louis College to a state charter as a university in 1832; others taught at the university or ministered to Native Americans and African Americans.

Records of the name, birthplace, and studies for the early Jesuits of Saint Louis University

The 1829 building erected for Saint Louis College, as depicted by Charles Bosseron Chambers, who graduated from the Commercial Course around 1900.

"BECAUSE THERE WAS A BLESSED FAITHFULNESS OF THE LORD TO WHAT BEGAN SO FRAILLY, THE BELGIANS BELIEVED WHAT OTHERS THOUGHT WAS FOLLY... ASSOCIATED WITH THEIR FAITH WAS A PASSION FOR THE POSSIBLE."

ROBERT T. COSTELLO, S.J. (PROVINCIAL)[35]

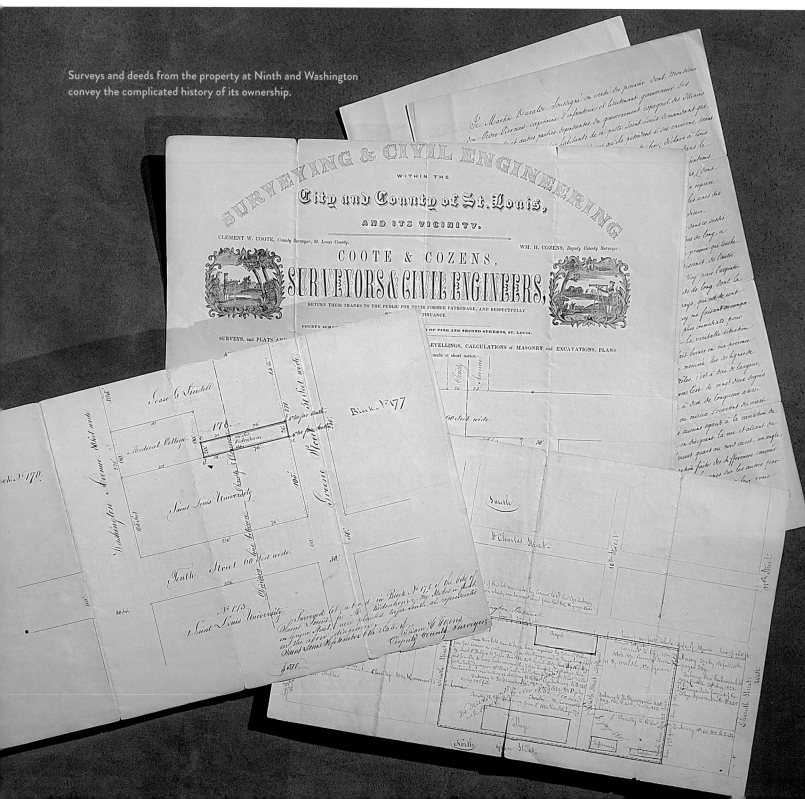

Surveys and deeds from the property at Ninth and Washington convey the complicated history of its ownership.

Through a complex series of land transactions dating back to 1772, a piece of land came into the possession of Bishop DuBourg in 1820. At the time, the land was called "Connor's Addition" and was considered remote: people spoke of it as that part of town where horses got mired in the mud. The German travel writer Johann Georg Kohl described the original property as "a piece of waste land."[36] When the Society of Jesus accepted the administration of St. Louis College, Bishop Rosati transferred to them this land: a lot on Ninth and Christy (now Washington). By then, Bishop DuBourg had left the United States. Using funds including $3,000 from Father De Smet's inheritance as well as money from Father Van Quickenborne's inheritance, ground was broken for a college. Van Quickenborne wrote in 1825 to DuBourg: "It will require a miracle to give us a college at St Louis, such as our institute demands, namely, one which is free for day-pupils and which for that reason must have an adequate revenue. Still I dare to hope it of the divine goodness."[37]

"ON THESE TERMS WE CAN ALL SUBSCRIBE…"

In 1828, Father Van Quickenborne began to solicit funds to build the new college. He knew that the school must have boarders in order to pay the expenses of the place and obey the requirement of free tuition that was a rule of the Society of Jesus. John F. Darby, a former mayor of St. Louis, had just finished dining with a few other men at the home of Major Thomas Biddle when "the reverend" was shown in; Van Quickenborne asked for subscriptions for building the college, saying that no one would be approached for their contribution until the "edifice reached the second story." Someone joked: "On these terms we can all subscribe, for I think it doubtful whether the proposed structure will ever reach that height." The group chuckled, and then signed up to contribute. By November 1829, classes were being offered in the new building.[38] Construction was still incomplete, so ladders were used to get to the second floor. The Jesuits later purchased the remaining portion of the square west of Ninth Street, bounded by Washington Avenue, and two-thirds of the next square, Tenth and Eleventh streets. In 1832, their previous college building on Second Street was converted by Bishop Rosati to a church for African American Catholics called St. Mary's Chapel, blessed that year by Father Peter Verhaegen, S.J. In 1834, it began to be used by German Catholics.[39] Three boys were hired to help at the new college, serving as sacristan, porter, and dormitory assistant. In addition, "two Negro slaves transferred from the Florissant farm, Ned and Thomas." Tom was employed as a buyer of supplies as well as a superintendent of the hired help, and Ned served as a cook.[40]

Father Van Quickenborne worked hard to obtain funds and equipment. He also crafted a September 1828 advertisement detailing the curriculum: Greek, Latin, English, and French languages; natural philosophy; mathematics; "geography and the use of globes"; reading, writing, etc. Music and drawing would be offered if "desired by any parents … the learning of profane history will be interwoven with the study of sacred and divine objects. In religious opinions, however, no undue influence shall be exercised on the mind of any pupil."[41]

In North America, the presumption in this period was that students would begin a college course in their early teens, study for six or seven years, and earn an A.B. (bachelor's degree) at an age of nineteen or twenty. Father Peter Verhaegen, S.J., first president as well as first professor of science at Saint Louis College, detailed a study schedule in a letter of November 13, 1829: "The culture of the heart and mind of youth constitutes the end of this institution. And, this important object can only be attained by establishing order … These rules are not imposed with the design of subjecting the scholars to a heavy and toilsome yoke, but of promoting their advancement in virtue and science … experience evinced that present suffering and future ignorance are the natural results of disorder."[42]

The schedule was written for boarders, but day students also followed it, and Verhaegen notes that they should also undertake additional hours of study both before arriving on campus and after returning home.

A.M.

5:30	Rising, washing, combing, etc.
6:00	Studies
7:30	Breakfast and Recreation
8:00	Mass
8:30	School [class]
10:30	Recreation
11:00	Studies
12:00	Angelus Domin., Dinner, Recreation

P.M.

1:30	Studies
2:00	School
4:00	Recreation
4:45	Studies
7:00	Lecture [Reading] of the Lives of the Saints
7:45	Supper, Recreation
8:30	Evening Prayer & Rest

Depending upon the day and time, specific subjects were studied, for example mathematics and geography at 10:30 a.m., cathechism in the chapel at 2:45 p.m. Silence was to be observed in the chapel, dormitory, and study hall.

"Lonely Journies"

Father Peter Kenney, S.J.'s detailed "Memorial" hints at the privations of the Missouri Mission. Even while affirming that humility and frugality should be observed in both abundance and poverty, he reproached the kitchen staff for "reprehensible" carelessness and uncleanliness in cooking and dressing meat and poultry. He was aghast at the service of meals, and pleaded that the members of the community not be fed "greasy hot water under the name of soup." Ironically, greasy gravy was still a complaint in some records from 1938.

Father Kenney recommended strong horses, warm clothing, and "a good watch" for the Jesuits' "lonely journies" when called out at night to minister to the community. While recognizing the "circumstances of this Mission" and the specific contexts "in this country" and making some adaptations to certain rules (for example adding July 4 as a holiday; allowing men to forego Litanies at night if wearied from travel and ministerial duties; and declaring: "no man should be obliged to go from the fatigues of class directly to dinner"), nevertheless he insisted that an infirmary be built, that the Society's rules regarding communications, prayers, feast days, possessions, penance, and numerous other customs be honored, and that book-keeping be improved, as the balances "are rather more probable than the exact result." Adhering to the Concordat, he cautioned against a mission to Native Americans on Salt River if it appeared to be "unnecessarily taking to ourselves a mission that could be supplied by Secular clergy."[43] These and other words of advice would have been very important to the men of the Mission, being so far from Rome and with much work to do.

The Jesuits of the Missouri Mission went far and wide, in St. Louis and throughout the American West. This travel cross, chalice, and flask belonged to Father De Smet.

"THINGS HERE, REVEREND FATHER, ARE ALL NEW
AND MUST BE MOULDED INTO SHAPE."

FATHER PETER VERHAEGEN, S.J.

"A PAINFUL UPHILL FIGHT FOR BARE EXISTENCE"
FATHER GILBERT
GARRAGHAN, S.J. [44]

In October 1831, Father Peter Kenney, S.J. arrived as an official Visitor from the Jesuit headquarters in Rome. The Society of Jesus periodically sent Visitors to assess its various missions around the world. Verhaegen worried that the school would be ordered closed. It was not thriving financially. In addition, some of the local citizens were growing more "American," that is to say: less interested in a classical education. Indians in the West had been asking for "Black Robes" since 1804, and new immigrants arrived daily. How could Verhaegen justify using Jesuits in a college when other forms of ministry were calling?

Not only did Kenney recommend keeping the school open, his remarks in a "Memorial" of May 1832 (see sidebar at left) provided astute and helpful comments that were read aloud at meals for decades. He also brought along Father Van de Velde, who proved to be an excellent addition to the staff. Van de Velde taught rhetoric and math, took his final vows in 1837, and served the university as president from 1840 to 1843.

The demand and need for Jesuits was significant, always outweighing the numbers of men and resources available. The Middle West Jesuits have been the subject of numerous accounts, both scholarly and popular; perhaps one of the most succinct descriptions can be found in a 1928 letter from Father Thomas Hughes, S.J. to Father Charles H. Cloud, S.J. Writing from Rome, Hughes refers to "a devouring missionary zeal among certain types of men from Fathers Damen and Weninger down, and behind them back to the founders of the Mission and Province."[45]

Leon Pomarède's 1832 "View of St. Louis from Illinois Town." A noted and prolific artist, he also painted (1856-7) the frescoes which decorated the university's auditorium.

In October 1832, Father General Jan Roothaan, S.J. wrote to Kenney of the college as "unpromising." While in St. Louis, Kenney wrote to Father John McElroy, S.J., who was in Fredericktown, Maryland, that religious studies at the college were good, but the teaching of the classics did not live up to the ambitious prospectus. He wondered if it was worthwhile for Jesuits to seek to cultivate "this stubborn soil" of cities like St. Louis. Yet, both Roothaan and Kenney had been instrumental in preventing the Maryland Province from taking the Missouri Mission back under its control in August 1832, thereby ensuring the independence of the western mission.[46]

While the Father General urged the wider promotion of Latin and Greek, Verhaegen negotiated by drawing attention to the flux of life in St. Louis. Verhaegen wrote: "We are placing on the pursuit of letters just that degree of emphasis which the state of our infant country allows. Things here, Reverend Father, are all new and must be moulded into shape. The study of languages, if you except English and French, has no great attraction for the young. This defect will be remedied only in the course of time, namely, when the family affairs of the inhabitants become more settled and an end be put to all these changes and shiftings of residence." William McGucken writes: "Latin was first taught in the session of 1830-31, and Greek probably at the end of the 1831-32 session," while Garraghan estimates thirty Latin students by 1833-1834, and eight in Greek class.[47]

The CHARTER of St. Louis University.

An Act
to incorporate the St. Louis University.

Whereas it is represented to the General Assembly that a literary institution called the St. Louis College, has, for several years past, been in successful operation, near the City of St. Louis, sustained and conducted by the voluntary association and private resources of individuals, without the aid of Government; And, whereas the President of the said College, in behalf of himself and the other professors and managers thereof, has solicited an act of incorporation, by the name and style of the St. Louis University: Now, in order to encourage learning, to extend the means of education, and to give dignity, permanency, and usefulness to the said institution,— Be it enacted by the General Assembly of the State of Missouri: That [1] P. J. Verhaegen, Theódore de Theux, P. W. Walsh, C. F. Van Quickenborne and James VandeVelde be and they are hereby constituted and appointed trustees of the said Literary insti-

By Christmas of 1832, when the university was granted its state charter, Verhaegen may have allowed himself to feel some relief. With this status, Saint Louis University became the first university to be established west of the Mississippi River. Also in 1832, Saint Louis University was officially the first Catholic university in the United States to offer the A.M. degree (a Master's degree) in the classical program. Divinity studies taking place at St. Louis Academy from the time of foundation arguably extend a claim even farther back. "Of the Catholic universities in the United States there is only one, Georgetown, that is older [than SLU] in point of origin… But though Georgetown was founded by the Jesuits at an earlier date, Saint Louis University was the first to establish the various schools and faculties which constitute a true university."[48]

Father Peter Verhaegen, S.J., the first president of Saint Louis University.

"THE PETITION OF P.J. VERHAEGEN"

The state charter of Saint Louis University was discussed amidst legislative considerations ranging from divorce decrees and the founding of a penitentiary to "A bill to provide for the killing of wolves." On Friday, November 23, 1832, Missouri Senator Edward Bates "presented the petition of P. J. Verhaegen, President of the St. Louis College, praying the incorporation of said institution by the name and style of the St. Louis University." The petition was referred to the committee on education; it was read out three times over the ensuing days, passing on November 29. The Missouri House of Representatives learned on November 27 that the bill had been introduced in the Senate, and learned of its passage on November 29. On December 3, the Senate bill was "taken up" by the House; Representative William Carr Lane moved that it be reviewed in committee. After committee review and three readings, it was passed on December 20. By the end of the month, it was passed to Governor Daniel Dunklin for his signature.

It was official: Bishop DuBourg's Academy had grown up into a university.

As the year 1832 drew to a close, the Missouri legislature reviewed and passed in less than one month "the petition of P.J. Verhaegen," incorporating Saint Louis University.

A true university

1833-1867

In his correspondence and journals, Saint Ignatius of Loyola often used the phrase: *cura animarum* (Latin: "to help souls/persons"). Living in a place that would one day be called "the Gateway City," the St. Louis Jesuits were positioned to do just that. From what we can discern across the decades, they were a complex group: pious, cheerful, bold, loving, serious, craving quiet. They served as teachers, missionaries, pastors, and university administrators. As teachers, they could be stern, if we can judge by the nickname: "The Inquisition," bestowed by students who started a secret newspaper. In this period, Saint Louis University increased the size of its campus: acquiring more land and erecting new buildings. Despite tight finances and anti-Catholic prejudice in the city, the Jesuits reached for a vision of a true university, establishing medical, law, and divinity schools. Financial straits, political revolutions, and crises mark the era, both in the United States and abroad. By 1867, the Jesuits had purchased for their university a plot of land at the corner of Grand and Lindell boulevards, but it was over twenty years before they could afford to move to the new site.

Students pose, with their hats, coats, and baseball bats, in the quadrangle of the downtown campus. Behind them is the original 1829 building, which gained new wings in 1832 and 1833.

"TIME WILL TEACH US WHAT IS TO BE DONE."
FATHER PETER VERHAEGEN, S.J.

In early 1833, Saint Louis University's administrators and faculty included the six Belgians who snuck out of their homeland, full of missionary zeal. They had trekked to Missouri, where they chopped down trees to build their new home: St. Stanislaus Seminary. They studied, taught, and worked in the fields of the seminary farm. Now they were running a college in a bustling, riverfront town, and expanding their mission widely (see page 48).

While Father Peter Kenney's counsel (see Chapter 1) buttressed morale in the Jesuit community, it was money—pure and simple—that ensured the survival of the university. Key funds were raised by Bishop DuBourg in his travels across Europe. In addition, Pope Gregory XVI approved Father General Jan Roothaan, S.J.'s *Ordinatio de Minervali* of February 1, 1833, allowing Jesuit colleges to charge tuition for the first time in the history of the order. Father Peter Verhaegen had lobbied Roothaan to change this rule, as Father Francis Neale, S.J., Jesuit superior in Maryland, had once fruitlessly entreated Father General Luigi Fortis, S.J.

One man: Father Peter John De Smet, S.J., played a crucial role in supporting the Middle Western Jesuits for decades. Gilbert Garraghan writes: "No other single individual among them was as active in maintaining the economic basis necessary for the activities they carried on."[1] He calculates that De Smet brought eighty-four recruits from Europe to St. Louis alone (he also recruited men for the mission in California). De Smet solicited about $250,000 (several million dollars in today's terms), mostly from Belgium and Holland, and secured low-interest loans at key times. He brought back gifts-in-kind including books, artwork, and equipment for the university as well as altar furniture and supplies for Indian missions in Kansas and the Rocky Mountains. Eight out of every ten colleges in the nation had closed by the end of the Civil War, but De Smet's wide network of friends, which included U.S. Secretary of War Edwin Stanton, helped the university to survive the war.[2]

As a missionary, Father De Smet produced many maps, sketches, and other materials regarding native life. In winter 1858-59, he used sepia ink to illustrate the Coeur d'Alene Mission of the Sacred Heart of Jesus. The sketch includes a list of twenty-three numbered sites within the mission.

"When one is sick among the Seneca..."

FATHER PETER JOHN DE SMET, S.J.
IN "GREAT MEDICINE DANCE AMONG THE SENECAS, AS RELATED TO ME BY THE CHIEF OF THE SIX NATIONS," 1867

Jesuits prize eloquence and have long respected the intersection of language and culture. The life and work of Father Peter John De Smet, S.J. demonstrate these values. A tireless missionary and careful ethnographer, he forged connections with people from many Native American tribes. He cherished relationships of mutual esteem with them. De Smet translated Christian prayers into seventeen different native languages, and produced a wealth of maps, drawings, stories, and concepts about native life.

Born in Dendermonde, Belgium in 1801, DeSmet was among the pioneer Jesuits recruited by Father Charles Nerinckx to come from Belgium to the United States in 1821, to serve in the Native American missions. An optimistic, sturdy soul, nicknamed "Samson" for his physical strength, De Smet chopped down trees and dragged logs through the woods along with his fellow Jesuits in order to construct the buildings of the St. Stanislaus Seminary in Florissant, Missouri. In 1829, De Smet was listed as "person in charge of the library" at Saint Louis College. He taught English, and in 1834, acquired for the university the entire library of an Augustinian monastery in Enghien, Belgium.

By 1840, the Missouri Vice Province had sufficient resources to take on new missions and De Smet was permitted to follow his heart's desire: he traveled to meet Flathead braves, who had repeatedly asked for "Blackrobes" to come and live with them. Thanks to his efforts, the Society's missions soon extended to areas that became the states of Idaho, Montana, Washington, and Wyoming.

Father Gilbert Garraghan, S.J. wrote of De Smet: "Probably no Jesuit since the restoration of the Order in 1814 had gained so widespread a celebrity." Through his extensive contacts, he gathered money, men, and resources that greatly advanced the Society of Jesus in North America. In 1837, he recruited Arnold Damen in Holland, who began a mission to Chicago in 1856 and later founded Loyola College (later University) of Chicago. In 1844, Father De Smet sailed from Europe with five Jesuits bound for Oregon, including Michael Accolti and John Nobili, the pioneers of the Jesuit apostolate in California. He ensured the survival of Saint Louis University during the Civil War. In addition, he was solicited by the U.S. government to assist in negotiating treaties with tribes.

Although he was highly skilled in handling finances for the university and the Missouri Province, De Smet was never happy at a desk. He loved travel, and covered an estimated 180,000 miles in the course of his life, often under arduous and even dangerous conditions. He knew many powerful and wealthy people in the United States and Europe. But his true joy was to sit on the ground with Native Americans, eating dog stew after sharing some tobacco. He played clarinet for the Indians, and used a "ladder" graphic to reinforce his lessons about God. De Smet's greatest sorrow in life was to witness exactly what he had foreseen and tried to stop: the decimation of the American Indians as whites encroached upon their land and way of life.

This 1864 photograph of Father De Smet is believed to have been taken by Matthew Brady, in his studio in Washington, D.C.

1834

ST. LOUIS UNIVERSITY.

1834

THE **FIFTH ANNUAL EXAMINATION** of the Students attached to this Institution, will take place on TUESDAY and WEDNESDAY, the 29th and 30th inst., from 8 till 10 o'clock, A. M., and from 5 till 7 o'clock, P. M., on both days. The EXHIBITION and DISTRIBUTION OF PREMIUMS, on THURSDAY, the 31st inst. at 9 o'clock, A. M., when the following pieces will be delivered by the Students whose names are affixed to them.

ORDER OF EXERCISES.

PROLOGUE,		John Haggerty,	New York.
VANITE DE L'HOMME		Detour Foucher,	New Orleans.
1 DIALOGUE, {Boniface,		Russel Curtis,	Alexandria, La.
{Aimwell,		Robert Beamon,	Do.
WM. TELL'S SOLILOQUY,		Louis Texada,	Rapides La.
L'OPTIQUE,		Omer Bouis,	Point Coupee, La.
		Eugene Biossat,	Alexandria.
2 DIALOGUE, {Yankee,		William Taylor,	St. Louis.
{Dandy,		A. Jackson Hyams,	Donaldson La.
EXTRACT FROM P. HENRY,		Jos. Larguier,	Baton Rouge La.
DESCRIPTION DU LAC		Robert Beamon,	Alexandria.
DEATH OF WASHINGTON,		Thrasimond Landry,	West Baton Rouge
3 DIALOGUE, {Le Bourgeois,		Peter Poursine,	Ascension La.
{Le Philosophe,		Charles Kennedy,	New Orleans.
STANZAS BY LORD BYRON,		Chérotte Laroque	Ascension.
MONOLOGUE D'ESTHER,		Victor Solis,	St. Bernard, La.
LA SOLEDAD,		John Walker,	Rapides La.
		Daniel Hicky,	Baton Rouge.
		William Hardey,	Opelousas, La.
4 KENTUCKY ELECTION,		Vassain Dupuy,	Plaquemine, La.
		Jules Hebert,	Iberville, La.
		Philip Hicky,	Baton Rouge.
		Fremon du Bouffay,	Missouri.
LE REVEUR DE'CONCERTE,		Théodule Bouis,	Pointe Coupee.
THE TORCH OF LIBERTY,		J. B. Quegles,	Natchez, Mis.
PHENOMENES DE LA NATURE,		Severin Braud,	Ascension.
BATTLE OF WARSAW,		John Walker,	Rapides.
	{Le Roi,	Joseph Duralde,	W. Baton Rouge.
	{Hemon,	Auguste Roche,	New Orleans.
5 SCENE TIREE DES FRERES ENNEMIS, {Eteocle,		Jean Lafaye,	Do.
	{Attale,	Louis Laroque,	Ascension.
	{Polynice,	Jules Hebert,	Iberville.
	{Soldat,	Charles Kennedy,	New Orleans.
COLUMBUS ON DISCOVERING AMERICA,		Israel R. Christy,	St. Charles.
IN DEGENEROS NOBILES,		Jose Puch y Bea,	Campeachy.
PASSAGE OF THE RED SEA,		Eugene Biossat,	Alexandria.
ELEGIE,		Louis Petit,	Plaquemine.
6 SCENE BY SIR WALTER SCOTT, {Fitz James,		Philip Hicky,	Baton Rouge.
	{Roderic Dhu,	Joseph Duralde,	W. Baton Rouge.
CONSEILS DE LA SAGESSE,		Thrasimond Landry,	Do.
DESTRUCTION OF POMPEII,		William Taylor,	St. Louis.
UTILITAS SCIENTIÆ,		Isidore Boudreaux,	New Orleans.
CHARACTERE DE NAPOLEON,		Joseph Duralde,	W. Baton Rouge.
	{King Henry,	Fremon du Bouffay,	Missouri.
	{Prince Henry,	John Walker,	Rapides.
	{Clarence,	Daniel Hicky,	Baton Rouge.
	{Humphry,	Adolph Sigur,	Iberville.
7 SCENE FROM HENRY 4TH., {Northumberland,		Louis Laroque,	Ascension.
	{Hotspur,	Jos. Duralde,	W. Baton Rouge.
	{Warwick,	William Hardey,	Opelousas.
	{Westmoreland,	Philip Hicky,	Baton Rouge.
	{Harcourt,	Jules Hebert,	Iberville.
CATO'S SOLILOQUY,		Charles Tessier,	Baton Rouge.
LE LEVER DU SOLEIL		Peter Poursine,	Ascension.
EIS TEN ELEUTHERIAN,		Chas. Kennedy,	New Orleans.
8 SCENE TIREE D'ANDROMAQUE, {Oreste,		Jean Lafaye,	New Orleans.
	{Pylade,	Adolphe Sigur,	Iberville.
GLADIATOR'S DREAM,		Philip Hicky,	Baton Rouge.
DESCRIPTION D'UN ORAGE,		Isidore Boudreaux,	New Orleans.
	{Artaxamenes,	Edward Manning	Cork, Ireland.
9 BOMBASTES FURIOSO, {Fusbos,		Adolph Sigur,	Iberville.
	{Bombastes,	Fremon du Bouffay,	Missouri.
	{Disposo,	Daniel Hicky,	Baton Rouge.
GRADUATES' ADDRESS,		Fremon du Bouffay,	Missouri.

Distribution of Premiums, and Collation of the Degree of A. B., on

P. A. FREMON DU BOUFFAY, MISSOURI, AND PETER A. WALSH, ST. LOUIS.

EPILOGUE, {John Quegles, {Eugene Biossat, {John Haggerty, *Natchez. Alexandria. New York.*

By order of the Faculty,

P. J. VERHAEGEN, PRESIDENT.

Students demonstrated their skills and received prizes at annual, public exhibits held when the school year ended. University historian Father Faherty reports that an M.A. was awarded in 1834.

While reporting in 1840 that "the intrepid missioner" Father De Smet had left to meet the Flathead tribe, who for years had been requesting "Black Robes," Verhaegen wondered in a letter: "I am afraid that, in this case we have run ourselves into danger by running too far. Time will teach us what is to be done." This last sentence likely reveals far less about Verhaegen's personal philosophy and more about the effort it required for him to be patient. He valued discipline and order, while possessing great personal magnetism and initiative. Born June 21, 1800, he was the second Jesuit priest ever ordained in Mis-

Father Peter
Verhaegen, S.J.

souri.[3] The first and youngest president in Saint Louis University's history, his face can be glimpsed in only a few surviving images, all rather serious. Some sense of his intellectual acuity, faith, and candor is evident in his extensive writings.

In 1840, Verhaegen confided to Bishop of Cincinnati John Baptist Purcell: "I, poor fellow, find myself again in my Purgatory" (emphasis in original).[4] In his journals, Verhaegen developed proofs for the proposition "the human soul is a substance altogether Spiritual" (distinct from matter). In one journal, he reasoned: "I grant that the idea of a Self-existent, eternal, infinitely intelligent and almighty being, distinct from this

material universe, is overwhelming; for a finite being, like man, cannot adequately or perfectly comprehend infinity, though he has an idea of it; but though the admission of an uncreated, eternal being of boundless power and wisdom, who formed, sustains and governs all things, cannot but fill the mind with awe, and show to man his own littleness and vanity, the mind finds repose; it recognizes an adequate cause for all the mighty wonders, the wonderfully varied and splendid effects which the universe exhibits. On every other supposition, we are lost in a labyrinth of endless mazes, and find ourselves bewildered among innumerable conjectures of contradiction and absurdities."

Verhaegen quotes "the holy author" in closing: "if, what is impossible we be deceived, Thou, O Lord hast deceived us!" And with that, the journal ends, as he underlines the sentence.

In 1858, Father De Smet traveled to Washington territory, accompanied by, from left, in front row: Victor, of the Kalispel tribe; Alexander, of the Pend Oreille; Adolphe, of the Flathead; and Andrew of the Coeur d'Alene. Back row: Dennis of the Colville; Bonaventure of the Coeur d'Alene; and Francis Xavier of the Flatheads.

[BOTTOM] Father Verhaegen corresponded frequently with the Jesuit superior-general, Father Jan Roothaan. This 1840 letter shows his easy usage of both French and Latin as well as his distinctive signature.

When Brother James Yates, a faculty member, fell ill in late 1832, Verhaegen faced a challenge. Losing a teacher and with no replacement, he was forced to cut twenty students. The university still relied upon boarding fees, as Jesuit schools were not yet permitted to charge tuition. He could not afford to cut boarding students. Yet, if he cut day students, he risked alienating the very community that had helped to fund the school. He took a remarkably independent position in this, the first week of the institution's official status as a university. He refused a $5,000 endowment from a prosperous local businessman named John Mullanphy knowing that its terms would bankrupt the school, and he chose to dismiss twenty of the "externs" or day students, rather than cut boarders.[5] Arranging the curriculum around the boarders was important. It maintained a commitment to moral education: the "formation in learning and virtue" to which a commission of Jesuits had given structure in the 1599 *Ratio Studiorum*.[6] For, as Father Lowrie Daly, S.J. writes: "it was not dreamed of that informational education could be divorced from moral education."[7] Verhaegen's strategy was both realistic and bold. After this, the university actually refused endowments for several decades, striving to maintain independence.

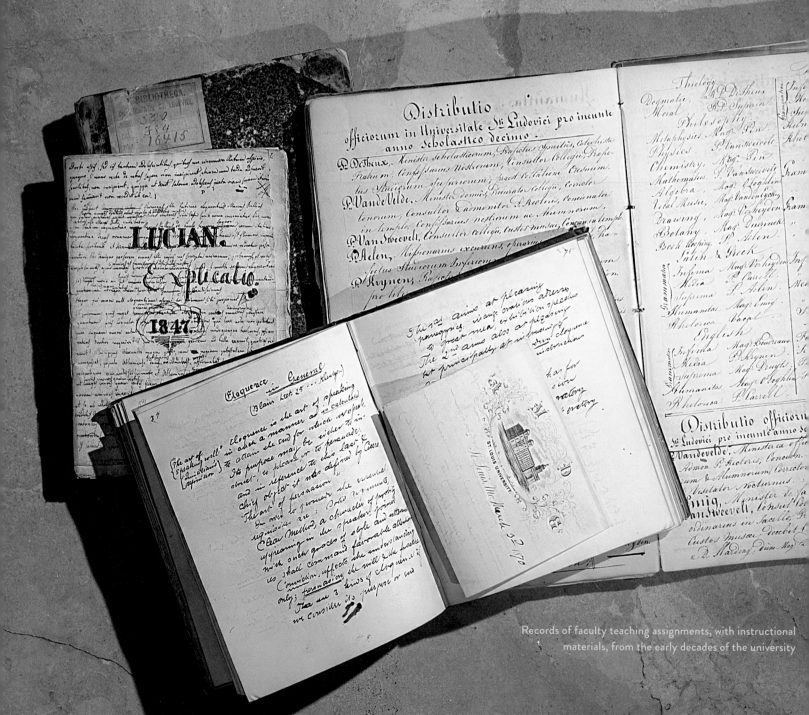

Records of faculty teaching assignments, with instructional materials, from the early decades of the university

"IS THERE ANY BETTER SCHOOL IN THE FAR WEST?"
WILLIAM CARR LANE, 1845[8]

All of the original structures of the university's campus at Ninth and Washington are gone, but life there is evoked in many records. Prefects' journals for this time are packed with daily reports of the arrivals and departures of the fathers: coming in from Chicago, California, Cincinnati, and Ecuador, or heading out to Kansas and leaving for Florissant, whether in carriages, on horseback, and even riding bicycles. Newspapers and scrapbooks track the many civic activities of the faculty and students. Patriotic parades took place on Independence Day, with medical students joining in the processions starting in 1838. The students marched to the church, and the Declaration of Independence was read aloud. In February 1847, the Chouteau family rode in a carriage in the anniversary parade of the city, while university students marched behind the wagon of D. Colver's Brewery. The *St. Louis Republican* on September 14, 1879 listed all the "old Creole families" and their sons who attended the university from 1828-1860.[9]

Minutes from the board of trustees demonstrate that discussion was crucial. The university's administrators met in spaces long since built over in downtown St. Louis. Gathered together in the office of the president at seven o'clock in the evening, the Jesuits addressed a range of topics: assigning realtors, considering bequests, fending off claims, planning a post-graduate course of lectures. Topics of concern included housing for boarders, and separating classical from mercantile students. Some periods were relatively smooth: at an annual board meeting in 1838, "no subject" was offered for consideration, and the meeting adjourned!

The founding members of the Society of Jesus admired the pedagogical system of the University of Paris, drawing upon this model when they opened their first college at Messina in 1548. They also integrated elements from the University of Alcalá and the Brethren of the Common Life. The "method of Paris," according to Father Gabriel Codina, S.J., includes these elements: (1) relatively more power was accorded to professors than to students (in contrast to the system in Bologna); (2) pedagogical methods included lectures, notes, planned questions, disputations, memorization, and study of a theme in pairs; (3) Students kept notebooks with cites of the best classical authors, under a principle of "healthy emulation"; and (4) the system used sequencing and progression: divisions by class, and advancement to the next class only after passing. Rewards included prizes in academic competitions. In addition, numerous rules were in force, including bans on "unwholesome" activities. Physical punishment was only to be used as a last resort, and was never to be administered by Jesuits.[10]

In 1853, Saint Francis Xavier Church (built 1841) faced Ninth Street. The original 1829 college structure is behind the church, and a classroom building is to the left, with two observatory towers, a museum, library, and lecture hall. Other buildings housed the medical school, boarding facilities, and classrooms. A nine foot high wall around the campus led students to dub their school: "Saint Louis Penitentiary."

John H. Reel (Class of 1856) was interviewed for the December 15, 1921 issue of the student newspaper, named at the time: *Varsity Breeze*. Decrying the haste and lack of fundamentals of current educational practices, Reel recalled the rigorous system used by his professors, "native Belgians." Students learned philosophy in Latin, spoke it fluently during their free moments, and even tried to conduct classes in classical Greek.

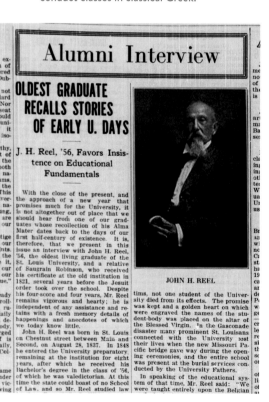

Distant in time and space, the nineteenth century campus of Saint Louis University was marked by many of these traits, including the culture of severity and "treats." Life was rigorous! One student wrote to his mother about a boy who was punished for sneaking a Bible into Church to read.[11] John H. Reel (Class of 1856, valedictorian) remembered "many a time" waking up to find that drifts of snowfall had come through the windows during the night. Even worse was "the ordeal of the pump"— carrying a basin to the pump and washing up with icy water. Students rose at five in the morning, except on Thursdays, when they were allowed another hour of sleep. Philosophy was studied in Latin. There was no honor system, so Reel notes that students lived under "perpetual surveillance" and "a huge spy system," which they resented. They tried many "rash escapades" simply to rebel, despite knowing they would be caught and punished.[12]

Saint Louis University's campus at first seemed remote. "When the first building went up in 1829, it stood isolated in suburban loneliness," writes Garraghan. The city limits stopped at Seventh Street. Soon, the building gained new wings on each side: to the east in 1832 and to the west in 1833.[13] Other buildings were added, as well as a gracious church: St. Francis Xavier, which was open by 1843 and served what was called "the College parish." And in 1855, the university finally had an auditorium with capacity to seat the many attendees at commencement and other events. Its walls were decorated with allegorical frescoes by the noted painter, Leon Pomarède.

The dream of quiet remained elusive, despite a rule of silence governing many spaces on campus. A noisy, growing city soon encroached upon the campus; the rumbling wagons of west-bound travelers passed nearby. The Jesuits eventually sought other property further out of town, including at Bellefontaine Road, finally choosing a parcel of land at Grand and Lindell boulevards.

In 1841, Lewis Foulk Thomas described the university in an illustrated publication about the city of St. Louis.[14] The system of instruction was "truly paternal." Regarding observation of faith at the university, Thomas writes: "The public exercises of religion are those of the Catholic Church; but pupils of all denominations are received."[15] Every Thursday was designated for recreation, and on the first Wednesday of each month, the university announced the ranks of pupils in their classes; top students received medals. Students could elect a mercantile course ("reading, writing, the English and French languages, poetry, rhetoric, history, geography, mythology, book-keeping, arithmetic, algebra, geometry, the use of the globes, trigonometry, mensuration and surveying") or a classical course (mercantile subjects, as well as Latin and Greek, logic, metaphysics, moral and natural philosophy and higher branches of mathematics). As the curriculum expanded to include business courses, more lay faculty began to be hired.[16]

Thomas praised the university's 8,000-volume library, which included a special edition of the Domesday Book issued in 1834 to American universities by the British government. Father Thomas Hughes, S.J., however, used the phrase "lumber room" to describe he university's nineteenth century library, referring to its state of neglect and even a degree of "danger" upon entry!

[RIGHT] Handwriting variations suggest that at least ten different people contributed entries to this, the university's first library catalog. It includes author, title, and publication data for over 2,000 titles. Estimates of the collection in this period range as high as 8,000 volumes. This catalog was never completed and after six years, it was abandoned. In the 1880s, two more attempts were made; the collection by then had over 25,000 titles.

Prior to 1839-40, the school year went from September 1 to July 31. In subsequent years, the schedule varied: sometimes from October 1 to mid-August, or late August to July 4. Student ages ranged from twelve to sixteen years old, and enrollment fluctuated: before the 1850's, it was never more than two hundred; it exceeded four hundred by the end of the nineteenth century.[17] The 2,911[th] student was admitted on July 2, 1860.

Students could try fencing, learn music, or join the brass band of the philharmonic. In the late 1830s, both French and English were spoken during recreational periods. Spanish was also commonly spoken in these years, as many of the students who came (via New Orleans) to study at Saint Louis University were from Mexico. However, by 1881, boarding had stopped.

In 1837, the noted orator Daniel Webster visited St. Louis. Mayor John Darby brought him to the university, where he was warmly welcomed. Webster grew quite moved by the student recitations: "poems and addresses from students in English, Latin, Greek, German, Italian, Spanish and French."[18] He was made an honorary member of the Philalethic Literary and Debating Society, which students had founded in 1832. Other notable guests included Martin Van Buren and Charles Dickens in 1842.

In 1855, students put out a clandestine paper called *The Sharp-Shooter*, calling the faculty "The Inquisition" for their attempts to curtail the paper. Also in that year, a German traveler, Johann Georg Kohl, visited the campus. From his book on travels in the northwest United States, the section on Saint Louis University was translated by Father Laurence Kenny, S.J.

Kohl was pleased by the sight of young people playing sports in the garden and the playground on a Sunday. He personally found the strictness of Protestant observances on Sundays to be tyrannical. Of the 240 students, fifty were Protestants; out of respect to them, the University fathers made sure that the game options did not include something as noisy and scandalous as football. Regarding Catholic schools in the United States, he writes: "I must say that the Jesuit schools have made the best impression on me both as regards the intelligence of the teachers as well as the careful and rich equipments of their plants." He also praised the library, the astronomical observatory, and the "courage" and daring of the priest who gave the sermon that evening in the college church.[19]

Catalogus 1mus

Omnium Librorum

Universitatis Sti Ludovici,

Diversarum facultatum auctoribus

ordine alphabetico in diversas

Classes distributis,

1836.

"Locust trees in yard begin to bloom"

The nineteenth century French astronomer, explorer, and geographer Joseph N. Nicollet conducted expeditions to territories which later became the states of Minnesota, Iowa, and North Dakota. He credited Saint Louis University's Father Peter Judocus Van Sweevelt, S.J. in his 1841 *Report Intended to Illustrate A Map of the Hydrographical Basin of the Upper Mississippi River* (submitted to Congress): "The absolute height of the barometer at this point was not known (the ordinary low water in the Mississippi at St. Louis); and my addressing myself to the reverend fathers, the Jesuits at the head of the University of St. Louis, and engaging them in making meteorological observations, was the first approach towards obtaining it. They acquiesced cheerfully in my proposal, as they do with everything tending to the advancement of learning. The late reverend Mr. Vansweevelt charged himself with the task, for which I gave him a fine cistern barometer of Troughton, and received afterwards nineteen months of observations, made five times a day, and followed as regularly as his official duties would permit, through the years 1835 and 1836." Nicollet also gave a barometer to Father De Smet, to take measurements at Council Bluffs, and encouraged him to write a dictionary of the Iroquois and a vocabulary for the Potawatomi.[1]

Some years later, meteorological observations were restarted at the university. From 1857 forward, Jesuits noted barometric pressure, wind speeds, and numerous other details from observation points including property at College Hill. More than simply a set of numbers, these notations are accompanied by evocative descriptions of other phenomena, such as snow and rain. In the winter of 1857, the Mississippi was gorged: "Ferry Boat can't cross," and a few days later, the community experienced "a heavy fall of snow." Soon the ice was "thawing rapidly." Father Ignatius Panken, S.J. observed in 1861 the lower and upper clouds moving in opposite directions to each other; others recorded one spring: "Locust trees in yard begin to bloom."

Meteorological phenomena were recorded at College Hill by many Jesuits, including Father Ignatius Panken, S.J.

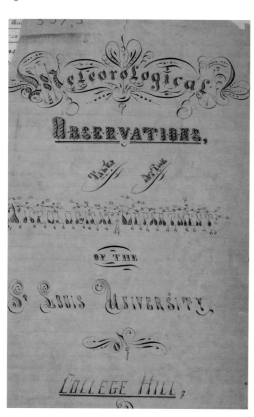

Joseph Nicollet led three expeditions to map the Upper Mississippi River basin. He used technical innovations and native place-names, producing highly accurate maps. The Chouteau family supported his first trip, in 1836.

As late as 1960, SLU had a May Day tradition in which a student would place this silver crown on the statue of Mary in St. Francis Xavier Church.

During this time period, various calamities beset the city of St. Louis: cholera epidemics in 1832, 1834, and 1849, major fires in 1839 and 1849, the Camp Jackson skirmish and the Civil War — but they seemed to sweep past the university without causing permanent damage. Students devoted themselves to the Blessed Virgin's care during one cholera outbreak that killed ten percent of the city population. They commissioned a silver crown for her in gratitude for what seemed like a miracle: not a single member of the university fell sick. The university closed early due to the 1864 small pox epidemic, but the Jesuits took their graduating class to Florissant, to study at the St. Stanislaus Seminary, so they could graduate.

By 1867, the first team sport at the university was organized: the baseball team "The Pickwicks" were led to a victory over Washington University by star pitcher Shepard Barclay.

The Pickwicks used two fields: the Red Stockings' field west of Compton, and the St. Louis Browns' field, at Grand and Sullivan.

In 1843, Dr. Moses Linton founded the first medical journal west of the Mississippi, the *St. Louis Medical and Surgical Journal*, pictured here with a catalog of the time, and medical equipment used at the school.

"SINCERELY ATTACHED TO THE PRIESTS OF THE COLLEGE."

Father Verhaegen soon set to work to expand courses of study. Within a few years of receiving its state charter, the university was approached by the St. Louis Medical Society of Missouri with a request to "attach a medical department." The request was debated by the board of trustees, and approved. Six professors were chosen: one for each branch of medicine that was planned for the school.[20] Verhaegen had cultivated contacts to support this goal, meeting with area physicians as early as 1835. The Board resolved to be "uninfluenced" by religious principles. Indeed, the school's leaders had initially planned and hoped for tolerance. They established a constitutionally determined, inter-denominational board of advisers, "in order to free the Department from all prejudices of a sectarian character." Faiths represented on the board were: Presbyterian, Catholic, Unitarian, Episcopalian, Methodist, Baptist, and Reformed Presbyterian. After some years of planning, classes in the "Medical College of St. Louis University" were offered in 1842. There were twenty-nine students, and the college was in a building on the north side of Washington Avenue, between Tenth and Eleventh.

In addition to these plans, the Jesuits took advantage of another opportunity. As described in subsequent memoirs, the generosity of Saint Louis University resulted in a new academic undertaking: a law college.

"AN ACADEMY WILL BE FORMED, IN WHICH SUBJECTS RELAT-
ING TO THE NATURAL LAW, AND TO MENTAL AND MORAL
PHILOSOPHY, WILL BE DISCUSSED FOR THE IMPROVEMENT OF
THE STUDENTS IN LAW AND PHILOSOPHY."

SAINT LOUIS UNIVERSITY CATALOG, 1844

The 1844 catalog describes the law courses offered. There may have been another professor, whose name is lost to history.

4

LAW DEPARTMENT.

Hon. RICHARD A. BUCKNER, Professor of Common Law,
" " Professor of Chancery Law.

The Law School opens on the first Monday of November, and closes in March.

The system of instruction, by close and frequent examination in the text books, is calculated to make the students thoroughly acquainted with their profession.

A Moot Court, for the discussion of legal questions, and for conducting cases in law and equity, is held weekly. The students may attend the classes of one or both professors. Diplomas will be given at the end of the session to those who will be deemed qualified.

The text books for the Common Law class are — Blackstone's Commentaries, Gould's Pleading, Chitty on Contracts, Chitty's Pleadings, Kent's Commentaries, and Smith's Commercial Law. Such as cannot conveniently procure Gould's Pleading, may get Stephen on Pleading.

The text books for the Chancery Law class are—Mitford on Pleading, and Maddock's Chancery.

TERMS.—Fee for the ticket of each Professor $20 00
Graduation Fee 5 00

The number of Students for the first course of Lectures was 18.

SOCIETIES.

Four societies, the Philalethic, the Orthological, the Phileuphradic, and the Philharmonic, exist among the students of the University.

The Philalethic Society was instituted in 1832, and subsequently sanctioned by the Board and Faculty of the University. Its principal object is to improve the members in public speaking. The honorary members are allowed to be present at their debates.

OFFICERS OF THE PHILALETHIC SOCIETY.

F. P. O'LOGHLEN, President.
D. H. GUYON, Vice-President.
WILLIAM G. COLEMAN, Secretary.
THOMAS O'NEIL, Treasurer.
PATRICK DONNELLY, Librarian.
F. P. LEAVENWORTH, First Censor.
THOMAS FINNEY, Second Censor.

The Orthological Society was instituted in 1840, and sanctioned by the Board and Faculty of the University. Its object is the improvement of its members by means of Literary Discussions and Speeches, calculated to accustom them to speak with ease and fluency.

In "the first great fire Sept 1839," writes Richard Aylett Barret, one St. Louis merchant on the levee named William D. Barret "lost heavily." He writes that Father Verhaegen offered to educate this merchant's three young sons "privilege to reimburse at some convenient future… Grateful for the kindness, desiring the success of the University, knowing the Faculty wished to obtain a man learned in the Law, to ground a Law School, recommended judge Buckner, an able lawyer, an experienced teacher of the law, suitable for the task."

According to Richard Barret's handwritten account, Father Verhaegen proposed a plan in 1841 to Richard Aylett Buckner of Kentucky. Buckner had served in the Kentucky House of Representatives and the U.S. Congress. Buckner was invited to come to St. Louis and "lay the basis of a Law Department." The school opened "with éclat," as the judge arrived "unheralded," and moved in with his son-in-law, Dr. Richard Farril

Barret. He was promptly visited by notable figures of the city, including Edward Bates, who later served on President Abraham Lincoln's cabinet. Although Buckner "considered it unprofessional to advertise," he drew eighteen students to classes in a two-story brick building on the north side of Washington Avenue between Ninth and Tenth streets. Courses in Common Law as well as Chancery Law were offered, and a Moot Court was held weekly. Other sources also credit Father Van de Velde and Father George Carrell for helping to create the first law school.

Boasting many notable alumni, including Thomas Sherman, S.J. the son of General William T. Sherman, the law school closed in 1847 upon Buckner's death, reopening in 1908. A brilliant orator, Buckner was remembered thus: "making Christianity and Christian virtues his object, his spirit soared [over] petty prejudices in religion and politics … Sincerely attached to the priests of the College, he esteemed their personal virtues, honored, loved them, whose lives were noble examples of Humility and Poverty."[21]

This sketch of the dissecting room is labeled: "Amphitheatre - 1853, at Seventh and Myrtle Ave. St. Louis University, Medical Department." The Latin inscription around the walls reads: "Ad caedes hominum prisca Amphitheatra patebant: Ut longum discant vivere, nostra patent," which translates as: "The old amphitheaters were opened for the slaughter of human beings; ours are opened so that they may learn how to live long lives." This Greek saying is noted by Richard Ford and John Murray in *The Handbook for Travellers in Spain*, 1862.

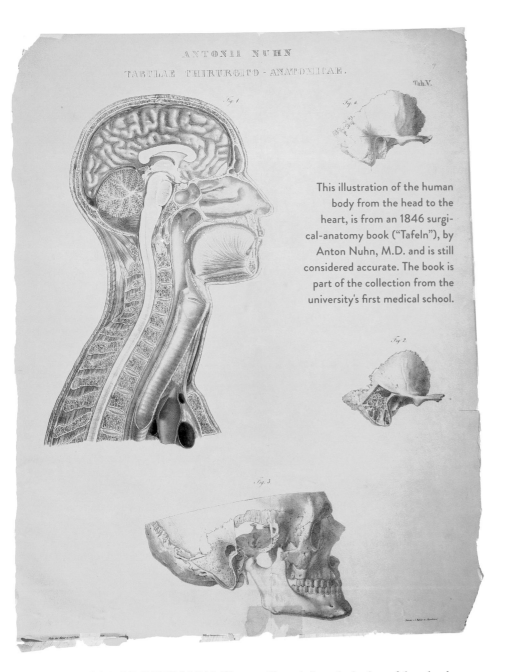

ANTONII NUHN

TABULAE THIRTREITD - ANATOMIIAE.

Tab.V.

This illustration of the human body from the head to the heart, is from an 1846 surgical-anatomy book ("Tafeln"), by Anton Nuhn, M.D. and is still considered accurate. The book is part of the collection from the university's first medical school.

"THE MEDICAL PROFESSION IS, THEN, A SACRED CALLING."
DR. ABRAM LITTON, 1851

Saint Louis University's medical college soon faced a serious challenge. Local, anti-Catholic sentiment flared into violence in 1844 and again in 1855. "Anti-Jesuit and anti-Catholic feeling had long percolated in Saint Louis."[22] This sentiment seems to have also been connected with ill will toward French residents, who as early as the 1830's, were criticized for playing the fiddle![23] Such prejudices were intensified by newspaper editorials, sensationalistic novels, and other media in St. Louis, and were given additional impetus by some groups among the new German immigrants. In February 1844, a mob gathered, angered by a rumor that the medical school was using corpses obtained through grave-robbing. They destroyed the dissecting room.

Nevertheless, the leaders of the school continued to be hopeful. The 1844-45 *Annual Announcement of the Medical Department of the St. Louis University* remarks: "The Anatomical Cabinet, which was destroyed last winter, has been replaced by one more extensive, more perfect, and more valuable in every respect." The tone of the text on dissections changes from previous *Announcements*, growing more positive: "Knowing the great advantages derived from dissections ..." Readers learn that new buildings were "in process of completion" and included a library, museum, chemical laboratory, tiered lecture hall, anatomical theatre, and dissecting rooms, "lit with skylights."

The 1845-46 *Announcement* contains even longer discourses on the value of dissection, while a November 4, 1845 introductory lecture by Dr. Linton critiques bigotry. The theme remained relevant: speaking to

graduates on February 28, 1851, Dr. Abram Litton remarked: "The medical profession is, then, a sacred calling. It elevates the thoughts, it refines the heart, it purifies the feelings. It cherishes a philanthropy that is not bounded by the confines of nations; it nurtures a love that is not restricted by the narrow circle of rank, and kindles a charity whose tender ministries are not fettered by the bigotry of sect."[24]

In 1850, the Medical College moved to a new building at Seventh Street and Myrtle Avenue (now Clark Street). New offices "within the paved district" are noted in the text of the 1851 *Announcement*, with plans to build "O'Fallon Clinic and Dispensary," offering free medicine and surgery for the poor. But during the early 1850s, St. Louisans heard reports that Jesuits were sinister and lecherous. As a Jesuit wrote with some irony at the time, Jesuits were seen as the "pest of all free institutions, and as something to be expelled completely from this glorious asylum of liberty."[25] A mob approached the university one evening in 1855, but lost their zeal when they saw the calm figure of Father John Druyts, S.J., pacing in front of the building with his breviary. Indeed, this period saw a great deal of anti-Catholicism, in St. Louis and well beyond.

Given such sentiments, combined with attacks from competing physicians, it was deemed best for the medical school and the university to separate in 1855. The board moved to incorporate St. Louis Medical College and to establish the tax-exempt O'Fallon Clinic and Dispensary. All parties agreed to the painful decision. In April 1855, Dr. Charles Alexander Pope sent a brief letter to the Jesuits, regretting "the unreasonable prejudices which render the separation expedient, and even necessary."[26]

During its short history, the university's medical college had granted over three hundred medical degrees. The Jesuits' costly foray into medical education was over, at least for the time being. By 1891, the original medical college of Saint Louis University had been absorbed into Washington University.

A painting of the Sacred Heart Mission among the Coeur d'Alene tribe, in Idaho, from the Linton album.

The Linton album contains many translations of Christian prayers by Father De Smet and others.

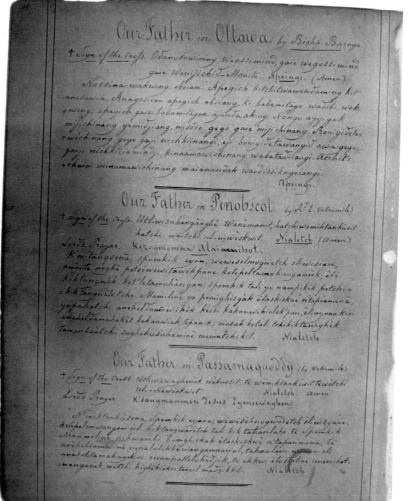

"SOMETHING MIRACULOUS ABOUT IT"
DR. MOSES L. LINTON, 1872

Dr. Moses L. Linton was professor of obstetrics and diseases, among other topics, at Saint Louis University Medical College. In 1843, he founded the *St. Louis Medical and Surgical Journal,* the first medical journal of the American West. Linton was attending physician both to the Jesuits and their students from 1858 to 1871.

Dr. Linton was a close friend of Father De Smet. They kept a remarkable scrapbook

which chronicles De Smet's extensive travels. It contains prayers, paintings, obituaries, observations about Native tribes, photographs, and verses.

In a tribute addressed to the Jesuits shortly before his death in 1872, Linton wrote: "the more I think about this organization, the more I am convinced that there is something miraculous about it."[27]

The key for this 1844 map notes: "College," as well as "Med University" and "St. Xavier Church."

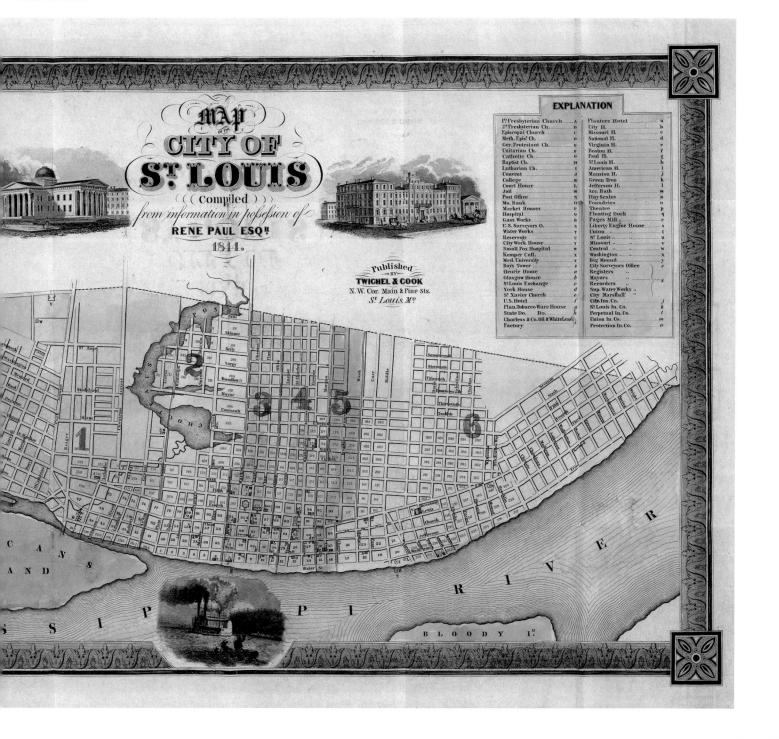

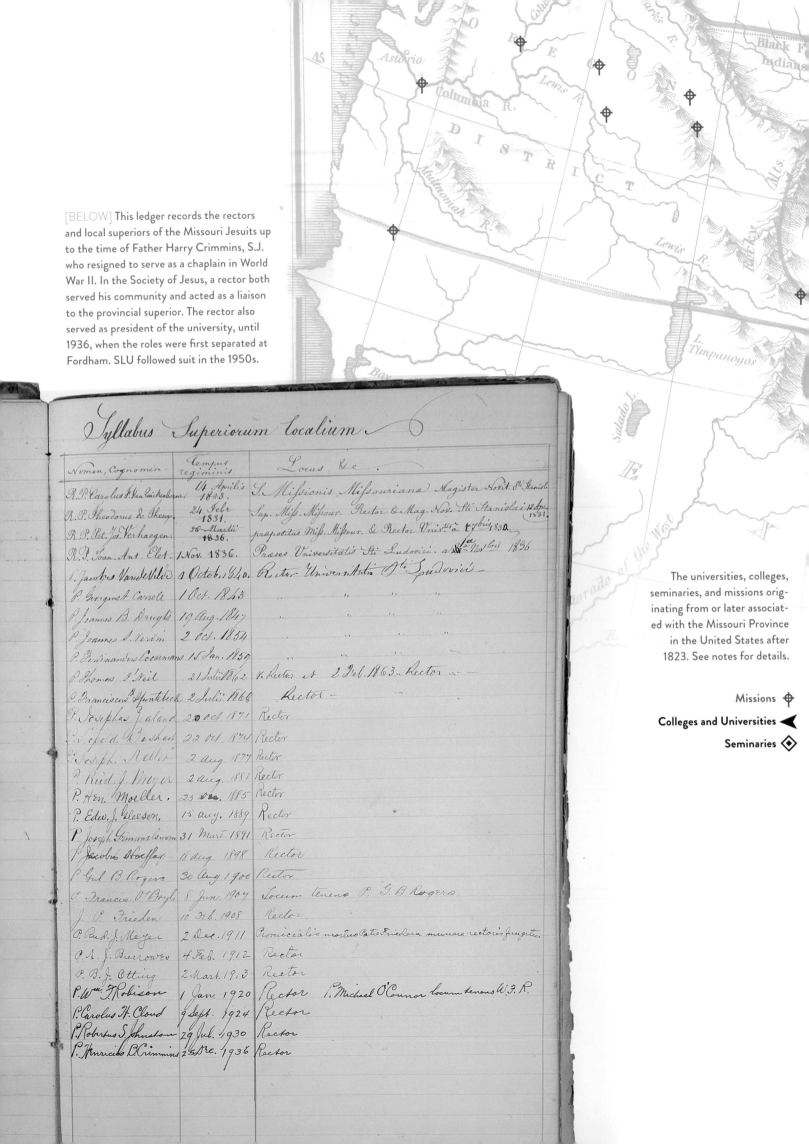

[BELOW] This ledger records the rectors and local superiors of the Missouri Jesuits up to the time of Father Harry Crimmins, S.J. who resigned to serve as a chaplain in World War II. In the Society of Jesus, a rector both served his community and acted as a liaison to the provincial superior. The rector also served as president of the university, until 1936, when the roles were first separated at Fordham. SLU followed suit in the 1950s.

The universities, colleges, seminaries, and missions originating from or later associated with the Missouri Province in the United States after 1823. See notes for details.

Missions ✠

Colleges and Universities ◄

Seminaries ◈

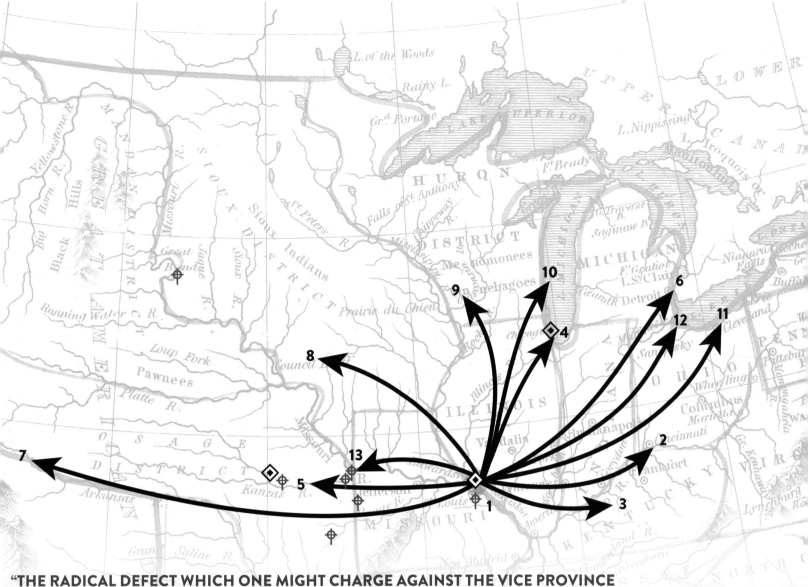

"THE RADICAL DEFECT WHICH ONE MIGHT CHARGE AGAINST THE VICE PROVINCE IS THAT IT DID TOO MUCH FOR OTHERS AND TOO LITTLE FOR OURSELVES."

FATHER ISIDORE BOUDREAUX, S.J. [28]

The Jesuits of the Middle West surely took on far more than was healthy. In a sense, perhaps this was inevitable. A few months before the Belgian novices arrived in St. Louis in late May 1823, the Society of Jesus had already accepted a weighty charge in the March 1823 Concordat: "All the Catholic population of Missouri west of St. Louis was in the care of Father Van Quickenborne."[29] In fact, the Vincentian, Bishop Joseph Rosati, shared tasks with the Society of Jesus. In 1824, he had been consecrated as coadjutor to Bishop DuBourg in New Orleans. After Bishop DuBourg's resignation in 1826, the Vatican split the territory (Upper and Lower Louisiana) and Rosati became the first bishop of St. Louis.

The Missouri Jesuits took up their endeavors with energy that is still astonishing. From St. Louis and Florissant, they went forth to start Indian missions, work as pastors in both rural

areas and cities, serve as superiors and rectors, establish parishes, schools, and universities, and serve as presidents of educational institutions. Father De Smet first became involved in the Rocky Mountain Missions when he established St. Mary's Mission among the Flatheads in 1841, near present day Stevensville, Montana. He also supported other missions in collaboration with Jesuits in the Pacific Northwest. Some are shown on the map above; see details in Notes.

The region is considered the second "staging area" in the American history of the Society of Jesus, the first being the Maryland Province/Georgetown University.[30] Educational institutions emanating from or taken on by the Missouri Mission (later Vice Province and Province) in this period often began as colleges. They are shown on the map above with numbered arrows, in chronological order.

1. **Missouri Mission** based at St. Stanislaus Seminary takes over **St. Louis College,** now University (St. Louis, Missouri), 1826-27

2. **Xavier University** (Cincinnati, Ohio), founded 1831, Jesuits took over 1840

3. **St. Joseph's College** (Bardstown, Kentucky), founded 1819, Jesuits took over 1848

4. **Loyola College,** now University (Chicago, Illinois), 1870

5. **St. Mary's College** (St. Marys, Kansas), 1870 (began as a mission school in 1848, became a seminary in 1931)

6. **University of Detroit Mercy** (1877 Jesuits founded Detroit College; 1941 Sisters of Mercy of the Americas founded Mercy College of Detroit; the schools merged in 1990)

7. **Las Vegas College,** now Regis University, (Denver, Colorado), 1877

8. **Creighton College,** now University, (Omaha, Nebraska), 1878

9. **Campion College of the Sacred Heart,** (Prairie du Chien, Wisconsin), 1880 (founded by Buffalo Mission, absorbed into Missouri Province in 1907 and became a high school)

10. **Marquette College,** now University (Milwaukee, Wisconsin), 1881

11. **St. Ignatius** (Cleveland, Ohio), 1886 (founded by Buffalo Mission, high school and college later split, latter became John Carroll University)

12. **St. John's College** (Toledo, Ohio), 1898 (founded by Buffalo Mission)

13. **Rockhurst College,** now University (Kansas City, Missouri), 1910

Close ties both personal and professional existed across the Jesuit and other Catholic schools. In 1848, Father Edward Sorin, C.S.C. of Notre Dame wrote to ask for advice on the curriculum in use at Saint Louis University. Father Nerinckx recruited Father Arnold Damen, S.J., who left St. Louis as a missionary to speak in Chicago for three weeks, and ended up founding Loyola College there. Nerinckx died with Damen at his bedside.

At the seminary in Florissant, an entry for "Regulations 11th Scholastic Year 1839" suggests the intensive study that helped to prepare men for their future roles. The men rose at 5 a.m., with meditation, Mass, and breakfast followed by study: "English, writing, Latin and Greek, Bookkeeping, French, Math, Spanish and German, Divinity and Metaphysics."

Father Verhaegen wrote in 1840: "Our mission has been raised to the rank of a <u>vice</u> Province! Yes, dear Father, and we consider it a great favor, but thus far, we have but a faint prospect of seeing the adjunct <u>vice</u> erased. The number of professed fathers here is so small, that if we be compelled to wait, until we shall have completed the number usually required for a Province before the little word can be struck out, we, old folks, shall be all dead and forgotten. This circumstance, however, does not disturb my own mind. We try to go ahead as fast as we prudently can without exposing ourselves to the danger of breaking down, and what more can be required of us?"[31] (emphasis in original). Despite this sober prediction, Verhaegen lived to see the elevation in status to a Province, which took place in 1863.

Until 1870, the superior of the Society of Jesus in the Missouri Province was *ex officio* president of the Saint Louis University board of trustees. The university remains to this day officially a mission of the Province, which is now called the Central and Southern Province of the United States.

Father Kenney's warnings (see Chapter 1) about the Missouri Mission taking on too much were echoed in this period by two superior generals: Father Jan Roothaan, S.J. and Father Peter Jan Beckx, S.J. Historian of the Society of Jesus, Father John W. Padberg, S.J. notes that the Jesuit superiors of this time constantly cautioned the Jesuits to go slowly, because unless a solid base of formation was established, there was a risk of "dooming ourselves to superficiality and a loss of people." He adds: "There is a common perception that Missouri took on things "too fast" as a frontier mission, and in a sense, this has remained true."[32]

There are many ways to interpret this quality. Of course, many programs have been initiated at Saint Louis University over two hundred years. Not all have had a smooth trajectory, in part due to the exigencies of the times and the need to be flexible. A School of Divinity began in 1834, was discontinued in 1860, reorganized in 1899, transferred to St. Mary's in Kansas in 1931, and then was brought back to St. Louis in 1967. It was closed in 1975 and some of its faculty joined the Department of Theological Studies. The School of Medicine began in 1836, as noted above, was disassociated from the univeresity in 1855, then was revived, as was the School of Law (originally lasting 1842-47), due to the efforts of Father William Banks Rogers, S.J. (see Chapter 3). Even in later decades, others may be said to have reached too far, driven by their respective visions of what a university should include.

Perhaps this tendency to dream big indicates the lingering influence of Bishop DuBourg?

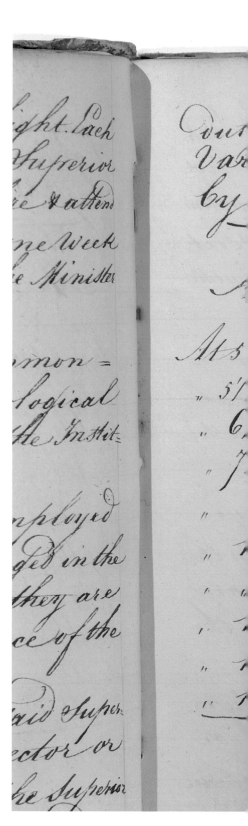

acquaint the Scholastics with the
appointments that may be made
Superior

Order of Exercices.

A. M.

...ck, Rising, etc	
Meditation	
Mass	
Breakfast	
English class	
Writing Class, &	
...tin & Greek till 11¾	
...Bookkeeping & Study	
Examen	
Dinner, visit & recreat	

P. M.

At 2 o'Clock,	End of Recreat.
„ 2¼ „	French Class.
„ 3¼ „	Mathematics & Arithm.
„ 4¼ „	Luncheon
„ 5¼ „	German & Spanish.
„ 6¼ „	Divinity & Metaphysics.
„ 7¼ „	Supper, Visit & recreat.
	at 8 on days of abstin...
„ 9 „	Litanies & preparat. for Med.
„ 9¼ „ Examen; 9¾ Visit & Bed tim...

NEGROES AND MULATTOES.

AN ACT respecting slaves, free negroes and mulattoes.

§ 1. Negreos or mulattoes not to be taught to read or write.
2. Where preacher is negro or mulatto; certain officers to be present at service.
3. Certain specified meetings unlawful; how suppressed.

§ 4. No free negro or mulatto to emigrate to this State.
5. Punishment for violation of this act.
6. Free negroes and mulatoes under twenty-one years; for certain causes, not to be bound out in this State.

Be it enacted by the General Assembly of the State of Missouri, as follows:

§ 1. No person shall keep or teach any school for the instruction of negroes or mulattoes, in reading or writing, in this State.

Among other harsh laws, the state of Missouri declared it illegal to teach reading and writing to any person of African American or "mulatto" (mixed race) heritage, *whether free or enslaved.*

"OUR SLUMBERING CITY"

As late as 1840-41, Father Verhaegen gave public lectures in the cathedral in the evening, partly in French. In 1842, he wrote in French to one of the town's eminent personages, Pierre Chouteau, about the financial needs of the university, sharing details about Father Van de Velde's travels to raise money in Belgium, New York and Boston.[33] Verhaegen was on good terms with the town's French and Creole elite, but their power was slowly eroding.[34] In addition, there were ongoing challenges for the Catholic Church. In 1842, Verhaegen wrote to Father Francis Vespre, S.J.: "Our new splendid church will be ready by the feast of the Sacred Name," expressing hope for "our slumbering city." After the great fire of May 17, 1849, French and even Spanish influence in St. Louis architecture and lifestyle was physically lost.

An act approved in February 1847 made it illegal in the state of Missouri for any person to "keep or teach any school for the instruction of negroes or mulattoes, in reading or writing, in this State." John Berry Meachum found a way around that law, setting up a Freedom School on a steamboat floating along the Mississippi River, with a library, desks, and chairs. Some Jesuits may have similarly worked around the law. There is an anonymous, handwritten document in the archives of the Jesuits of the Central and Southern Province regarding Father Ignatius Panken, S.J. The author writes that: "The Fathers of College Church began to teach Negroes at 10th and Morgan in 1856."

In 1860, the state of Missouri had just under 1.2 million residents, and of these, 114,500 were slaves. The city of St. Louis has been characterized by scholars as very "fluid," as "a free-thinking city" within a slave-owning, border state, a gateway for invasion by either side during the Civil War, and a place where the "line between slavery and freedom" was attenuated. Indeed, St. Louis was the site of a civil rights protest as early as 1819, when free blacks and "a few liberal white friends" rallied against the Missouri Compromise.[35]

From 1724 to 1804, the lives of African Americans in Missouri were controlled through the French-instituted *Code Noir*, the Black Code. In its 1847 law forbidding any Negro or "mulatto" (mixed race), free or slave, to be taught reading, writing, or arithmetic, the Missouri General Assembly also levied harsh fines on and forbade: "any black religious services unless some 'sheriff, constable, marshal, police officer, or justice of the peace was present during all the time of such meeting or assemblage in order to prevent all seditious speeches and disorderly conduct.'"[36]

But St. Louis was "fluid," as noted. The Missouri Province Jesuits were independent-minded, and the city was home to wealthy, free black persons, some of whom were successful entrepreneurs.[37] Many hints of Jesuit ministry to black Catholics are evident, despite the strict rules. In 1832, Bishop Rosati had converted the college's first building on Second and Walnut streets (which the Jesuits had ceased using after 1827) to be a chapel for African Americans. It was named

St. Mary's Chapel, and was blessed by Father Verhaegen. After two years, German Catholics began to use it.[38] In 1843, Father Joseph Joset, S.J. begged his superiors for permission to minister to African Americans. He had been assigned to Oregon, but had arrived in St. Louis too late for the trip and was about to spend a year studying German. In August 1849, buildings were taken down at St. Stanislaus that had been built "by the hands of the pioneer Fathers;" some of the structures were preserved for "a chapel for the Negroes."[39] In this case, the chapel would have served the slaves who lived and worked at the seminary in Florissant, and possibly other black Catholics from the region.

In 1858, Father William Koning S.J. created a chapel for "his wards," i.e. African Americans, in St. Francis Xavier Church. Jesuits serving the black community in the 1860s included: Father Ignatius May, Father Henry Baselmans, Father Philip Colleton, Father James M. Hayes, Father Michael Callaghan, and Father W.B. Van der Heyden. By 1873, St. Elizabeth's was established as the first African American parish in St. Louis, and remained the only black parish in the city until 1927 (see Chapter 3). It was founded by Father Ignatius Panken, S.J.

"ENGAGED WITHOUT MOLESTATION IN THEIR ORDINARY ROUND OF ACTIVITIES"

On April 25, 1861, the university trustees' minutes reflect the "impending national troubles," as the board decides to send home without delay all students from the south. The next month, a skirmish at Camp Jackson resulted in a Union takeover of a store of weapons. In St. Louis in 1860, there were 170,000 people; of that total, 60,000 were Germans, Alsatians, or Swiss. The Germans were loyal to the Union. Close knit and unified, they made the capture of Camp Jackson possible. Once the camp was held by Union forces, the city became something of a haven. Many rural citizens fled to the towns "made relatively safe by sizable Union garrisons, especially to St. Louis, physically the most secure place in the state."[40]

In September 1861, Vice Provincial William Stack Murphy, S.J. issued a circular letter citing Superior General Beckx and urging "scrupulous observance" of the Jesuit rule about showing no partiality "towards either party in national difficulties."[41] For the Jesuits: "the war became a forbidden topic in Jesuit communities, lest it rupture the bond of fraternal charity and revive the anti-Cath-

FORTIFICATIONS THROWN UP TO PROTECT THE UNITED STATES ARSENAL AT ST. LOUIS, MISSOURI.—[See Page 295.]

The St. Louis arsenal was of great strategic importance as war loomed. In May 1861, volunteer Confederate militia gathered at Camp Jackson, preparing to attack the arsenal. They were arrested by pro-Union forces led by Nathaniel Lyon. The arsenal is illustrated in this 1861 issue of *Harper's Weekly*.

olic crusade that nativism had mounted in the 1850s."[42] Jesuits tried to abide by Father Beckx's wishes; some served as chaplains to soldiers on both sides of the conflict. Both Father De Smet and Father Francis Xavier Weninger, S.J. admired President Abraham Lincoln and supported the Union. The nuances of public opinion were complex. Writing to Charles Drake and others in October 1863, Lincoln observed that one group advocated for the Union with slavery, another for the Union without slavery, one for gradual emancipation, and one for immediate emancipation.[43]

Although an abolitionist and Unionist, De Smet was also a consummate networker. He maintained ties with people on all sides of the issue of slavery, and secured draft exemptions for the university's students and faculty. In 1861, he wrote to Beckx: "The city of St. Louis is in great danger of being sacked and burned in case the secessionists get the upper hand in Missouri." He added: "Several of Ours without regard to the instructions of your Paternity, as published by the Provincial, continue to manifest secessionist sentiments, at least in the house. No good and much harm can result from manifestations of this sort. Indiscretions are filling the prisons more and more every day."[44]

NO MASTER BUT GOD

"No person within the jurisdiction of this State shall ever … know any master but God." On January 11, 1865, Governor Thomas Fletcher of Missouri declared the end of slavery in the state with these words.

Finally, the "evils and disaster of the time" had come to an end, as Father Hill observes in his history of the university. Garraghan writes: "The close of the war found the Jesuit houses of the Middle West if not in a state of prosperity at least engaged without molestation in their ordinary round of activities."[45] De Smet reflected that the Missouri Jesuits kept their "tranquility."

A few years after the war's end, the Jesuits of St. Louis had purchased property that would one day become the permanent campus of the university. The board's minutes for May 10, 1867 contain this brief phrase: "offer made to the univ of one Lot of ground on the west side of Grand Ave for $54,650 446 feet 5.5" front and 360' deep."[46]

A promising, new era was in sight.

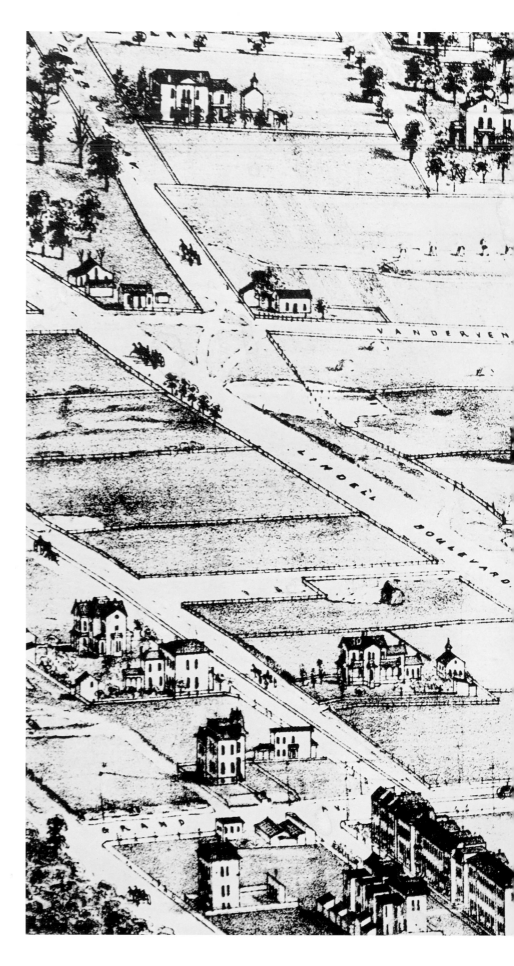

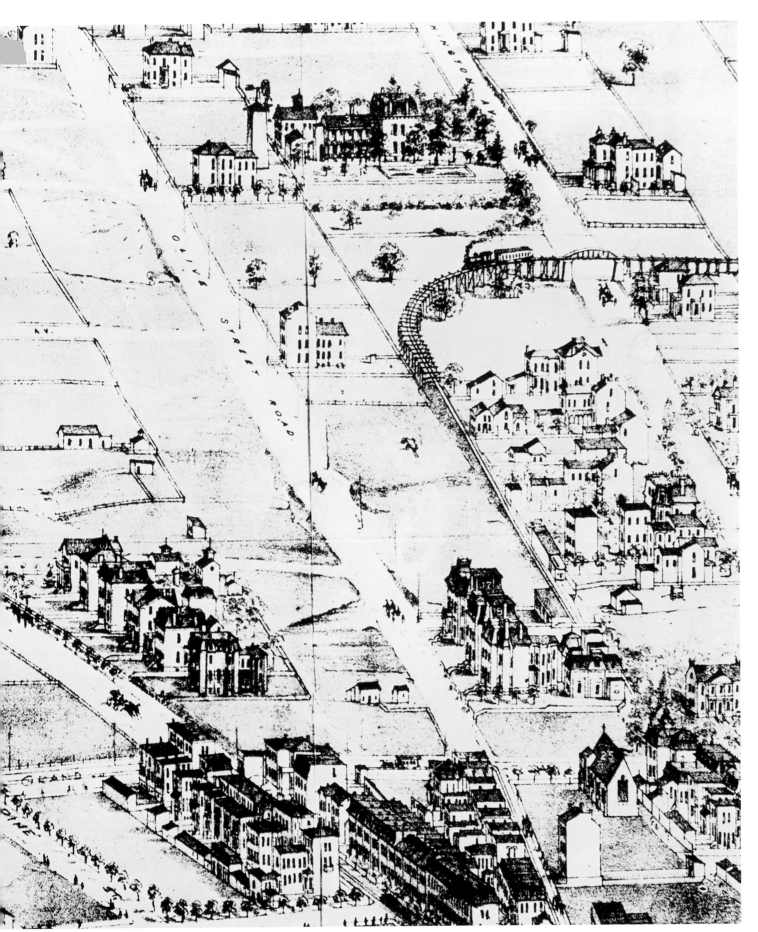

This 1867 sketch depicts the region surrounding a piece of property purchased in that year by the Jesuits. They moved to this property, at the corner of Grand and Lindell, in 1888.

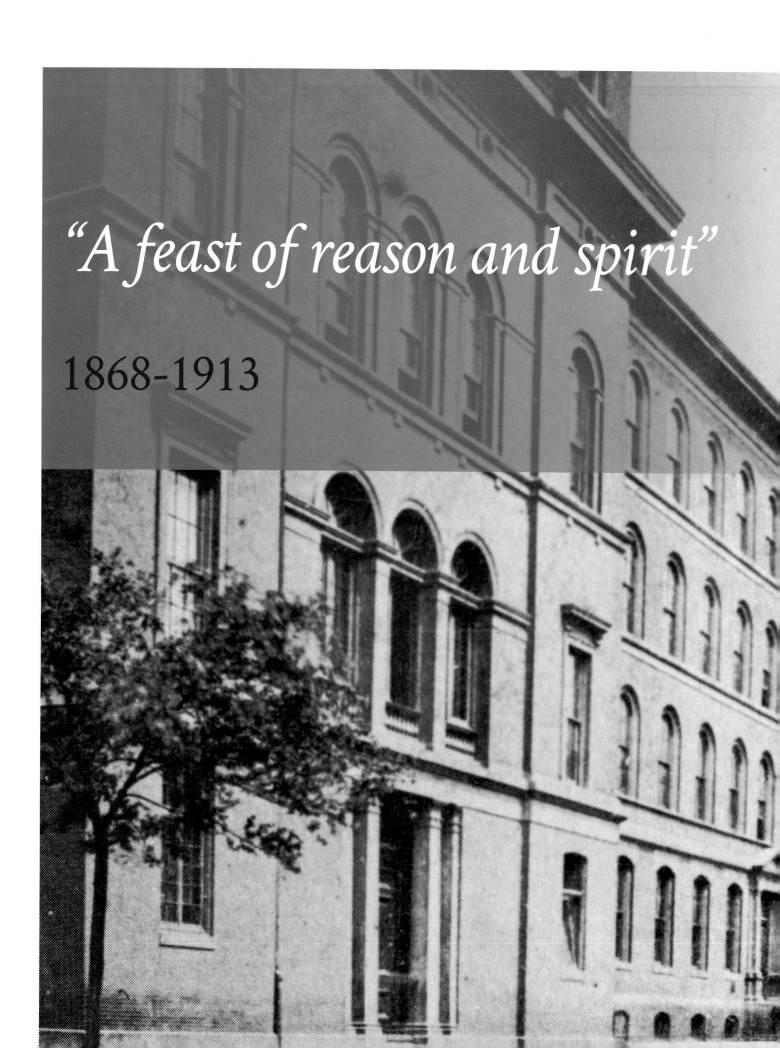

CHAPTER 3

"A feast of reason and spirit"

1868-1913

In 1864, a four-story building was erected between the 1853 classroom building and St. Francis Xavier Church. This photograph from the 1870s shows the resulting row of buildings as they faced Ninth Street.

In 1867, the Missouri Province of the Society of Jesus purchased property at the corner of Grand and Lindell boulevards in St. Louis. Their university was growing beyond the limits of its downtown campus. Moreover, the Jesuits longed to provide a more "salubrious" environment for their pupils. But before they could move, they had to wait for permission from Archbishop Peter Kenrick in St. Louis and from Father General Peter Jan Beckx in Rome. They also had to wait for a buyer. At last, having secured permissions, and with a purchaser in 1886, the Old College was able to move in 1888 to the new site, where it remains to this day.

During this period, curricular reform began in the Midwest Jesuit schools, as one part of national changes in Catholic higher education. Father Rudolph Meyer, S.J., (president from 1881 to 1885), Father William Banks Rogers, S.J., (president from 1900 to 1908), and Father Alexander J. Burrowes, S.J. (president from 1911 to 1913) played key roles in this effort. Father Rogers earned the epithet: "Saint Louis University's Second Founder" by reviving the Medical and Law Colleges, guiding an increased emphasis on science at the university, and adding a Dental School. He strengthened relationships both with local Catholic clergy and with the administrators of the city's Catholic hospitals, and promoted Jesuit education as a theme at the 1904 World's Fair: the Louisiana Purchase Exposition.

In 1908, women were admitted to the law school. They could attend the professional schools by 1920; this policy expanded to all programs by 1925. *Officially* coeducational classes at the university as a whole began in 1949, but women studied in various programs prior to that date. In 1889, a College of Philosophy and Letters was established and by 1910, the School of Commerce and Finance opened. Organized athletics were underway: baseball had started in 1867, track had a short stint from 1870 to 1880, and football began in 1886, lasting until 1949. The football teams included medical and law students!

Reading Horace — in Latin and in silence during study periods — nineteenth century pupils at Saint Louis University must have anticipated with great joy the celebrations hinted at in their prefects' journals. On New Year's Day in 1869, the "treat" was "Sangaree" (now called Sangria) for "the boys" as well as "two kinds of cakes"! For the Jesuits, there was eggnog, cakes, nuts and candies, fruit and cigars. On February 7 of that year: "coffee and pousse café in the Rectory." The latter drink is a complex, layered digestif. Its inclusion reflects the European upbringing of many St. Louis Jesuits.

Gracious turns of phrase in the journals cap-ture prosaic as well as whimsical moments. In December 1869, the prefect observed: "Today we were saluted in the morning by a clever snow storm," and: "Today our baker commenced to bake bread in the new oven." In late June and early July that year, fireworks were let off "in the yard" (at the city campus) and later, at "the Farm," probably referring to the College Hill Farm property in North St. Louis. In November 1871, the "little boys flooded their yard for a skating rink" and organized entertainment "in the large study hall." Just after Christmas, there was: "eggnog in the evening for boys and men at their supper."

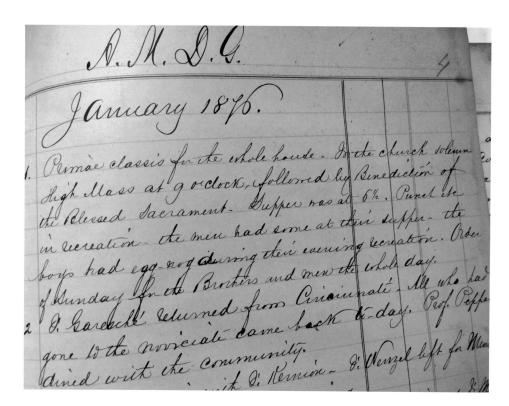

Entries in this 1876 prefect's diary chronicle daily life: religious holidays, celebratory meals, and the constant travel of the Jesuits.

[RIGHT] The talents of Father Charles Charropin, S.J. preserved photographs of the downtown campus, as well as solar and lunar eclipses, and life at the seminary. His photo albums use different languages to warn viewers: "Do Not Touch!"

Ne me touchez pas!

'play-room, Parish school, Class rooms, Main building.'

"SEPTEMBER 29, 1870. BOYS WENT TO SEE THE MATCH BETWEEN RED STOCKINGS AND EMPIRE. R.S.7 - E. 5. IT RAINED AT THE FIFTH INNING."

In 1870, the opening entry for the prefect diary records that on September 2, the prefects "Mr. Charroppin and Weinman" left the College Farm in north St. Louis, where they had spent the summer. They began the academic year on September 5, with 168 boys making up the student body. But, as archivist John Waide notes: "book learning and spiritual guidance were not the first concerns of Jesuit educators at the beginning of the year," for already on the first day of school the "boys got their tickets" for an upcoming baseball game. The St. Louis Red Stockings took on the Empire Baseball Club. These were early amateur baseball teams in St. Louis, although the Red Stockings did play professionally for one year in 1875 as part of the National Association of Professional Base Ball Players. The Red Stockings' field, which was known as Compton Field, was located on the west side of Compton Avenue at Gratiot Street, several hundred yards north of the intersection of Chouteau and Compton avenues. In 2014, Saint Louis University laid out a new baseball diamond near that very site.[1]

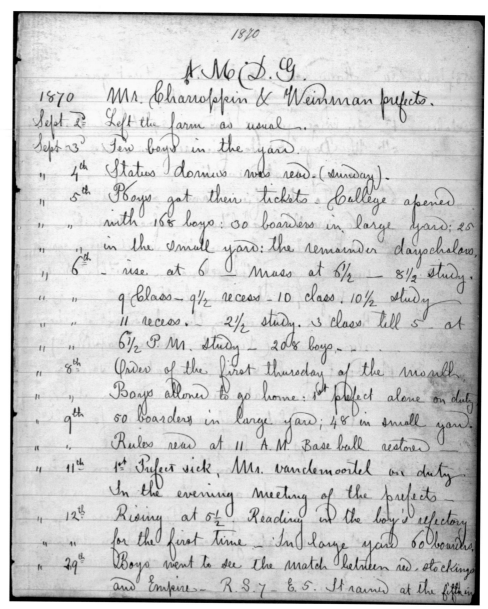

[ABOVE] As recorded in this diary, baseball was a beloved sport: students both played it, and eagerly watched local teams.

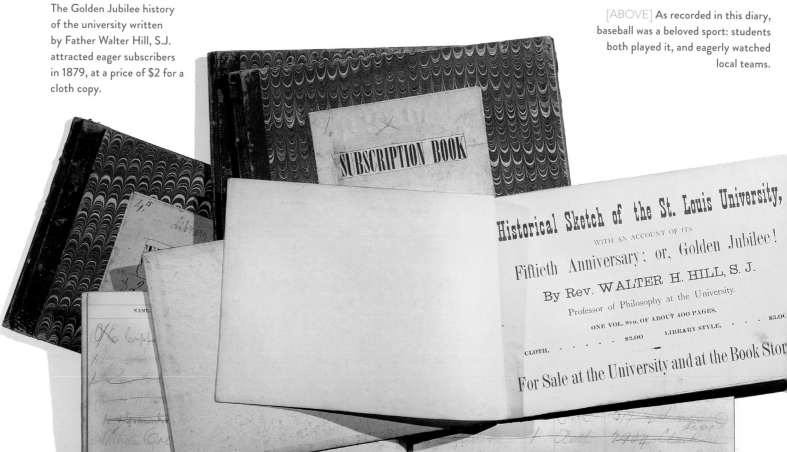

The Golden Jubilee history of the university written by Father Walter Hill, S.J. attracted eager subscribers in 1879, at a price of $2 for a cloth copy.

The university's prospectus in the early part of this period begins: "This Literary Institution, situated in an agreeable and airy part of the city of St. Louis..." In 1868, the 14,000 volumes in its library were also highlighted, although students could only use half of them.

Around 1858, a distinction which had been in place for decades began to be framed as: the classical and commercial course. In the past, these two paths had sometimes been designated as "scientific" or "literary" versus "mercantile." Each course required six years of study. In 1858, a classical student in Latin would be expected to start with *Epitome Historiae Sacrae* and proceed in the next years to Nepos, Horace, and Cicero. Ten years later, the names of the years had changed slightly (from Grammar to Humanities) but many of the assigned readings were similar. The first three years were denoted: First Year "Third Humanities," Second Year "Second Humanities," and Third Year "First Humanities." The next three years were denoted: Fourth Year: Poetry, Fifth: Rhetoric, and Sixth: Philosophy. In Greek, a student would progress over the first three years from Brooks' *First Lessons* to Bullion's *Grammar,* Arnold's *Greek,* Xenophon, and St. Chrysostom. In the Poetry and Rhetoric years, he would proceed in

Greek from Prosody, Dialects, Arnold's *Exercises* (continued), Homer, and Demosthenes to Plato, Euripedes or Sophocles, and then Composition. The five years of formal study in Latin proceeded from Brooks' *Epitome Historiae Sacrae* to Bullion's *Grammar,* Arnold's *Latin Exercises,* Ovid, and Cicero *de Senectute et Amicitia.* Study culminated with Virgil, Livy, Horace, and Tacitus. In the sixth year, although students were finished with formal study of Greek, Latin, and English, their texts in Logic, Metaphysics, and Ethics included materials in these languages, for example Tongiorgi's *Institutiones Philosophicae.*[2]

While students in the commercial course studied many of the same subjects as classical students, such as Arithmetic, English, Writing, Catechism, Evidence of Christianity, and Physics, they did not study Latin or Greek; they also took a class in "Book-keeping." In 1856, the study of French, Spanish, German, and Italian was made optional for either course. Previously, these were offered only in the commercial course.

"Gentlemanly" and decorous behavior was rewarded. Order sustained the university culture, and when that culture was shared with the public, citizens responded eagerly. Indeed, the public "exhibitions" and "disputations" held by the Jesuits at Messina and Palermo in the sixteenth century were very popular.[3] Some three centuries later, St. Louis citizens thronged to the university's philosophical lectures, festivities, contests, and parades. In 1879, the Jubilee celebration (at the time, university origins were calculated as 1829) included "a grand Pontifical Mass ... the doors were opened shortly before nine o'clock, and the large crowd made a rush for them," although unfortunately only those with tickets could enter. The Bishop of Peoria, John Lancaster Spalding, was a long-time supporter of the university. In his sermon at the celebratory Mass, he praised Saint Ignatius of Loyola for his belief that "they should win who, through God's mercy, were able to lead the highest moral and intellectual life."[4]

Notes inside an 1864 edition of *Institutiones Philosophicae*, by Salvatore Tongiorgi, S.J. This book was used by students in their final year of studies.

Prospectus.

This Literary Institution, situated in an agreeable and airy part of the city of St. Louis, was founded in 1829, by members of the Society of Jesus, incorporated by an Act of the State Legislature in 1832, under the name and style of "St. Louis University," and empowered to confer degrees and academical honors in all the learned professions, and generally "to have and enjoy all the powers, rights and privileges exercised by literary institutions of the same rank." It has experienced uninterrupted prosperity, and has steadily advanced, and offers the student every facility for acquiring a liberal education.

The Institution possesses a valuable Museum, which contains a great variety of specimens, both of nature and of art, collected from various quarters of the globe, especially from our own country; also a very beautiful and complete Philosophical and Chemical Apparatus. The Library belonging to the Institution numbers over 14,000 volumes, embracing almost every branch of literature and science, and containing many rare and interesting works. The select libraries, open to the students, form a collection of over 7,000 volumes.

The College Villa, situated near the city, is large and beautiful, with ample buildings, spacious groves, and recreation grounds. Here the students may spend their weekly holiday and the summer vacation in a manner conducive alike to health and relaxation.

General Regulations.

The Academic Year consists of one session, beginning on the first Monday of September, and ending on the last Thursday of June, when the annual commencement, the conferring of degrees, and the distribution of premiums take place.

The session is divided into two terms, the first ending on the first of February, and the second on the last Thursday of June. A thorough

The introduction to Saint Louis University's prospectus in 1868

The *St. Louis Globe-Democrat* reported in June 1881: "The usual immense audience filled University Hall last night" for the 52nd Annual Commencement Exercise, deemed a "grand success." For St. Louisans, the author observed: "an evening at University Hall means a feast of reason and spirit." The university's students eagerly joined in public festivities. In 1877, a procession of 12,000 persons formed to honor the golden jubilee of the election of Pius IX as pope. When they passed by the university, they were joined by an estimated five hundred young men. The Philalethic Society celebrated the 150th anniversary of George Washington's birthday in 1882. Already in 1882, newspapers referred to Saint Louis University as "the Old College." The university's indoor track meets even became something of a social event, according to university historian Father William B. Faherty, S.J.

In 1879, Father Thomas Hughes, S.J. organized a post-graduate program of lectures

Rev. Thomas A. Hughes, S.J.

for "All gentleman who can follow the lectures with profit and interest." Topics included psychology, ethics, history, physics, and philosophy. Students could earn either a bachelor's degree or if they already had one, a master's degree after "a year or two" of attending. The program drew praise from Chancellor William Greenleaf Eliot of Washington University and President James McCosh of Princeton.[5]

From 1868 to 1913, twelve different men served as president of Saint Louis University. The maximum term of a major religious superior in the Society of Jesus was two three-year terms, and the rector of the community was also the president of the university. Aging, illness, and death were factors in the turnover; moreover, men circulated, as they were assigned to roles around the region, nation, and world. Father James F. X. Hoeffer, S.J. was president at Creighton College from 1891 to 1895, founding a medical school there, before serving as president at Saint Louis University from 1898 to 1900. Father Joseph Grimmelsman, S.J. was president at Marquette College (which became a university in 1907) from 1889 to 1891 and 1911 to 1915, serving St. Louis from 1890 to 1898. Father Alexander J. Burrowes, S.J. was president at Marquette from 1900 to 1908, then president at St. Louis from 1911 to 1913. He became provincial when Meyer died. This turnover may have hurt the university locally. Grimmelsman rebuffed requests to reopen a medical school in St. Louis. In May 1888, Father Henry Moeller, S.J. (president at St. Louis from 1885 to 1889) had the vision to offer a free scholarship to one successful com-

petitor from each parochial school in the city limits, but perhaps due to a lack of sustained effort from his successors, the clergy did not respond with applicants until pressed years later by William Banks Rogers, S.J. Certainly, the changes in leadership assured a circulation of fresh ideas and energy.

Connections between Rome and St. Louis were significant. In 1883, Father Anton Anderledy, S.J., who had studied theology at Saint Louis University and was ordained in St. Louis, was elected as the 23rd Superior General of the Society. Father Rudolph Meyer, S.J. studied at Florissant, was selected twice as Missouri provincial, and was selected to be English assistant in Rome, working with Father Luis Martín García, S.J., the 24th Superior General of the Society. Meyer's skills drew attention as a possible superior general, but he was ultimately not chosen. He served as rector of Saint Louis University in the 1880s, and applied his talents to incorporate part of the German-led Buffalo Mission into the Missouri Province in 1907. "Just as truly as Peter Verhaegen was the builder of the Missouri Province, Rudolph J. Meyer was its rebuilder," according to university historian Father William B. Faherty, S.J.

"To fit man for the duties of life, by the full and harmonious development of all his faculties"
FATHER RUDOLPH MEYER, S.J., 1908

There were many challenges for Catholic and Jesuit higher education in this period. Free public high schools, increased enrollment, new standards and accreditation bodies, and the phenomenon of research universities – all demanded careful thought and responses. Philip Gleason writes: "The full story of Catholic colleges in the nineteenth century is yet to be told, but it is certainly safe to say that the Jesuits were by far the most influential Catholic teaching order."[6] This influence was due to the fact that the Jesuits had more personnel and more colleges, the longest tradition, and the most developed pedagogy.

Jesuits hoped to maintain their centuries-long commitment to humanism, the liberal arts, and the *Ratio Studiorum* (or Plan of Study). On a structural level, the six year, European model of education brought to the United States by the Jesuits was at odds with the American model of four years in high school and four years in college. Catholic colleges and universities adapted, in part because their fusion of secondary and collegiate education had begun to harm student enrollment.

In addition, a new trend toward "electivism" was developing. Catholic and specifically Jesuit educators soon found themselves defending their methods. In 1900, Father Timothy Brosnahan, S.J.'s "Course leading to the Baccalaureate" was published as a rebuttal to the troubling announcement that Harvard Law would accept students from a list that included only two Catholic colleges: George-town University and the University of Notre Dame.

From the earliest days of Saint Louis University, teachers and administrators sought to hold true to the *Ratio* foundations, for example

FATHER MEYER

in the use of precepts and a pedagogy based in Ciceronian Latin. But change pressed upon the institution. St. Louis-born Father Rudolph Meyer, S.J. possessed the intellectual acumen, eloquence, and organizational skills to respond to that change, and to advance successfully the issue of curricular reform at the university and well beyond.[7] He was dedicated to the task of promoting Catholic education, which he saw as urgently needed in society.

Meyer served as president of Saint Louis University from 1881 to 1885, and was twice chosen by superiors to lead the Missouri Province. As Provincial in 1887, he charged a committee with writing a "Course of Studies" for the seven colleges of the Province, encouraging them to adhere to the *Ratio*. A four year college curriculum was tested first in St. Louis, in 1887-1888. The "St. Louis plan" became a model for Jesuit colleges, but "its influence went far beyond the Jesuit circle of colleges to affect every Catholic college seriously concerned with keeping abreast of curricular trends in higher education."[8] Father William Banks Rogers, S.J., who was president of Saint Louis University from 1900 to 1908, undertook further reforms, for example, changing the designations of the class years to freshman, etc. from Humanities, Poetry, Rhetoric, and Philosophy, and formally separating the university from its high school. Father Alexander J. Burrowes, S.J. was president from 1911 to 1913 and is also credited with efforts in this regard. Jesuit high schools were coordinated with other schools by 1915, while higher education reforms continued to be a topic in subsequent years. Father James B. Macelwane, S.J. and others later took up issues of reform, as well (see Chapters 4 and 5).

ST. LOUIS.

CINCINNATI

CHICAGO.

ST MARYS

DETROIT

MILWAUKEE.

OMAHA

In 1889, Saint Louis University's Dr. Conde B. Pallen suggested that the Jesuit colleges' alumni adopt a badge. In 1895, a design was created at St. Ignatius College of Chicago, from the Oñaz y Loyola family coat of arms in the time of Ignatius. Two gray wolves rest their paws on a kettle suspended from black pot-hooks, symbolizing both the name and generosity of the family. Seven gold bands on a red field honor seven family members killed in battle in 1321. The seven colleges of the Missouri Province adapted the design. Saint Louis University incorporated gold, blue, and white (representing the Pope and the Blessed Virgin), and a *fleur-de-lis* (the standard of Saint Louis).

Osage children at the mission run by the Missouri Province Jesuits in Kansas. The essay by Christy Finsel (Chapter 1) describes the long relationship between Osage and the Society of Jesus.

Indian boys & Girls after the vacation of 1867 Osage mission Kansas.

"THE GREAT ISSUES OF THE DAY ARE ELUCIDATED AND DISCUSSED."

1895 SAINT LOUIS UNIVERSITY COURSE CATALOG

National economic crises in this period were accompanied by business and banking scandals that included price-fixing by meat industry owners in Missouri. Social harm, even lawlessness, from excessive individualism was a threat to community perceived early on by members of the Society of Jesus.[9] Now this phenomenon was becoming more widely understood. In response, reformers began the progressive movement in the United States, fighting to end child labor, among other efforts. Pope Leo XIII's 1891 encyclical on "Rights and Duties of Capital and Labor," *Rerum Novarum*, established an important, early foundation for the Catholic social movement.

Entire worlds were changing in North America: ways of conceptualizing family, community, work, and education. The last of the Native American tribes were removed from the state of Missouri, constituting a major loss of local knowledge. In 1872, the beloved Dr. Moses L. Linton died. He taught at the university's first medical college, and was the attending physician to the Jesuits and their students from 1858 to 1871. His dear friend Father De Smet died in 1873; De Smet's passing was deeply mourned by his Native American friends. As ideologies from the "Manifest Destiny" and Civil War periods ebbed, dreams of grandeur emerged in St. Louis. These aspirations were expressed in the 1904 World's Fair, but well before then, civic pride was evident. In 1858, Cyprian Clamorgan profiled prosperous African-Americans, including women, in his book: *The Colored Aristocracy of St. Louis.* In 1875, L.U. Reavis's *Saint Louis: The Future Great City of the World* presented glowing biographies of the city's powerful, white men.

Yet, many people were left out of such visions. The sensationalistic *Mysteries of Saint Louis* by Joseph Dacus and James Buel, published in 1878, provides a glimpse into the lives of the poor. The cover promises "the particulars" on topics including: "Disappearances," "Ways that are Dark," and "Crimes of a Great City." The authors characterize the part of town near the university — Washington, Locust, Olive, and Chestnut streets in the neighborhood intersecting Eighth to Eleventh streets — as papered with signs for "sample rooms," attracting illicit activities. Even allowing for exaggeration, this atmosphere suggests another reason why the Jesuit fathers longed to move the university to a location more suitable for their pupils.

In 1890, Father Thomas Hughes, S. J. reported in the *Woodstock Letters* about the old and new campuses. After the summary, he regrets that he lacks the space to speak: "of our relations with the poor, and of the great floating population of men, with whom we had so much to do in the old location; also of the German church which we left behind us there, and the colored congregation and church which are no longer in the college neighborhood; of the Young Men's Sodality, and the Marquette Club."[10] Records of bequests and donations confirm that others were aware of social needs: in 1870, Mrs. Jane Graham gave land to the university trustees for a "Church for Catholic Colored population of St. Louis," and John Doyle gave a bequest for poor children.

In one of the last photographs of the downtown campus, taken in 1888, the original 1829 building is visible at the center left.

"To respect in every man his dignity as a person ennobled by Christian character"

POPE LEO XIII, 1891

A profound shift occurred in American society from the late nineteenth to early twentieth century. In part due to changes wrought by the Industrial Revolution, Americans "were passing from a use-value world permeated by familial/communal ties and God's everyday presence to a market world that takes the competitive ego for human nature and rationality for revelation."[11] It is this atomizing influence which Pope Leo XIII sought to identify broadly in the world, and to resist, in his May 15, 1891 encyclical, *Rerum Novarum* (On Capital and Labor). The Pope decries "the enormous fortunes" of some and "utter poverty" of others. He argues that the right to possess property is a right of nature, noting that, while the lot of humanity is to suffer and endure, harmony should exist between capital and labor. Among many points, he asserts that laborers should have proper work conditions and the right to organize.

Efforts to teach and learn in community—the ideal of life within the Society of Jesus and other orders—constitute an important response to the alienation of modern society. Howard Gray, S.J. writes: "To be a Jesuit is to learn from one another." He suggests further that *union*, not simply community, has for centuries been built by the Society through selectivity, obedience, exclusion of those who undermine the unity, and communication by letter.[12] Public lectures and sermons in St. Louis from this and later decades constitute additional responses to alienating forces, in a call for renewed faith. Father Henry M. Calmer, S.J. offered sixteen lectures to the general public at St. Francis Xavier Church from 1891 to 1900. In his first lecture, on Oc-

tober 12, Calmer addressed the topic: 'What is Vexing the Men of the Age." Criticizing the common view that "Money is king," he warned that humanity was living in a time of *material*, but not spiritual or intellectual progress. Against the period's doubt and uncertainty about faith, he reminded the audience: "Jesus Christ is the truth ... the Author of the life of grace."

Others at this time lectured on the importance of the family, and the role of women as mothers. Father Laurence J. Kenny, S.J., who loved the university (his nickname was "Father Saint Louis University") and spoke of his few years at another school as "exile," saw the alumni as filling a special role. He wrote in 1922: "wherever they go, they are a light in the darkness, strength to the weak ... The joists in the walls of your homes do not serve a more useful purpose – although unseen – than the scattered fragments exercise in sustaining the national standard of morals."[13] Father Michael Martin, S.J. taught a course in Moral Theology that addressed labor and human dignity, drawing from *Rerum Novarum*.[14] One of his students, Father Joseph C. Husslein, S.J., went on to a noteworthy career (see Chapter 4).

Even when sympathetic to labor, most Jesuits in the post-*Rerum Novarum* decades opposed socialism and communism as both authoritarian and anti-religious. They, along with many other Catholics, actively sought a more humane form of capitalism. The reverberations of *Rerum Novarum* continue at Saint Louis University to this day, evident in the university tagline ("Higher Purpose, Greater Good") and spanning all programs and colleges.

"LAND ENOUGH TO LAY OUR FATHERS BONES UPON"

COMMITTEE OF FREEDMEN
ON EDISTO ISLAND,
SOUTH CAROLINA, 1865

Now legally free and recognized as persons, African Americans nevertheless continued to struggle for equality in every aspect of life. Newly freed blacks in Missouri were spared the terrible system of re-enslavement that developed throughout the former Confederate states immediately after the Civil War.[15] Racial and social class prejudices impacted the experiences of black St. Louisans in homes, neighborhoods, schools, jobs, churches, stores, theaters, restaurants, and hospitals. Without "colored" maternity wards, births in African American families took place at home; even embalming had to be performed in private homes.[16] The city and county were separated in a move by the city leaders for home rule in 1876; this decision proved very problematic in later decades.[17]

After the Civil War, Catholic clergy had not been widely involved in helping black Catholics to organize churches. Blacks were seen by many as in need of evangelization, like Native Americans.[18] Father Ignatius Panken, S.J. was an important figure in ministering to both groups, and he laid the foundations for cultural change that led to the university's integration (see Chapter 4). Born in 1832, he entered the novitiate at Florissant in 1857, and founded Sacred Heart Church there. He was Professor of Modern Languages and taught in the Commercial Course at the university. He later went to the Indian missions with Father De Smet, and then was recalled from Leavenworth City, Kansas to teach at Saint Louis University in 1872. In 1873, he founded St. Elizabeth's parish in St. Louis, which remained the only church for black Catholics in the city until 1926. From 1873 to 1950, Jesuits staffed this church. It never had an African American pastor. Indeed, only two black priests were ordained during the entire nineteenth century in the United States.[19] It is notable that the first Native American to join the Jesuit order was James Bouchard,

who was so moved by a catechism class being given by Father Arnold Damen, S.J. that he joined the Society of Jesus. He was ordained in St. Louis in 1855 and ministered to miners in California.

In 1858, a separate chapel was created for African Americans in St. Francis Xavier Church at Ninth and Green streets (see Chapter 2). After the Civil War, the black congregation outgrew this chapel and decided to raise funds to build a church, with the assistance of Father Panken. However, plans changed when Panken attended a holiday fair held in "Vinegar Hill Hall," a former Protestant church on Fourteenth and Gay streets. Built by Southern Methodists in 1849, it was once known as "Asbury Chapel." Father Panken saw its potential for his congregation, and persuaded the Province not only to buy the building but to pay for its renovation. On May 18, 1873, over 10,000 people processed to the dedication of St. Elizabeth's Church by Archbishop Kenrick. Worshippers were numerous: "about eight hundred persons compose the congregation, and all attend the Sunday services with considerable regularity."[20] Some whites attended, as well.

In September 1873, Panken opened a school in the church basement with the Oblate Sisters; over ninety African American pupils applied to study there. The parish bought a bell, as well as a lot in Calvary Cemetery for the graves of African Americans.[21] Panken remained as pastor until he was sent in 1890 to help Father Paul Ponziglione, S.J. at St. Stephen's Indian Mission. As of 1928, records state: "the Jesuit Father Arnold J. Garvey of St. Stanislaus Seminary has charge of two Catholic Congregations of colored folk, one at Anglum consisting mainly of former slaves of the Seminary, and the other at South Kinloch."[22] Father William Markoe, S.J., a prominent advocate for racial equality, was pastor of St. Elizabeth's from 1927 to 1940 (see Chapter 4).

Besides Panken, of course other parish priests were working with black Catholics across the nation. Yet a lack of imagination was evident in 1884, when the Third Plenary

Father Ignatius Panken, S.J.

The Linton album (see Chapter 2) contains this photograph of Jesuit James C. Bouchard, and a note he wrote to Father De Smet reading "Dear Father, as another proof of the sincere friendship and love of your ever devoted child." It is signed with Bouchard's Indian name, Wa-tom-i-ka.

... INSTITUTION
OF THE UNITED STATES
Governor's Island,
New York City.

Entered at New York Post Office as Second Class Matter.

[RIGHT] On an envelope sent to Father Panken in Minnesota and then to Wisconsin, the writing across the top indicates it was later reused for "Papers concerning Colored Church and School."

This photograph of Father Panken and two other men was taken at St. Stephen's Mission in Kansas. Panken was superior at the mission from 1890 to 1891.

Council of Baltimore created a commission to aid missions among Indians and African Americans in the United States. By this point, the very notion of a population requiring a "mission" should have been subsumed by an attitude of inclusion and welcome for blacks at existing Catholic parishes, argues Jeffrey Dorr, S.J. He writes: "The bishops failed to arrive at a national plan for the evangelization of and ministry to African Americans," in effect, making blacks a 'racialized other' and fostering a sense of exclusion that "placed them in the category that demanded the attention of missionaries."[23]

Through the work of this Council, "In the archdiocese of St. Louis the colored people of the city and its vicinity were placed in charge of the Society of Jesus with headquarters at the St. Louis University."[24] This policy seems to have affirmed an existing pastoral relationship, but without providing guidance from the bishops on racial integration in existing parishes. Dorr writes that the color line in St. Louis "ran right through the heart of the Catholic community" until the arrival of Archbishop Joseph Ritter in 1946.[25] Meanwhile, an official policy to admit African Americans at Saint Louis University was still three decades away. In 1911, the trustees' minutes state: "The question of receiving negroes into the classes of the University was discussed but action was deferred."[26] However, attitudes were beginning to shift. And indeed, as the transition was made from "convert-making" and interracial programs in the 1930s (see Chapter 4) to community organization and direct action in the 1960s, Catholics of all ethnicities became increasingly engaged by the middle of the twentieth century in the struggle for racial equality.[27]

Photographs of the downtown campus exist thanks to the talented Father Charles M. Charropin, S.J. Born to French parents in 1840 in the West Indies, Charropin entered Florissant seminary in 1863, and was ordained in 1875. From 1875 to 1890, he was professor of chemistry, mathematics, and astronomy at the university, in addition to teaching rhetoric; he also lived for five years at the Missouri Province's mission in Belize. Charropin used photograph stereopticons in a post-graduate lecture course. He was vice president of the St. Louis Camera Club and head of the Lantern Slide Committee; his correspondence with astronomers around the nation includes references to their frequent "Eclipse parties." Astro-photography was new, but of course Jesuits have a long interest in astronomy. They established observatories in Peking and Paris in the seventeenth century.

[LEFT] Father Charoppin (seated, with white hat) and his colleagues, as they prepare to photograph an eclipse.

The forlorn-looking downtown campus, after the Jesuits moved to their new property at Grand and Lindell in 1888.

1888

Sept. 3ᵈ Opened the new College with a great
rush of new-comers, most of whom
were recruited during vacation...
Quite a number of boys otherwise
old enough, were turned away
as below the standard.

4ᵗʰ 315 boys actually present,
as far as could be ascertained
amidst the confusion

5ᵗʰ 327 boys actually present.
Mr. Condé B. Pallen today
entered upon his engagement
to Teach the Special class and
2ᵈ Commercial P.M.
Mr. Luersman, S.J. Takes charge
of one division of 3ᵈ Academic.

10ᵗʰ Mass of the Holy Ghost at 9 o'clock.
Second hour P.M. Reading Rules.
332 present; 13 absent.

11ᵗʰ Begin Catechism. 344 present;
8 absent; 1 left

12ᵗʰ 357 boys.

Oct. 3. Holiday; We...
" 30 Holiday in hon...
Nov. 19. 399 boys in...
Private specimens...
most of the classes th...
way of contests.
Nov. 26ᵗʰ Holiday for...
honor of St...
410 boys on the...
Dec. 3ᵈ Holiday. Hig...
the Church at...
few boys attend...
Dec. 7ᵗʰ Dismissed...
to give time for...
Dec. 8ᵗʰ Mass for...
the Chapel a...
attendance...

Saint Francis Xavier Church, or "College Church," was modeled after St. Colman's Cathedral in Cobh, Ireland. A ceremony to lay the foundation stone was held in 1884, drawing a large crowd. From this angle, the buildings that existed at the time to the south and east of the church are visible. The arches face Lindell Boulevard.

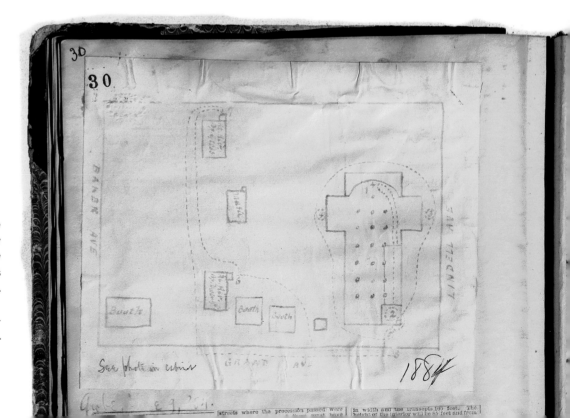

In 1883, the Jesuits assigned a realtor to sell the campus property, while also soliciting bids on construction of a new church. The following year, thousands of people processed to the corner of Grand and Lindell boulevards to witness the placement of the cornerstone of St. Francis Xavier Church. A local newspaper characterized the event as a "Gathering Such as Has Seldom Been Seen in This Country."[28] A careful sketch pasted in a scrapbook demonstrates one vision for the new campus, including a square marked for "Du Bourg Hall." A few years later, trustee records state simply that the old property "found purchasers" on May 24, 1886.

By 1888, the new campus was ready, and was duly celebrated with a procession from downtown, as "millionaires and laborers, Irish and German, white men and negroes" all formed in line with the clergy. Father Faherty describes DuBourg Hall: "A four story brick building looked towards the center of the city … the front wing housed classrooms to the left of the main entrance, and laboratory, chapel and library on successive floors to the right."[29] The Jesuits lived in a section that was two stories high at the time, parallel to the beautiful new church, which was dedicated on January 10, 1898. The whole structure formed an L shape. In September, classes began at the new site, with 435 students enrolled, according to Faherty. This was "a new high" for the university. A scholasticate was built about one year later; that building is now called Verhaegen Hall. A building erected in 1898, later called De Smet Hall, housed the College of Philosophy and Letters (also called the School of Philosophy and Science in some periods), and formed a U shape around the quad.

Recording the first months at the new location, the prefect observes that many hopeful students "were turned away as below the standard." The Mass of the Holy Spirit was held on September 10, 1888.

[RIGHT] An 1884 sketch in blue ink demonstrates a vision of the future campus.

"THE INSTITUTION ... AIMS AT LAYING A SOLID FOUNDATION IN THE ELEMENTS OF KNOWLEDGE AND AT OPENING THE MIND TO A GENEROUS SHARE IN THE CULTURE OF LIFE."

SAINT LOUIS UNIVERSITY COURSE CATALOG, 1913
INTRODUCTORY STATEMENT: SCOPE, 227

In 1888, students could still choose either a classical or commercial program of study for the baccalaureate. An "Academic Department" served what we now call "high school." The "Collegiate Department" was for undergraduate studies. The years were named, in descending order: Philosophy, Rhetoric, Poetry, and Humanities. Students were still learning Latin through the *Epitome Historiae Sacrae,* as they had for decades. They studied English, arithmetic, history, Christian doctrine, geography, penmanship and elocution, but Greek was not offered until the second year, with a text by Yenni. In their last year of formal study in Greek and Latin (the fifth year of the total of six), they still read Cicero, Horace, Tacitus, Demosthenes, St. Chrysostom, and Sophocles. In the course catalog of 1898-1899, the words "Senior" and "Junior" appear in parentheses next to the old designations. Soon the old names: Poetry, Rhetoric, etc. – disappear.

In 1901, for the first time "Departments" are explicitly listed in the course catalog: College, Academy, Commercial, Military Science, School of Philosophy and Science, and School of Divinity. By 1913, Latin and Greek continue to be offered in the classical course. Even with new colleges and divisions, curricular changes and reforms, the school's Jesuit heritage remains clear in this statement of aims: "laying a solid foundation in the elements of knowledge and at opening the mind to a generous share in the culture of life." The appearance of this quote on *page 237* of the *Course Catalog* indicates just how complex the university had become by that time.

Thanks in part to purchases of over one thousand volumes in Europe by Father Joseph Keller, S.J., the library's holdings increased by thousands of volumes in this period. Brother Henry Eils, S.J. catalogued over 50,000 books, writing cards out by hand. By this time, the library had begun a separate collection for its rare books. Talk of another medical college began to circulate, but the trustees decided "to take more time" with this.

In 1893, the "stringent financial condition of the century" meant that work ceased for a time on the church. Donations helped in later years: in 1898 and 1899, local citizens donated the Mass Altar (from Mr. Moffit, who had it imported) and the Altar of the Virgin (from Caroline Rose).

This photograph shows a portion of Pine Street that was east of Grand Avenue, at the time that the university moved in 1888.

St. Louis University - College of Arts and Sciences

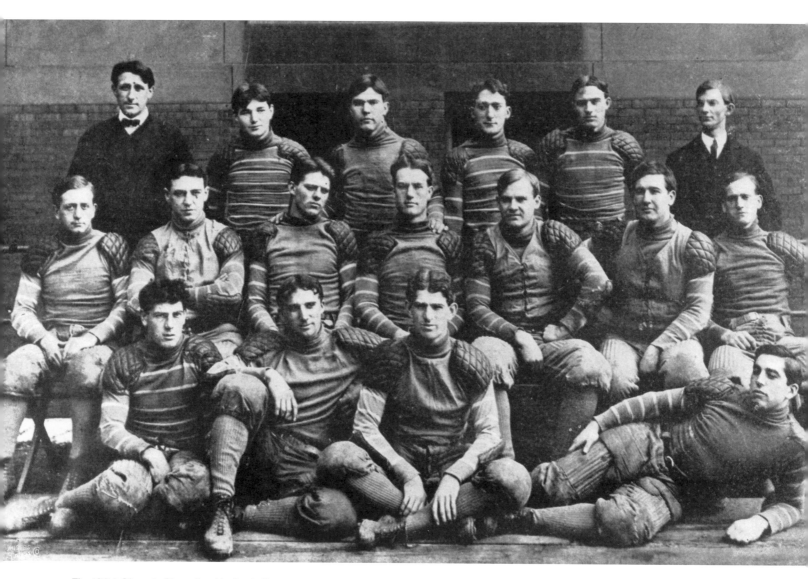

The 1904 Olympic Championship football team

[RIGHT] The genial Coach John Bender bore an uncanny resemblance to the popular good luck symbol, the Billiken, shown here on a 1909 postcard.

A kindly word, a smile of cheer,
An open sympathetic ear,
And you can have the world less drear,
And make another glad "you're here."
—BILLIKEN.

In the 1901-1902 edition of a new university publication called *Fleur de Lis* (in later years this same name was used for a literary magazine), reference was made to the "stout and honest college spirit." Indeed, a robust tone marks this era. Studies were rigorous, but fun and competition were a part of campus life: "snow ball battles" among the students, debates in the Philalethic Society, and pride in the 1904 football team as Olympic Football champion, which at the time meant amateur football champion of the world. Students admired the "wonder teams" in football of 1906 and 1907. The university issued its first year book in 1907, and in 1908, a bulletin by Father William Fanning, S.J. that summarized the university history. It was accompanied by a news release, stating that "new" findings proved the university's origins dated to 1818, not 1829.

During this era, the "Billiken" was a popular good luck charm. Legend has it that when law student Charles McNamara saw one, he thought it looked like football coach John Bender. He drew a picture of a Billiken, placed it in a window in a drugstore near campus, and a mascot was born. The team became known as "Bender's Billikens." On September 5, 1906, the first forward pass ever was thrown in the game of football. This was a strategy invented by Coach Eddie Cochems, called a "projectile." Bradbury Robinson threw the pass, in a game against Carroll College, surprising all in attendance.

In 1911, President William Howard Taft shared a box with the president of the university, Father John Pierre Frieden, S.J. Taft tossed out a new football to team captain Earl Painter. Also in 1911, Saint Louis University was designated by Father General Franz Xavier Wernz, S.J. as the highest kind of Jesuit school, *Collegium Maximum,* due to its possession of a faculty of divinity.

Eddie Cochems became athletic director in 1905, and in 1906, invented the forward pass. He coached the "wonder teams" of 1906 and 1907, and also studied law.

Father William Fanning, S.J. published new information on the origins of the university.

President William Howard Taft attends the first game of the 1911 season. Saint Louis University's Blue and White defeated Shurtleff College 11-0.

"The highest honor"

ST. LOUIS GLOBE DEMOCRAT, 1900

Father William Banks, Rogers, S.J. in a relaxed mood, is shown seated outside.

During "the quite revolutionary Rogers years,"[30] the university advanced in many ways. Father William Banks Rogers, S.J. was familiarly known as "Banks." His fellow Jesuits called him "the Presbyterian," alluding to his famous penury in official matters. Rogers was astute, personally generous, and conscientious. A dogged promoter of both Saint Louis University and of Jesuit education, he echoed Caesar Augustus, saying that he found a place "of brick and left [one] of marble."[31] He took on many challenges, including the "extraordinary unpopularity of the Society of Jesus in St. Louis at the close of the last century."[32] This sentiment was likely due to the Jesuits' neutrality in the case of divisions among the local clergy, according to this source. Catholic clergy were initially cold, even hostile to Rogers, but through outreach, letters, and invitations, he slowly won them over.

Rogers was "eminently practical," sincere, unostentatious, and admired for his good motives. Born in Cincinnati, Ohio in 1857, he entered Florissant in 1875, studied at Woodstock and at Louvain, then taught in Chicago and Cincinnati. Ordained in 1890 by Cardinal Gibbons, he served as president at Marquette from 1898 to 1900, already making educational reforms and even introducing a football team and riding a bicycle. Rogers took over the presidency at Saint Louis University due to the illness of Father James F. X. Hoeffer, S.J. in the autumn of 1900. Announcing his appointment, the *St. Louis Globe Democrat* observed: "the charge of St. Louis University is always assigned to the one considered an authority on theology and philosophy," and one who also has executive abilities. The post is "considered the highest honor."

Rogers is known for outreach and "Americanizing" the university. He promoted Jesuit education at the 1904 World's Fair in St. Louis, developed informational materials such as the "Academic History of Newly Appointed Instructors" to demonstrate the university's excellence, supported the football program, and established at Saint Louis University the custom of the annual Requiem Mass for deceased friends and benefactors. During his administration, enrollment went from 200 to 1,000. He oversaw the 1903 Grand Act, which was visited by President Theodore Roosevelt, whose associates later praised the event as "the best ordered and most dignified" of all events Roosevelt attended. (A "Grand Act" is a theological disputation conducted in Latin.) He also hosted Catholic educators, which led to the foundation of the National Catholic Educational Association in 1904, and was quick to join the Missouri College Union when invited in 1902.

Father Rogers was persistent, successfully cultivating relationships to advance the university. This is demonstrated in the remarkable tale of his revival of the medical college. Among the many doubters was John Fitzgerald Lee of St. Louis, who at first opposed the idea, but later left $750,000 for the cause in his will. Superioresses of the orders running hospitals in St. Louis were reluctant to cooperate at first yet, again, Rogers persevered. He believed that "the Catholic doctor" was second only to the priest in promoting God's glory; he saw the medical school as truly part of a Catholic *moral force*. If he couldn't persuade a person to work with him, then he sent someone else who could. He secured the cooperation of St. John's Hospital when Dr. Augustus Van Liew Brochaw left his position at Washington University to come and help with the new medical college. By March 1907, Rebekah Hospital, St. Mary's Infirmary, and many others had agreed to cooperate.

Long-term university supporter and banker Festus Wade helped Rogers to raise money for the medical school. There were several early donors; the sale of some property at "College Hill Farm" (a piece of land where the Jesuits ran a scholasticate in North St. Louis) also helped to generate cash. Rogers' biographer says that countless prayers to St. Joseph surely also helped.

Generally, Rogers saw that an endowment was needed for the university. He even issued a financial statement to the public, seeking to counter the perception that the university was wealthy (see Chapter 4).

Father Rogers suffered a stroke after a trip to Rome in 1906. The effects rendered him unable to continue as president. His positive and enduring impact on the university cannot be overstated, although he himself believed that he "did not succeed even partially" in his many aims.

THE OLDEST UNIVERSITY IN THE LOUISIANA PURCHASE

Turn of the century St. Louis was full of hopes to "win" at last against the city of Chicago, a long-time rival. Perhaps some of the woes of the past, like Charles Dickens' sneers about the city or the Gasconade train wreck of 1855, could be forgotten in new expressions of grandeur. Civic authorities, teams of engineers and designers, businessmen, and officials all helped to plan the 1904 World's Fair.

Father William Banks Rogers, S.J., as president of Saint Louis University, organized an exhibition to promote Jesuit higher education at the World's Fair. All seven of the colleges and universities in the Missouri Province were represented. The exhibit was designed by Father John C. Burke, S.J. and featured academic and laboratory work by students, anatomical drawings, maps, a collection of crystals used to teach chemistry, and relics. The exhibit won numerous awards. October 18 was designated "St. Louis University Day at the Fair."[33] On that day, the Fair drew 140,000 visitors.

Knowing that President Theodore Roosevelt was coming to St. Louis in 1903 to dedicate the Louisiana Purchase Exposition, Father Rogers arranged for a "Grand Act." Rogers invited Roosevelt to this very rare event: a public debate on questions of theology and philosophy conducted in Latin. A fourth-year theology student named Joachim Villalonga , S.J. was "chief protagonist," according to Father Faherty. This photograph shows the decorations of the library for the event. Images are superimposed on it of Rogers, Roosevelt, and Villalonga.

A photograph of the De Smet bridge in a pamphlet from the World's Fair

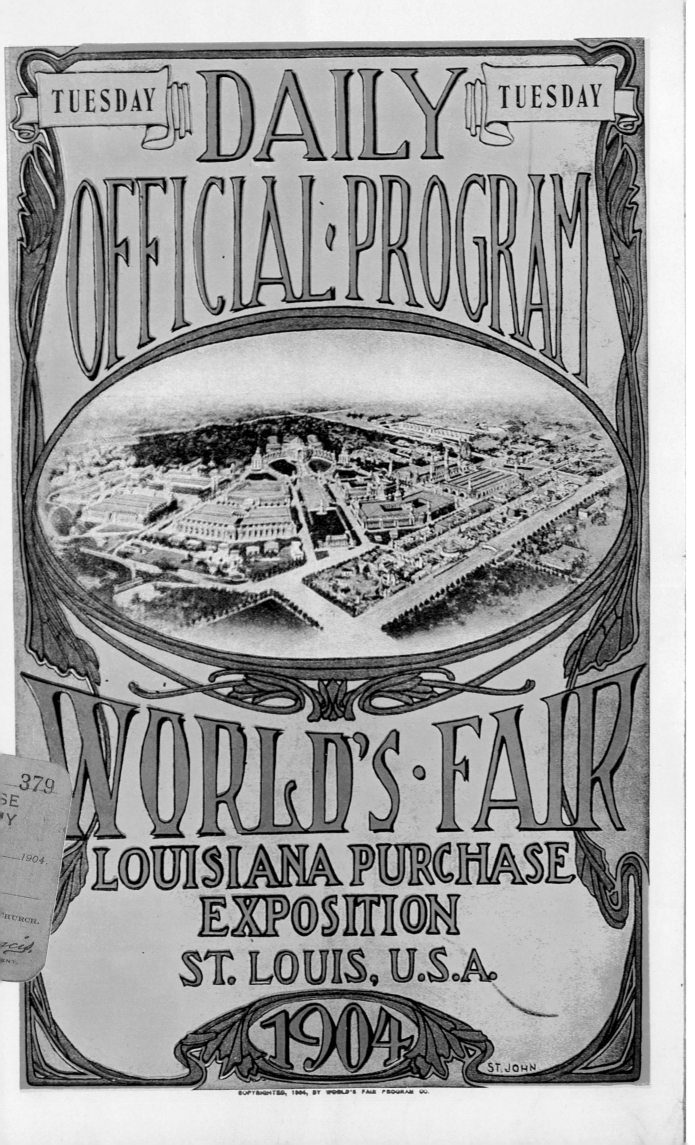

TUESDAY

DAILY

TUESDAY

OFFICIAL·PROGRAM

WORLD'S·FAIR

LOUISIANA PURCHASE
EXPOSITION
ST. LOUIS, U.S.A.
1904

ST. JOHN

Jesuit Seismological Service
Record
of the
Earthquake Station, St. Louis University
St. Louis, Mo., U. S. A.

LATITUDE: 38° 38′ 17″ N.
LONGITUDE: 90° 13′ 58″.5 or 6ʰ 0ᵐ 55ˢ.9 W. Gr.
TIME: Mean Greenwich, midnight to midnight.
INSTRUMENT: Wiechert 80 kg., astatic, horizontal pendulum.
NOMENCLATURE: Goettingen.

From May '23. 1914 to June 20th 1914.

DATE.	CHAR.	PHASE.	TIME.	PERIOD. T.	AMPLITUDE. AE	AMPLITUDE. AN	REMARKS.
			h. m. s.	s.			
May 26th	ƒƒƒ IIIu	L ?	14:44:18 to 15:16:12				N-S cannot be determined. Very irregular. No P and S, only long waves recorded. Disturbance strongly felt at Sidney, N.S.W.
		L	15:30:15 to 15:37:00				
		L	15:38:06 to 15':45:00				
		L	15:47:00 to 16:30:00				
		M 1E	15:33:50	19	1.2		
		M 2E	15:41:46	20	1.5		
		F	16:45:00				
y 27.	IIr	iP	3:30:09				Δ = 3300 Km. Probably Columbia, S.A. Felt very severely at Panama.
		RP 1	30±55				
		RP 3	31:10				
		eS ?	35:04				
		M 1E	35:09	5	.6		
		M 1N	35:10	5		.5	
		iL	37:10				
		M 2E	38:05	7	.7		
		F	3:57:00				

Records of seismic activity have been maintained at the university since 1909. The first notations in this record are from the magnitude 7.9 earthquake that struck near Papua, Indonesia on May 26, 1914.

A PROFUSION OF NEW IDEAS

Father John Pierre Frieden, S.J., president of Saint Louis University from 1908 to 1911, presided over a significant period in the university's growth. Specialized financial management was still in the future, but Frieden was careful. He tabulates students in a handwritten document: "1,181 total," including "251 Med, 167 Law and 144 Dental." In a 1901 letter, he anticipates the space needs of the law school: "expecting continuous growth as the years pass." In a 1910 memorandum, he emphasized the need for the university to get a "fixed sum" as "stimulus to grow," in other words, to establish an endowment. He believed that, if invested, it "would forever place us beyond the possibility of disaster or retrogression." Hand-written along the bottom, he cites the "good work of Seismography and Meteorology and learned and careful work around Halley's Comet." Indeed, even later years suggest a relatively calm view regarding budgets. Trustees' minutes in 1952 note: "Father Reinert mentioned that the preliminary survey of the operating income and expenses of the University for the current year revealed that, with care, we might balance the budget."

Frieden's efforts were supported by members of the local community, who dedicated themselves to the "advance of higher education" through an Advisory Board that met at the Mercantile Trust Company. Notes from this group in June 1, 1909 state: "Father Monahan reviewed the general conditions, showing especially the necessity for developing the engineering department and class of biology in the college department." The group concluded that separating high school from college was important; this separation occurred in 1924 to create Saint Louis University High School.

Also in 1908, Father James I. Shannon, S.J. returned from his doctoral studies in physics at Johns Hopkins and created an academy of science for lay students. He also organized summer field courses in the Rocky Mountains. The young Alphonse Schwitalla summarized the trip in *Science* magazine, providing an early example of precise, research-oriented writing by a man who would come to be a prolific and nationally-respected health educator (see Chapter 4).

Meteorological observations at Saint Louis University were undertaken from 1835 to 1836, in support of research by the explorer, Joseph Nicollet (see Chapter 2). These observations began again in 1857, at the College Hill site in north St. Louis. In 1908, Brother George E. Rueppel, S.J. came to the university, and with Frieden's support, organized a seismological station. Financed by the mother of Father John Bernard Goesse, S.J., a new Weichert 80 kilogram, horizontal-component, inverted pendulum seismograph was installed in the basement of DuBourg Hall. It recorded its first earthquake on October 9, 1909.[34]

By 1900, plans emerged to revive the Law Department. A group of alumni informed the trustees of their plans to help, and the trustees approved of the idea. Space was rented on the corner of Locust Street and Leffingwell Avenue. Father Frieden supported Father James Conway, S.J. in opening the school in 1908. Father Conway purchased a library in Chicago, and soon the faculty included some forty judges and lawyers with active practices, who served without compensation! In this period, night schools were seen by some as inferior; nevertheless, the university offered them. Night classes in the law school were very helpful for the poor and immigrants of the community and for all law students who worked full-time.

In 1908, the first women were admitted to the university at the School of Law: Bertha Breuning, Adele M. Doyle, Mary A. Maguire, Rose O'Boyle, and Anna L. Ross. Soon, two more women enrolled: Aurelia Hollos and Margaret Elizabeth Wood. In 1911, the original

Father James Conway, S.J. was the first white to attend St. Mary's Mission School in Kansas. He spoke eight languages and was a popular preacher in College Church.

When the law school reopened, this group of students was first to enroll and graduate.

five women received LL.B degrees, and in 1913, three women received the LL.M. degree from the School of Law. There followed a period when no women enrolled.

In 1910, an idea for a school of commerce and finance was advanced by Father Joseph "Buck" Davis, S.J., who emphasized the historic role of St. Louis in commerce and the need to render economic institutions "genuinely serviceable to society," while shaping lives to the "light of charitable purpose" and fostering research toward those ends.[35] From its origins in night school sessions that met on the ground floor of DuBourg Hall, the school advanced by 1931 to the imposing Davis-Shaughnessy Hall.

Also in 1910, and on a lighter note, Alfred Robyn wrote the "Varsity Song," which was used for nearly fifty years at sports events.

O'Neill Ryan, a fiery debater, was dean of the School of Law from 1908 to 1915. As a judge, he was so passionate regarding the Irish Republic that he would not allow court decisions of the British to be cited in his court.[36]

Joseph L. Davis, S.J. founded the School of Commerce and Finance in 1910; the school's first graduate was in 1913.

Thanks to the care and persistence of Father William Banks Rogers, S.J., Saint Louis University Medical College was revived in 1903. Its initial catalog notes affiliations with over a dozen hospitals. Father Rogers convinced Dr. Young H. Bond, dean of Marion-Sims-Beaumont College, and the MSB faculty, to work with Saint Louis University. MSB, located at Grand Avenue and Caroline Street, was the result of the 1901 merger of Beaumont Hospital Medical College (founded 1886) and Marion-Sims College (founded 1890, by Dr. Bond).

In May 1903, MSB became "the Medical Department of the St. Louis University." Dr. Bond was the first dean of the new medical school. He recruited excellent doctors. From Rush Medical College came Dr. Elias Potter Lyon and Dr. Albert Eycleshymer. From Harvard came Dr. Ralph Thompson, and from the University of Missouri: Dr. Peter Potter. "The group was young and aggressive," Father Alphonse Schwitalla, S.J. later wrote; all were laboratory-trained, not administrators, yet thanks to Father Rogers' "keenness of judgment," the group thrived.[37]

Although the Catholic, Jesuit environment was new to them, they were productive, with "no evidence of intolerance or factions." Schwitalla credits Rogers for proceeding "with serenity and assurance and with a word of encouragement for everyone." The doctors were constantly being recruited to leave for what Lyon later called "greatly increased salaries," but they stayed because they loved "the spirit" of Saint Louis University.

Bond served as dean until 1907, when Dr. Lyon took over, making physical changes to the building to add laboratory space. In 1909, Father John Burke, the regent of the school, reported that Saint Louis University medical students' failure rate was 3% before the State boards, while the percentage for both Harvard and Johns Hopkins was 3.7%, and Washington University's was 5.4%. The letter ends: "What could we not accomplish if the difficulties mainly pecuniary under which the University is now laboring, were removed."[38]

Rogers also negotiated with the Marion-Sims Dental College (founded 1894), which was purchased by the university in 1903. Doctor C.D. Lukens, D.D.S. became dean in 1908. Courses were offered in anatomy, bacteriology, chemistry, dental jurisprudence, and oral surgery, among other topics, for $150 per year. The university catalog notes that "the Infirmary is visited daily by patients from all over the city." Lukens was succeeded in 1911 by Dr. J.P. Harper, D.D.S.[39]

In 1910, the famous Abraham Flexner Report on medical education was published. This report was prepared for the Carnegie Foundation for the Advancement of Teaching, and contained scathing reviews of institutions of medical education across the United States and Canada. SLU's new medical

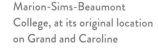

Marion-Sims-Beaumont College, at its original location on Grand and Caroline

school received a surprisingly positive review in this notably rigorous study: "St. Louis University affords an excellent example of a brave, uphill contest, by no means barren of result. Unable for the moment to do all it wishes, it has, like a good general, concentrated its effort at critical points. It secures a pervasive scientific atmosphere in the first two years through intensive cultivation of anatomy and physiology. The departmental head of the former subject stipulated that his routine work be kept in close bounds: with wise liberality he has been provided with an assistant professor, a draughtsman, and a competent helper; the productive department thus created has invigorated the entire school on the laboratory side." In 1911, Dr. Lyon provided the following, humble list in a Dean's Report as the "reasons for the existence" of the medical school: "Our location in St. Louis; Good doctors, but we accept Washington University has more money; Research."[40]

That year there were just under three hundred students, and the school had a budget of $43,000. In 1912, the Sisters of St. Mary (now known as the Franciscan Sisters of Mary) opened a free, walk-in clinic with a dispensary. It was staffed by faculty members from Saint Louis University School of Medicine. Since about 1903, Father Rogers, Father John C. Burke, S.J. (regent of the SOM), and Mother Mary Seraphia Schlochtermeyer and Mother Mary Aloysia Schruefer of the SSM, had established a foundation of trust that led to the partnership at Firmin Desloge Hospital (see Chapter 4). Soon the medical college was to enter a phase of dramatic growth and increasing professionalization, under the leadership of Father Alphonse Schwitalla, S.J. Another important figure in the advance of the school was Dr. Hanau W. Loeb, who came to the Marion-Sims College of Medicine in 1891, later worked with Rogers on the medical school negotiations, and in 1913, became dean of the School of Medicine.

The free clinic at 1507 Chouteau [TOP] was staffed by faculty from the university's School of Medicine. Cooperation between the Sisters of St. Mary and the Jesuits was forged by, from left: Mother Mary Seraphia Schlochtermeyer, S.S.M., Mother Mary Aloysia Schruefer, S.S.M., and Father John Burke, S.J. Burke was regent of both the medical and dental schools. (Images of the clinic and two Sisters: courtesy of Franciscan Sisters of Mary. Used with permission.)

Dr. Hanau Loeb was a member of the medical school governing faculty in 1903.

CHAPTER 4

"*Beyond the possibility of disaster or retrogression*"

1914-1948

The title of this chapter is taken from a memorandum written in 1910 by Father John Pierre Frieden, S.J., who was president of Saint Louis University from 1908 to 1911. Frieden expressed the modest hope that the creation and investment of an endowment fund might protect the university from harm. His words anticipate a cautious, even sober, time. The decades to come were marked by the Great Depression and two world wars. SLU's leaders fretted over the budget, but they also initiated new programs: a School of Education, a School of Nursing, a School of Social Service, an Institute of Technology, and an Aviation Engineering Program. Saint Louis University continued to serve as a rich source of thinkers, leaders, and ideas. Its impact was felt in the reform of Jesuit higher education, in policies on both coeducation and integration, and in the development of Catholic social thought and action.

African American students had attended the university on an unofficial basis for many years, but a university-wide policy of admission for black students became official in 1944. Similarly, women had often been admitted with certain caveats or only to certain programs, but the entire university officially became coeducational by 1949. In 1924, the process of separating Saint Louis University High School from the university was completed. The high school students began to attend classes in the Backer Memorial building, located a few miles from the university.

ST. LOUIS UNIVERSITY, ST. LOUIS, MO.

Page 28

DuBourg Hall and St. Francis Xavier Church, 1918: The church is of fourteenth century English Gothic design, and was built in three stages. The steeple and bells were completed in 1914. Pastor Henry Bronsgeest, S.J., facilitated construction and was one of many men recruited by Father De Smet.

"THINGS ARE LOOKING GOOD FOR THE OLD SCHOOL. NOW IF ONLY WE HAD SOME GRASS."

EDITORIAL, *THE UNIVERSITY NEWS*, 1947

The quadrangle formed by DuBourg Hall and De Smet Hall served as a recreation field sheltered from the busy corner of Grand and Lindell. This scene is from 1913. The quadrangle is still present on campus, but now boasts grass and hammocks.

[RIGHT] This sketch shows a student's humorous view of the campus and its environs. It appeared in the 1914 edition of the *Archive*, the university yearbook.

In 1904, Father William Banks Rogers, S.J. issued the university's first-ever public financial statement. It is, in effect, a fund-raising letter. He began: "St. Louis University is commonly thought to be rich." He noted an annual deficit of about $11,000; in some years, that deficit was not recovered. After detailing the university's many contributions, he asked graduates to contribute $25 per year, so that the university might "broaden the scope of its usefulness" and be an institution "to which all might point with pride." By June 1914, the university announced a major bequest from James Campbell, signaling the onset of financial stability. A series of other grants followed, and by 1938, an endowment of $1.24 million was recorded: a relatively small but important achievement for the school. University historian Father William B. Faherty, S.J., notes that the endowment of Tulane at the time was $10 million, and Stanford's was over $30 million.[1]

In 1915, Saint Louis University's seven colleges were: Arts and Sciences; Commerce and Finance; Dentistry; Divinity (including courses in Dogmatic Theology and Moral Theology); Law; Medicine; and Philosophy and Sciences. Applicants to the College of Arts and Sciences who lacked a high

school certificate were required to undertake examinations in all four books of Caesar's *Gallic Wars* (or *Nepos' Lives* in place of two of the four books); Cicero's Orations against Catiline; works by Virgil and Ovid; and a host of other subjects. In addition: "All applicants must present evidence of good moral character."

In 1915, most of the 1,427 enrolled students were from Missouri. Among those from outside the state, thirty-five states and eighteen countries were represented. Saint Louis University was: "a compact campus covering the half-block on the west side of Grand between Lindell and Pine." As Faherty describes it, walking east on Lindell toward Grand, one passed the Law School, the School of Philosophy, and the parish rectory. Next to the administration building, there was a quadrangle or recreation field comprised of dirt. A School of Theology was behind the Law School, and the Sodality Hall was located about a half block south of the campus.[2]

DON'T NEGLECT YOUR "INNER MAN"
VISIT THE
CAFETERIA
AT THE ADMINISTRATION BUILDING

[LEFT] On Thanksgiving Day in 1923, Saint Louis University held Notre Dame to a score of 13-0!

DuBourg Hall and Saint Francis Xavier College Church are presented in the 1914 university yearbook along with the "Varsity Song."

'VARSITY SONG

Sons of a royal name,
Dear 'Varsity,
For aye our faith and love
We pledge to thee.
Guardian of truth and light
Our fathers knew,
Thou whom the years have crowned,
Saint Louis U.!

CHORUS:

All hail, Saint Louis U.!
Valiant and strong,
Noble old 'Varsity,
Hark to our song!
Proudly our colors fly,
Brave White and Blue,
Loud let the chorus swell,
Saint Louis U.!

Great is thy noble heart,
Tender and true,
Dear to thy loyal sons,
Saint Louis U.!
Bear we with pride and love
Thy White and Blue.
Sweet are thy memories,
Saint Louis U.!

Truth and nobility
Thy halls inshrine,
Guarding the hallowed name
Forever thine.
May we with heart and hand,
Through life renew
Thy noble victories,
Saint Louis U.!

Graduates in a 1925 procession

Students in the pathology lab, from August 1915 *Dental School Bulletin*

As this period proceeded, campus construction and expansion were guided, above all, by pragmatism.

Boarding had ceased in 1881. After the move to the Grand and Lindell location in 1888, students rented rooms in private homes, or lived in fraternities or club houses, including the Knights of Columbus club house on Lindell. Students pressed for more options: a 1931 editorial in *The University News,* the student newspaper, argued that campus-based student housing was needed for non-local students, and to promote friendships. In the 1930s, enrollment increased despite the Depression, and many students commuted. Amidst reports of "these our distressing times" in 1932, a headline observed: "Police Warn Students about Parking in Alley."

In 1920, the university purchased land on the south side of Oakland west of Kingshighway, and by 1930, a student journalist reported on construction at the site: "Osborn Company Already at Work on Our New Stadium."

While on campus, students ate in a cafeteria located on the ground floor of the administration building. When that cafeteria closed in 1930, a "Union House" opened in the basement of the gymnasium. The Union House remained open each day until five o'clock p.m. If there was a dance in the gym, the cafeteria reopened at night. A student journalist described it as "a smoke-filled cafeteria, pool hall and ping-pong room all in one." Pool cost two and a half cents a cue, with longer ones costing ten cents a stick. "It is the only eating place, of any type, that graces the University campus," offering fresh sandwiches, pies, cakes and cookies, as well as milk shakes and sodas. He made sure to mention the "candy counter with two penny nut vendors." By December 1940, the students' longed-for smoking room in the Commerce School was finally a reality. A room was converted to a "jelly-joint atmosphere" for the "future business wolves" with a dense cloud of smoke and a jukebox, and was praised for attracting even the "co-eds" away from their books.[3]

A 1937 editorial in the student newspaper acknowledges that the school will never be a "summer resort type of university." Improvements and growth continued, nevertheless. The school reached an all-time record in 1938, when 666 students graduated. Post-war enrollment was high, and by autumn 1947, a sentence above *The University News* masthead proclaimed: "11,500 expected to sign up for University's 130th Year." A map and accompanying text provided information on the latest renovations, highlighting the new freshman dormitory, Clemens Hall. Summarizing the changes, the writer concluded: "You can only say, "Things are looking good for the old school, now if only we had some grass.""

The 1947 student newspaper praised the new freshman dormitory, Clemens Hall. The intimate campus was soon to be greatly expanded.

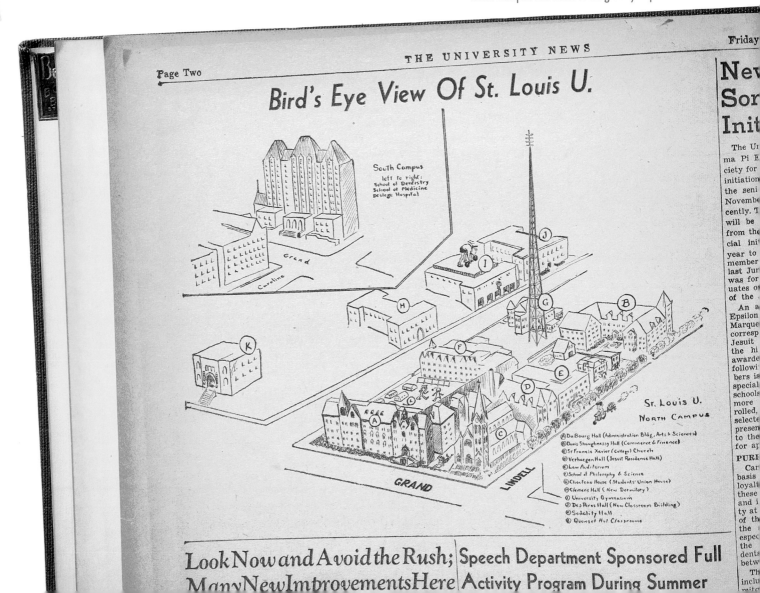

"Our poor, war-torn world"
FATHER BERNARD OTTING, S.J., 1917

On June 28, 1914, Archduke Franz Ferdinand of Austria (heir to the throne of Austria-Hungary) was assassinated. World War I officially began July 28 of that year, and ended November 11, 1918. Although it was not until April 6, 1917 that the United States declared war on Germany, as early as 1915, the Saint Louis University School of Medicine was planning to send a unit for service in Europe, while the university trustees' minutes for March 28, 1917 report that students "wished to form a military unit among themselves."[4]

Students did indeed join "the fight for France" even before the U.S. declaration of war. In addition, the university began a School of Telegraphy which sent many trained men to the war effort. Fourteen of twenty-one surgical faculty went into the medical corps, and hundreds of alumni were commissioned. "Four Minute Speakers" (volunteers nationwide, who promoted the war under government auspices) were trained by Father Robert S. Johnston, S.J., and alumnus Major Albert Bond Lambert was in charge of "the first national balloon school," offering a course at the university. Divinity students preached, joined the Red Cross, and volunteered as chaplains. In May, 1917, four university professors made themselves available for the National Security League: "to arouse patriotism" and instruct people "upon the reasons for the war." In December of that same year, Chancellor Frederick Aldon Hall of Washington University asked if Saint Louis University could assist in the training of wounded soldiers. In response, the trustees decided they would "do all in our power."

Local heroism was also evident. Fourth-year medical students volunteered to go to the Barracks in St. Louis to battle influenza in 1918. Father Laurence Kenny, S.J. wrote: "The young men who were within a few months of graduation at the medical school of St. Louis University – and no other – asked in that spirit of generosity that this school stands for to be permitted to assist the doctors at the Barracks. In a very brief time the Barracks was under control, and the city and the State of Missouri got off with perhaps fewer deaths than any location similarly situated in America. How many of your people would have died of the flu if these young men had not come to the rescue in time! I am convinced that they saved the lives of thousands in Missouri. No other medical school in America, so far as I can learn, certainly none in Missouri did like St. Louis."[5]

To local banker Festus Wade's Christmas Eve, 1917 note urging him to "<u>serve our Country the coming year</u>" in order to win the war "more speedily" (emphasis in original), Father Bernard Otting, S.J. replied graciously. Otting prayed that "a just and honorable and lasting peace be granted soon to our poor war-torn world."[6] Father Otting had planned to raise funds to celebrate the centennial of "the old college," but this endeavor was delayed when the board decided in March 1918: "war conditions make the time inopportune." The plans were revived by May 1920.

There were thirty casualties among Saint Louis University alumni in World War I. In at least one case, service in the war exacerbated a health condition and proved fatal. Powhatan Hughes Clarke, born in 1893, graduated from SLU in 1913, going on to earn his law degree in 1918. He served with the 21st Aero Squadron and the Labor Bureau, A.E.F. during World War I, then sailed for the United States in 1919, and was discharged at Camp Dix, New Jersey. He died from tuberculosis August 20, 1920.

Father Bernard Otting, S.J.

Festus Wade

An Officer's Club in Issoudun, France - photograph by Powhatan Hughes Clark, who earned his B.A. and law degrees at SLU and then served in World War I.

The cover for sheet music from a 1917 song about World War I

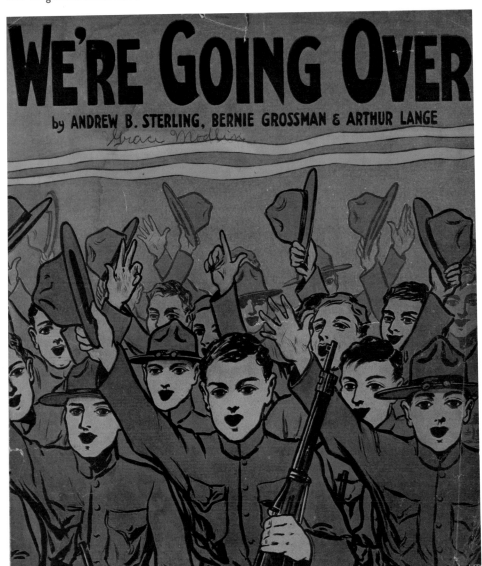

Three brothers: Charles, John and Joseph, from the Holten family are pictured. They all served in WWI. Joseph, in the lowest photo, went to Saint Louis University High School and donated his photographs to the university.

"THAT WAS WHEN WE STARTED TAKING OVER."

MARY BRUEMMER, 2017

It was women religious in the early twentieth century who paved the way for these School of Education students, pictured here in the 1950s.

In 1929, Pope Pius XI issued his encyclical *Divini Ilius Magistri* ("On Christian Education of Youth"). The document included criticism of coeducation. But Missouri Jesuits had already been experimenting with some forms of coeducation for several years. Women were accepted at the law school in 1908, and progress also took place through "extension" and summer courses. Father Alexander Burrowes, S.J. served only two years as president before becoming provincial upon the death of Father Meyer in 1912. Burrowes was succeeded by Father Otting. At least by 1915, Burrowes was advocating for coeducation in the Missouri Province. In summer 1913, the university's Father Hubert Gruender, S.J. taught experimental psychology for women religious at St. Mary's College in Leavenworth, Kansas. Father James Shannon, S.J. taught science at Visitation Convent in St. Louis in 1916, and extension courses offered at the Academy of the Sacred Heart included psychology, ethics, Latin, geometry, trigonometry, and education. In addition, in 1924,

a system of "corporate colleges" was created, to support Catholic women's colleges in the granting of degrees. Saint Louis University partnered with three four-year colleges (now known as) Fontbonne University, Maryville University, and Webster University, as well as three junior colleges, Maryhurst Normal College, Notre Dame, and St. Mary's, in a relationship that endured until 1957.

In 1925, the university founded a School of Education. Classes were held in Sodality Hall, and the first dean was Father George Deglman, S.J. Out of over 250 initial students, more than half were public school teachers. The school was designed to prepare teachers who would shape both the intellect and character of young people, encouraging "a sound outlook upon life." Dr. Francis M. Crowley was dean from 1930 to 1937. He published *The Catholic High School Principal* in 1935, analyzing data from 243 principals. When Leo Kennedy became dean in 1937, there were over five hundred students enrolled.

In part, the school came to function as a surreptitious means to register female students; the university was able to report to Rome for two decades that there were no women in the College of Arts and Sciences.[7]

Another strand of this story is woven through the Catholic hospitals of the city. One group in particular has a long history with the Missouri Jesuits. Mary Odilia Berger, the foundress of the Sisters of St. Mary, had left Germany with her companions in 1872, bound for St. Louis, and five years later, the sisters opened a hospital called Saint Mary's Infirmary. By 1907, their partnership with the Jesuits led to a plan whereby Saint Louis University High School offered a high school education to the sisters, in order that those seeking to become nurses could fulfill

Missouri state requirements (see also Chapter 3). In 1921, School of Medicine dean Dr. Hanau W. Loeb sought advice from nursing educators nationally on opening a nursing school. He did not live to see the realization of his dream, but his inquiries were fruitful. By 1924, Saint Louis University and the Sisters of St. Mary (now known as the Franciscan Sisters of Mary) agreed that three hospitals run by the Sisters would be teaching hospitals of the university: Saint Mary's Infirmary, Mount Saint Rose Sanitarium, and Saint Mary's Hospital. The agreement was signed by Father William J. Robison, S.J., president of Saint Louis University, and the Reverend Mother Mary Concordia Puppendahl, S.S.M., Superior General of the Congregation of the Sisters of St. Mary of the Third Order of St. Francis.

Mother Marie Kernaghan, R.S.C.J. was the first woman to graduate from Saint Louis University with a Ph.D. Her degree was in physics and was issued in 1929.

Sodality Hall housed the School of Education when it was founded in 1925.

[RIGHT] Father Schwitalla proudly wrote that the February 13, 1924 agreement was believed to be "one of the most far reaching and large-visioned documents ever drafted in the history of medical education under Catholic auspices."

AND

TERMINATION.

...eement is to be considered binding upon the
... for both St. Louis University and St. Mary's
..., and upon their successors in office, and
that it is to be modified or terminated only by mutual
agreement of those same signees or their successors
in office.

For St. Louis University,

W. F. Robison S.J. Pres.

For the Sisters of St. Mary,
of the Third Order of
St. Francis,

Mother M. Concordia

St. Louis, Missouri,

Feb. 13   1924

m. E. Mc Donald - E. Hoing - L. R. Schmitz - D. O'Meara - M. Conway - G. E.
A. M. Koetting - J. Werner - A. Mc Grail - M. Heitz - K. Cummins - R. Witt
L. Fagan

The first graduating class of SLU's School of Nursing is shown here in 1931. This photo was taken outside of Mother Concordia Hall at Saint Mary's Hospital on Clayton Road, where classes were held.

[RIGHT] Mary Bruemmer in the 1939 yearbook, along with her fellow sophomores in SLU's School of Education. She is second from right, in the first row.

The partnership was successful; in 1928, it led to the establishment of a School of Nursing at Saint Louis University, run by the sisters at Mother Concordia Hall in Clayton. They had begun a School of Nursing for sisters at St. Mary's Infirmary in 1907, which opened to laypersons in 1927. In 1937, the school was restructured into two divisions: Nursing and Nursing Education; and Health and Hospital Services, under which all of the allied health programs were housed. The curriculum for the new venture expanded by 1938 to include Laboratory Technology, Dietetics, Physical Therapy Technology, Hospital Administration, Radiological Technology, Public Health Nursing, and Medical Records Library Science. In addition, as early as 1926, Medical Social Services was both a program and a practice for the sisters. Father Alphonse Schwitalla, S.J. and Reverend Mother Concordia worked closely on this and other projects.[8] These programs marked the beginning of the Allied Health programs, which later became the Doisy College of Health Sciences.

In the 1930s and 1940s, American Jesuits disagreed with Superior General Wlodimir Ledochowski and his assistant, Father Zacheus Maher, S.J., on the issue of coeducation.

THE UNIVERSITY NE

MISS NANCY RING

Ring In The New---We Have A Woman Dean

In September 1943, Nancy McNeir Ring was appointed as the first female Dean of Women. The university's president at the time, Father Patrick Holloran, S.J., established a University Council of the Dean of Women to work with Ring.

Father William J. McGucken, S.J.

In 1938, the university's Father William J. McGucken, S.J., who served on the Executive Committee of the Jesuit Educational Association, wrote a brief essay on the matter. McGucken acknowledged Pius XI's view in *Divini Ilius Magistri* ("On Christian Education of Youth"), agreeing that coeducation at the elementary and high school level was not "ideal," but he argued for its practicality due to limited resources. For graduate and professional studies, coeducation was essential "as women are taking their places alongside men in important positions of responsibility." For undergraduates, it was a "danger," but one that "is recognized and guarded against, and in no way comparable to coeducation in a materialistic university." Young people should "receive that contact with Catholic thought and Catholic culture that will make them intelligent leaders in Catholic Action."[9] The debate went on for years; ultimately, Saint Louis University, Creighton, and Gonzaga led the Jesuit schools in making university-wide coeducation official in 1949.[10]

Page five of *The University News* of November 15, 1940 states that Mary Bruemmer spoke "at last Friday's first annual Parents' Day Dinner." Note the phrase: "first annual." This event had been called the "Dad's Day Dinner" for years. Ms. Bruemmer was still just a junior, majoring in Education. Two weeks later, a newspaper article refers to her as a prefect, and later pieces reflect her success, as she began editing news and organizing events. She was to have an enduring impact on the university community, with a career spanning seven decades (see also Chapter 6).

"TALK WITH FRIENDS ABOUT
WHAT YOU LEARN."

In April 1921, WEW became the first radio station west of the Mississippi to send weather reports; Brother George E. Rueppel, S.J. was the station's first "DJ" in a sense, playing records in between providing reports on the state of the weather and the Mississippi river. WEW introduced a "radiophone" rather than using the "spark method." Another local experimenter was William Evans Woods, who used a wireless telephone to report the election returns of the 1920 Harding-Cox Presidential Election from his home in St. Louis.

In 1926, scholastics presented a series on the university's radio station, WEW. They gave six popular lectures, covering Logic, Ontology, Psychology, Cosmology, Theodicy, and Ethics. Law students even got involved in the broadcasts, when the radio station expanded into the locker room area on the first floor

In the *Ratio Studiorum* ("Plan of Studies") of the Society of Jesus, principles such as "*Eloquentia perfecta*" (write and speak well) are elaborated. One simple but profound proposal is: "Talk with friends about what you learn."[11] This ideal was certainly in evidence at Saint Louis University in this period.

Students and faculty wrestled with urgent themes, including the global role of the United States, the idea of a national "social security" system, and the need for community studies to inform medical care. There were also less weighty topics. In 1931, the student debate team took up the proposition: "Resolved. That the Eighteenth Amendment should be repealed and control of the liquor traffic be left to the several States."

Brother George E. Rueppel, S.J. is pictured here next to his "sending station." He was the first "DJ" at WEW. He called it the "Little Flower's Station," acknowledging Saint Thérèse of Lisieux as its patron saint [LEFT].

of the law school in 1928. Law professor and regent Father Linus Augustine Lilly, S.J., who taught constitutional law, took advantage of the proximity. He enlisted law students to present programs on the radio regarding current events, continuing as the country underwent financial reconstruction after the Depression. Topics included "the Ethics of War." In 1931, WEW played a role in the first broadcast by any pope—Pope Pius XI. The station broadcast extensive lectures, and starting in 1932, hosted an "Interracial Hour."

The journal of philosophy, *The Modern Schoolman,* was founded as "a mimeographed sheet" by students, issued for the first time in January 1925. Its name was changed to *Res Philosophica* in 2013. The editors refer to "The recently inaugurated seminars in the Philosophy department" the aim of which was "to really know Scholasticism... Soon the students

formed 'logic study clubs.'" The paper was an outgrowth of this activity. The editors invited professors of philosophy in the Province to submit articles; over the decades, international submissions and book reviews expanded its scope. It became an established quarterly by May 1932, one of a few neo-scholastic journals in the United States; another was *Thought* at Fordham University.

The Modern Schoolman offers a sophisticated intellectual journey, spanning disciplines of evolution, biology, geology, behaviorism, philosophy, physics, and physiology. By April of the first year of publication, "Chuck Heithaus," or Father Claude Heithaus, S.J. (who advised the student newspaper and in 1944, gave a fiery speech urging integration), had already contributed a piece on freedom. In November 1928, Father Bernard Dempsey, S.J. reviewed philosopher Jacques Maritain;

in subsequent issues, there are essays on philosophers from Plato and St. Thomas Aquinas through Immanuel Kant and René Descartes to Karl Marx, Rudolf Carnap, John Dewey, and Erich Fromm. A summary of scholasticism in selected countries in Europe is presented, as well as an essay on the ethics of Bolshevism, and in one issue, nearly twenty pages are devoted to a bibliography of scholarship on existentialism. A veritable "who's who" of important scholars and authors is evident in *TMS.* In 1938, the path-breaking historian of philosophy Étienne Gilson contributed a piece (see Chapter 6 for more on his impact). In 1939, Father Louis Twomey, S.J. (who in subsequent years was a prominent activist at Loyola University New Orleans) offers a book review, and Father John La Farge, Jr., S.J., (another prominent activist, who edited the progressive journal *America* in varying capacities for thirty-seven years) offers an essay. In 1940, Father Walter Ong, S.J. critiques a book on the history of aesthetics for neglecting to include scholasticism, noting: "St. Louis University alone has nearly one hundred students in its graduate school taking ten to fifteen hours of Scholastic philosophy each semester."[12]

Other student publications reflect the lively spirit of discussion on campus. The *Fleur de Lis* was initially published in 1899 as a news magazine for the university and the high school. In October 1919, a paper called *The Billiken* was produced, with Claude Heithaus as managing editor. It was soon renamed the *Fleur de Lis,* then *The Varsity Breeze,* and later, *The University News.*[13]

Dry wit characterizes many stories: after the "relatively disastrous football season" of 1923, a scoreless final game is heralded by student headline writers as "little less than a triumph." In 1940, a sports columnist chided students for not cheering for the football team. He teasingly alleges they may disdain: "such bourgeois activity as cheering which was designed for the masses." Story topics range from tips on "Proper Costume for a Barn Dance," to cautions against being a "cad," news on dances, "smokers," and the federal government depository at the law library.

MISSOURI PROVINCE **CLASSICAL BULLETIN**

FOR PRIVATE CIRCULATION

February, 1925

ST. LOUIS, MISSOURI

Vol. I, No. 1.

The Loyola Service Cards

By reason of financial embarrassment and difficulty in securing suitable "copy," the editors of the Loyola Service cards were forced to suspend publication for this year. Although some members of the Association considered the cards to be of but doubtful value, there are others who regret that the work was not continued. The matter will be brought up for discussion at the summer convention and it is hoped that a feasible modus agendi will be arrived at. In the meantime the publication of one or two issues of a printed bulletin has been decided upon as a means of keeping the members of the Association in touch with another. Should the members who attend the convention decide that a bulletin [...] permanent substitute [...] look upon [...]

The Classical Association.

On January 17, the St. Louis Branch of the Missouri Province Classical Association held its second meeting of the year. Father O'Neill read a short paper on "Type Sentences in Language Study" in which he advocated a judicious use of Yenni's method of teaching syntax by the aid of model sentences, which the pupil should be required to memorize in connection with abstract rules. He argued that if concrete examples are necessary for the initial understanding of the abstract rule, they are no less necessary in the practical application of these rules in theme work. In translation work, a familiar type sentence will often suggest not only the proper construction, but also the mood and tense forms of the verb, etc. An abstract rule is a barren thing; it does not guide or suggest. Its function is to prove the correctness of the construction suggested by the type sentence [...] the use of type sentences [...] mechanical process [...] program was [...]

The survey recommends that 80 pages of easy reading matter be seen in the first year and a half. The matter recommended is almost identical with the reading matter in the back of the old Yenni's Latin Grammar, and Yenni is nothing but the ratio personified. Not nearly so good a choice is in the back of Bennett's First Year Latin. Bennett gives Caesar Book II. Most teachers would consider that too difficult. In Canada our old "Historia Sacra" is prescribed for reading in First Year. In St. Jerome's College conducted by the Resurrectionists. Get a copy out of the House Library and look it over. If there is a sufficient number of copies, give them to the better boys for a little "supplementary reading" and see what happens. You may have something interesting to report at the Convention next summer.

The survey recommends that we lighten the burden in First Year by postponing the study of the subjunctive mood to Second Year. We have been doing that in the province for nearly ten years.

Caesar. The survey reports that most teachers think that Caesar is too hard for Second Year. They then proceed to recommend a host of substitutions. If they try such some of these substitutes, they [find] that they are harder than Caesar. [...] of our High Schools this year tried [...]'s Lives. They were too hard. They [...] tried other matter from the beginning [...] Beeson and Scott's Second Latin Book [...] much better success. Caesar Book I in the First Semester of Second Year is too hard. Book I is harder than Book II. Book II is usually not too hard. Several years ago a mimeographed course of studies from Province Headquarters allowed the use of selections from Beeson and Scott in place of Book I. It works. In the Ratio and in the Canadian Course of Studies referred to above, Caesar is taken in Fourth Year.

Latin Grammar. The survey recommends that the grammar be spread out over all four years. In Second Semester of Fourth High therefore, a boy will see some points of Case and Mood Syntax for the first time. Our present course comes very close to the Ratio, that is—complete the grammar by the end of Second Year, review it thoroughly in Third Year, and take it for granted in Fourth Year.

Latin Composition. The survey recommends theme work in First, Second and Third Years but adds that "it may well be omitted from Fourth Year." The discussion of this topic brought out a lively criticism of some points regarding the arrangement of Bennett's Latin Composition Book. It is not designed in a way to give sufficient

THE **MODERN SCHOOLMAN**

ST. LOUIS UNIVERSITY

VOL. 1   JANUARY—1925   NO. 1

THE SEMINAR IDEA

A SEVENTEENTH-CENTURY DIVORCE

A VISION OF EMPIRE

SALVAGE THE DUM-DUM THOUGHT

THE SEVENTH AGE

BULLETIN OF THE PHILOSOPHY SEMINAR OF ST LOUIS UNIVERSITY

In 1925, the first issue of *Classical Bulletin* reported on a lecture given by Father T.S. Bowdern about the teaching of Latin. He called for, among other things, postponing the study of the subjunctive mood to Second Year.

[LEFT] The "divorce" between Scholastic Philosophy and modern science was among the themes discussed in the first issue of *The Modern Schoolman*.

THE CONSCIOUS DEVELOPMENT OF CATHOLIC THOUGHT AND ACTION

John and William Markoe with their mother, Mary Prince Markoe. The two brothers spent their lives battling racism and played key roles in the integration of Saint Louis University.

A highly talented man with a genius for connecting with young people, Daniel Lord left home to join the Jesuits at Florissant, Missouri in July 1909, was ordained in 1923, and while still a novice, wrote and produced a play called "College Heroes." He was assigned to help Father Edward F. Garesché, S.J. with a publication called *The Queen's Work* (first published in May 1913) and also to assist generally with a national organization called the Sodality of Our Lady, which published *TQW*. This was a turning point in his career. Father Lord's talent for organization combined with

his charismatic energy to lead numerous projects. He offered a popular program called the Summer School of Catholic Action, which began at Saint Louis University in 1930 and spread nationally. Lord also helped to run the Institute of Social Order while it was in St. Louis. The ISO was created by American Jesuits in response to a mandate from General Congregation 28 (held in 1938), which called for centers of social research and action to be established, staffed by Jesuit staff with graduate training.

Lord was a prolific author, and also found time to advise Hollywood filmmakers on Catholic values, organize the university's student conclave, and lecture nuns on Saturday mornings about the fundamentals of teaching.[14] Among Lord's many important contributions, perhaps the most direct was his production of musicals in St. Louis. Many were held at the university's gymnasium. By staging theatrical events including the musical comedy "Lala," written by Richard Hudlin, "Flying Feet" in the Odeon, and "High Lights," Father Lord raised funds for St. Elizabeth's, St. Louis's first parish for black Catholics. The pastor of St. Elizabeth's, Father William Markoe, S.J., greatly appreciated Father Lord's steady support, especially when the Depression hit and plans for fund-raising were undermined. In addition, Markoe stated: "I believe the most important advances were the integration of our Young People Sodality members into Father Lord's pageants with white students," which paved the way for integration.[15]

Saint Louis University students in a pageant, written by Father Dan Lord, S.J. and presented at the Muny Opera in St. Louis, circa 1920s.

PRICE 10¢

The WAR and Ourselves

by

DANIEL A. LORD, S.J.

THE QUEEN'S WORK
3742 West Pine Boulevard
ST. LOUIS, MO.

Lord was just one among an extraordinary group of individuals who lived and worked in St. Louis during this period. Especially notable are these Jesuits: Leo Brown, Charles 'Dismas' Clark, Bernard Dempsey, George Dunne, Claude Heithaus, Joseph Husslein, James Macelwane, John and William Markoe, and Louis Twomey. Teaching and preaching, writing articles, producing interracial musicals, conducting research and scholarship, undertaking ministry and activism — they lived lives of courage and conscience. Many had an impact on the nation and the world. And yet, reflecting the complexity of the times, some of them were reprimanded by Jesuit superiors and peers, as seen later in this chapter.

Father Lord produced ninety books, forty-five dramas, thirteen musicals, about three hundred pamphlets, and hundreds of articles in newspapers and magazines.

[RIGHT] An overhead, artistic shot of the entrance to the gymnasium captures the jazzy feel of the 1933 campus. In February of that year, the *Interracial Review* sponsored an integrated dance in the gym. St. Louis jazz legend Dewey Jackson and his orchestra performed.

Father Daniel Lord, S.J. ensured that both the casts and audiences of his St. Louis productions were interracial.

[BELOW] Father Lord and Father Markoe cooperated extensively on fund-raising for St. Elizabeth's Parish through the production of musicals.

ATHOLIC CHURCH IN ST. LOUIS   1930
MISCELLANEOUS COLLECTION   April 3
                                        St. Louis

L.S. Wm. M. Markoe, S.J.

To:

Subject: Form letter sending out tickets to Flying Feet, a musical
to be presented by young people of St. Elizabeth's Church in effort
to raise money for mission work of Jesuit Fathers among the colored
people of St. Louis.

                                        Places:
                                        St. Louis

Persons:

Daniel A. Lord, S.J.

They were part of a growing social movement in the Catholic community, inspired by *Rerum Novarum* (see Chapter 3) and eager to act "in defense especially of the poor and the weak"—as Pope Pius XI urged in his 1931 encyclical: *Quadragesimo Anno*—"On Reconstruction of the Social Order." The Pope's thoughts resonated on the campus, intensified by experiences of the Depression. For example, in February 1932, the topic of the intercollegiate Essay Contest announced in the student newspaper was: "the present labor problem and economic crisis and its solution as taken up in Quadragesimo Anno." Every student was eligible to submit an essay. "Students will have to show how Catholic students can apply the principles of the encyclical." In that same issue, a front page headline summarized a recent conference at the university: "Economic Woes cause Wars, say Peace Speakers." A front page headline in *The University News* on January 6, 1933 reads: "Redistribution of Wealth Urged by Fr. Husslein." In 1931, the university's president, Father Robert Johnston, S.J., gave an address about charity on its radio station WEW, stating: "The dire specter of depression stalks pitilessly throughout the land spreading everywhere its ravages of suffering." He asked listeners to reflect upon their own role in the neglect of the needy. In December of that year, WEW broadcast a lecture by Father Joseph Casper Husslein, S.J. titled: "Can Christians be Socialists?"

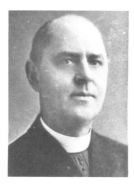

Father Joseph Casper Husslein, S.J. was a prolific author and lecturer. A typical lecture by Father Husslein, titled: "Can Christians be Socialists?" was broadcast by WEW in December, 1931.

Father Husslein's presence on the campus, his extensive writings, and his many lectures in public and on the radio helped citizens to understand Catholic social thought on labor and justice. Husslein was born in 1873, entered the Society of Jesus in 1891 at Florissant, and was ordained in 1905. In 1911, he moved to New York and became associate editor and secretary of the journal *America*. He wrote hundreds of articles and book reviews, developing his ideas on economic justice. He included the notion of "preferential option for the poor" in his writings on the highlights of *Rerum Novarum*.[16] In 1929, the Society of Jesus sent him back to Saint Louis University, where he founded the School of Social Service. In 1939, this school admitted its first African American student: Mrs. Felicia Stevens Alexander.

In 1931, Husslein began to edit "A University in Print," a highly regarded collection of books that ultimately included over 200 texts, organized into three series: Science and Culture; Religion and Culture; and Science and Culture Texts. He was also involved in the university's summer sessions, which began in 1916. In 1931 alone, eighty-two courses were offered. By 1941, twenty-seven different departments at the university were involved.

Regarding this solitary, prolific writer, one anecdote is particularly informative. The fervent advocate for racial equality, Father William Markoe, S.J., recalled a conversation with one of the Jesuits who taught at SLU, who boasted that he could "always" tell when a person had any "Negro blood." Markoe mischievously asked him the identity of his brightest pupil and he replied at once: "Imogene Lee." Markoe smiled, revealing that Ms. Lee was African American. Markoe and Dr. John A. Ryan had sponsored her application and she was able to "pass," that is, she was "light-skinned" and able to be accepted at the university as if she were white. In this subterfuge, they also had the help of Father Husslein, "who could never be a racist," recalled Markoe.[17]

Father Leo Brown, S.J. was born in 1900, entered the Society of Jesus in 1921, earned his Ph.D. in economics at Harvard, and in 1942, began to teach economics at Saint Louis University. He organized a labor school, as part of the national movement initiated by the U.S. Assistancy of the Society to foster harmonious industrial relations and provide an alternative to Communism. Brown also played a role at the Institute of Social Order, including service as director. He was known for his skill at both statistics and poker. Father Brown was a highly trusted mediator, famed for resolving the Granite City Steel strike and Monsanto Chemical Company strike. He arbitrated over 4,000 disputes in his lifetime. Along with his fellow Jesuits who instituted labor-management studies around the nation, Father Brown believed that "social justice is a definable good to which society can aspire."[18]

Brown met Father Bernard Dempsey, S.J. when they were studying at St Mary's; they formed the Catholic Economic Association in 1942. Born in Milwaukee in 1903, Dempsey entered the Society of Jesus in 1922. He showed an early interest in both history and economics. He organized a group to study *Quadragesimo Anno* while at St. Mary's (for Jesuit theology studies, which took place in Kansas from 1931 to 1967), studied at Harvard after being ordained in 1935, and after completing his doctorate, taught economics at SLU and later served in administrative roles in the School of Commerce and Finance. In 1943, he published an important work titled *Interest and Usury*, with a foreword by Joseph Schumpeter. Dempsey was uniquely qualified to write on the topic of usury, as an economist trained in theology. Adam Smith, John Maynard Keynes, and Schumpeter himself had written about usury and its prohibition by the medieval church. Father Dempsey was inspired by both *Rerum Novarum* and *Quadragesimo Anno* to develop thinking "for the restoration of the social order."[19] Dempsey worked with the Markoe brothers to help African American students attend the university, advised political leaders, and had the foresight to begin plans for the Knights of Columbus Vatican Film Library (see Chapter 5).

Students may have grown a bit jaded regarding economic theory. Budding journalist Bolen J. Carter summarized an interview that Dorothy Day, the founder of the Catholic

Father Leo Brown, S.J. taught economics at SLU and was a highly regarded labor arbitrator.

Despite a global economic depression, the university was able to raise funds for a new home for the School of Commerce and Finance. The cornerstone for the imposing Davis-Shaughnessy Hall was placed in 1931, and the building quickly took shape.

As an economist trained in theology, Father Bernard Dempsey, S.J. was uniquely qualified to write on the topic of usury and interest.

Worker newspaper and movement, granted to *The University News*. Carter leads with a quote from Day on the need to spread the teachings of the Catholic Church and the doctrines of Christ in support of "the working man" and "to withstand the attacks of Communism." Impressed by Day's humility, nevertheless he notes: "Such words have been heard by students again and again." An October 15, 1937 *University News* editorial titled "Challenge" grumbles that talk in the "new Arts School Lounge" can be disheartening: "If you endeavor to discuss views on labor, on property, on wages, on unions, and more importantly, on the principles of sane corporative order, all of which can be summed up in the word of Father Pesch, "Christian Solidarism," you are regarded as a radical if you fail to mention the Pope as authority for these views, and as an idealist if you do." (This was a reference to the philosopher Heinrich Pesch, S.J.) In 1946, Father Dempsey addressed the Mortgage Bankers' Association of St. Louis at their monthly dinner meeting at Park Plaza Hotel. *The University News* reported somewhat wearily: "The talk centered around Father Dempsey's belief that the present inflationary problem is unnecessary and has resulted from misguided policies that could have been avoided. He further holds that there is little hope that this problem will be handled with the care it deserves."[20]

"I have a wonderful view here.
I can see my hospital and my medical school."
FATHER ALPHONSE SCHWITALLA, S.J., 1950

In 1908, SLU physicist Father James I. Shannon, S.J. organized a summer field course in the Rocky Mountains. Joining the group was an avid young student named Alphonse Schwitalla. He went on to a powerful role at Saint Louis University's School of Medicine. In his lifetime, he advanced medical education and health care in the region, supported nurses, improved health care for African Americans, met with two popes, gave numerous addresses and retreats, and published widely. He lived until the end of his life in a bare room with a single cot in the Jesuit quarters. Savoring the panorama from his room on the top floor of DuBourg Hall, he told an interviewer in 1950: "I have a wonderful view here. I can see my hospital and my medical school."[21]

Schwitalla was born in Germany in 1882, then was brought to the United States by his parents when he was three years old. The son of a tailor, he attended SLU high school. He described himself as "smart and bookish as a youth."[22] He went to Saint Stanislaus Seminary in Florissant in 1900, and was ordained in 1915. In August of that same year, Schwitalla was in the British Honduras on a SLU expedition to study tropical diseases. He was delayed in returning to the shore and missed his ship back to the United States. That vessel, the Marowijne, left the coast of Belize, and was never seen again. The ship, along with sixty-five crew members and twenty-eight passengers, was lost in a hurricane.

Schwitalla received his Ph.D. in zoology at Johns Hopkins University in 1921, and along the way, earned the distinction of being the first Jesuit ever to study in that university's biology department. He was acting dean of the Saint Louis University Graduate School from 1926 to 1929. An excellent administrator, Schwitalla was also very active in organizations like the North Central Association; from 1934 to 1939, he was part of a four-man team to study medical training for the American Medical Association. He assisted with a minority report to the 1928-1933 Committee on the Costs of Medical Care. He expanded the university's School of Medicine building in 1948.

Schwitalla was a prolific scholar and lecturer, contributing over a hundred medical papers as well as editorials and popular articles. One of his favorite themes was individual responsibility to community. In addition, he opposed the trend toward "commercialization" in health care, believing that it undermined medical ethics. He opposed divorce and birth control. Because he saw medicine as more of a "personal service," he reasoned that it was best to keep the government out of that realm. He valued the "dignity of the individual" and "voluntary initiative" in medicine, seeing socialized medicine or other such trends as "compulsion." Like Father William Banks Rogers, S.J., who revived SLU's medical school (see Chapter 3), Schwitalla esteemed the physician-patient connection. He saw it as a "priestly" relationship.

In 1927, Schwitalla invited a prominent advocate for racial justice, Father William Markoe, S.J., to address the faculty of the medical school on "the race question." Yet Schwitalla himself was still learning a great deal about race. In 1928, he addressed a banquet attended by members of St. Elizabeth's Parish, which primarily served black Catholics. Schwitalla used phrases about coming "down here" to talk to "you people," and emphasized themes of morality. Markoe described the banquet in his memoirs, noting that after he finished speaking, Schwitalla was effectively rebutted by a young woman named Hazel McDaniel. (She eventually became an assistant to Markoe, and was later known by her married name of Tebeau). Schwitalla listened, but Markoe writes that he didn't really understand what he had done wrong; "he asked about it later in the car." But by 1933, Schwitalla assisted in the reorganization of Saint Mary's Infirmary as a private hospital for African Americans; Markoe wondered if his growth was a result of Ms. McDaniel's rebuke. In 1928, Schwitalla addressed a gathering of African Americans, giving a far better speech, according to Father Bill.[23]

Schwitalla carefully handled arrangements regarding a critical donation for the hospital made by the family of lead magnate Firmin Desloge. Although Schwitalla grumbled about the "annoying qualifications" relating to the donation, the advantages of a teaching hospital located close to the medical school were recognized by all. In 1930, he sailed to Europe in order to take the hospital plans to Pope Pius XI for approval.

Schwitalla resigned in 1948 due to ill health. That year, author Bob Schulman published an interview with him, capturing the warm and humorous side of a powerful man whom some found imperious. Schwitalla's nickname with fellow Jesuits was "Schweets" because he took coffee with three or four tablespoons of sugar, yet he was also disciplined, avoiding meat and eggs. He decided one day in July to give up his beloved pipes and "Jesuit stogies," and in edits to a draft of the interview, someone (probably Schwitalla) wrote in "3:22 pm" near the sentence about quitting smoking. He was stern, and a perfectionist who "insists on compliance with rules," but Schulman writes that those who are in awe of him "do him a disservice." He actually enjoyed being "ribbed" by students, and had a great sense of humor and integrity. The local medical community called him the "beau ideal," and he had a reputation for supporting nurses. His personal files at SLU archives are packed with the correspondence that he undertook with students who were stationed overseas during the war.

Father Alphonse Schwitalla, S.J. oversaw the successful expansion of medical education and healthcare at SLU, and in St. Louis.

"IT WAS ONE OF THE BEAUTIFUL TIMES. WE WERE POOR WITH THE POOR."

SISTER MARGARET MARY JARVIS, S.S.M., 1977[24]

During the first two decades of SLU's new medical school, "the one great outstanding and unsolved problem of the SOM" was the development of clinical facilities. The school had an extensive network of hospital relationships, but these were not always stable. Father John Burke, S.J. had started discussions with local religious orders about the development of a medical hospital. He shared this goal with Father Schwitalla, for whom the establishment of a teaching hospital was "his greatest concern."[25]

The Jesuits' hopes synchronized with the dreams of Mother Concordia, who had longed to renovate the St. Mary's Infirmary as a hospital for African Americans. She wrote: "Would to God that we might do something for the poor negroes here in St. Louis who are so absolutely forsaken, especially the sick." The sisters also hoped to incorporate a School of Nursing for African Americans, as part of the renovated hospital. But first, they needed a new hospital to replace the infirmary, which handled over 39,000 treatments in 1929. Mother Concordia estimated that they had provided $100,000 of free services in that year.

The Sisters of St. Mary had a long relationship with Firmin Desloge, a wealthy local man, and in late January of 1929, Mother Concordia wrote to him to ask for a donation for a new hospital. She called upon his feeling of "a sympathetic heart for suffering hu-

manity," remarking that "one or two million dollars for charity" was not a lot for one of his wealth. She reminded him: "our dear Lord has promised to reward a hundredfold a cup of cold water given in His Name." After his death, the Desloge heirs honored this relationship. A series of complex legal arrangements ensued, as the bequest was managed. The hospital was to be vested in the university and run by the Sisters of St. Mary.

The cornerstone for the beautiful new hospital was laid in 1931, with a Latin inscription that translates thus: "To honor Christ our King upon the Cross, To Bring health to the Afflicted, Light to those in Ignorance and Charity to All this Stone is laid in Deathless Memory of Firmin Desloge by St. Louis University and the Sisters of Saint Mary." By 1933, the hospital was open. Patients of moderate means paid a flat rate of $3 or $4 per day; for others, the hospital was free. One sister recalled: "It was one of the beautiful times. We were poor with the poor."

"A sinkhole of heretical racism"

FATHER WILLIAM MARKOE, S.J.

The Young Catholic Crusaders was a group at St. Elizabeth's, formed by Father William Markoe, S.J. (seated at far right) and his brother John, (standing at far left). This undated photograph is probably from the 1930s.

A student named Jane Maginnis began a January 28, 1944 feature article in *The University News* thus: "Hidden away in the colored slum district of downtown St. Louis is St. Malachy's Catholic Church run by the Jesuits." She described "Cap" Markoe, the pastor of St. Malachy's: "consumed with a burning interest to see justice done." That man was Father John Markoe, S.J. He was to play a crucial role in the integration of SLU. Father John was born in 1890 and his brother, William, was born in 1892. Bill became a novice in the Society of Jesus in 1913, and John entered in 1917. While still at Saint Stanislaus Seminary, the two brothers and two of their friends, Austin Bork and Horace Frommelt, "consecrated their lives to the salvation of the Negro in the U.S.," as Father Bill put it in his memoirs. They believed that racism was not only a heresy, it was a sin. The provincial at the time, Father Alexander Burrowes, S.J., agreed to their pledge.[26]

But the story of SLU's integration begins even farther back in time. When Father Ignatius Panken, S.J. founded St. Louis's first black parish, St. Elizabeth's, in 1873 (see Chapter 3), he also took steps to create schools for African American children, putting in place a culture of Catholic education for blacks in the city. In 1911, admission of African Americans had been discussed by SLU's board of trustees, but no decision was reached.[27]

In the early 1900s, life in St. Louis and across the nation was racially segregated, and the struggle for change required effort on many levels. Dr. Hanau W. Loeb, M.D. was dean of SLU's Medical Sschool from 1913 to 1924. A 1921 report to the trustees noted that facilities for teaching at City Hospital #2 (the "Negro hospital") were "altogether inadequate," and Loeb was instructed by the trustees to insist on "some division of the clinical material at City Hospital No. 1." He did do so, but "found decided opposition."[28]

Even before their ordination, the Markoe brothers were active opponents of racism. They held secret meetings in the basement cafeteria of DuBourg Hall, directly under the rooms of then-president Father Charles Cloud, S.J., to plan a group called "the Knights of Peter Claver." Claver, a sixteenth century Jesuit, was the patron saint of slaves. Father Bill writes: it was "strictly an underground operation," so they had to have the meetings late at night. Sometimes after a speech there would be applause, and Cloud started to get suspicious about the sounds at night, so they soon had to move the meetings.

In 1927, Father William Markoe, S.J. became pastor of St. Elizabeth's, and remained until 1940, when the Society of Jesus sent him to Minnesota; his brother was pastor at St. Malachy's from 1943 until the Society sent him to Creighton in 1946. Although a number of light-skinned African Americans were able to "pass" as white and thereby to gain admission to SLU through the assistance of key facilitators, an official policy of admission for blacks was still not in place.

In 1931, the Markoe brothers secured permissions for a convention in St. Louis of the Federation of Colored Catholics. Saint Louis University president, Father Robert Johnston, S.J., allowed the group to use the university auditorium and gym for the event, and Aquinas Hall for priest lodgings. Father Joseph Husslein, Father John LaFarge, Archbishop John Glennon, and leaders from around the United States participated in the three-day event. In his remarks, Reverend Stephen L. Theobald, one of only three black priests in the United States at the time, referred to the "closed doors in Catholic Universities." Father Bill Markoe wrote later that Father Johnston was unhappy with the remarks, but Markoe rejoiced that "we invaded the lily white campus" of SLU with the convention. Father Bill was outspoken and fierce, to the point of referring to SLU as a "sinkhole of heretical racism."

SLU's first officially admitted black student was Henry Schmandt, who was admitted to the College of Arts and Sciences in the fall of 1935. In January 1936, an editorial titled "Shackles" in the student newspaper makes a plea for racial equality: "Beneath the mad cacophony of the city-mad noises, pulses the slow rhythm of a song for freedom ... The picture of St. Louis street cars with "whites" standing because the only vacant seats are those next to Negroes ... the Negro is excluded by people who go to Mass and dare call themselves Catholic ... If we Catholics would shield ourselves from the justified

charge of hypocrisy, we must recognize the position of the Negro as a brother in Christ." In 1939, SLU's School of Social Service, founded by Father Husslein, S.J., admitted its first African American student: Mrs. Felicia Stevens Alexander.

In February 1943, SLU's trustees heard a report from the Committee on the Admission of Negro Students, which was created at the recommendation of the provincial, Father Peter A. Brooks, S.J. The committee suggested that the medical school accept Negroes "as an experiment." Also in 1943, Father John appealed to SLU's president, Father Patrick Holloran, S.J., to admit Ethel Williams of St. Malachy's parish. John Markoe asked Raymond Crowley, City Editor at the *St. Louis Post-Dispatch*, for help in raising awareness through the media and the newspaper's owner, Joseph Pulitzer II, agreed. The newspaper was already on a campaign against segregation at the University of Missouri. St. Louis's Race Relations Commission, meanwhile, proposed that SLU admit blacks in order to set an example for the region.[29] Father John also distributed an article about the rejection of a black applicant to Webster College. It was a piece by Ted Le Berthon: "An Open Letter to Mother Edwarda." She was the Superior General of the Sisters of Loretto, who ran Webster.

The combined pressure generated a two hour meeting at SLU; two of the fifteen faculty members present supported the appeal on behalf of Ethel Williams: Bernard Dempsey of the School of Commerce and Finance, and Dean Thomas Purcell of the Dental School. According to Father Bill, when Father Claude Heithaus, S.J. read "An Open Letter to Mother Edwarda," he was inspired to write his 1944 sermon, at which the entire student congregation rose to pledge themselves against racial discrimination. After the outcry

Father Claude Heithaus, S.J., was inspired by the Markoe brothers to fight for integration at SLU.

resulting from Father Claude's sermon, Father Patrick Holloran, S.J. told his staff to accept black applicants, but no official statement was made. When Father John learned that a black applicant from Saint Joseph's High School had been rejected by the university, he and Father Heithaus appealed to Father Joseph Zuercher, S.J., the Provincial of the Missouri Province. Zuercher promised to urge Father Holloran to reverse the decision, and after further meetings, the university announced that five African American students were admitted. Their names were: Mary Ann Jones, Margaret Simms, Clemmie Smith, Sylvester Smith, and Fredda Witherspoon. As Father Bill wrote: "Cap blew the doors of Saint Louis University wide open to Negroes."[30]

In 1946, newly arrived Archbishop Joseph Ritter demanded the integration of all of the Catholic schools in the St. Louis Archdiocese, helping to generate the repeal of the law on segregation of public schools in Missouri. By 1947, SLU had 150 black students, the most of any Jesuit school (second was Fordham with 102 students).[31]

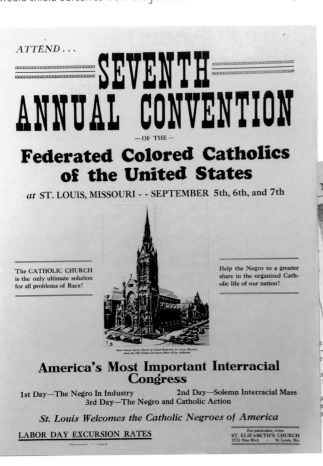

In December 1948, the first African American doctors were appointed at the medical school: Dr. Henry Hudson Weathers (Surgery), Dr. Walter A. Younge (Medicine), and Dr. Arthur N. Vaughn (Surgery).

MULTIPLY TALENTED

In January 1923, the medical school board voted to recommend Dr. Edward A. Doisy as Professor of Biological Chemistry. Dr. Doisy received his Ph.D. at Harvard in 1920, then served in the Army. In December 1929, Dr. Doisy isolated the active principle of the follicular hormone. He spent virtually his entire career at SLU. He served as professor and chairman of the Biochemistry Department until he retired in 1965, working on discoveries that included estrone and vitamin K, and winning a Nobel Prize in 1943. (For more details on Dr. Doisy, see Chapter 5.)

Minutes from this period suggest the university's engagement in the community. In October, 1930, it was reported that the Hospital Commission asked "our School" to take on teaching Physiology, Bacteriology, and Anatomy to "colored nurses at City #2." SLU agreed. The trustees discussed a sliding scale of payments for the patient of "moder-

In 1929, Dr. Edward A. Doisy initiated the field of research into steroid hormones. He won the Nobel Prize in 1943 for his work on the chemistry of vitamin K.

ate means." Factors included the number of dependents, the disease, and "paying capacity" depending on "social data." In 1932, the University of Missouri had to cease offering medical school classes, so they reached out to SLU to take on their students. SLU agreed.

From 1919 to 1925, Father Cloud served as regent of the Dental School, which in 1920 was rated a "Class A" school by the Educational Council. The school gained a new building in 1922, and enrollment grew to over three hundred by 1924. When Schwitalla became regent in 1925, the dental course took five years to complete, including a pre-dental year. Under the leadership of Dr. Thomas Purcell, D.D.S. as dean from 1933 to 1945, new department heads were appointed and pre-dental studies were increased to two years. Addressing graduates in 1944, Purcell said: "That each of you may be successful in bringing comfort to suffering humanity and credit to your calling is my fervent wish."

Another remarkable talent who began to make a mark in this era was Goronwy O. Broun, Sr., a scholarship student from Alabama. Born in 1895, he earned his medical degree at SLU in 1918, and devoted over fifty years to his research at SLU, studying infectious diseases and specifically influenza. He was beloved as an exemplary teacher. Broun became an assistant to Dr. Ralph Kinsella on a federal grant in 1919. Kinsella was studying infectious diseases and emphysema. From 1933 to 1938, Broun delineated the epidemiology of St. Louis encephalitis as part of a World Health Organization Influenza Study. His team isolated the strain of Hong Kong influenza virus in 1972. He understood the importance of family and neighborhood contexts in the training of doctors and provision of health care. Broun contributed to a report on the Department of Community Medicine, noting details as parts of the city grew poor. Even in his eighties, he was active at SLU's ambulatory care facility serving low-income residents (see Chapter 6). His son, Goronwy Broun, Jr. was associate professor of internal medicine and director of hematology at the school of medicine for decades.

Early seismography at SLU (see Chapter 3) became fully established by Father James B. Macelwane, S.J. Born in 1883, he grew up in a large family. Macelwane joined the Society of Jesus, choosing the Buffalo Mission because he wanted to learn German. When the Province split, he came to SLU. In 1910, Father John Bernard Goesse, S.J. asked the third year Jesuit philosophers if they wanted to learn meteorology and seismology. Macel-

wane was interested, and thanks to his German skills, he was able to correspond with a noted German scientist, Dr. Ernst Tams, sharing a table of travel times for tremors. In 1911, he published a piece on the physics of the seismograph, and that summer, led a geological summer school in the Rocky Mountains, beginning a lifelong interest. Among many endeavors and accomplishments, he invented "microbarographs," and in 1925, organized and headed the first department of geophysics in the Western Hemisphere, based at Saint Louis University.

In addition to his scientific work, Macelwane played an important role nationally, in the reform of American Jesuit institutions of higher education. As chair of the Commission on Higher Studies of the American Assistancy of the Society of Jesus, he directed the committee's 1931-1932 report, which cited foundational Jesuit texts like the *Ratio* and Part 4 of Ignatius's important foundational work, the *Constitutions*. The Macelwane Report noted goals such as: providing a "foundation of truth" through pedagogy, and cultivating in students the ability to organize language and express themselves "in accordance with high ideals."[32] The report called for a centralized coordinating body, trained administrators, development of young Jesuits as doctoral students, increased resources for libraries, and a host of other improvements. It led to changes that raised the Jesuit schools' academic profile in the ensuing decades.

By 1911, the lease expired on the building that the university was leasing for the law college, so it moved to Lindell and Grand. Alphonse George Eberle, a graduate of the school, became the first full-time dean. In 1924, it became the first accredited night law school in the country.[33] As the system of apprenticeship in law faded away, new standards of professional education emerged. One form of response was "the lawyer-scholar," exemplified by Father Linus Augustine Lilly, S.J., who taught constitutional law. As law professor and regent, Father Lilly headed the school until his death in 1943. It closed due to low enrollment during WWII, then reopened in 1946.

The brilliant humanist and scholar, Father Walter Ong, S.J, begins to shine in this period. In 1941, Ong wrote his master's thesis at SLU under the supervision of Marshall McLuhan, then in 1954 completed his dissertation on Peter Ramus at Harvard, and spent the rest of his career at SLU. He produced a staggering amount of scholarship across numerous disciplines, often with quite original insights. In 1944, the genial, visionary Father Paul Reinert, S.J. was appointed dean of the College of Arts and Sciences. He went on to lead the university for decades, while also playing an important role in national Catholic higher education and in the social movements of the day. These two men are discussed in more detail in Chapter 5.

Father Macelwane (at far left), had a lifelong interest in geology which led to his organization of field trips and excursions.

"LEARNING BY DOING"

In 1927, a former car salesman nicknamed "Lafe" opened an aviation college. Shortly after beginning his new venture, he crashed a Laird Swallow bi-plane in a fateful incident near the Florissant seminary. His full name was Oliver Lafayette Parks, and his school was the Parks College of Aviation at Lambert Field. Parks was the first federally certified aviation school in the United States.

The Jesuits helped Parks to recover, and in gratitude, he offered his school to Saint Louis University in 1946. By then it had operated in Cahokia, Illinois for about twenty years, and was to remain there until 1997, when it moved to SLU's north campus in St. Louis. At the time of his injury, Parks received a special blessing from the rector at St. Stanislaus, Father Richard Rooney, S.J. This led to his conversion. Father Paul Reinert, S.J. recalled in a 1994 interview that President Holloran asked him to take on arrangements for the new program. In Reinert's words: Oliver Parks said to the Jesuits in 1946 that he would give them the college "if you teach the core curriculum as well over there as you do over here."[34] There were numerous challenges, including sheer logistics of distance, but both groups of educators set to work on the collaboration.

By 1948, SLU enfolded an Aviation Engineering Program in its offerings. Administrators sorted out the Latin for "Bachelor of Science in Aeronautics" for the diplomas. The Parks Air College students joined the jovial spirit of the university. In 1948, they announced plans to put on a musical review by the "Take offs." Parks students also performed in "The Parksters," described as a "fave quartet." Profiled in *The University News* in 1953, Parks College students joked about the reason for cordial relations they had with faculty: "We repair the planes they fly."[35]

Oliver Lafayette "Lafe" Parks

WORLD WAR II, AND BEYOND

In May 1941, the university's president Father Harry B. Crimmins, S.J. urged students to continue their studies "as the highest form of patriotism," but by 1942, his own patriotism took a dramatic turn, when he resigned the office of president to serve as a chaplain in the 70th General Hospital which was created for the Army. He spent the remainder of the war stationed abroad, first in North Africa and later in Italy.

The impact of World War II on the university was extensive. In 1942, the United States Army chose SLU as the center for the new Army Air Force Radio Instructors School. Students joined the Reserve Officers' Training Corps (ROTC) drilling teams, and twelve "defense courses" were offered, covering physics, chemistry, and management.

Father Charles Robinson S.J. introduced a phonograph in his class to teach the Japanese language. In March 1942, the formation of the Flying Billikens was announced: a naval aviation unit formed entirely of SLU students and alumni.

In the early days of WWII, there was great concern that typhus fever would wreak havoc among soldiers and civilians, as it had during wartime for centuries. In 1944, SLU's Dr. Donald Greiff, Dr. Vicente Moragues, and Dr. Henry Pinkerton announced the discovery of a cure for typhus fever.[36]

The university yearbook, *The Archive*, was canceled for several years due to the war. A three-year accelerated degree program was offered, while rationing and shortages also had an impact. In April 1943, the trustees discussed closing the law school "for the duration" because twenty-two students were enrolled, with fifteen set to graduate and the rest called to military service. Yet, campus life carried on.

Rueppel Hall on Olive Street housed The Institute of Geophysical Technology, which opened in 1944 under Father Macelwane and Father Victor Blum, S.J.

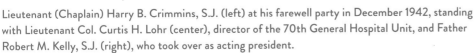

Lieutenant (Chaplain) Harry B. Crimmins, S.J. (left) at his farewell party in December 1942, standing with Lieutenant Col. Curtis H. Lohr (center), director of the 70th General Hospital Unit, and Father Robert M. Kelly, S.J. (right), who took over as acting president.

Professor Gustav Kadysh Klausner was hired to teach at the School of Commerce and Finance school in 1915 by Father Joseph L. Davis, S.J. While still in Russia, Klausner's life was saved by a Catholic neighbor; he then left Russia because of the czar's pogroms, found refuge in the United States, and ended up teaching at SLU for thirty-five years. He loved the Jesuits, and they cherished him as well. He was an excellent, beloved teacher and recipient of the university's highest honors. Of Jewish faith, he famously told his students: "Go to Mass, or you'll all turn out to be Bolsheviks."

Father Otto Kuhnmuench, S.J., pictured above, was one of the stellar faculty members in the 1930s and 1940s who, under Father Thurber Montgomery Smith, S.J. as dean of graduate studies, inspired countless students.

For example, student activities in 1942 included: Conclave (student government), Glee Club, a wide range of Sodality organizations, student publications, Playhouse Club, junior and senior debate squads, fraternities, a social sorority, Philalethic, Book & Quill, Classical Club, French Club, German Club, La Union Pan Americana, International Relations Club, Civics group, and Rho Theta, the mathematics honor society.

Some strong personalities left a lasting impact on students in this era. Father Otto Kuhnmuench, S.J. was born in Milwaukee in 1876. He studied at Marquette, was ordained in 1907, and was assigned to teach at SLU in 1912. Over the course of a productive career, Father Kuhnmuench launched the Friday morning student Mass and annual student retreat. Nicknamed "The Old Roman," he taught Latin for thirty years. Another devoted scholar in the classics field, Father Claude Heithaus, S.J., was born in St. Louis in 1898. He joined the Society of Jesus in 1920, and earned his doctorate in anthropology at the University of London. Subject to violence while he was doing research in the Middle East, Father Heithaus became a fervent opponent of racism.[37] He was a brilliant teacher of classical languages and English, and was

the faculty advisor to *The University News.* Heithaus was fondly described by students in a column about their office renovation in 1944: "Clad in a cheerful birds-eye blue sport shirt and mournful crepe trousers, our moderator … with the assistance of the staff athletes, muscled massive furniture in all directions simultaneously." Father Heithaus knew the Markoe brothers, who also opposed racism. The views of these younger men, however, were not included when a committee was appointed in 1942 to study integration at SLU.[38] The group, which included Kuhnmuench, recommended only that the medical school undertake an experiment of admissions for black applicants.

Father Kuhnmuench died in December 1943. In the homily at his funeral in January 1944, his colleague Father Heithaus heralded him as "a living edition of the Ratio Studiorum." The very next month, Heithaus stunned the university with a fiery, anti-racist sermon.[39] In July of that year, students from SLU and Eden Seminary stood outside of downtown stores and passed out thousands of leaflets in support of the sit-in protests undertaken by forty black women and fifteen white women. The women were seeking to integrate lunch counters at St. Louis department stores.[40]

In Spring 1945, Father Heithaus refused to run an ad in *The University News* for a "whites-only" dance, and was publicly chastised by his Jesuit superiors, although his peers demonstrated support. He was ordered to leave the city. Remembered as humble, brave, and deeply conscientious, Father Claude borrowed a suitcase and left town on a midnight train. He said little about the incident. Relatives say Father Claude did not see himself as "so far ahead of his time, just more willing to speak out." About the banishment, "he didn't care, he didn't fight. He had total trust in God."[41]

Father Heithaus was banished "temporarily," but was ultimately gone for fourteen years. Returning to the university in 1958, Father Claude collected the artifacts he had once salvaged, and, together with Father William Faherty, obtained permission to create the Museum of the Western Jesuit Missions at St. Stanislaus Seminary. These materials were later moved to the university's museum on Lindell.[42] They became part of the university's tribute to the Jesuits who led missions among Native Americans and white settlers (see Chapters 2 and 3).

Like the Markoe brothers, Father Heithaus was honored as a "pioneer" only later in his life. Auxiliary Bishop Harold R. Perry of New Orleans (the only Negro Catholic bishop in the United States at the time) said at the Golden Jubilee dinner held for Father John Markoe, S.J. at Creighton University in Omaha in 1967: "He was the leader and the crusader ... spreading that simple, yet transcendent doctrine of the God-given dignity of each individual human being."[43] These words certainly apply to Father Heithaus, as well.

With the end of World War II, SLU began to experience record enrollment. There were 6,118 students in attendance as of February, 1946, in large part due to returning veterans. That August, construction began on a new residence hall for men (the first residence hall constructed as such), to be located at 3636 West Pine.

Extracurricular activities in the immediate postwar period included golf, soccer, teas, "Coke and Carol" parties for women at Christmas, a TB drive, and dances. In January 1947, a school of public administration was announced, to be led by Dr. Carl F. Taeusch; the next month, plans were announced for the annual symposium and Mass for Feast Day of St. Thomas. In September 1948, SLU's medical school heralded its first female students: Mary Francis Nawrocki and Catherine J. Carroll. Campus life was proceeding with distinction and growing complexity. Saint Louis University was well-positioned for the coming decades.

Since the early days of the university, students have engaged in theatrical pursuits. The Playhouse Club considers its first season to be 1946-1947. That year, they presented *Mary Queen of Scotland* [BELOW], as well as *Our Town*, *The Terrible Meek*, *Revelations of 1947*, *Aria DaCapo*, *Overtones*, and *The Rising of the Moon*.

Father Heithaus lines up a shot at an archeological dig in Lebanon. He is reported to have once hung by his legs from a plane in order to take photographs.

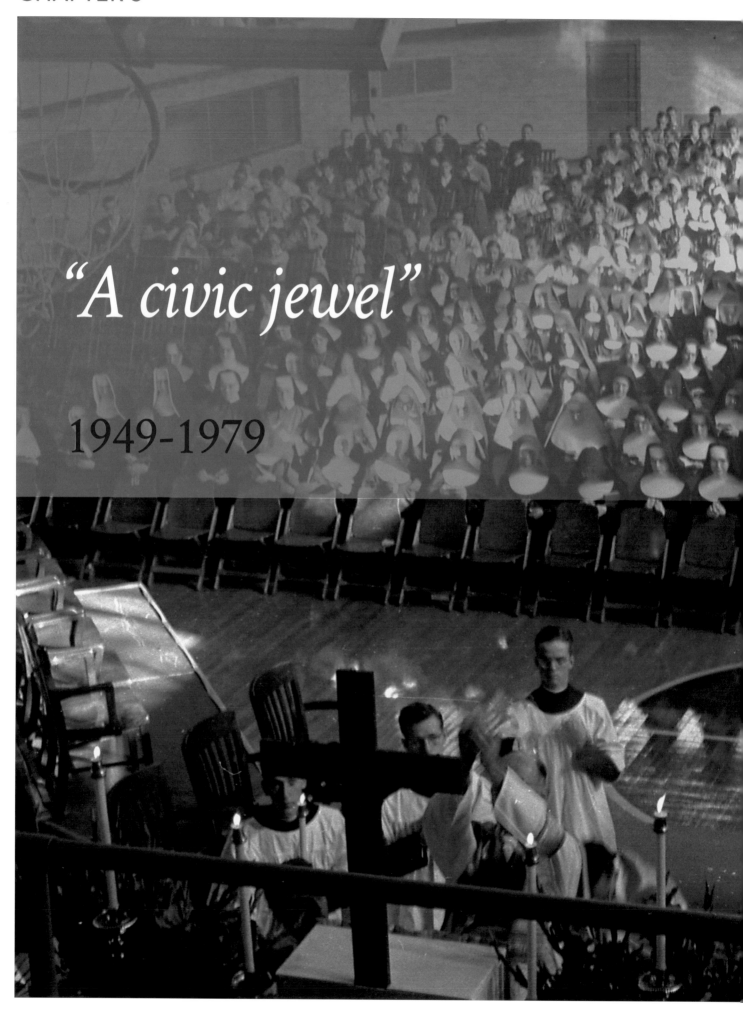

CHAPTER 5

"A civic jewel"

1949-1979

As a Saint Louis University booster, Father Paul C. Reinert, S.J. surpassed even the tireless Father William Banks Rogers, S.J. Former dean Mary Bruemmer has remarked: "Father Reinert saw the university as a civic jewel." A highly respected president and nationally recognized leader in Catholic higher education, Reinert devoted over fifty years of service to SLU. As dean of the College of Arts and Sciences and then as president of SLU from 1949 to 1974, Reinert advanced the core values of Catholic colleges and universities in the post-Vatican II world.

Reinert's biographer, Maureen Wangard, describes him as a "pragmatic visionary." He was a pioneer, inviting laypersons to serve on the board of trustees, and reaching out to engage entirely new partners for the university. In 1959, Father Reinert named an outside group, headed by local businessman August Busch, to support SLU's development. The yearbook motto for 1959 was: "The university as an integral part of the whole urban community." Total enrollment in that year was just over 8,000, across all of the divisions of the university: Arts and Sciences, Commerce and Finance, Dentistry, Graduate, Law, Medicine, Nursing, Parks College of Aviation, Philosophy and Letters, and Technology.

In 1962, Reinert initiated a program to reach non-traditional students: Metropolitan College. In the mid 1960s, a study abroad program in Madrid, Spain was established by Father Raymond Sullivant, S.J. By the late 1970s, SLU had 11,000 students and 2,000 faculty members, programs had been restructured in response to realities of the time, and the physical plant of the campus was greatly transformed. In this period, scholars including Father John F. Bannon, S.J., Dr. Edward Doisy, and Father Walter Ong, S.J., were among the many members of the university community who contributed their gifts of intellect and wisdom. Serving as presidents toward the end of this period, Father Daniel O'Connell, S.J. (1974-1978) and Father Edward Drummond, S.J. (1978-1979), provided steady leadership during challenging times.

Major ceremonies and events were often held in the gymnasium. This photo is from the 1952 Convocation.

Physics major Dan McAuliffe adjusts an electron diffraction camera, pictured in the 1945 yearbook.

"THE COLLEGE'S OBLIGATION TO TRUTH IS ITS OBLIGATION TO SOCIETY."

FATHER ROBERT G. HENLE, S.J., 1955[1]

Both the speed and the scope of social change in this period are breathtaking. Along with developments in science, technology, and medicine, members of social movements broadened the struggle for liberty and justice both in the United States and abroad. Detailed critiques of inequality emerged, complicating the assumptions and methods of traditional academic disciplines. Discourse analysis, post-modernism, race theory, African-American studies, feminist theory, subaltern studies, and liberation theology had a revolutionary impact across the humanities and social sciences in particular. They also affected law, medicine, the natural sciences, and even accounting.[2] Amidst changing values and skepticism toward any and all claims of authority, those in Catholic, Jesuit higher education sought to remain true to their purpose. But how to define that purpose, for new times? In 1956, SLU trustees moved to end the requirement of attendance by Catholic students at weekly Mass. The community wondered: was this the beginning of a loss of identity?

University enrollment increased across the United States after World War II, as veterans returned home and took advantage of the G.I. Bill of Rights. Enrollment at Catholic colleges and universities went from 162,000 in 1940 to 400,000 in 1967.[3] After decades of stereotyping as an urban, immigrant people beholden to a "foreign power," American Catholics saw an improvement in their social status. This ascent was symbolized in the 1960 election of the nation's first Catholic president, a senator from Massachusetts named John F. Kennedy. And in terms of global and national politics, the Catholic Church wielded significant political influence.[4] In St. Louis, this sense of heightened respect found an interesting expression: in the connection between Catholics and soccer.

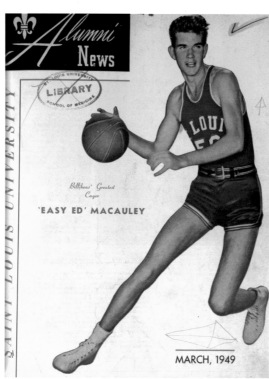

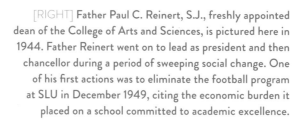

[LEFT]The first all-color front page of the alumni magazine was issued in March 1949. It featured "Easy Ed" Macauley, who led the Billikens to the 1948 National Invitation Tournament championship in Madison Square Garden. He was the Associated Press "Player of the Year" in 1949, and later played professionally in the NBA.

[RIGHT] Father Paul C. Reinert, S.J., freshly appointed dean of the College of Arts and Sciences, is pictured here in 1944. Father Reinert went on to lead as president and then chancellor during a period of sweeping social change. One of his first actions was to eliminate the football program at SLU in December 1949, citing the economic burden it placed on a school committed to academic excellence.

"A Soccer Hotbed"
Catholics, St. Louis, and the SLU dynasty
By John Waide

SLU beat UCLA 2-1 in this championship game in 1973, the last year of their streak. Bob Matteson (#6) reaches for the ball against Sergio Velazquez (#11), with Mark Demling on the ground.

In the history of men's collegiate soccer, no program rivals the success of the Saint Louis University Billikens. SLU won ten of the first fifteen NCAA men's tournament championships ever held: from 1959 to 1973. SLU holds the following NCAA Soccer Division I records: ten national championships, six successive appearances in the NCAA championship match, forty-eight total NCAA tournament appearances, and the most rapid ascent to six hundred victories of any college soccer team. In addition, SLU men's soccer boasts: more than seven hundred soccer alumni; over one hundred players who played professional soccer; more than fifty All-American players; ten U. S. Olympic team players; three U. S. World Cup team players; two players who played in the National Football League; four players who coached professional soccer; and five players who coached collegiate soccer.

"St. Louis is a Catholic town and soccer is a Catholic-supported game," the student newspaper asserted in 1961. Indeed, the scrappy Catholic boys from "the Hill" were audacious. As early as December 1905, men at Saint Louis University had been plucky: showing up as an "association team" to take on the Christian Brothers College team. CBC won 2-0, and two weeks later, beat SLU students 3-0. SLU's team was not sponsored by the university; in fact, at first there was doubt that the SLU players would be allowed

to play, since they were not wearing official soccer uniforms.

SLU men continued to play soccer from 1910 through the 1930s, against local schools or soccer clubs, but it wasn't until after World War II that the university began to sponsor its own intramural soccer league, playing on a field at Tower Grove Park. Then, in 1953, Bob Guelker, the physical education instructor at Saint Louis Preparatory Seminary, and Walter C. "Doc" Eberhardt, SLU's director of physical education, arranged a game and started discussions about the future of soccer at the university. When Bob Stewart became athletic director in 1958, he and Guelker created the first "soccer club." It was so successful that the university agreed to make men's soccer a varsity sport in 1959. The team had a total budget of $200. The university supplied the players with their uniforms, but the players had to provide their own soccer shoes. With Guelker as their unpaid coach, they won eleven games in their first season, outscoring opponents by an amazing combined score of *71 to 10*. In 1959, the NCAA sponsored the first-ever Division I Men's Soccer Championship tournament, in order to determine the national champion. With only one loss in their whole season, SLU won the tourney, defeating the University of Bridgeport 5-2. SLU's team featured three All-American players: Jack Dueker, Jerry Knobbe, and Tom Trost.

Another great coach associated with SLU's dynasty is St. Louisan Harry Keough, who coached from 1967 to 1982. His 1950 World Cup team, which included five St. Louis players, defeated England 1-0, against 500 to 1 odds. This legendary game is depicted in the 2005 film, *The Game of Their Lives*. Keough coached at SLU for sixteen seasons, compiling a 213-50-22 record that included fifteen appearances by the Billikens in the NCAA tournament. SLU ended its championship run in 1974, losing 2-1 to Howard University, but they had enjoyed a stunning record of success, and left an inspiring heritage.

Bob Engler of SLU men's soccer club fights for the ball in a November 1958 game, as Don Range approaches. Men's soccer went to varsity status in 1959, and went on to win ten of the next fifteen NCAA Division I championships.

"NEW STUDENTS STARTED THEIR CAMPUS CAREERS WITH THE USUAL ENTHUSIASM AND 'FALL FEVER' STARTED AT THE UNIVERSITY."

SAINT LOUIS UNIVERSITY MAGAZINE, OCTOBER 15, 1954

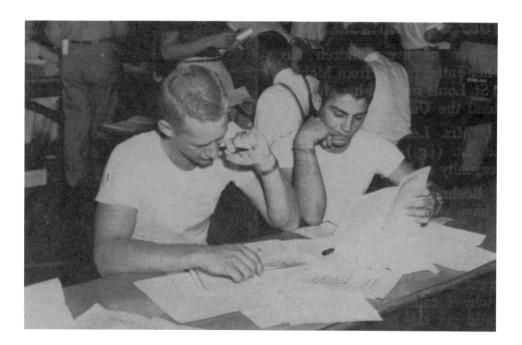

[LEFT] Students review their registration materials in 1954.

Miss Jean Clark of East St. Louis, selected as 1954 freshman queen, receives with dignity her crown of pencils.

As this period began, Saint Louis University students were busy with dances, blood drives, sports, clubs, seasonal festivities, and fraternities and sororities, in addition to their studies. The "crowning" traditions continued: the freshman queen was honored with a crown made of pencils, and the "Karrot Krown" was bestowed upon the "Kampus King" at the Sadie Hawkins dance. Every May Day, a student placed upon the head of the Blessed Virgin in College Church the crown commissioned by students in gratitude, after the 1849 cholera outbreak bypassed the university.

At the "icebreaker" for first-year students, there was a search for the secretly designated persons known only as "Mr. X" and "Miss X." The president hosted an annual tea party for students from overseas. Students attended the Mass of the Holy Spirit, and a Christmas Ball with a choral concert. The Parks College "Cloudhounds," formed in 1946, were just one of many student groups busy with activities, in this case, the construction of model aircraft. In March 1949, the novelist Evelyn Waugh spoke at the school gym regarding "Three Convert Writers," namely: G.K. Chesterton, Monsignor Ronald Knox, and Graham Greene.

When the academic year began in fall 1949, SLU's communications department started KBIL, an AM radio station and forerunner of today's KSLU. WEW, the university's first radio station, had closed in 1949; the trustees decided to sell it in 1954.

Students register for classes in the West Pine gym, an ordeal that was the subject of frequent, ironic comment in SLU student publications.

Father Paul Reinert, S.J., at right in this photograph, welcomes students during 1952 freshman orientation week.

[BELOW] Ivory Lee Herron was the first African American woman to win a scholarship at SLU.

After the long wait for an official policy of admission, African American students quickly excelled at SLU. In February 1949, Theodore McMillian became the first African American man at the university to be selected for the Jesuit honor society for men (Alpha Sigma Nu). McMillian went on to be a student and later faculty member at SLU's School of Law. He was the first African American to serve on the Missouri Court of Appeals, as well as the first African American to serve on the United States Court of Appeals for the Eighth Circuit. Also in February 1949, Anita Lyons became the first African American woman selected for the Jesuit honor society for women (Gamma Pi Epsilon). The next month, Stan Harris, SLU's first African American tennis player, received a varsity athletic award. In June 1949, the *Globe Democrat* announced "First Negro Girl Wins St. Louis

Theodore McMillian was the first African American man at SLU to be accepted into the Jesuit honor society for men.

In 1953, Father Maurice McNamee, S.J. announced that the Quonset huts (erected as temporary classrooms during the post WWII boom years and fondly called "sweat boxes") and asphalt in the quadrangle would be replaced with grass. Philosophy faculty member Vernon Bourke, wrote in 1975: "these abominable huts ... were floored with broken boards separated by wide gaps ... heated by stoves that burned oil but produced no real heat ... Many student coats had burn marks at stove-top level."[6]

U. Scholarship," as business student Ivory Lee Herron, the second-ranking senior in the graduating class of Vashon High School, joined the SLU community. That autumn, SLU medical school welcomed its pioneer black student: Joseph Gathe, who later had a successful career in St. Louis and Houston, Texas.

However, despite these advances, racial discrimination persisted locally. While they were medical students, Joseph Gathe (mentioned above) and Ronald Hoffman (a white medical student) played bridge and golf together, and became close friends. Gathe was welcomed by Hoffman's family at meals and slept overnight at their home. Hoffman recalls that Joe lived in "the colored Y near the Fox Theater" and although the two were able to golf at Forest Park, they were not welcome in many locations. Students at SLU learned more about the discrimination in local restaurants and other businesses from an investigative report launched by *The University News* in the fall of 1950. Students decided to mount opposition to the local "jim crowism" and their actions earned praise from the magazine *America,* as "democratic and Christlike."[5]

As Clyde Cahill, Jr. observed in a 1950 letter to the student newspaper editor: "A Negro student must go at least ten blocks to get a meal if the university cafeteria is closed." Gathe had been accepted as a student, but he could not join a medical school fraternity despite Hoffman's pleas with the national organization. Indeed, Hoffman was reprimanded by a SLU administrator. The school relied upon a faculty comprised of practicing physicians who taught for free. SLU could not afford to jeopardize these relationships. Cahill later attended SLU's School of Law and had a distinguished career, including appointment as a federal judge by President Jimmy Carter in 1980.

Looking south toward Clemens Hall (at left) in 1952, this photograph captures a Jesuit crossing West Pine Street and heading toward the quadrangle. The abandoned building was demolished soon after this photograph was taken. Students had long joked about the danger of crossing the street; it was eventually closed to traffic (see Chapter 6).

Billikens men's basketball was called on the radio by star announcer Harry Caray. The team played in a range of venues over the years, including: the First Regiment Armory (1920-25), West Pine Gym (1926-45), Kiel Auditorium (1945-68, 1973-78, 1983-91), and St. Louis Arena (1968-73, 1978-82, 1991-94), until 2008, with the construction of Chaifetz Arena.

Students at the School of Social Service in the early 1960s

As a Jesuit and as a university leader, Father Paul C. Reinert, S.J. sought to understand his times. He was in a position to shape discussion about and responses to change by Catholic educators. Moreover, he possessed the personal and intellectual qualities that rendered these responses both inclusive and thoughtful. In 1944, Father Reinert was appointed dean of the College of Arts and Sciences at Saint Louis University. He was made academic vice president in 1948, served as SLU's 27th president from 1949 to 1974, and then served as chancellor from 1974 to 1990.

In the Society of Jesus, the rector is responsible for maintaining a connection with every individual in his Jesuit community. Dating from the first days of Saint Louis University, the rector had always had the additional task of serving as president. Many Jesuits were realizing that the sheer complexity of running a university made it difficult to perform both functions well. Much discussion and some experiments regarding issues of governance took place, including a 1936 structure adopted at Fordham with a rector-president, assisted by a local dependent superior. In 1954, Father Reinert adopted this model, working with Father William Fitzgerald, S.J.[7]

SLU's leaders had resisted the limits to their autonomy presented by financial contributions; even the first president, Father Peter Verhaegen, sought balance in this regard. In August 1944, Father William Murphy, S.J. of Boston College and director of the National Catholic Educational Association (NCEA), remarked upon the "disturbing financial crisis" in private colleges. Discussing Murphy's comments, SLU trustees agreed there was a need for "federal emergency support." Just as this and other critical topics were being discussed by Catholic educators, Father Reinert was coming into a leadership role at Saint Louis University.

In 1949, Pope Pius XII approved the creation of the International Association of Catholic Universities, renamed in 1965 as the International Federation of Catholic Universities (IFCU). The Second Ecumenical Vatican Council was held from 1962 to 1965, initiating sweeping changes in the Church. An early hint of change came in the 1963 encyclical, *Pacem in Terris,* which notably was addressed to "all men of good will"and signaled an open and ecumenical attitude.[8] In July 1967, IFCU president Theodore M. Hesburgh, C.S.C. hosted a discussion at Land O' Lakes, Wisconsin. Father Reinert played a key role at this meeting (see sidebar on facing page), as did Father Robert Henle, S.J. (see page 128 and Chapter 6). As president of the University of Notre Dame, Father Hesburgh knew the challenges of pursuing research excellence while also being bound to pursue appropriate permissions from religious authorities. The group issued a still-controversial document: "Statement on the Nature of the Contemporary Catholic University," calling for "true autonomy and academic freedom in the face of authority of whatever kind, lay or clerical, external to the academic community itself."

Reinert ably managed these and other major changes: the shift to a lay-led board of trustees in 1967; the separate incorporation of the university and the Jesuit community; and the restructuring of the Jesuit Educational Association (JEA) to its present form as the Association of Jesuit Colleges and Universities (AJCU).

Father Paul Reinert, S.J. - A Prolific Visionary
By Maureen Wangard, Ph.D.

Faculty, staff, and alumni of Saint Louis University remember Father Paul Reinert for his impact on the university and the city of Saint Louis. Under his leadership, the student body grew exponentially, the size of the campus doubled, and SLU erected multiple buildings to accommodate this growth. One of his most important legacies was guiding the transition to a lay-led board. Father Reinert understood that Catholic colleges and universities needed the expertise of business, civic, and legal experts. Consequently, in 1967, the board of trustees went from consisting of a board of five Jesuits who administered the university to twenty-eight members, only ten of whom were Jesuits. Father Reinert also influenced the neighborhoods surrounding Saint Louis University. As chancellor, he established non-profit organizations to drive reinvestment in the Midtown area. Business leaders, politicians, developers, and philanthropists supported the rehabilitation of abandoned properties, and over the course of many years, Midtown once again became the cultural hub of Saint Louis with the renovation of the Fox Theatre and Powell Symphony Hall.

Less well known is the important role Father Reinert played in shaping the direction of Catholic higher education. As president of the Jesuit Educational Association, Father Reinert influenced other Jesuit colleges and universities nationwide in convincing them that their very survival depended on incorporating lay people into the leadership of Catholic educational institutions. Because Jesuit colleges and universities dominate Catholic higher education worldwide, Father Reinert's advocacy affected many Catholic universities founded by other religious orders. SLU forged the way in establishing a lay-led board of trustees, and by the early 1970s, other institutions followed SLU's example.

Father Reinert worked together with Father Theodore Hesburgh, C.S.C., president of the University of Notre Dame at the time, to promote lay leadership at Catholic institutions. In addition, they collaborated to foster independence from Vatican control for Catholic colleges and universities worldwide. In the early 1960s, Catholic colleges and universities were struggling to maintain a balance between operating autonomously while still retaining a strong Catholic identity.

Father Reinert and Father Hesburgh guided the International Federation of Catholic Colleges and Universities in establishing academic freedom and institutional autonomy from the Vatican. Father Hesburgh organized a meeting at a retreat house in Land O' Lakes, Wisconsin. At this meeting, participants drafted a ground-breaking document which would later become known as "The Catholic University and the Modern World." The group outlined ways for Catholic higher education to preserve its Catholicity but operate independently from papal control. The partnership between Hesburgh and Reinert was crucial to the success of establishing academic freedom and autonomy. Although Hesburgh was well-known and respected across the United States and in Vatican circles, he needed support from most Catholic colleges and universities to have any chance at creating lasting success. Father Reinert's ability to convince other Jesuit institutions to push for autonomy and academic freedom gave Father Hesburgh the broad support needed to advocate for changes in how church officials and Catholic colleges and universities interacted.

Father Reinert also demonstrated national leadership during his presidency of the Association of American Colleges. By the late 1960s, private colleges and universities across the nation faced financial ruin in part because they received no federal funding to award students in work study programs, not to mention grants and loans to cover tuition. With financial support from the Danforth Foundation, Father Reinert directed Project SEARCH, a national effort to solve the financial dilemma facing private colleges and universities. He took a year's leave of absence from SLU during the 1971-72 academic year and during that time, met with men and women in Congress, business leaders, and college presidents across the United States to better understand the financial problems and to seek solutions that would keep private institutions from closing. During his travels, he rallied support for the Higher Education Amendment of 1972 because the law awarded federal financial aid directly to students, allowing them to choose where to attend college. After the law passed, finances at many private colleges and universities improved because students at private institutions were given the same opportunities for federal financial aid as students attending publicly supported colleges and universities.

People who knew Fr. Reinert personally remember him as a humble leader who embraced change and demonstrated genuine concern for students, faculty, and staff at SLU. He was well known for his friendly demeanor and his ability to recall names and information about people he encountered. As president, he successfully navigated tense situations on campus stemming from social changes occurring around the country. However, he should also be remembered for his work outside of Saint Louis University. Without his influence, higher education, particularly at Catholic colleges and universities, would be very different in the 21st century. His actions and achievements demonstrate the way he lived SLU's motto by being a man for others.

Father Reinert reading his breviary in the walkway between DuBourg Hall and St. Francis Xavier Church.

> ## "WE CAN NO LONGER PRETEND THAT THE INEQUALITIES AND INJUSTICES OF OUR WORLD MUST BE BORNE AS PART OF THE INEVITABLE ORDER OF THINGS."
>
> SOCIETY OF JESUS GENERAL CONGREGATION 32, DECREE 4, 1974-1975

Great change took place in this period for the Society of Jesus, indeed, the intellectual and spiritual trajectory of the order is a story of profound and still emerging historical significance. In 1891, Pope Leo XIII had issued *Rerum Novarum,* an encyclical defending the dignity of the laborer (see Chapter 3). The title of the encyclical is Latin for "of revolutionary change." In the course of the ensuing century, this connotation of revolution has only grown stronger for many Jesuits. It has evolved into a call to dismantle oppressive structures.

The ultimate governing body of the Society of Jesus is known as the General Congregation or GC. The first thirty general congregations were occasions at which, over four hundred years, "constancy overwhelmed innovation," indeed, to the point of "immobility."[9] The GC's were generally more responsive, rather than leading through change. They were concerned with such

matters as the conservation and deepening of religious life and discipline; the preparation, formation, and education of younger members; apostolic activity; and the structure of congregations themselves. Suddenly, a radical shift emerged. At the GC 31 (held May to July 1965 and September to November 1966), Father Pedro Arrupe, S.J. was elected as superior general, a position he held until 1983. Born in 1907 in Bilbao, Spain, Father Arrupe received medical training and later served as provincial of the Japan Province in Hiroshima, Japan. In August 1945, he was among the first to arrive on the scene to help treat civilians injured by the United States' explosion of a nuclear bomb.

At GC 31, the group discussed Jesuit spiritual formation, as well as the rules on poverty; they enacted a decree on scholarship and research. As they headed toward the famous GC 32 in 1974, the delegates knew something new was afoot. It was rare to convoke solely to discuss governance. The issues for

discussion included prayer life and obedience, but then Father General Arrupe addressed the group on justice: "we will find ourselves accused of Marxism or subversion."[10] With these words, he anticipated the response to GC 32's document *Our Mission Today: The Service of Faith and the Promotion of Justice.* It is just one of an important body of documents that proclaims an unmistakable call for peace in relation to economic justice.

Father Reinert was an elected delegate to GC 31; he knew and respected Father Arrupe. In addition to many other actions, Reinert attended a 1963 conference on civil rights convened at the White House by President Kennedy, worked to promote civil rights in St. Louis, established SLU's Metropolitan College in 1962 for "the distinct purpose of serving adults living in the metropolitan area,"[11] and in 1971, invited Roy Wilkins, executive director of the National Association for the Advancement of Colored People from 1955 to 1976, to serve on SLU's board of trustees.

The University News

BILL SAYS: LEFT, RIGHT, LEFT

"America's Best Catholic College Newspaper"

Vol. XLIV, No. 20   Saint Louis University, St. Louis, Mo., March 26, 1965   Entered As Second Class Material at the Post Office at St. Louis, Mo.

Students And Faculty March At Montgomery

Students Start South

Southern White Citizens Meet Marchers With Stunned Silence

By JAMES LUTZ

MONTGOMERY, ALABAMA (Special) — Over 100 University students and faculty together with 50,000 of their fellow citizens helped to write a page of history today. Hoarse from singing they joined arm in arm with disenfranchised Negroes in the quest for the right to vote.

It was a long day marked by a triumphant march through three miles of central Montgomery and topped with several hours of singing and speeches in front of Alabama's state capitol.

Marchers walked from St. Judes hospital to the capitol waving to thousands of cheering Negroes along the streets. White citizens of Montgomery were strangely absent until we reached the downtown area when we were met by a few jeers but mainly stunned silence.

Color Ended At Curb

The color line ended at the curb for all of us here. A sense of brotherhood was overwhelming. It was something like the liberation of Paris, the same welcome, kids grinning at you, plenty of waving and handshaking along the way.

Green helmeted state troopers

Ten Seniors Receive Conclave Service Awards

The seniors were awarded Senior Service Awards by Conclave in their meeting this week. Eight Arts students, one Tech and one Nursing student were selected by the representatives. The recipients are:

Robert Beekman of Arts who served as editor-in-chief of the University News was a member

"THE POSTWAR FACULTY WERE TRULY 'CHARACTERS,' BUT THEY HAD ONE THING IN COMMON: THEY LOVED THE LAW AND SLU LAW SCHOOL."
JOSEPH SIMEONE, 2011[12]

Although some Jesuits had been reluctant to reopen SLU's law school in 1908, on the theory that law was "too secular,"[13] the study and teaching of law were quickly re-established after a temporary closure during World War II. The school reopened in January 1946, retaining its practice of offering classes in the evening. Paul Fitzsimmons was dean; he started the *Intramural Law Review* in 1948, which later became *Saint Louis University Law Journal.* He also hired a young job-seeker named Joseph Simeone to teach, for $300 per month, conflicts of law, civil procedure and property. Simeone stayed for twenty-five years. By 1948, Father Leo C. Brown, S.J. was acting regent of the law school. He brought his profound understanding of labor arbitration issues to bear on the revived school (see Chapter 4 for more details on Father Brown.)

Joseph J. Simeone later wrote of himself as being too "diffident," but he had an impressive career, and is credited with modernizing legal practice in Missouri. He was born in Quincy, Illinois and began to teach at Saint Louis University in 1947. In 1971, Simeone was appointed to the Missouri Court of Appeals, and in 1977 was appointed to the Missouri Supreme Court. He acted as a senior judge for the Missouri Court of Appeals from 1986 to 1990 and served as an administrative law judge for the Social Security Administration from 1990 to 2007. He served as professor emeritus at SLU Law until his death at age 93, in 2015. He was also counsel for two Missouri governors and the legal advisor for the Judiciary Committee of the Missouri House of Representatives. He is the principal author and draftsman of the Judicial Article of the Missouri Constitution, the original Missouri Public Defender Act, the Controlled Substances Law, various environmental laws and other legislation. Simeone authored more than sixty legal articles, published in various legal journals, and wrote more than three hundred judicial opinions. Among many

[LEFT] Joseph Simeone is credited with modernizing legal practice in Missouri.

[BELOW] Dean Childress at left, speaking with a student

honors, he earned a Lifetime Achievement Award from the Missouri Supreme Court for his more than fifty years of dedication to the field of law.

Teaching some three hundred students along with Simeone in 1947 was a fascinating group of young full- and part-time faculty, many just returned from the war. They included: Charles Brown, James Higgins, Thomas Quinn, Walter Rafalko, Joseph Sinclitico, Robert Vining, and Walter Dakin Williams. Also among them was Richard Childress, who was legendary with peers for his kindness, great teaching, running (never walking) to class, perennial lateness in grading papers, and setting his coat on fire due to placing a burning match in his pocket after lighting a cigarette (while teaching!). Kentucky-born Childress served at SLU for nearly thirty years, and for fifteen of those years was associate dean and dean. He gave the current name to the *Saint Louis University Law Journal,* and helped expand the law library as well as interdisciplinary programs. Childress was active in civil rights, was a respected professor, and performed legal service for the American Law Institute and the Missouri Bar Committee on the Bill of Rights. He was also a renowned constitutional law scholar. He arranged to pay tuition for black students from Arkansas and other states. Childress was instrumental in the movement to ratify

Vince Immel was dean of Saint Louis University School of Law from 1962 to 1969, managing expansion of faculty and students, while also supporting the Legal Aid Society. He was known as the most "feared" teacher on the faculty.

the Equal Rights Amendment, and served as director of the St. Louis Urban League, St. Louis Conference on Religion and Race, and as chair of the Archdiocesan Commission on Human Rights. In March 6, 1957, Father Edward Dowling, S.J. oversaw a wreath-laying ceremony at Dred Scott's grave organized by the Student Bar Association at SLU. Scott's remains had been moved to Calvary Cemetery in 1867 by SLU alumnus Taylor Blow, from the old Wesleyan Cemetery at Grand and Laclede. Richard Childress spoke at the ceremony, and the Scotts' descendants were present.

Alvin Evans, of Kentucky, was asked to serve as dean after Fitzsimmons; he recruited senior lawyers who balanced the youthful faculty. In 1962, Jesuit-educated Vincent Immel became dean, taking charge as the law school had risen from "a minimal trade school to the upper third of the country."[14] He and Donald King began a juvenile law "forum clinic" in 1967. Its success led to the establishment in fall 1969 of SLU's legal clinic, collaborating with the Legal Aid Society, the city, and county. Childress, King, Richard Power, and Peter Salsich later worked to establish a national juvenile law center at SLU. Also in this period, Kurt von Schuschnigg, former chancellor of Austria, taught International Law, and was a member of SLU's Department of Political Science.

In 1965, about one hundred SLU students and faculty (including Childress) participated in the Selma-to-Montgomery march for civil rights.

THE UNIVERSITY AS A "FRONTIER POST"

Father John W. Padberg, S.J. has contributed many publications. He was honored with the George Ganss, S.J. Award by the Institute for Advanced Jesuit Studies at Boston College in 2016.

Academic life at SLU was shaped by innumerable, highly gifted people in this period. Among them was Father Robert John Henle, S.J., who was born in Muscatine, Iowa in 1909. He finished his secondary studies at the Jesuit high school in Mobile, Alabama, an experience which generated a continuing interest in racial justice. Henle completed degrees in theology and philosophy at SLU, was ordained in 1940, received his doctorate in philosophy from the University of Toronto in 1944, and became an instructor in philosophy at SLU. Father Henle was a Thomist scholar and prolific author; he also taught at SLU's law school and was honored as the first holder of the McDonnell Professorship in Justice in American Society. His instructional manuals in Latin, originally published in the 1930s, remain in print and are considered unparalleled. In 1956, his work *Saint Thomas and Platonism* was published, fostering significant change to scholarly thinking. A passionate teacher and gifted speaker and counsellor, Father Henle made scholarly contributions in the fields of law, philosophy, education, public service, foreign policy, business ethics, energy, and classics. He served in several administrative roles at SLU including dean of the College of Philosophy and Letters (see also Chapter 6). Father Henle became dean of SLU's graduate school in 1950. He also led a nine-member board of directors created at the Jesuit Educational Association (JEA) to plan a 1962 "Workshop on the Role of Philosophy and Theology" which was held at Loyola Marymount University in Los Angeles. The experience was important in demonstrating the "potential rewards of union and cooperation among the American provinces."[15] Father Henle's progressive approach to graduate education, coupled with skills in planning and innovation, and his expertise on Latin America and issues of social justice,

made him a force for much positive change in this period. Henle established SLU's Latin American program in 1960, and developed programs to train Peace Corps volunteers for service in Honduras and Panama. At Henle's instigation, SLU initiated a cooperative assistance program through the Agency for International Development (AID) with various Latin American universities. Henle was president of the JEA from 1966 to 1970.

From 1969 to 1974, Father Henle served as the 46th President of Georgetown, then returned to SLU to finish his career. Undeterred by blindness, his last scholarly book in philosophy was published when he was ninety years old.

Another significant presence, Father John W. Padberg, S.J., is a prolific scholar who has carefully elucidated the Society of Jesus and its long history. Father Padberg was born in 1926 in St. Louis, and entered the Society in 1944, when he was not quite 18 years old. He studied at Florissant, and was taught almost entirely by Jesuit professors, from 1948 to 1951. After his master's degree in history at SLU, he studied in Paris, received his doctorate at Harvard in 1965, then taught at Saint Louis University. In 1969, he received the Danforth Foundation's E. Harris Harbison Award for Distinguished Teaching.

A few years after receiving this honor, he averred in a speech to student and faculty members of Phi Beta Kappa that a Jesuit university should be a "frontier post … out in the forefront of educational theory and practice. In this exposed and lonely position they will be most truly in touch with their historical traditions."[16] Padberg generously shares his understanding of the Society of Jesus: its history and its role. He was instrumental in building SLU's Rare Book Collection when he acquired material from several French, Jesuit libraries in and around Toulouse, France for the cost of shipping to St. Louis. Father Padberg has held administrative posts including academic vice president at Saint Louis University, served as president of Weston Jesuit School of Theology in Cambridge, Massachusetts from 1975 to 1985, and directed the Institute of Jesuit Sources from 1986 to 2014.

Another key figure in this period was Father Trafford Maher, S.J. who was ordained in 1946, earned his Ph.D. at Catholic University in 1952, and joined the faculty at SLU in 1952, later serving as chair of the Department of Education and in other administrative roles. He founded the first Human Relations Center, conducted numerous summer workshops abroad, and in 1958 was the first chairman of the Missouri Commission on Human Rights. Maher produced research that contributed to Vatican II, specifically in the writing of materials on ecumenism.

FATHER ROBERT HENLE, S.J.

FATHER TRAFFORD P. MAHER, S.J.

"This is where I am needed."
Edward A. Doisy

Edward Adelbert Doisy was born in 1893 in Hume, Illinois. He received his B.S. and M.S. degrees at the University of Illinois, then studied at Harvard under Otto Folin, completing his Ph.D. in 1920. He spent two years in the Army, then taught at Washington University before being recruited by SLU's Medical School dean, Dr. Hanau Loeb. In 1924, Doisy became chair of the newly created Department of Biochemistry, a position he held until 1965.

Early in his career, Dr. Doisy famously presented a bill for $750 to Dr. Loeb. That was the amount Doisy had spent on the processing equipment he needed as he sought to isolate ovarian hormones. He sincerely expected to be fired. Loeb paid the bill, albeit with a slight gulp. But Loeb never learned the results of the investment, because he passed away in 1927.[17] Doisy went on to pioneering research in female hormones. In 1955, he and his junior colleague, Dr. Phillip Katzman, assigned the patents associated with these discoveries to SLU, generating a foundation that is now worth over $100 million. Besides his work on estrogens, Doisy also extracted vitamin K from alfalfa and fish meal in 1939; for that discovery, he shared the 1943/1944 Nobel Prize in Physiology or Medicine with Dr. Henryk Dam.

Throughout his life, Doisy always credited his mother: Ada Alley Doisy, as well as his first wife, Alice Ackert (who died in 1964) and his second wife, Margaret McCormick Doisy, for his success. He was frequently recruited by other universities and research centers, but he always firmly declined, saying that SLU is "where I am needed." Dr. Doisy died in 1986. His generosity throughout his life, and that of his family, have earned them the honor of being the largest benefactors in the university's history.

Father Paul Reinert, S.J., presents Dr. Edward Doisy with the highest honor of the university: the Fleur de Lis.

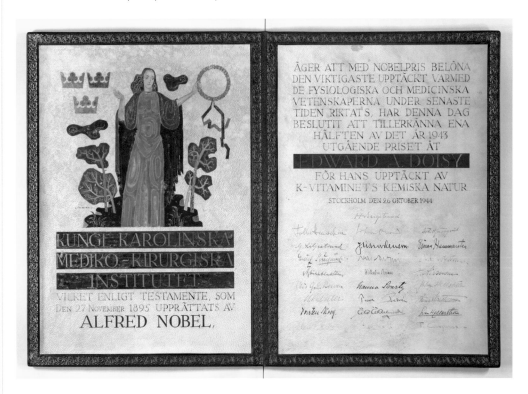

The citation issued to Dr. Doisy with his Nobel award in 1944

Eileen Searls directed SLU's law school library for decades. In a 2016 interview, Searls noted: "the university relies upon excellence speaking for itself, it does not swagger."

When Eileen Haughey Searls was hired at SLU's law library in 1952, the collection numbered 23,000 volumes. There was no air conditioning. The law faculty was small, as the program had recently reopened after World War II. When Searls, described as a globe-trotting, adventurous bibliophile, retired in 2000, the law library contained over 585,000 volumes, microforms, rare books, audio and video cassettes, and software. Searls was a visionary regarding technology, networking, and the usage of space. She advised architects, secured the library status as a federal government depository site, and was the sole reason SLU was among the first ten users of Westlaw and Lexis/Nexis in the United States. She was especially committed to interlibrary cooperation. Working with a tight budget, Searls built an impressive collection including numerous titles in international law, supporting specialized centers: the Jewish Law Center, the Smurfit Irish Law Center, and the Polish Law Collection.

As the first tenured, female member of the law school faculty, Searls was important as a mentor to female faculty. She was a true "trailblazer," in every sense of the word.[18]

A portrait of Eileen Searls hangs near a reading room named in her honor at the Saint Louis University Law School.

"THE UNIVERSITY ... MISSION IS TO BE A CENTER RADIATING INTELLECTUAL LIFE FOR THE BENEFIT OF THE NATIONAL COMMUNITY, IN THAT ATMOSPHERE OF HEALTHY FREEDOM THAT IS PROPER TO ALL CULTURE."
POPE PIUS XII

In the early 1950s, issues discussed by the trustees of Saint Louis University ranged widely. The board discussed the cancer research wing at Desloge hospital, the possibility of obtaining federal funds to construct dorms, a way to honor Dr. Edward A. Doisy, a policy on prayers before class, and the need for an improved space for the library. SLU's renowned library collection had over 580,000 volumes and 3,000 periodicals. Plans for the Vatican Film Library (VFL) were already underway (see pages 132-33). Father Reinert telephoned President Harry S. Truman for assistance in acquiring a large automatic developer for the VFL because, during the Korean War, the military had priority in acquiring cameras, developers, and film in the United States.[19]

Students in the old library, which was located on the second floor of DuBourg Hall. The open floor seating area was at the base of four tiered levels of bookshelves. This gorgeous space was renovated in 1995, and is now called Père Marquette Gallery. It boasts numerous artistic and religious treasures, as well as stunning stained glass windows.

Vatican Film Library

by Gregory A. Pass, Ph.D., MALS
Assistant Dean, Special Collections
Director, Vatican Film Library

Saint Louis University took a leading role in the preservation of world heritage humanities collections in the 1950s with its Vatican Film Library project. An audacious undertaking—proposed and directed by SLU history professor Father Lowrie Daly, S.J., sanctioned by Pope Pius XII, and funded by the Knights of Columbus—this project captured on microfilm almost half of the 80,000 medieval and Renaissance manuscripts contained in the Biblioteca Apostolica Vaticana. The Vatican Library is one of the world's most important manuscript collections and one of the oldest libraries in continuous operation, having been established by Pope Nicholas V (1447–55). Its collections represent a fundamental store of original materials preserving and transmitting many of the ideas, texts, and works of the pre-modern world: some of the oldest copies of the Christian Bible in Greek (Codex Vaticanus), as well as copies of the Qu'ran and the Torah; works from ancient Greece and Rome (some of them the sole copies to survive); and a wealth of medieval and Renaissance authors, such as Thomas Aquinas, Michelangelo, and Galileo.

Microfilm was the most advanced imaging technology of its day, and the VFL project was the largest scale application of this technology to the humanities yet attempted, capturing more than twelve million manuscript pages. This monumental effort not only preserved valuable manuscripts from potential loss, such as had been threatened during World War II, but also made this unique and vital collection more easily accessible to scholars in the Western Hemisphere. It was a major contribution to scholarship and the preservation of cultural heritage. Filming proceeded from 1951 to 1957, and with Dr. Charles Ermatinger, professor of philosophy, as its librarian the VFL opened to the public in 1953 in DuBourg Hall. It moved to its current space in Pius Library in 1959 when the new library was constructed. Today, the Vatican Film Library is known internationally as a research collection for manuscript studies, attracting scholars and students from the United States and abroad. It is expanding its original mission through METAscripta, an online initiative to both digitize the microfilm collection and crowd-source the collection of descriptive information about these manuscripts.

Father Daly's ambitions were not limited to Vatican Library manuscripts. With the understanding that a new library was necessary to support Saint Louis University's rapid expansion in the post-war years (the old library in DuBourg Hall, now Pére Marquette Gallery, was no longer sufficient) and wishing to equip it with the richest resources possible, he sought and was granted permission to microfilm volumes from the Vatican Library's outstanding collections of incunabula and early printed books, many of which were unavailable to scholars in North America. Daly's passion to preserve and make accessible vital historical sources had an even greater impact. While still microfilming manuscripts and printed books in the Vatican Library in the 1950s, he also visited the Central Jesuit Archives in Rome (Archivum Romanum Societatis Iesu), the official repository of all reports, correspondence, and other historical documentation sent back and forth to the headquarters of the Society of Jesus. He conceived what was to become another great project: to microfilm all surviving historical documents relating to the missionary activities of the Jesuit Order in the New World. Starting with the Jesuit's central archive in Rome, and later working with Ernest J. Burrus, S.J., and others, this project grew through the 1970s to encompass materials in the national archives of Spain and in archives of South, Central, and North America, as well as the Philippines. Saint Louis University now holds in the microfilm collections of the Vatican Film Library many thousands of documents fundamental to the history and identity of the Jesuit Order.

Example of a Vatican Library manuscript in the VFL microfilm collection: a 5th- to 6th-century manuscript of works by the Roman poet Virgil, containing his *Aeneid, Georgics,* and *Eclogues* (Vatican City, Biblioteca Apostolica Vaticana, MS Vat. lat. 3867, fol. 44v)

Example of a Vatican Library manuscript in the VFL microfilm collection: a mid-13th-century manuscript of the *De arte venandi cum avibus* (On the Art of Hunting with Birds) by the Holy Roman Emperor Frederick II (Vatican City, Biblioteca Apostolica Vaticana, MS Pal. lat. 1071, fols. 42v-43r)

[ABOVE] Father Lowrie Daly, S.J., and Dr. Charles Ermatinger consult microfilms in the original Vatican Film Library reading room in DuBourg Hall, ca. 1953-1958.

A 1959 image of the new Vatican Film Library reading room, from a series of postcards celebrating the opening of Pius library

The library's original design was altered, alternating glass windows with panels to reduce the impact of sunlight on the books, as shown in the architectural rendering below.

On October 9, 1959, a striking statue of Pope Pius XII, sculpted by Ivan Mestrovic, was blessed by Bishop Leo C Byrne. Mestrovic used the chair or "cathedra" to symbolize teaching, and enlarged the Pope's right hand in a Byzantine gesture of the rhetorician or teacher, to emphasize the point.[20]

Work on the Vatican Film Library spurred action on the new library. The university contracted the Omaha-based firm of Leo A. Daly Co. to design a space capable of holding one million volumes. Ground was broken in June 1957, the cornerstone was placed in February 1958, and the doors opened in May 1959. Pius XII Memorial Library was dedicated in November 1959. A major supporter of the library, Morton May, agreed to exhibit his extraordinary collection of German expressionist art at the dedication; this event was featured in *Time* magazine.

This period saw additional, new construction on campus, as well as new speakers and events. In 1954, the Jesuit House of Studies (now Fusz Hall), opened for seminarians. It was built on the West Pine Boulevard, now West Pine Mall, and was also designed by Leo A. Daly Co. The building was the location for the first ever Founders Day event held at Saint Louis University, which took place in November 1955 and was chaired by Morton May. In 1958, Dorothy Day visited SLU's campus for the third time, continuing to

spread her message of mercy, and the next year, President Lyndon B. Johnson spoke at the law school. A streak of independence is evident in speakers in this period, for example, Robert Kennedy in 1960 and the controversial theologian Hans Küng in 1963. Küng's lecture tour that year addressed the issue of freedom in the Catholic Church. He refuted papal infallibility, and claimed that lack of freedom in the Church undermined its credibility. In a piece in *Commonweal,* the Swiss priest argued: "What is bad is that even today the spirit of the Inquisition and unfreedom has not died out." In his view, there cannot be freedom without order; obedience is good, but it should not be merely "blind obedience." He called upon the Vatican Council to eliminate the Index of Forbidden Books. Küng received an interdict from Catholic University, and was not allowed to teach theology officially. He received an honorary degree from SLU in 1963.[21]

FIRST FLOOR PLAN

LOBBY
113

CIRCULATION OFFICE
114

BIBLIOGRAPHY
113

PROCESSING 116

BINDING & MENDING 118

DUCT SHAFT

ELEV. NO.

REST RM.
103

WOMEN
104

WOMEN
105

JANITOR

CORRIDOR 101

TYPING RM.
106

TELEPHONE 107

CHECK ROOM

VEST.

MICROFILM RM.
131

RECEPTION & OFFICE
133

VATICAN READING 134

REFERENCE ROOM 131

TELETYPE ROOM 128

OFFICE

CARD CATALOG
132

TYPING ROOM 129 135

OFFICE

FIRST FLOOR PLAN

NOTE: ELEVATIONS SHOWN FOR TOP OF FINISH FLOOR

FIRST FLOOR PLAN

PIUS XII LIBRARY
ST. LOUIS UNIVERSITY
ST. LOUIS, MO.

LEO A. DALY CO.
ARCHITECTS — ENGINEERS
LOUIS   OMAHA   SEATTLE

A2

Father Bannon filming his history program on KETC. It was on the air from 1955 to 1960.

"THIS APPROACH TO LITERATURE, THE SOARING LECTURES AND HARD WORK APPROACH..."

MARK J. CURRAN, 2012[22]

The alliance against Germany and the Axis powers had been instrumental during World War II, but proved to be short-lived; the United States and the Union of Soviet Socialist Republics (USSR) soon entered a period of nuclear détente and diplomatic "Cold War." The impact of World War II and the Cold War was felt on American college campuses, for example in a new field of study: international relations. In 1946, the Fulbright Program was founded in the United States in an effort to foster international understanding through scholarly and cultural exchange. By 1961, President John F. Kennedy had started the Peace Corps. During this period, SLU students and faculty greatly expanded their awareness and understanding of other cultures, reaching out to fellow students from abroad, and applying for Fulbright scholarships to study overseas.

Reflecting the rise of academic interest in international relations during the post-war era, Father John Francis Bannon, S.J. lobbied for a Latin American Affairs Institute at SLU. He taught history at SLU from 1939 to 1973, and served as chair of the History Department

for twenty-eight of those years. John Bannon was born in 1905 in St. Joseph, Missouri, and entered the Society of Jesus at St. Stanislaus Seminary in 1922. He received his bachelor's and master's degrees at SLU. Ordained in 1935, he undertook doctoral studies at the University of California at Berkeley. His mentor was Herbert Eugene Bolton, who pioneered the study of the American Borderlands. Bannon's doctoral research on Jesuit missions in Mexico developed his interest in archival study and Latin American history. He returned to SLU to begin a career as teacher, scholar, and administrator. In 1955, he began to appear on a TV program called: "Before There was a USA." The first installment was titled: "How There Happened to be American History."

As a frontier post in a global order, the Missouri Province of Jesuits had always cultivated international connections, including a mission in Belize. In addition, the university had an important opportunity in the 1960s. Soon a program was underway in Madrid, Spain.

"A valuable intercultural experience"
Saint Louis University in Spain: 1982-1983 catalog

The tale of the origins of the Madrid campus of Saint Louis University is exactly as mysterious as its founder. How did a lone Jesuit, (who seems to have been a rather complicated man, if some stories are to be believed), navigate the Spanish bureaucracy during the dictatorship of Francisco Franco, who ruled from 1939 until his death in 1975, in order to establish a campus for an American university? The answer may be lost to history; Father Raymond Sullivant, S.J. died in Spain after spending thirty-eight of his forty-five years as a Jesuit in Europe. There is no trace of his personal papers. However, there are many hints about who he was as a man and as a Jesuit.

Some basic facts are clear: Father Sullivant was born in 1925, in Waverly, Kansas. He entered the Army and was a volunteer medic, landing at Utah Beach on D-Day. He studied at Kansas State University, the University of Poitiers in France on a Fulbright Fellowship, and the Sorbonne. He entered the Society of Jesus in 1959, studying at the seminary in Florissant, then was ordained in Lyon, France in 1966, and took final vows in 1975. He earned his master's and doctoral degrees in French literature at Washington University, taught in the United States and abroad, and was fluent in Spanish and French. In 1966, Father Walter Ong. S.J. wrote that Sullivant was "a fine teacher and a promising young scholar."[23] As assistant professor of modern languages at Saint Louis University, he is reported to have been working with homeless people in Madrid when he saw a need for more intercultural awareness. He began a study abroad program in 1967 on what was described as an "extension" campus of Saint Louis University at Madrid's *Ciudad Universitaria.*

Classes were offered in conjunction with the *Universidad Pontificia Comillas,* a Spanish Jesuit university. SLU later established an independent, permanent program. Spanish students were drawn by the liberal arts curriculum, enrollment grew, and soon the program had a full range of courses, a library, and a system in which Spanish and European students could

This photograph from 1982-83 was taken in Father Sullivant's English class, which was a requirement for all freshmen. It was taken in what was then called AULA 1 (Classroom 1), one of the three classrooms of the Madrid Campus in Calle de la Viña no.3. Sullivant is seated at center, with a student placing a hand on his shoulder.

complete the first two years of their undergraduate studies in Madrid. Its success and distinctive position, as the American Jesuit university in Spain, prompted Saint Louis University to build a campus. In 1990, SLU purchased two buildings now called Padre Rubio and Padre Arrupe halls. By the 1990s, there were over 1,200 students at SLU's Madrid campus, most of whom were Spanish-born.

Sullivant later stepped down as academic dean to become director of development, charged with oversight of a new campus headquarters. In 1996, SLU Madrid was the first U.S. university to receive official recognition from the *Consejeria de Educación y Cultura,* Madrid's higher education authority.

Along the way, Sullivant also built up an English-language parish in Madrid that attracted a large and loyal following at Our Lady of Mercy Church.

Students remember him as kind but strict. He possessed an extensive network of contacts in Spain; this greatly helped to strengthen the SLU program in Madrid. He forbade students to take drugs or engage in protests, and he was careful to reassure students that they were not targets, after a 1974 terrorist attack at a nearby cafe. Father Michael Marchlewski, S.J., wrote the following in honor of Sullivant's life: "He was a very driven man, extremely generous, yet demanding. He had a temper, but it was a front. He was a softy for the poor ... extremely compassionate, yet he could not accept praise. He was a man you could count on and lean on. I will miss him like an older brother."[24]

FATHER RAYMOND
SULLIVANT, S.J.

A college campus reflects larger trends, as scholars and researchers not only communicate knowledge gleaned from the past, but also investigate contemporary issues and prepare students for the future. For example, the widespread suffering and inequity caused by the Depression were factors in the creation of SLU's programs in social service and education (see Chapter 4). In this period, the very notion of "administration"—planning, using data for policy-making, and so forth—was becoming increasingly professionalized. Investment in scientific research and technology was driven in part by security concerns associated with a global condition termed by analysts: "a bipolar world." SLU's geophysical, biochemical, and health sciences strands of research were soon supplemented by library and computer technology studies, beginning with the Yalem Center. From its $200,000 "electric brain" donated by Charles Yalem in 1962 (which students gleefully taught to play blackjack and calculate marriage odds), the school progressed quickly. The 1969 collaboration between the university and Control Data Institute, a private school for programmers, gave SLU students access to a $1 million Control Data Corporation 3300 computer. Edward Gotway, director of the Yalem Scientific Computing Center, said the arrangement provided "access to a far more sophisticated research tool than we could afford on our own." Located in the basement of Des Peres Hall, the computer had an optical card reader able to scan data processing cards at a rate of 1,200 per minute. The institute also offered $25,000 per year of scholarships to young people from "the Inner City," and Yalem staff gave programming seminars (for Fortran and Cobol) to SLU personnel, so they could use the computer for academic research.[25]

Postwar developments also impacted Parks College, as the "space race" got underway. In October 1957, the launch of Sputnik 1 spurred the National Aeronautics and Space Administration (NASA) to invest more resources in space travel. In December of that year, Willy Ley, the author of *Rockets, Missiles*

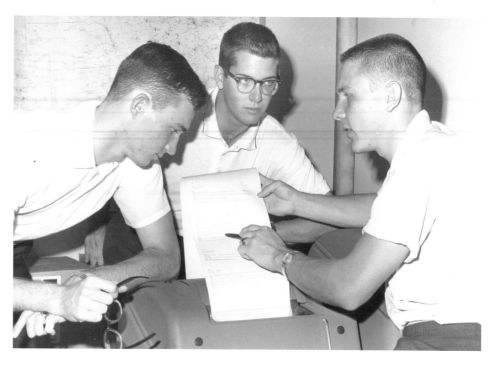

and Space Travel, spoke at the Parks College Commencement. (Parks College moved to the north campus in St. Louis from Cahokia, Ilinois in 1997.) Parks alumni have been involved in every NASA space mission since the Mercury Redstone 3/Freedom 7 launch on May 5, 1961.

With the dazzling changes in technology that took place in this era, many philosophers and humanists reflected upon the relation between human thought and the use of technology. Marshall McLuhan arrived at SLU in 1937 as a young English instructor from Cambridge still working on his dissertation. He taught "New Criticism" and then left in 1944, later earning fame as a media theorist. One of his most accomplished students was Father Walter Ong, S.J.

Students discuss a printout from the CDC computer in the Yalem Center.

At Parks College, Father Jonathan C. Choppesky, S.J., (right) prepares for takeoff, as Father John Higgins, S.J., bids him safe travels. Photo courtesy of *Life Magazine*, October 1954 issue.

Father Walter Ong, S.J., possessed the gift of cherishing human connections in every moment. This gift is clear even in his writing. A remarkable scholar, Father Ong wove themes of love and community into his brilliant observations on literature, philosophy, intellectual history, cultural anthropology, and communication, to name just a few of the disciplines to which he contributed. He focused expertly on a given topic, while tossing nuggets of spectacular insight along the way; these asides merit entire works on their own.

Father Ong was born in 1912, entered the Society in 1935, and in 1941, received his master's degree in English at Saint Louis University. His master's thesis on sprung rhythm, as used in the poetry of Gerard Manley Hopkins, was supervised by Marshall McLuhan. Father Ong studied at Harvard under Perry Miller, returned to SLU in 1954, and received his Ph.D. in English from Harvard in 1955. He remained at SLU as a teacher and prodigious scholar for the next thirty years, publishing hundreds of books, chapters, reviews, articles, and poems.

Father Ong tackled important themes early; in May 1940, his piece on "Imitation and the Object of Art" was published in *The Modern Schoolman.* In January 1942, he published "The Province of Rhetoric and Poetic" in that same journal. Soon he began to study the sixteenth-century thinker, Petrus Ramus, which allowed him to explore deeply the realms of dialectic, rhetoric, and the impact of writing upon human thought. Among his many concerns was the shift away from habits of thinking based on *listening to voices,* which for him meant living with people, to thought as affected by *looking at surfaces.* The two-part, Socratic exchange was lost, and so was even the monologue of the teacher: persons and voice are simply *gone.* "An art is now a 'thing,' not a possession of the mind but something

This 1957 photograph of Father Walter J. Ong, S.J. was taken in De Smet Hall. The hall was built in 1889 to house the College of Philosophy and Letters.

with surface, like the rest of the coming Newtonian world."27 Father Ong rejected the silence of this isolation, this absence both of community and of God's voice. He was especially interested in media ecology, the interplay of media that surrounds us every day, and famously argued that different modes of language—oral, written, electronic—shape consciousness.

Fortunately for Pius XII Library, Father Ong had a "library addiction." He donated his speaking honoraria to the Rare Book Fund; with two consecutive Guggenheim fellowships and a love of bookstores, he traveled widely in Europe and the British Isles, acquiring rare books. He sent ninety-one packages of books back to SLU; 430 books in the collection can be traced to him. SLU librarian of rare books Jennifer Lowe observes: "Acquiring books and acquiring understanding were to him one and the same."28 A brilliant scholar, he was also a kind, loving human being and above all, a priest.

Father Ong's "Route book" refers to this atlas, marked on numerous pages with the dates and sites of his travels.

"WE HAVE LABORED STRENUOUSLY TO MERGE CAMPUS LIFE WITH THE LIFE OF THE INNER CITY WHICH ALMOST ENCIRCLES US."

FATHER PAUL REINERT, S.J., 1970[29]

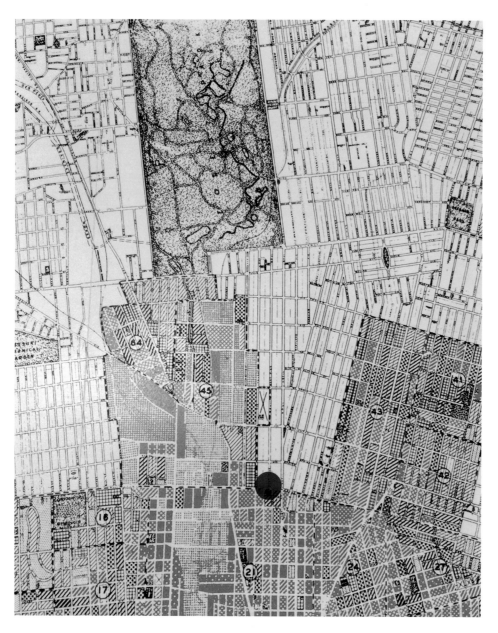

The red and black marks indicate "substandard" and "blighted" neighborhoods in this 1947 City Plan. SLU's campus is marked with a blue circle.

In 1888, the university moved from its campus at Ninth and Washington in the downtown section of St. Louis (Chapter 3). The Jesuits sought a more suitable location for many reasons, including an escape from the bustle and noise of commerce. In an essay printed in the 1919 St. Louis *Zone Plan,* I.H. Lionberger described his six consecutive moves of residence, starting from Sixth and Chestnut in the 1860s and ultimately ending at Westmoreland Place. He explained: "The causes which induced these various removals were simple: coal, smoke, dirt, dust, noise, the intrusion of various retail establishments, livery stables, saloons and other objectionable businesses, and the wish to live under comfortable conditions." He praised the idea of zoning districts, as a way to separate factories and other business establishments from homes. He added: "I think the crying need of the time, however, is cleanliness, noiselessness and something pleasant to look at. The town is a very ugly town, and the downtown part of it is not only excessively ugly but excessively dirty."[30]

As warehouses and businesses grew unchecked, they blocked light, and created other unhealthy conditions. Zoning was intended to place some limits on commercial development, while protecting the property values of homes. The idea was admirable: to promote healthy community life. However, other zoning practices in St. Louis and across the nation were far less benign. Racially restrictive covenants developed in the housing real estate market, preventing African Americans

Mill Creek Valley Tract Purchased By University

University Land Totals 21 Acres; Law Suit Pending

The University purchased a 21.3-acre tract Tuesday in the first sale of land in the Mill Creek Valley.

Papers were signed by officials of the St. Louis Land Clearance for Redevelopment Authority and the University.

The University purchased two tracts, totaling 929,686 square feet from Grand boulevard to Channing street between Laclede avenue and a point near Lindell boulevard, at a cost ranging from 55 to 60 cents per square foot, for a total of $535,743.

The Very Rev. Paul C. Reinert, S.J., president, signed papers for the tract on which the University hopes to expand its present campus. Its purchase of land from the Land Clearance Authority has been challenged in a law suit pending here.

Mill Creek Signing

—Globe-Democrat Photo

THE FIRST UNIVERSITY WEST OF THE MISSISSIPPI took a step eastward this week when the University purchased a tract of land in the Mill Creek area. Seated are (left to right) the Very Rev. Paul C. Reinert, S.J., president, James H. Scheuer, Eugene C. Farrell and Mayor Raymond Tucker. Standing are

Five Campus Religious Leaders Voice Criticism of Mass Cards

By GERALD MEYER
Copy Editor

The leaders of five campus religious organizations are critical of the present IBM-card system of checking Mass attendance, a poll by The University News revealed this week.

Two said that they do not believe the University should require weekly Mass attendance of undergraduate students.

The leader of another religious group, James Stanley, Commerce Sodality prefect, said he favors both compulsory Mass attendance and the card-checking system.

Jo Ann Resch, president of the Handmaids of the Blessed Virgin, was unwilling to express any opinion.

Russell Bley, president of the Sodality Union, said that he is not opposed to the Mass regulations but believes the IBM-card system is "inadequate and ineffective."

"When people who understand theology much more than I see fit to require Mass attendance, I ably be a better method of checking Mass attendance than is presently in effect, but until a more satisfactory one is found, the present method must be continued to accomplish the purpose," she said.

"If a student finds out what the Church has to say about Mass attendance and still objects," she said, "well, there are many other schools he can attend."

James Hitchcock, Arts Sodality prefect, expressed disapproval of both mandatory attendance at Mass and the present checking system.

"Whatever good is accomplished by way of promoting solidarity or attracting otherwise reluctant worshipers is, I believe, outweighed by two factors," he

---

from buying or renting homes in specific neighborhoods. In 1948, the U.S. Supreme Court ruled in *Shelley v. Kraemer,* a case originating with a family in St. Louis, that such practices violated the equal protection clause of the Fourteenth Amendment. But other patterns systematized and reinforced racial segregation; after *Kraemer,* housing discrimination persisted, through more subtle means.[31] Over time, both large-scale industrial disinvestment and white flight reshaped

the city of St. Louis. The city's population peaked in 1950 at 850,000, then declined over the ensuing decades, as the population in the surrounding municipalities grew. These realities pressed upon Saint Louis University, and SLU's president Father Reinert was determined not to ignore them.

For decades, university leaders had been concerned about the poverty of the surrounding community, including people living across Grand to the east of the campus. This section

of the city was part of Mill Creek Valley (MCV), a 465-acre neighborhood that was home to 20,000 working-class black residents.

In 1947, maps produced by the city of St. Louis showed designations of "substandard housing, a measure of obsolescence and blight." MCV received this designation. Problems included outdoor privies and vermin. Planning for the revitalization of the urban core through industrial development, St. Louis mayor Raymond Tucker decided to clear this "slum" area. The city worked with Civic Progress, a group of local business leaders, gained federal financing, and in the 1950s undertook an urban renewal project in MCV on a scale that was unprecedented in the nation at the time. The St. Louis chapter of the National Association for the Advancement of Colored People (NAACP) supported MCV redevelopment, but with several conditions that, ultimately, were not met. City leaders were not only concerned with the dwindling tax base. They also sought to thwart "small-time slumlords" who had allowed such neglect of housing conditions in the first place.[32]

An aerial view of Mill Creek Valley and the surrounding region in 1959, with DuBourg Hall and the College Church visible at the top center of the image.

At this time, Father Reinert was under pressure from lay advisors to move the university out of the city of St. Louis.[33] The city offered to sell the university land east of Grand, but Reinert could not afford to purchase it. He asked for help from a long-time SLU supporter: Harriet Frost Fordyce, who asked that the campus be named after her father, Daniel Marsh Frost. General Frost had defended Camp Jackson on that very piece of land in May 1861. He was a Confederate general, but resigned in 1864 and went to Canada. Father De Smet helped to arrange his pardon by President Andrew Johnson. In 1865, Frost swore an oath of loyalty to the Union and was permitted to return to St. Louis.[34]

SLU's purchase in 1960 of one portion of the Mill Creek Valley land (Tracts 29 and 30 in MCV) amounted to just over twenty acres. A suit was filed to block the purchase on grounds relating to religion, but the university won the ruling in the Missouri Supreme Court. Around this time, local leaders had formed St. Louis Research Council (RC) and St. Louis Regional Industrial Development Corporation (RIDC); Father Reinert was among the "pioneers" serving on these groups, which developed the east-west corridor of the city. In the late 1950s and early 1960s, SLU expanded its science education and research on the land it had purchased in MCV, supported by millions of dollars of federal funds and private donations. Supporters included Monsanto, Emerson, the National Science Foundation (NSF), and SLU's Development Council. These and other organiza-

tions anchored the science-based industrial sector of St. Louis.[35]

Yet, the relocation of over 4,000 families and 1,300 individuals from MCV was bungled by local government agencies, troubling Reinert and others. Black citizens bore the brunt of urban renewal projects in St. Louis, and did not benefit from the anticipated new jobs. Indeed, the city continued to lose industrial jobs regardless of its efforts, in part due to competition from the suburbs, but also because of the wider trend of industrial relocations to the Sun Belt. The campus was named after Frost in 1965. A nearby statue of his old rival, pro-Union Nathaniel Lyon (see Chapter 2) had been moved in 1960 to Lyon Park, across town.

Scholars who have researched American urban life in order to improve public policy and planning include SLU's Dr. George Wendel. Termed a "visionary" and even a "legend," Wendel joined the Political Science Department in 1956. He founded the university's Center for Urban Programs in 1968, serving as its director until 1992. The center's 1971 proposal for consolidation of services led to the city's creation of the Community Development Agency, which exists to this day.[36] Wendel gained national renown for his extensive studies of urbanization, but was also known as an excellent teacher and engaging story-teller. His research topics included governance, public health, and poverty, among other issues, in St. Louis, Detroit, and Philadelphia.

In 1968, SLU held a conference "Toward an Understanding of Campus Community" as part of its 150th anniversary celebrations. One goal was assuaging the fears of local business people, whom Father Reinert later observed were worried about their profits in the light of "urban problems."[37] He sought a way to change perceptions so that people could understand racial and economic injustice in the United States. Father Reinert made a choice to stay in the city of St. Louis. He completed a necessary purchase, gaining space for a major expansion. He sincerely believed in the promise of urban renewal; Father Reinert maintained a space for thought on an urban site, and that may be enough of a legacy in itself.

Researcher of urban planning, Dr. George Wendel, describes Father Reinert's idea for a "New Town in the City." (*Archive* 1976)

This image of a bus is from SLU's 1974 yearbook. The Falstaff beer advertisement on its side reads: "Because we are all in this together."

This iconic photograph of Father Paul Reinert, S.J. addressing a group of student protesters in 1970, was taken on the front steps of Cupples House. The ROTC office was in Cupples (then called Chouteau House) and students who opposed the war in Vietnam demanded its removal. Father Reinert resolved the protest with a peaceful approach.

STUDENT PROTESTS

In March 1951, Father Reinert announced that participation in the Air Force Reserve Officers' Training Corps (ROTC) program or some other form of military training would be required of all male freshmen who entered the university. The United States engaged in the Korean War from June 25, 1950 to July 27, 1953. SLU's plan was for students to render service during "this emergency period" for two years. In 1968, when Reinert reflected to an audience about the "student power" movement, he demonstrated a clear grasp of student perspectives on peace in Vietnam, racial justice, and an end to the inequities in the draft law. In 1970, protesters led by

student body president Michael Forster gathered at Chouteau House (now called Cupples House) to protest the presence of the ROTC office in the building. When Father Reinert arrived to address the militant group, they parted to form a path for him, and the meeting ended with peaceful compromise.

That demonstration was just one of many protests across the United States against American involvement in the Vietnam War. Although other protests in the nation and city had generated property damage and violence, Reinert staved off such action at SLU. He agreed to move ROTC to another building, but refused to penalize SLU's ROTC students in any way.[38] In another protest, the

Association of Black Collegians occupied a SLU dean's office for eleven hours. Reinert listened, and took actions to address civil rights demands and educational access for disadvantaged persons. In 1969, he addressed a group on the need for teaching styles that would be relevant to a student from the "ghetto," in an early form of the movement for inclusiveness and diversity.

Another of Reinert's enduring contributions to the university was to advocate for service as part of a university's educational role in a community. While he did remark in one interview that "a university should not be a soup kitchen," he also valued "service as intrinsic to the mission of a Jesuit university."[39]

"MAKING A WORLD THAT IS MORE HUMAN AND MORE DIVINE."

FATHER LEO WEBER, S.J., 1978[40]

In October 1957, the university's trustees discussed a looming deficit, as they sought to pay for a new boiler and heating plant. Father Reinert told the group that he had hoped to "establish a principle of adjusting faculty salaries before spending money for physical facilities."[41] Such an ideal was difficult to maintain, as challenges continued. In 1967, the board decided to close SLU's Dental School. However, the orthodontics section was preserved and remains now as the Center for Advanced Dental Education in Dreiling-Marshall Hall (see Chapter 6). Kenneth Marshall, D.D.S., who had been hired to lead SLU's orthodontia program in 1947, rallied support from loyal alumni to ensure its survival. In 1968, Father Reinert changed the Institute of Geophysical Technology to the School of Engineering and Earth Science, which was ultimately combined with other programs to become Parks College of Engineering, Aviation and Technology.

In 1972, SLU's hospital made history as the site of the first heart transplant in the Midwest. And indeed, successes continued, yet the presidents who followed Father Reinert also faced fiscal challenges. In 1974, Father Daniel O'Connell, S.J. was appointed as president, accepting the post with some reluctance. He eschewed pomp; in 1966, he said in an interview that he would be satisfied as a "happy hod-carrier."[42] Born in 1929, O'Connell joined the Society of Jesus in 1945, earned his bachelor's and master's degrees at SLU, and his Ph.D. at the University of Illinois, Urbana. A professor of psychology at SLU, O'Connell published widely in psycholinguistics.

The School of Divinity had several iterations in the nineteenth century (see page 50), but when it returned to St. Louis after being located for over forty years at St. Mary's in Kansas, problems developed. Father O'Connell closed it, and some of its faculty joined the Department of Theological Studies in 1975.[43] As noted, O'Connell had not sought to be president; he stepped down in 1978. Also in that year, SLU researchers led by Duane Grandgenett, Ph.D., professor at SLU's Institute for Molecular Virology, discovered integrase, the basis of the class of drugs that now treats HIV.

In 1979 the university appointed Father Edward Drummond, S.J. as president. A highly capable administrator who was also active in national higher education, Drummond had served eleven years as vice president of SLU's medical center, among other roles. He was born in 1906, entered the Society of Jesus in 1924, and was ordained in 1937. In 1942, he received his Ph.D. in English from the

Dr. Martin Luther King, Jr. spoke about the power of "agape" (creative, redemptive love) at SLU in 1964.

Friday, October 16, 1964   THE UNIVERSITY NEWS

"We Shall Overcome"

Long Way To Go

Doctor King Says Much Work Still Needed In Civil Right

By MAUREEN CLEARY

Speaking before a standing room only crowd at the University gymnasium, the Rev. Dr. Martin Luther King stated that there are three basic attitudes toward the question of progress in the area of race relations: extreme optimism, extreme pessimism and realism. Announcing his topic as "The Future of Integration" Dr. King stated adherents to the first two positions agree on one point: both are convinced that "we should sit down and do nothing.

"However," he said, "the realistic position admits that we have come a long, long way; but, we have a long, long way to go before this problem is solved."

Not only has the attitude of the white people toward the Negro changed but Dr. King pointed out that "the Negro himself has come a long, long way in reevaluating his own intrinsic worth. Slavery's greatest damage to the Negro was inflicted on the soul and mind. It ended up giving the segregated a false sense of inferiority." But this atitude has changed. A new Negro has come into being with a new sense of dignity and a new sense of self respect."

The nation, too, has come a long way: "in our age we have seen the walls of racial segregation crumble . . . I have no doubt

are 500,000 eligible yet only 23,000 registered to vote.

Concerning legislation Dr. King noted that, "While the law can change the hearts of men, it does change the habits; and, in time habits change atitudes."

In the context of the three Greek words for love: eros, philein, and agape, Dr. King stressed his own belief that non-violence is a strong method to use in gaining integration. Agape is the love which inspires the non-violence approach. It is "understanding, creative, redemptive good will toward men . . . It rises to the point of loving the person who does the deed while hating the deed." Going on in an impassiond way, he said "You may beat us until we're half dead . . . charge that we are not intellectually and culturally

Pi Lambda Theta is one of the many honor societies at SLU which recognize excellent students. Pi Lambda Theta is for graduate students in education; its name was later changed to Lambda Pi Eta. Members in May 1969 included the women below.

Dorothy Pillman

SLU's first modern residence hall for women was open in 1956, named after Marguerite of Provence, who was the wife of Saint Louis of France.

Alice W. Smith

University of Iowa. He established a historical archive at SLU, and directed the renovation of Fusz Memorial Pavilion, which at the time housed the College of Philosophy and Letters. This college, founded in 1889, originally provided philosophy training for Jesuits and now prepares Catholic priests generally in philosophy. Marking the 160th celebration of SLU's founding, Father Drummond told an audience that the university's goals were unchanged since its early days. He quoted Father Leo Weber, S.J., who had summarized those goals as: "Making a world that is more human and more divine." Even amidst fiscal challenges, this important ideal prevailed.

Loren M. Williams

CHAPTER 6

"Our campus is the community."

1979-2018

The story of Saint Louis University has never been simply a tale of pioneer missionaries, bookish presidents, or the construction of new buildings. But in contemporary times, the complexity of the university seems especially striking. Ideas and action flourish in countless ways, across campuses. SLU's mission statement remains compelling: the pursuit of truth for the greater glory of God and for the service of humanity. It is taken to heart by students, staff, clinicians, and faculty.

There were many important milestones in this period. For example, in 1994, SLU was designated as a Research II institution by the Carnegie Commission on Higher Education. Alongside fame and distinction, everyday stories are lived out in celebrations, awards, and ministry; in scholarship, teaching, and research; in service projects and partnerships locally and abroad.

As this period began, Father Paul Reinert, S.J. remained in a significant role as chancellor of Saint Louis University. He devoted himself to projects including the revival of Midtown, a neighborhood in St. Louis known for arts and culture. Major physical change was driven by Father Thomas Fitzgerald, S.J., who served as president from 1979 to 1987, and by Father Lawrence Biondi, S.J., who served from 1987 to 2013. In an historic shift, SLU appointed its first-ever permanent lay president, Dr. Fred Pestello, in 2014.

As this period ends, many resources and perspectives contribute to visions of the future. The university's oldest schools and colleges are, appropriately, derived from classical arrangements of higher education: Arts and Sciences; Law; Medicine; and the College of Philosophy and Letters. The university's various lecture series for adults in a sense anticipated today's School for Professional Studies. During the twentieth century, a campus in Madrid and new colleges and departments expanded offerings: aviation science, business, education, engineering, nursing and allied health professions, social work, and technology. In time, the College for Public Health and Social Justice, and the Center for Health Outcomes Research, have developed. Each expansion would have been a great joy to Father Rogers, S.J., who dreamed of Saint Louis University as an institution that would be "useful," one "to which all might point with pride."

This gathering of SLU's Graduate Student Association (circa 1990) includes Julie Saker (at left in white shirt), then dean of student development, and Sandra Norman, director of the community service department (behind woman with folder). Student-run diversity programs in this period included a group called S.T.A.R.T. (Students Together Against Racial Tension, a name borrowed from Northwestern University).

FATHER JOHN KAVANAUGH, S.J.

In the nineteenth century, the university's leaders and teachers sought to promote "virtue and science" among students. How to articulate such goals in new times? Father Edward Drummond, S.J. saw SLU's identity: "In the witness given to our Jesuit traditions and values … in our belief that we have a common father who gives persons a radical worth. It's that kind of value that makes the human person important."[2] He hoped to encourage students: "to undertake some risks as well as trusts; to involve themselves for the good of others." Drummond stepped down as president in August 1979, as Father Thomas Fitzgerald, S.J. was appointed president. That winter, SLU's first-ever lay chairman of the board of trustees, Daniel Schlafly, resigned after twelve years. He hoped the Jesuits would always stay in "the education business," noting in an interview at the time: "I can't begin to tell you what it's meant for me to work with these men over the years … I never saw one who wasn't superbly trained for his, and the Society's, educational mission."[3] Superb training, the common good, God's gift of each person's radical worth: these phrases can shed light on the aspirations of subsequent decades.

Many undergraduate students' experiences are shaped by faculty members in the Department of Theology (known as the Religion Department until 1964). Although the 1975 closure of the Divinity School was difficult, some of its faculty members joined the Theological Studies Department, which also in this period benefited from thoughtful leaders and reforms. When Woodstock Theological Jesuit Seminary closed, SLU's Department of Theological Studies took on increased prominence locally and nationally. William Shea, a former priest with a Ph.D. from Columbia University, chaired the department from 1991 to 2005. He implemented important administrative reforms, recruited many new faculty members, and strengthened graduate programs. Father J.J. Mueller, S.J. (chair from 1997-2003) provided a genial balance, emphasizing undergraduates. In 2007, he published a widely admired introductory

textbook: *Theological Foundations.* Father J. A. Wayne Hellmann, O.F.M. (2002 to 2011) expanded the faculty cohort and its research profile.[4]

Reaching beyond the classroom, Father Frank Cleary, S.J. of the Theology Department wrote popular articles in the *St. Louis Review,* a weekly Catholic newspaper, together with Father John Kavanaugh, S.J., who came to SLU's Department of Philosophy in 1974. In 2003, Kavanaugh won the Best Regular Column Award from the National Catholic Press Association for his "Ethics Notebook," a feature in *America Magazine.* His 1981 book, *Following Christ in a Consumer Society,* is a powerful argument for human dignity. A more recent example of outreach is the degree program created in 2007 at the Correctional Center in Bonne Terre, Missouri by theology professor Dr. Kenneth Parker. Father Hellmann was supportive of Parker's project, which enables men who are incarcerated, as well as their guards (in separate courses), to engage questions such as: "How does humanity encounter the divine?" As Parker notes: "It really was about reclaiming their humanity."[5] The program is now run by Dr. Mary Gould and others.

In this period, the College of Arts and Sciences continued to offer and expand its programs in social, behavioral, and physical sciences. Its departments include history, mathematics, and computer science. At the same time, interdisciplinarity is cultivated in endeavors such as the Center for Medieval and Renaissance Studies and the Center for Digital Humanities. The School of Education has done yeoman service in training teachers and administrators who serve in the region. Meanwhile, research in the biological and physical sciences has produced many significant contributions, including the pioneering work with Cyberknife radiation surgery, a more precise way to treat cancer. SLU installed this technology in 2004, with the efforts of Doctors Richard Bucholz, Bruce Walz, and John Dombrowski. Other contributions include: Dr. Shelley Minteer's work on biofuel cells, Dr. Richard Mayden's research on biodiversity, and Dr. William Sly's work in the field of molecular genetics.

Dr. Eleonore Stump joined SLU's Philosophy Department in 1992. Her 2010 work, *Wandering in Darkness: Narrative and the Problem of Suffering,* asks: in the face of the heart-breaking suffering we see all around us, where is God?

Stump considers this question with the help of the thought of Thomas Aquinas and with a detailed look at stories in the Bible about human suffering. Stump's logic forms a natural fit with the line of reasoning developed by Father Kavanaugh, with both scholars tending toward an emphasis on love and hope. Stump suggests that we can move away from alienation, "willed loneliness," and shame by integrating ourselves around the common good. Kavanaugh sees, in alienation caused by capitalist modes and in the brokenness caused by evil and suffering, a path to love: "It is no shame to be a frail and contingent human being. In fact, it is priceless to be so. It is, necessarily, to be loved into existence."[6]

Together, Stump and Kavanaugh founded the Alexandrian Society at SLU: a community of faculty and students that gathered regularly for years for prayer and theological discussion. Stump has also partnered with Father John Foley, S.J., Distinguished Liturgical Scholar in the Theology Department and past director of SLU's Center for Liturgy, to develop a course called "Beauty as a Road to God." Stump is coordinator for Foley's internationally read Saint Louis University Sunday Web Site (liturgy.slu.edu), for which she writes a weekly column on the Sunday Mass readings. Father Foley is a founding member of the St. Louis Jesuits. In the late 1960s, a group of Jesuits in training for ordination were living at Fusz Memorial Hall. When new liturgical directives emerged from Vatican II, this group of Jesuits began to compose music based on the psalms and Gospels, and singing at Sunday Mass in the Fusz chapel. Their music gained international fame, and is still sung around the world today, including at the 9:00 p.m. Sunday Mass at College Church—the "student Mass"—sung by the Mass choir.

In 1982, Father Walter Ong, S.J. published *Orality and Literacy.* It is only one of his hundreds of publications, but is the most often acclaimed as a "classic." Ong, Stump, Foley, and Kavanaugh are among the many faculty members who have sustained the powerful culture of intellectual inquiry, community, and love at Saint Louis University. While that culture may not entirely explain why so many people devote their lives and careers over so many decades at SLU, it certainly must be reckoned as a factor.

Dr. Eleonore Stump is a world-renowned philosopher who has been Robert J. Henle Professor of Philosophy at Saint Louis University since 1992.

The original St. Louis Jesuits were from left: John Foley, Bob Dufford, Dan Schutte, Roc O'Connor, and Tim Manion.

Saint Louis University's early history includes various forays into graduate studies, including the "post-graduate" lectures (see Chapter 3). As Provincial, Father Meyer established the scholasticate at the university in the late nineteenth century and encouraged young Jesuits to pursue graduate degrees.[7] Although graduae degrees were conferred as early as 1834 at the university, a formal graduate studies structure at SLU dates to 1925 and the appointment of Father Alphonse Schwitalla, S.J. as first "acting dean" of the graduate school. Schwitalla was a national leader in this domain, advising on the evaluation of graduate programs. In 1927, he read the first formal paper on graduate education ever presented at a meeting of the National Catholic Educational Association. He also chaired an NCEA data-gathering committee, reporting its findings in 1928. In part due to his efforts, SLU was recognized as "a leader in the field" in graduate studies.[8] When Schwitalla became dean of SLU's medical school in 1927 (see Chapter 4), Father James Macelwane, S.J. became the first full-time dean of the graduate school. Macelwane was appointed to head a committee to study reforms in Jesuit higher education (on the Macelwane Report, see Chapter 4). He served as graduate dean at SLU until the appointment of Thurber Montgomery Smith, S.J. in 1933. These three men established a rigorous culture for SLU's graduate programs.[9]

In 1950, Father Robert Henle, S.J. became dean of SLU's graduate school. He also served as dean of the College of Philosophy and Letters, and in 1959, he was appointed university research administrator. Six years later he was made vice president for academic affairs (see also Chapter 5). In 1955, Henle wrote: "the university is, in our culture, the one institution that is formally dedicated to truth as such; that is, to intellectual knowledge, to its extension and development, to its preservation and communication ... there is no other."[10] Trustee minutes and other sources document that Henle frequently articulated this special role. Henle saw the graduate dean as "a kind of administrative maverick" who must ensure that students understand research as "the intellectual mode of discovery in their field."[11] His progressive approach also had an impact at SLU in dentistry, nursing, and hospital administration.

Student humor in this 1951 April Fool's Day edition suggests that Thomism has been rejected by the faculty.

The **University News**

APRIL FOOL EDITION

"NEWSPAPER"

VOL. XXX   ST. LOUIS U., ST. LOUIS, MO., FRIDAY, MARCH 30, 1951   No. 20

ROTC Disbanded, Big Fraud Bared

Philosophy Dept. Rejects Thomism After Beer Brawl

By JOHN WHEALEN

The Department of Philosophy today announced it had rejected the teaching of St. Thomas Aquinas and would henceforth confine itself to doing scholarly work on the writings of Bertrand Russell and Immanuel Kant with a view to producing a synthesis in fifty or sixty years. The decision came after what one of the members of the department described as "one of the most hectic meetings to which my Id has ever been submitted."

What looks to be one of the most revolutionary about-faces in the history of the University actually began in the most casual manner, the regular monthly meeting of the department faculty last Monday evening at 11 o'clock. (The usual subject-matter of these meetings deals with such prosaic subjects as "Ten easy ways to make philosophy harder," and "How to get philosophers recognized as members of the human race.")

After the regular business of the meeting was concluded, during which time "great quantities of beer were changed from potency to act," the Rev. William L. Wade, formerly head of the department, casually mentioned to a subordi-

Finds Parking Space

No Military Ball

Due to the putrefaction of the AF ROTC, the Military Ball scheduled for this evening has been cancelled. Instead, a tacky party sponsored by the revamped Arnold Society will be held at Union Station preparatory for the ex-cadets' departure for boot camp. The Arnold Society has been renamed after Benedict Arnold, the famous American traitor. Girls recently elected by the society to serve as honorary officers at the ball are asked to stay home and knit socks for the new inductees.

No Testimony From Law Teacher Until He Gets Lawyer

Special to the University News

WASHINGTON, Mar. 29, (PU)—A law professor from St. Louis, Missouri, today refused to answer key questions at the Kefauver Crime Hearings here until he could get a lawyer.

The tight-lipped, tough-talking man was Richard J. Childress, assistant professor of Law at St. Louis University. Childress pro-

611 Cadets Drafted; FBI Jails Three

Mass arrests and widespread confusion gripped the campus early yesterday afternoon as officers of the Federal Bureau of Investigation revealed the University Air Force Reserve Officers Training Corps as a "magnificent hoax." Intelligence officers of the Army Air Force and the *University News* aided in the investigation. The group simultaneously disbanded and 611 "cadets," victims of the hoax, were notified of their immediate induction as privates in the Army infantry.

"Major" Aubrey (Light-finger) Bouck and his cohorts "Major" Robert E. (Greasy-Thumb) Whaley and "Captain" H. Allen Graham, alias "Sugar-Ray" Graham, alias Ma Perkins, alias Julius Caesar, were taken into custody while counting their "ill-gotten gains" in the AF ROTC vault in their headquarters on West Pine.

The arrests were not made without a fight. Leaping out of five armored cars and two helicopters, FBI officers bombarded the office with napalm, jet rockets, hand grenades and cafeteria hamburgers. Bouck, Whaley and Graham, however, could not return the fire

This image of St. Thomas Aquinas writing is from a 1734 work, published in Dillingen an der Donau (Germany). Its bookplate and accession number indicate that it has been in SLU's library for over one hundred years. It is now in the special collection of rare books. Its title is: *"Pietas quotidiana erga divinissimum humani generis redemptorem fidei authorem salutis consummatorem Jesum crucifixum ..."* which is best understood as: "Daily devotions honoring the most divine redeemer of the human race, the author of faith, and the completer of salvation, Jesus crucified," and the author is Franz J. Molindes, S.J.

By the 1950s, SLU was known nationally for the excellence of its geophysics department, and its neo-scholastic philosophy department.[12] This was significant; many in American Jesuit higher education had been alarmed in the 1930s, sensing that they were being eclipsed in academic excellence by well-funded, secular research universities.[13] The Society of Jesus had worked hard in the intervening decades to raise standards.

In 1964, SLU appointed its first-ever lay dean of the graduate school: Dr. Harold Howe. Another notable graduate school dean was Donald Brennan, who was born in 1945, studied communication disorders at SLU, and earned his Ph.D. at the University of Oklahoma Medical Center. He returned to SLU in 1957 and soon moved into leadership roles; as dean of graduate studies, Brennan promoted Jesuit values and in particular, advocated for multicultural education.

In 1995, Philip Gleason suggested that Catholic colleges and universities must forge a vision that will provide, as neo-scholasticism had, "a theoretical rationale for the existence of Catholic colleges and universities as a distinctive element of American higher education."[14] The full story of that developing vision will include Saint Louis University. Its programs in medieval philosophy and the philosophy of religion rank among the best in the United States and in the world. A painfully brief summary of the Philosophy Department's history can only hint at reasons for this success. After World War I, neo-Thomism grew in influence in the United States and Europe. This movement stemmed from new understandings of Aquinas, explored by Étienne Gilson and Jacques Maritain, among others.

Father William Wade, S.J. was born in 1907, entered the Society of Jesus in 1924, earned his doctorate in philosophy at SLU, and was chair of the philosophy department from 1943 to 1966. He was a wonderful, if challenging and even eccentric teacher, and is the subject of many amusing stories in Father James Meara, S.J.'s *For the Sake of Argument.* A reviewer noted: "Alumni of the University, even those he flunked, would not attempt to improve on the title."[15] Wade recruited impressive faculty members, including James Collins, who was born in 1917 in Holyoke, Massachusetts, earned his bachelor's, master's, and doctoral degrees at Catholic University, and became an instructor at SLU in 1945. Collins published fourteen books and also served as chair of the department of philosophy for twenty years. Some of the new SLU faculty had studied under Gilson at the University of Toronto. Father Henle, George Klubertanz, S.J., Leonard Eslick, Linus Thro, S.J., and Vernon Bourke were among the luminaries of the philosophy department who developed "Missouri Valley Thomism." The department of philosophy is now entering a new "post-Wade" phase, according to Father Theodore Vitali, C.P. In 2017, Vitali resigned as chair after twenty-eight years. He observes: "I wanted the department to reflect and be an active member of the mainstream of philosophy as practiced in America today, while retaining and advancing our Catholic intellectual heritage and tradition." Vitali predicts the department "will continue to engage the great Catholic questions: God's existence, freedom, and morality."[16]

WILLIAM WADE, S.J.

GEORGE KLUBERTANZ, S.J.

JAMES COLLINS

DONALD BRENNAN

Father Thomas Fitzgerald, S.J., at left, shakes hands with Father Thomas Lay, S.J. The steeple of College Church is visible, under scaffolding, in the background.

"IT LOOKED FOR ALL THE WORLD LIKE A PRISON YARD."
MAURICE MCNAMEE, S.J., 2001[17]

It is only in the past forty years or so that major physical changes have taken place across all of Saint Louis University's campuses. In 1927, a young novice named Maurice McNamee arrived in St. Louis to begin his training as a Jesuit. Of the "grim-looking institution" with its soot-blackened buildings and quadrangle enclosed by a high cement wall, he wrote: "There was no semblance of a campus, no grass, no trees." By 1947, the first student dormitory had been built, but students were still ironically commenting "Now if only we had some grass." (see Chapter 4). It is a very recent phenomenon that the campus has become a place of natural beauty. Three presidents are particularly notable for their efforts in this regard: Father Paul Reinert, S.J., Father Thomas Fitzgerald, S.J., and Father Lawrence Biondi, S.J. Father Reinert, discussed in Chapter 5, laid the foundation for future development. Father Reinert was followed by Father Thomas Fitzgerald, S.J.,

who served as the 30th president of Saint Louis University from 1979 to 1987. Like Father Reinert, he was considered "a students' president." Father Fitzgerald, nicknamed "Fitz," was born in 1922, entered the Society of Jesus in 1939, and was ordained at Louvain in 1952. He earned his doctorate in classical languages at the University of Chicago. Over the course of his career, he held administrative roles at Georgetown University, was president of Fairfield University, and taught at Loyola University Maryland.

Father Fitzgerald strongly valued sound fiscal management. The endowment increased under his watch: from $57 million in 1977 to $90 million in 1987. Despite tight budgetary limits, Father Fitzgerald achieved his original, extensive goals, including the renovation and expansion of the hospital.[18] He oversaw the construction of Morrissey Hall for the law school, where enrollment had increased exponentially. From a graduating class in 1965 numbering about sixty persons; a class of three hundred students was enrolled a few years later. The law school administrators eventually settled on a level of about two hundred students as an optimal class size.[19]

Father Fitzgerald also managed the expansion of Pius XII Library, renovations of the business and aviation schools, campus-wide improvements to computer systems, the creation of new laboratories for the medical school, and the development of the Simon Recreation Center. When he worked with the city to close West Pine Street from Grand to Spring, he created a new sense of intimacy on the campus. Father Fitzgerald was forced to make some painful cuts to academic programs, but his contribution overall was to stabilize operations.

Father Barry McGannon, S.J. was a successful administrator and fund-raiser in this period at SLU. McGannon was born in Humboldt, Kansas in 1924, entered the Society of Jesus in 1942, and was ordained in 1955. At first, he did not expect to succeed in development, but his efforts nearly doubled the university's endowment. Father Jerome Marchetti, S.J. was another key figure. Born in Osage, Kansas in 1916, he entered the Society of Jesus in 1935. He earned his doctorate at the University of Minnesota. He was dean of the College of Arts and Sciences at SLU from 1953 to 1955, then executive vice president from 1958 to 1972 and secretary treasurer from 1972 to 1982. Serving as executive vice president while Father Padberg was academic vice president, during a time of great challenge in the late 1960s and early 1970s, Marchetti helped to provide organizational stability and a clear sense of purpose.

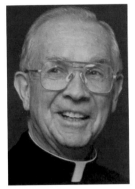

FATHER BARRY
McGANNON, S.J.

FATHER JEROME
MARCHETTI, S.J.

Thanks to Father Thomas Fitzgerald, S.J., the law school found a home in Morrissey Hall for its greatly increased enrollment. SLU's law school was in Morrissey Hall from 1980 to 2013, when it moved to Scott Hall in downtown St. Louis. [BELOW] A fountain graces the courtyard near Morrissey Hall and Queen's Daughters Hall.

[BELOW] Clemens Hall was built in 1947, and served as the first residence hall ever built on the Grand and Lindell campus. It is shown here in 1957 facing West Pine Street. Father Fitzgerald arranged for West Pine Street to be closed to traffic from Grand to Spring, beginning to create a central, pedestrian corridor through the campus. In the background of the 2007 photograph [LEFT] Griesedieck Hall, opened in 1963, towers over Clemens.

While still president of Saint Louis University, Father Paul Reinert, S.J. was urged by his lay advisors to move the north campus out of the city of St. Louis. He calmly resisted this counsel. He later described the decision to stay in the city as: "an altruistic and sincere effort by [the university] to establish ourselves as a community-based institution, with our interests not only in the University, but in Midtown … The area from Union Station to Forest Park could have become a no-man's land. We were the only major institution that chose to stay—and to stay not as a walled city, but as one working to revitalize the whole community, for our mutual benefit."[20] (For more details, see Chapter 5). In 1971, Father Reinert's vision was this: "A time, a place will emerge where residents of the city and students at the University will more likely be one and the same … where young and old, black and white will no longer form 'academic' and 'outside' communities, but one learning society."[21]

When Father Reinert stepped down as president in 1974, he continued to pursue this aim of community development. As chancellor, he promoted the revival of Midtown's theater district by establishing the Grand Center arts district with Leon Strauss and Stanley Goodman. He applied to the Federal Communications Commission for a license for an educational television station, working with physicist Arthur Holly Compton, who was chancellor of Washington University from 1946 to 1954. The project required extensive and challenging negotiations across all of the stakeholders of the region, but the outcome was worthwhile—the public broadcasting station Channel 9 (KETC). Reinert also helped to raise money for the new station's building, which opened in 1998 in Grand Center. His national and international activity continued, as well. He was part of a group which conducted a fact-finding mission to El Salvador in 1982, and he advocated against United States-sponsored political violence taking place in Central America.[22]

The once-popular arts district of Grand Boulevard is shown here in 1940, before it fell into relative decline. Father Reinert was determined to revive it. In subsequent years, Father Biondi continued these efforts, for example supporting the renovation of the iconic Continental Life building.

Dr. Kim was first to be honored as Paul G. Lorenzini Endowed Professor of International Business. He came to SLU in 1970, and is a highly accomplished scholar and visionary leader.

Dr. Ellen Harshman came to SLU in 1972, and has both taught and served in administrative posts. Appointed in 2003 as the first woman to serve as dean of the business school, Harshman initiated an annual service day open to all Cook School students, alumni, faculty, and staff.

The impact of remaining in the city of St. Louis could be the subject of extensive analysis for each of SLU's colleges and divisions. Both through its programs and its people, the business school cultivates local entrepreneurship, responsible business practices, and global connections which both advance knowledge and support the region. In 1984, Dr. Seung Hee Kim of the Finance Department was appointed to head SLU's first Institute of International Business. Among his many professional activities, he was the founding chairman of the World Trade Center of St. Louis board of directors from 1998 to 2000. He was appointed by the U.S. Secretary of Commerce to the Missouri District Export Council, and the Governor of Missouri appointed him as the founding chair of the Missouri Leadership Council. Relationships with campuses abroad have developed through the Institute, on SLU's Madrid campus as well as in France and Japan. In 1997 it was renamed as the Boeing Institute of International Business.

In 1987, Dr. Robert Brockhaus began the Institute for Entrepreneurial Studies at SLU, drawing national recognition. In 1990, it was renamed the Jefferson Smurfit Center for Entrepreneurial Studies. Now known as the Center for Entrepreneurship, it is directed by Dr. Jerry Katz and Tim Hayden. Its undergraduate and graduate degree programs are consistently highly ranked in the nation. A gift from alumnus John Cook led to the construction of a stunning addition: John and Lucy Cook Hall.

Dr. Ellen Harshman has emphasized the university's mission at the business school, for example, initiating mission liaison as a permanent faculty role. As associate dean, she founded the Service Leadership certificate program, through which undergraduate students direct their business skills to nonprofits serving people of low income. During her tenure as dean, the school advanced in national and international recognition for programs at the undergraduate and master's levels. Harshman also fostered innovative formats including the one-year MBA, and other programs responding to market demands and student and employer needs.

As an undergraduate student at SLU, Dr. Richard Chaifetz (A&S '75) struggled with tuition. Father Reinert enabled him to remain; as Chaifetz noted in a 2007 *Universitas* interview: "Father Reinert told me he believed in me." Chaifetz vowed to find a way to express his gratitude, and he did so with a $12 million gift to name Chaifetz Arena. The arena opened in 2008; it is home to Billiken basketball and is also used as an entertainment venue.

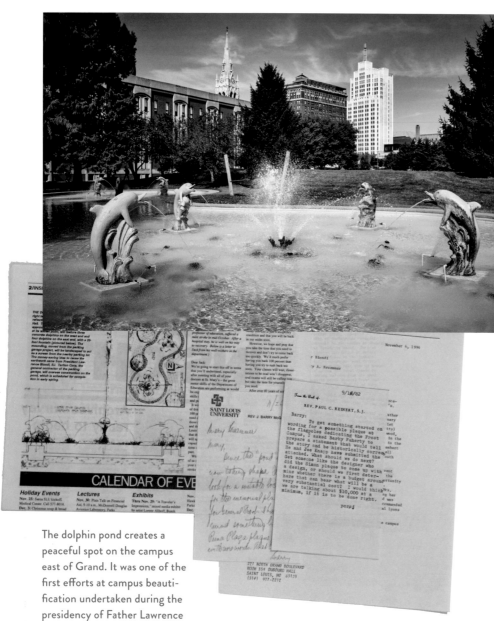

The dolphin pond creates a peaceful spot on the campus east of Grand. It was one of the first efforts at campus beautification undertaken during the presidency of Father Lawrence Biondi, S.J. Correspondence about its construction is shown above.

Inaugurated as president in September 1987, Father Lawrence Biondi, S.J. was also a driving force in campus transformation. Over a period of twenty-six years as president, Father Biondi directed truly spectacular improvements across all of SLU's campuses.

Father Biondi was born in Chicago in 1938, and recalled in a 2007 interview that he flunked first grade because he grew up speaking Italian. His humble background notwithstanding, he was to have a long, remarkable career at Saint Louis University.

Biondi entered the Society of Jesus at age nineteen, was ordained in 1970, and earned his doctorate in sociolinguistics at Georgetown University. He taught at Loyola Chicago, and held several roles in higher education administration before coming to St. Louis. Determined to make Saint Louis University the finest Catholic university in the country, he led the university to numerous milestones and achievements, including the designation in 1994 of SLU as a Research II institution in the Carnegie ratings. He also led important, sweeping projects such as: The University's Plan for the 1990s, SLU 2000, and the Presidential Research Fund. A team of excellent faculty members and administrators: Gregory Beabout; Robert Belshe; Donald Brennan; Father Michael Garanzini, S.J.; Sandra Johnson; and Father Walter Ong, S.J., were among those who helped to implement the University's Plan for the 1990s. It supported the core curriculum, attracted high-achieving faculty and students, and greatly raised the reputation of SLU nationally.

"I WAS ONE OF THOSE KIDS IN THE SHADOWS."

FATHER LAWRENCE BIONDI, S.J., 2007

After his investiture and speech in 1987, President Biondi is welcomed with applause. Seated next to him are William Bush, president of SLU's board of trustees (left) and St. Louis Auxiliary Bishop Edward F. O'Donnell.

Father Lawrence Biondi, S.J. marches with actor Martin Sheen during a 2000 protest held at the School of the Americas. Eleven members of the SLU group were arrested and detained, including Father Biondi.

[LEFT] Scott Hall in downtown St. Louis, renovated by the university, became the new home for the law school in 2013. The building was a gift to the university from Joseph and Loretta Scott. The original building was worth $17 million, and SLU invested $30 million into its renovation.

"FATHER BIONDI BROUGHT ALL OF HIS CAPABILITIES THROUGH THE JESUITS INTO SAINT LOUIS UNIVERSITY; HE PRESENTED AN OPPORTUNITY TO TAKE A WIDER PERSPECTIVE THAT WAS RESPONSIBLE TO THE CATHOLIC CHURCH AND THAT WORKED THROUGH THE UNIVERSITY MISSION."

FORMER TRUSTEE AL LITTEKEN, 2017

Father Biondi in his office with his two golden retrievers, Gancia (at left) and Iggy.

[RIGHT] Ranked fourth among "the most amazing college museums" in the United States, Saint Louis University Museum of Art is housed in a 1900, Beaux Arts-style building that was originally home to the St. Louis Club. Father Biondi was key to the purchase and renovation of the building.

It is easy to be dazzled by the sheer numbers and span of achievements associated with Father Biondi. As president, he ran three successful capital campaigns, raising millions of dollars in 1989, 1997, and 2009. His actions generated an upgrade in the university's credit rating and increased the endowment from $90 million in 1987 to $1 billion in September 2013, placing SLU among the nation's top Catholic universities (in terms of endowment) after Notre Dame, Boston College, and Georgetown. Enrollment in 2013 was the fourth highest of all 234 Catholic universities and colleges in the United States.[23] Yet, four years after his retirement, Father Biondi still wishes he had achieved two of his dreams: a program in "ethics across the curriculum" for both undergraduate and graduate students, and a program in "writing across the curriculum," incorporating public speaking and logic, similar to the one he began at Loyola University in Chicago.

In 1966, SLU's Jesuit trustees considered requiring that "professional scholars" serve on the board.[24] At the same time, the university's leaders have always recognized that it was important to collaborate with people in business fields. Father Biondi understood this balance. Under his watch, the number of doctorates awarded at Saint Louis University (Ph.D., M.D., J.D.) more than doubled. He increased the number of endowed chairs and named professorships, established new scholarships, and greatly increased financial aid. Meanwhile, as quantifiable measures were increasingly demanded of institutions of higher education, he hired an outside firm to

Workers prepare to lift the distinctive fleur-de-lis to its place atop the Doisy Research Center.

examine SLU's regional presence. They found that, in 2011, SLU created $715.5 million in economic impact and sustained more than 6,800 jobs in the St. Louis metropolitan region. In the city of St. Louis alone that year, spending from SLU operations, employees, students, and visitors generated $12.4 million in government revenue. The university's employees and students donated over $26 million in cash and over one million volunteer service hours to over 1,800 organizations and individuals.[25]

Father Biondi dreamed big: for example, he took actions that more than doubled the number of SLU-owned buildings and acres in Midtown St. Louis. In 2005, he was honored as "Citizen of the Year" by the *St. Louis Post-Dispatch,* as his "determination, energy, and vision" were heralded. In a city with an abundance of architectural treasures, the $82 million Edward A. Doisy Research Center, dedicated in 2007, is a stunning addition to the urban landscape. The largest building on SLU's campus, it houses research that complements the Cortex Innovation Community, a 200-acre project supporting bioscience and technology research. SLU is a founding member of Cortex. Father Biondi also directed renovations at the John Cook School of Business; Parks College of Engineering, Aviation and Technology; Marvin and Harlene Wool Center; and the Center for Advanced Dental Education. No detail escaped his attention,

as evidenced in landscaping, statues, archways, and buildings limned at night with blue lights. His value on aesthetics is clear in the Père Marquette Gallery renovation in DuBourg Hall, as well as at the Museum of Contemporary Religious Art, Samuel Cupples House, Boileau Hall, and Cartier Hall, among others.

Father Biondi cultivated relationships, like a friendship with Alberto Gnägi, a Swiss lawyer and businessmen. This led to a collaboration with SSM Health president and CEO Sister Mary Jean Ryan, F.S.M. and trustee Joseph Adorjan, establishing SLU's Center for Health Care Ethics. SLU Law graduate Henry Lay, a successful businessman, built a 350-acre complex of buildings, lakes, and trails that, through the influence of Father Biondi, Lay donated to the university. Anheuser-Busch executive (and later SLU trustee) Aloys "Al" Litteken first met Father Biondi during planning stages for Chaifetz Arena. Their partnership was successful on many other projects, including the Busch Student Center renovation and work on the Center for Global Citizenship, Scott Hall, and Pius XII Memorial Library. Trustee Robert Fox and his wife Maxine Clark were passionate about education and immigration; Biondi worked with them to change the discourse about "illegal aliens" into a broader understanding about new immigrants, as part of their joint efforts to create the health center called *Casa de Salud.*

Paul Loewenstein, assistant research professor at the Institute for Molecular Virology, signs the final beam in a ceremony held during construction of the Doisy Research Center.

"WE'RE TEACHING THOSE WHO ARE THE FUTURE TO 'LIGHT THE WORLD ON FIRE'…TO MAKE CHANGE. WE DON'T ALWAYS SUCCEED, BUT WE'RE COMMITTED TO TRYING TO CHANGE HOW OUR STUDENTS SEE THEMSELVES AND THEIR PLACE, THEIR RESPONSIBILITY, IN THE WORLD."

PAUL VITA, 2016

Father Frank Reale, S.J.'s arrival in 2008 was valuable in many ways. He worked with Kathleen Brady, vice president for Facilities Management at the time, and trustee Al Litteken, to acquire San Ignacio Hall (shown above), doubling the size of the Madrid campus. This allowed for a much larger library, a cafeteria, an auditorium, and a fine arts center.

Father Frank Reale, S.J. worked closely with Paul Vita to restructure SLU's Madrid campus.

In 1988, Father John Gray, S.J. was named as the first vice president of SLU-Madrid. Gray had been academic vice president on the St. Louis, north campus under Father Fitzgerald. Prior to his arrival, the Madrid program relied upon rented property, but faced with increasing enrollment levels, Gray undertook expansion including the purchase and renovation of two new buildings: Padre Arrupe and Padre Rubio halls. These are now historically protected sites at Avenida Del Valle. In 1992, Dr. Rick Chaney, a tenured professor at SLU's business school, became vice president and academic dean. He oversaw changes that earned the program official recognition by the Spanish government in 1996. He also marketed the program more broadly while expanding the number of degrees in Madrid.

Hired in 1999 as an English professor, Dr. Paul Vita was charged with developing a master's degree in English program in Madrid. He became chair of the department of English and Communication, working on the early degrees that were introduced. Another key figure in the Madrid program in this period was Father Frank Reale, S.J. Reale arrived as vice president and rector in 2008. He oversaw administrative reorganization, building renovation, and a renewed emphasis both on the Jesuit mission and on ties with the St. Louis campus.

Degrees are offered now in fields including: art history, international business, economics, and international relations, among others. In 2008, Dr. Vita became academic dean, then three years later, interim director, and the following year, director. Vita was also named a vice president in 2015. He oversaw the project of renovating San Ignacio Hall, greatly expanding the campus size. Dr. Vita sees SLU-Madrid as "part of a broader effort undertaken intentionally by the university to foster a global perspective among young people."[26] SLU-Madrid draws students from sixty-five countries, providing a rich opportunity to learn about the world. At the same time, the existence of the Madrid campus makes the university look further afield when making decisions, Vita suggests. Reflecting on SLU's role in the world, both historically and in the future, he emphasizes that Jesuit, values-based education is critical. "The U.S. model of liberal arts education is under a lot of pressure to provide 'measurable outcomes,' as is SLU itself. What can't be measured that effectively are some of the values embedded in the experiences we are offering students. Through Madrid, SLU is helping form more international 'men and women for others.'"

Dr. Paul Vita began at SLU-Madrid in 1999, and became a vice president in 2015.

The images above depict students and the campus of SLU-Madrid, including Padre Arrupe Hall. [ABOVE]

THROUGH CHRIST, A RECOGNITION OF BEAUTY

THEME FOR A PORTRAIT OF FATHER MCNAMEE, PAINTED BY ROB DREYER

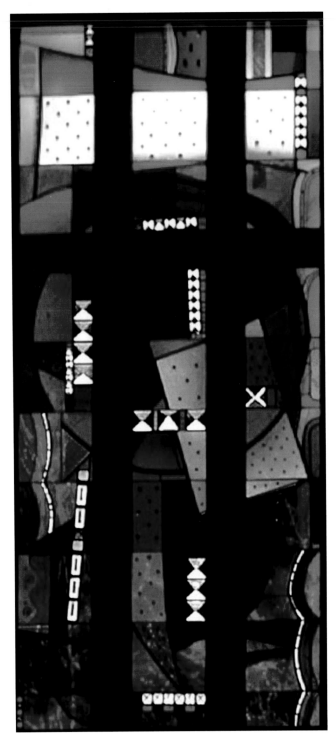

The Red Window at the Sheldon Gallery in Grand Center was created in honor of Father McNamee, and dedicated in 2001.

Father Maurice McNamee, S.J. was devoted to the cultivation of beauty, on SLU's campus and beyond. For nearly seventy-five years, "Father Mac" was associated with Saint Louis University as a student or teacher. He was a professor of English and art history for over thirty of those years. He was cherished by students and colleagues, and was an accomplished scholar and true visionary. Yet, stories about Father Mac most often invoke his humility and service. He was especially dedicated to the Samuel Cupples House, tending its gardens or scraping its tile floors free of debris after parties. Legend has it that the house was set to be demolished, but he said to administrators: "Give me six months and I'll save it." He then proceeded to paint its forty-two rooms himself, and attracted a crowd of thousands for its opening.

Father McNamee was born in 1909 and entered the Society of Jesus in 1927. He was ordained in 1940 and took his final vows in 1945. Father McNamee's real love was art history, but there were no programs in Jesuit schools at the time of his graduate studies, so he studied English. With Father Walter Ong, S.J. (see Chapter 5), Father McNamee's research was guided by Marshall McLuhan when the latter was a young English instructor at SLU from 1937 to 1944. "Mac's directing of my dissertation consisting of coming over into that building right over there, plopping himself down on the bed, and talking for three hours a night about his own studies," McNamee recounted.[27] (This was early in McLuhan's career, before his fame as a media theorist.) McNamee retained his interest in art, helping to found SLU's art history program in the 1970s; it was the first of its kind at a Jesuit institution. Saint Louis University gave him an honorary degree in fine arts in 2006.

Father Maurice McNamee, S.J., stands near his beloved Cupples House.

In the St. Louis area, McNamee was considered a "champion of the arts." He was also director, curator, and "odd-job man" at Cupples House. Designed by Robert Annan and built from 1888 to 1890, the building was purchased in 1946 by the university from the Order of Railroad Telegraphers. Renamed "Chouteau House" for a time, it served as a student center and later, it housed the Reserve Officers' Training Corps (ROTC) as well as Metropolitan College. It is recognized as one of the best examples of Richardsonian Romanesque domestic architecture in the United States. In 1976, it was placed on the National Register of Historic Places. Father McNamee also made it his mission to track down the paintings which Father De Smet had shipped to St. Louis from Europe in the nineteenth century. His luminous memoir: *Recollections in Tranquility,* provides an important glimpse into the formation of Jesuits in the early twentieth century. In addition, Father McNamee played a major role in developing the modern and contemporary art collection at the university, through the purchase of many works of art during his travels in Europe.

The Museum of Contemporary Religious Art, the world's first inter-religious contemporary art museum, opened in 1993. It was a dream realized by Father Terrence Dempsey, S.J., through sheer inspiration and a series of providential contacts.[28] Dempsey was born in 1945, entered the Society of Jesus in 1977 and was ordained in 1985. During graduate studies at SLU in the late 1960s, he studied under Father McNamee, then headed to Berkeley for doctoral work in the field of art and religion. Upon returning to SLU in 1990 to teach art history, he began to curate small exhibits in Cupples House's basement gallery, now called the McNamee Gallery. With encouragement from Father McNamee and others, he proposed to Father Biondi to use a vacated, large chapel space in Fusz Hall as a museum. The proposal was accepted, and a unique museum was born.

The stunning interior of Cupples House is a testament to hard work and careful restoration. Early on in the process of renovation, Father Mac famously pulled out miles of cord that snaked through the walls of rooms, left behind by the Order of Railroad Telegraphers. Legend has it that Samuel Cupples vowed that Saint Louis University would never own his home, through some dislike of the Jesuits for moving nearby and ruining his "view."

The former Fusz Hall chapel provides a striking setting for the Museum of Contemporary Religious Art's exploration of the ways in which today's artists engage the religious and spiritual dimensions. Since the inaugural exhibition in 1993, *Sanctuaries: Recovering the Holy in Contemporary Art* (pictured here), MOCRA has presented over fifty exhibitions and work by hundreds of artists from a breadth of religious and cultural backgrounds.

"THE UNDERLYING PHILOSOPHY OF THE LAW SCHOOL OF ST. LOUIS UNIVERSITY IS THAT THE LAW RESTS ON MORAL PRINCIPLES, RECOGNIZING THE PERSONAL DIGNITY OF THE INDIVIDUAL MAN AND HIS SOCIAL RESPONSIBILITIES ... IT AIMS TO KEEP ORIENTED TO THE GREAT NEED FOR SOCIAL JUSTICE."

FIRST DRAFT OF CASE STATEMENT, 1964

As this period began, laypersons had become fully integrated across the campus as faculty, staff, clinicians, and administrators. By fall 1979, Dr. John Slosar of the School of Social Work organized the first faculty senate at SLU, promoting faculty governance. Laypersons are now active collaborators in the Jesuit mission, at SLU and across all of the Jesuit schools.

The Jesuit emphasis on responding to the times and promoting the dignity of each person was evident in the founding of SLU's School of Social Service by Father Husslein, S.J. (see Chapter 4). In 1940, Father Aloysius Scheller, S.J. became its director, as the program evolved to one for graduate programs only, and was renamed as the School of Social Work. Skipping forward to more contemporary times, in 1991 Dr. James Kimmey was the founding dean of SLU's School of Public Health. This was the first accredited school of public health in Missouri, and remains the only one at a Jesuit university. It evolved from the Center for Health Services Education and Research, and has worked with the federal government's Center for Disease Control and the World Health Organization of the United Nations. Kimmey notes that there were few such schools in the United States when his idea developed; SLU was "at the front of the wave," building upon a strong program that had developed in the 1960s, training administrators for Catholic hospitals. He thrives on risk-taking and initiative, and so the project suited him well. The school trained state officials in Jefferson City, a remarkable exposure to practitioners that strengthened the program. In 2011, it was combined with the School of Social Work and the criminal justice program to create the College for Public Health and Social Justice, uniting the public health school's strengths in maternal and child health at a global level with the social work school's expertise in community organization, geriatrics, and mental health. Kimmey recalls that deans at public universities said to him, regarding the new school: "We'd like to do that, but we can't," and indeed, the feeling among the health education community was that "only Jesuits could and should do this."[29]

Dr. James Kimmey, in founding Missouri's first School of Public Health, saw that its "very core" is "to serve the disenfranchised and marginalized through the discovery and dissemination of knowledge."

SLU Law is another important forum for promoting the dignity of each person. In 1982, the Center for Health Law was established. The program has been ranked among the top in the country for many years, and indeed has been number one throughout at least the past decade as of this writing. Former Missouri Supreme Court judge and chief justice Michael A. Wolff is professor and dean emeritus at SLU Law. He served as dean from 2013 to 2017, providing crucial leadership. His successor, William Johnson, embraces the school's centrality to justice work in the region. In addition to its excellent, highly ranked academic programs, the law school runs a clinic which dates to the late 1960s. In 1967, SLU law faculty members Donald King and Vincent Immel created a juvenile law "forum clinic" that was so successful it led the university to establish the

Students in the law library, with the St. Louis civil courts building visible nearby. Its proximity facilitates internships and court experience.

legal clinic, partnering with the Legal Aid Society and the city and county of St. Louis (see also Chapter 5). It was staffed initially by sixteen students and led by Raymond White, and later David Lander, Jesse Goldner, and John O'Brien.[30] The clinic now has six emphases: Civil Advocacy, Criminal Defense, Entrepreneurship and Community Development, Mediation, Field Placement, and Judicial Process, as well as two new projects since 2017: Juvenile Reentry Assistance Program and Death Penalty Program. Students participate in field placements and in-house clinics, and partner organizations include the Catholic Legal Assistance Ministry and the judiciary. Litigation filed by the clinic includes cases to: challenge debtor prisons and illegal warrant fees, and advocate for those who are blind, disabled, homeless, or mentally ill. SLU Law professor John Am-

mann has long been associated with the clinic and explains its history thus: "We adapted to whatever the demand was," because it was important to respond to the needs of the community, "whether people were being locked up for mental health issues, or unemployment cases were surging, whether debtor prisons or Medicaid cases emerged."[31]

SLU Law professor Patricia Hureston Lee has served as the clinic director since 2014 and adds that, "The social justice mission today is aimed at helping those most in need and doing so in very proactive, collaborative and innovative ways … the types of matters the law clinics handle have also expanded to include pro bono legal services in litigation (civil and criminal), transactional matters and conflict resolution."[32] Helping to defend families whose homes have been condemned is a particularly urgent piece of their work.

St. Louis-born Roger Goldman returned to the city after earning his law degree at the University of Pennsylvania, and was assigned to the city's Legal Aid clinic as a volunteer with the AmeriCorps Volunteers in Service to America (VISTA) program. From there, he was recruited to teach at SLU, and agreed because, as he later recounted, Saint Louis University, and the Jesuits generally, were known for their welcoming approach to those who profess Jewish faith.[33] He went on to a career as a national expert in police licensing, driven by his awareness of abuses being suffered by local people who had been incarcerated. In 2009, SLU Law alumni Thomas Harvey and Michael-John Voss started the ArchCity Defenders in an effort to break the cycle of "revolving door justice" and serve the most the vulnerable citizens of the region.

Current staff at *Casa de Salud* include, from left to right: Gordon Goldman, M.D.; Enrique Toro, M.D.; Ratna Thakur, M.D.; and Kenneth Zehnder, M.D. The facility was created by trustee Robert Fox and Father Biondi.

In this 2010 photograph from *Universitas*, second-year medical student Monica Mitcheff takes the blood pressure of a patient at the student-run Health Resource Center in North St. Louis.

In the health professions, there are countless examples of excellence in clinical practice, teaching, and research as well as critical partnerships to address public health issues locally. It is impossible to mention every person and program, but a few examples can illustrate the initiative and passion of the SLU community.

At SLU's medical school, new cures and treatments are sought in five areas: cancer, liver disease, heart/lung disease, aging and brain disease, and infectious diseases. In the academic year 1989-1990, SLU's Center for Vaccine Development was one of five centers in the United States selected to conduct research for AIDS vaccines. The world's first dengue vaccine was developed from work at Saint Louis University, which holds the patent on the vaccine, developed in 1997 by Thomas Chambers, M.D., then an associate professor of molecular microbiology and immunology.

In 1994, Dr. Patricia Monteleone, M.D. was one of the first women appointed to lead a U.S. medical school when she was named eleventh dean of the School of Medicine. After thirteen years of service, she announced her retirement in 2007; she was at the time the longest continuously serving woman dean in the history of U.S. medical schools. Dr. Monteleone was a pediatrician with expertise in medical genetics. She restructured the curriculum, expanded research funding, and created SLUCare in 1995. This is an innovative way to offer medical care in connection with the university hospital. A subsidiary of the university was created to manage clinical operations, while still supporting the educational activities of the university. Monteleone received a Lifetime Achievement Award from the *St. Louis Business Journal* as a "Health-Care Hero."

In 2002, SLU's Cancer Center emerged as a joint initiative of SLUCare and Tenet Healthcare, led by Dr. Douglas Miller, M.D. In 2016, the center was designated by the National Pancreas Foundation as an NPF Cancer Center, the only cancer center to receive that honor in the region. The university accepted a bid from Tenet in 1997 to purchase its hospital, but by September 2015 bought it back, and rekindled a partnership with SSM Health. See Chapters 3 and 4 for more on the history of relations between SLU and the Franciscan Sisters of Mary.

Dr. Goronwy Broun, Sr. taught an estimated 5,000 doctors over the course of his decades-long career at SLU Medical School. He left Alabama and came to SLU as a scholarship student in 1914. In this photograph, he plots out health needs by zip code on a map, as part of his support for the ambulatory care facility in 1976. He carried on the long tradition of care for the poor spearheaded by the Sisters of St. Mary and Father Schwitalla (see Chapters 3 and 4).

Dr. Robert Belshe is the Dianna and J. Joseph Adorjan Endowed Professor of Infectious Diseases and Immunology at Saint Louis University School of Medicine. Belshe is one of the foremost vaccine researchers in the country. He came to SLU in 1989. He and his colleagues were so excited to move into their new lab at the Doisy Research Center in 2008, they showed up at dawn.

In 1994, SLU medical students started the student-run Health Resource Center in the St. Augustine Parish. The center offers clinical services in North St. Louis. Another critical site is *Casa de Salud*. Volunteer medical providers at *Casa de Salud* offer healthcare for uninsured and underinsured patients, specifically focusing on the immigrant and refugee community in the greater St. Louis area.

The Center for Advanced Dental Education (CADE) both conducts research and offers substantial discounts on its specialized services for members of the community. In 1998, the center moved into an impressive facility that receives over 35,000 patient visits per year. The building, once a wood-working plant, was renovated thanks in part to the lottery winnings of a major donor, along with alumni who raised $3.6 million. Dr. John Hatton, executive director of the center, notes of Father Biondi: "He is what made this place." CADE offers programs in Orthodontics, Periodontics, and Endodontics, and in 2017, introduced a Pediatric Dentistry program. It prepares students while also improving the oral health of young children in the region, a positive change that impacts the rest of their lives.

From creative responses to aging, post-traumatic stress disorder (PTSD), and student stress, to research on pandemic awareness, sepsis, radiation medicine, wound healing, and a cure for the Zika virus, the SLU medical community responds to health needs with a powerful sense of mission.

When Jaye Shyken, M.D. founded WISH (Women and Infant Substance Abuse Help) in 2016, she led the way in the fight against a deadly new scourge. SLU and SSM Health now run the only clinic of its kind in the region. From its origins as a half-day clinic in 2014, WISH grew to a full-time effort dedicated to assisting pregnant women who are addicted to opioids. Opioid addiction and the resulting deaths reached historic, crisis proportions in 2016, according to the U.S. Centers for Disease Control. WISH is a classic example of SLU and SSM Health partnering to respond to urgent needs and to serve the most vulnerable people in society. As Shyken notes: "It's so easy as a society to look at drug addiction as a personal failure, but the very definition of addiction is that of a primary, neurobiological disorder that involves the reward pathways in the brain. Drugs permanently alter the brain and have many far-reaching effects that are medical, spiritual, psychological and social. Our mission is to really start to address all of these things. It's important that we normalize treatment for this 'disorder.'"[34]

Dr. Patricia Monteleone was hailed in St. Louis as a "Health-Care Hero," and ran SLU's School of Medicine for thirteen years.

This period has seen new challenges emerge in science, technology, health, and medicine. To address the complex problems of the times, SLU's divisions frequently collaborate; for example, through the student-initiated program "MEDLaunch," Parks College of Engineering, Aviation and Technology students work with SLU's medical and business students to design and market solutions to problems arising in a clinical setting, such as the monitoring of health measures. MED-Launch was founded in 2015 by SLU medical students: Andrew Hayden, Anthony Grzeda, and Rusdeep Mundae.

In 1997, Parks College undertook a major move from its long-time campus in Cahokia, Illinois to SLU's north campus in midtown St. Louis. Still somewhat controversial to those who cherished their old location, the move benefits students. They are more fully integrated into university life, exposed to a wider range of academic options, and able to participate in more sports and student organizations.

Parks College is unique. It is the only program of its kind at a Jesuit school, and its alumni have been involved in every NASA mission ever undertaken. Behind the walls of an unassuming building easily overlooked on the bustling campus, Parks College runs a set of massive wind, supersonic, and water tunnels. The supersonic wind tunnel tests flight vehicles; some have re-entry speeds of 25 times the speed of sound. Parks students prepare to address issues ranging from energy, transportation, and water to health care and information security. They seek to improve the world around them and value the atmosphere of a Jesuit campus, notes Dean Michelle Sabick. She adds: "Parks started in a way that was very specific and cool, and it's still cool."[35]

Parks students have always been known for whimsy and fascinating activities, like the annual pumpkin launch.

Emily Growney Kalaf (Ph.D. Biomedical Engineering, SLU 2017) examines stained cultures of her novel tissue engineering scaffold, developed in Dr. Scott Sell's Tissue Fabrication lab.

Father James Sebesta, S.J. entered the Society of Jesus in 1958, worked in Alaska for nearly thirty years as a Jesuit, and has taught aviation science at Parks College since 1994. Sebesta is a pilot, and flew extensively as part of his service to missions in Alaska.

Students learn to reface valves, with instructor Murphy Shedenhelm at left, in 1929.

Nancy McNeir Ring (see Chapter 4) was the first Dean of Women at SLU. In her honor, SLU's chapter of Alpha Sigma Nu in 1966 established the Nancy McNeir Ring award for excellence in teaching. The many educators who have received this award span a wide range of disciplines. Past recipients of the Ring Award were profiled in *Universitas* in 2003. From right to left, from front to back, they are: 1st row: Dr. Vincent Immel (law), Dr. Nelly Grosswasser (modern languages), Dr. Michael C. Shaner (management), Dr. John A. George (Parks College); 2nd row: Joel K. Goldstein (law), John Kavanaugh, S.J. (philosophy), Dr. Avis Meyer (communication), Dr. Cheryl Cavallo (physical therapy); 3d row: Dr. Belden Lane (theological studies), Dr. Gregory Beabout (philosophy); Dr. John Doyle (philosophy), Dr. John Slosar (social service); 4th row: Dr. Daniel Finucane (theological studies), Dr. James Gilsinan (public service), Dr. T. Michael Ruddy (history).

In this 2016 photo, graduate student Alayna Sibert works in the urban garden started in 2002 by Millie Matfeldt Beman. Beman also started the Doisy College's Nutrition and Dietetics program. The garden provides food to seven local schools through a Farm to Table initiative, and offers a culinary camp for young people in summer. It is accessible, and thus ideal for special needs teachers, occupational and physical therapy students, and for students who are disabled.

Dr. Joan Hrubetz was dean of SLU's School of Nursing for twenty-two years. She established a doctoral program in 1989 and a distance learning program that was one of the first at the university.

Dr. Teri Murray was named director of the School of Nursing in 2006 and dean of the school in 2008. She has held significant state and national leadership positions including serving as president of the Missouri State Board of Nursing,

"WE REFLECT ON *WHY* WE DO WHAT WE DO."

JOAN HRUBETZ, 1989 ADDRESS TO NEW FACULTY MEMBERS

In 1982, Joan Hrubetz became the first lay dean of SLU's School of Nursing. With a B.S.N. from SLU, as well as a master's and Ph.D. in education/counseling, she worked at St. John's Hospital School of Nursing and in other settings before returning to SLU in 1975. Hrubetz served as dean for twenty-two years, and was critical to the success of the program. She cherished her students as well as "the sense of hospitality" that she found unique to SLU's campus. Polio confined her to a wheelchair for most of her career, but never held her back from her goals.

Historically connected to the School of Nursing (see Chapter 4), the School of Allied Health Professions has seen many name changes. By 1971, a program in Physician Assistant Education had been added, with new academic departments soon to follow, including Medical Imaging and Radiation Therapeutics (1981) and Occupational Science and Occupational Therapy in 1992. In 1979, the division of Health and Hospital Services became its own entity and its name was changed to the School of Allied Health Professions (SAHP). Dr. Frances Horvath, M.D. was appointed dean in 1980. The SAHP outgrew its space, so a new building was

constructed and opened in the fall of 1998. In 2001, SAHP became the Edward and Margaret Doisy College of Health Sciences thanks to the generous support of Margaret Doisy. It has grown to be a comprehensive college of allied health programs that is unique among American, Jesuit institutions of higher education. In 2014, Dr. Mardell Wilson became dean, and has spearheaded changes including the addition in 2016 of the Department of Communication Sciences and Disorders, formerly in the College of Arts and Sciences. By 2017, the college was offering twenty degree programs to nearly 1,800 students, making it one of the largest colleges at Saint Louis University.

Dr. Teri Murray became dean of the School of Nursing in 2008, creating the first local Doctor of Nursing Practice program that year. She began the first accelerated M.S. in Nursing in Missouri in 2010, as well as the first state-of-the-art clinical simulation lab with a public health simulation component, and the first endowed professorship in nursing. Murray's work garnered International Heiskell Award Special Recognition for the international nursing program in Madrid. She led SLU to become one of the first schools nationwide to establish the White Coat Ceremony for Nurses, and established the first-ever School of Nursing magazine, *Cura Personalis,* connecting with over 10,000 graduates.

"WE HAVE TO KEEP AN OPEN HEART."

In this period, many have come to conceptualize humanity as both global and interdependent. There has been a major shift in the way young people think about the world, and their role in it, as journalists and humanitarian groups draw attention to the pressing needs of people who are suffering around the world.

It is not possible to describe all of the service initiatives and partnerships in which the people of Saint Louis University engage. From starting a traveling bus to take fresh produce to food deserts in town, to gathering supplies for servicemen and servicewomen, there is a steady flow of heart, ideas, and help. At SLU, the academic component of reflection by students on the experience of their participation is the unifying thread.

In 1998, Father Bill Hutchison, S.J., dean of the School of Social Work, founded Northside Revitalization. This region of the city continues to struggle with economic and structural disadvantage. Some of the current projects of what is now called the North Saint Louis Initiative include: after school boys' programs in math and science; geriatric workforce enhancement; physical therapy, and other health programs; and job training. Another important local initiative is the Micah program, begun by Father Michael Garanzini, S.J. Micah is a learning community of students who connect with neighborhoods in St. Louis. The program emphasizes "faith in service." First-year students who are accepted into Micah live together on one floor of Marguerite Hall, take a distinctive academic program focused on theology and social justice, and do service each week in the city. Participants frequently engage in continuing service after graduation.

The Labre program of outreach to homeless persons, and hundreds of other SLU projects as well, serve the residents of St. Louis city and county, and people around the world.

Christelle Ilboudo, M.D., [AT LEFT] a 2012 graduate of the pediatric residency program at SLU, assists a mother and child in Burkina Faso. She was a participant in the Riley Endowed Medicine Abroad Program in 2011.

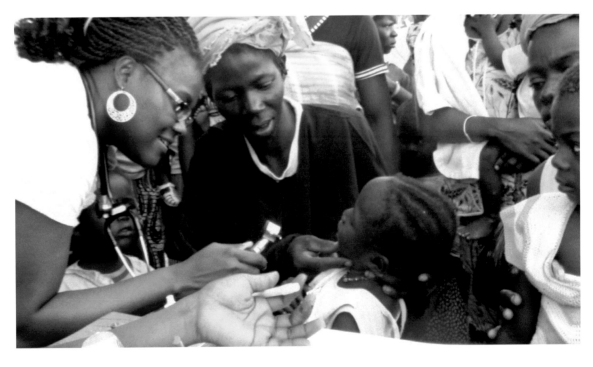

Father Boleslaus Lukaszewski, S.J., captured life at Saint Louis University in thousands of photographs.

The preamble to the 1832 charter incorporating Saint Louis University justifies the decision thus: "Now, in order to encourage learning, to extend the means of education, and to give dignity, permanency, and usefulness to the said institution." Perhaps the writer of those words could not have guessed that the "permanency" of the university would have lasted for so many years. Yet, it has indeed done so, and not always through easy times.

There are many Jesuits whose talent and dedication ensure that SLU can continue to learn from and draw upon its own rich history as an institution. Among them, two historians are of special note: Walter Hill and Gilbert Garraghan. Hill wrote the earliest full history of the university up to that time, and Garraghan's several scholarly volumes on the Jesuits of the

Middle West make clear how centrally Saint Louis University was a part of that extraordinarily varied history. Three have shared incredible photography skills, in addition to their teaching and scholarly activities: Charles Charroppin, Boleslaus "Luke" Lukaszewski, and "JJ" Mueller. From Charroppin in the nineteenth century, Luke in the twentieth, and Mueller up to the present century, the university has received a rich visual record of its life and activities. The talented Father William Faherty also played an important role in chronicling SLU stories. He taught history at SLU, served as director of the Museum of Western Jesuit Missions at the old "Rock" building (at the site of the St. Stanislaus Seminary in Florissant, Missouri) from 1976 to 2002, and wrote numerous books, including the highly detailed and engaging sesquicentennial history of the university titled *Better the Dream.*

A proud sense of history is clear at the university and among its 125,000 living alumni. More than 100,000 students have benefited from SLU's scholarship programs; nearly 1,100 active scholarship funds are supported by donors including alumni. SLU's Black Alumni Association established the Pioneers of Inclusion Endowed Scholarship in 2014 to mark the 70th anniversary of integration at SLU, and in 2015, the university established the St. Peter Claver, S.J., Service Endowed Scholarship, named after the patron saint of black Catholics.

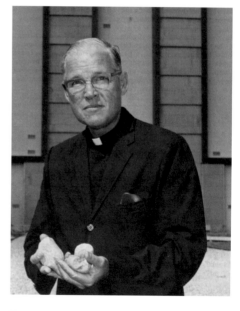

Father Faherty holding rocks from the moon during a visit to Cape Canaveral.

In 2000, university archivist John Waide presents Thierry Verhaegen, a descendant of a nephew of Father Peter Verhaegen, S.J., with a framed poem by Father Verhaegen, the university's first president.

[ABOVE] The university's first museum on the 1888 campus was located in DuBourg Hall. Treasures salvaged by Father Heithaus and Father Faherty from Saint Stanislaus Seminary were combined with many of these materials and are on display in the Saint Louis University Museum of Art, thanks to a gift from Mrs. Jessie Heithaus.

A PROCLAMATION

WHEREAS, since the start of our recorded history, the Wah-Zha-Zhe (the Osage people) have had a relationship with the Society of Jesus, beginning with Father Marquette's 1673 exploration of the Missouri section of our ancestral homeland,

AND WHEREAS, since its founding by the Society of Jesus in 1818, Saint Louis University has been a bastion of higher education west of the Mississippi River, holding title to many firsts of the west, the first college, the first medical school, the first law school, and many others,

AND WHEREAS, also since its founding in 1818 and to present day, many of the Wah-Zha-Zhe have been educated by Jesuits at Saint Louis University, learning that has benefitted our entire Nation as a whole,

AND WHEREAS, in the year 2018, Saint Louis University will celebrate its bicentennial.

NOW, THEREFORE, I, GEOFFREY MONGRAIN STANDING BEAR, Principal Chief of the Osage Nation, do herby commemorate and laud the two hundred year bond between the Wha-Zha-Zhe and

SAINT LOUIS UNIVERSITY

IN WITNESS WHEREOF, I have hereunto set my hand and caused to be affixed the Great Seal of the Osage Nation.

Geoffrey M. Standing Bear
Principal Chief of the Osage Nation

This proclamation from the Osage congratulates SLU on its bicentennial and heralds the long relationship between the Osage Nation and the Society of Jesus. For details on the complex history of the university's founding, see Chapter 1.

As noted elsewhere in this chapter, interdisciplinary endeavors are highly productive at SLU. The Center for Health Outcomes Research (SLUCOR) began as a unit of the Internal Medicine department, originally intended to provide statistics support. Projects included contracts and grants to evaluate projects, many relating to kidney transplants and diabetes. Collaboration developed with the College for Public Health and Social Justice, and as students evinced increasing interest in health outcomes, the program evolved. By 2011, the center accepted its first cohort in a master's degree program; it now offers several dual degree programs and certificates, and it cooperates with the School of Nursing, Doisy College of Health Sciences, and the School of Medicine. By supporting both research and teaching, the center staff are positioned to observe patterns in research across the campus. Driving the innovations: "It's the students," says Deputy Director Dr. Leslie Hinyard, "and their passion for social justice."

This focus on students and on a broad vision also characterizes the School for Professional Studies, which traces its origins to the 1962 Metropolitan College. In contemporary times, estimates are that thirty million adults in the United States have begun a higher degree, but have not finished. Dr. Tracy Chapman, current dean of the school, sees her role as making a SLU education accessible to that highly diverse group: "We are doing what St. Ignatius did and what he urged his followers to do: to meet people where they are." To best reach these busy adult learners, SPS offers fully online programs.

Dr. Fred Pestello sets up a "selfie" photo shoot with SLU students.

[BELOW] Dr. Pestello at an Oriflamme event with Mary Bruemmer (see also Chapter 4) who served as Dean of Women, in other administrative roles for decades, and as a volunteer until 2016. In 1963, Father Thomas McQueeny, S.J. started Oriflamme (recent members pictured here). The group assists new students as they arrive at SLU and adapt to college life. Bruemmer was advisor to Oriflamme for nearly twenty years.

Tawanda Quintanilla is a student at SLU's School for Professional Studies. She is working on a degree in Organizational Studies, and is shown here with her granddaughter, Lola Berry. (used with family permission)

The Society of Jesus had recognized for decades that formal lay collaboration would ensure the continued success of Jesuit colleges and universities. After Father Biondi's retirement, trustee James Smith chaired a diverse and representative presidential search committee. William Kauffman served as interim president. At the time, he had been SLU's general counsel for over eighteen years. He accepted the interim post because, as he put it quite simply, "I believe in this university."

Challenges included a divided university community, but Smith's search committee used the process as a way to unify the campus. They held meetings across all of the schools and colleges to ascertain the qualities sought in the new president. Among these were dedication to Jesuit identity and mission, and commitment to transparent and inclusive governance. Out of over one hundred candidates, Dr. Fred P. Pestello met all of the criteria. He was a graduate of John Carroll University, the Jesuit university in Cleveland, Ohio; he spent twenty-five years at the University of Dayton, a Catholic, Marianist university, holding virtually every position from associate professor to provost; and spent six years as president of Le Moyne College, the Jesuit college in Syracuse, New York, with a strong record. He was universally supported by the Jesuit community.

As Father Christopher Collins, S.J., Special Assistant to the President for Mission and identity, remarks: "Early on, Dr. Pestello stressed three goals: to know who we are as a Catholic and Jesuit university, to improve access and affordability, and to be a better neighbor in the region. These goals are not simply to gain prestige for our own sake. Every one of them has to do with relationship, with living a mission that is both self-reflective while looking outward to needs beyond its borders. Dr. Pestello is open to others and reliant upon genuine dialogue."

In 2017, SLU students hailed from all fifty states and seventy-eight countries. This breadth ensures that the university will continue to have an impact that is both local and global.

WRITING THE INTRODUCTION TO THE NEXT TWO HUNDRED YEARS

During his inaugural address in October 2014, Dr. Fred Pestello reflected upon the pursuit of truth as a defining aspect of being human. He also addressed the community, asking: "What must we become?" To answer that question, he initiated listening sessions across all of university's colleges, schools, and programs. He appointed Dr. James Kimmey as the strategic planning coordinator for a steadfastly "bottom-up" project that resulted in a strategic plan titled: *"Magis"* (Latin for "More"), a word that encapsulates a concept in Jesuit thought to do with "the more universal good." Kimmey describes it as "the most participative planning process SLU ever tried as far as I know," crediting its success to the two co-chairs: Dr. Joseph Weixlmann, professor of English and former provost, and Dr. Kent Porterfield, vice president for student development.[36]

Despite a period of fiscal challenge, the university is using this plan to shape its future. The Saint Louis University community has identified five broad aspirations: to be a national exemplar of transformative educational and research excellence; to be a market leader in health promotion and highest quality medical care; to be a leading catalyst for groundbreaking change in the region, nation, and world; to be both innovative and entrepreneurial; and to be efficient and effective in operations, while grounded in mission and values.

Dr. Christopher Duncan, dean of the College of Arts and Sciences, reflects that ancient questions of "who we are" and "how to be present" remain central to humanity, no matter how complex the world becomes. The university exists to help students consider these questions, in an environment shaped by Jesuit emphases on dialogue, companionship, and "creative fidelity." William Kauffman, former interim president, remains in a key role as a vice president, and is fascinated by the challenge of considering the "digital generation" and the kinds of training that will best prepare it for the future. A lawyer, he is especially concerned with new evidence that young people do not fully understand First Amendment rights. Amidst modern-day problems, the university remains mindful of its mission. As SLU's provost, Dr. Nancy Brickhouse observes: "Saint Louis University today is a community of students, teachers, and scholars living a contemporary version of a 200-year-old, Jesuit-inspired educational vision. We are stewards of an historically profound academic mission, grounded in the perpetual pursuit of truth that prepares students for lives of meaning, service, and success. We are embedded in the history and future of St. Louis as we work to change the world. And we are the authors of the introduction to the story of SLU's next 200 years."

"We met peace with peace and we must continue to do so."

Dr. Fred Pestello, 2014

For generations, unfair laws and practices have harmed citizens in the St. Louis region. These systems fall hardest on people who lack power, especially those who are impoverished and of African American descent. SLU as an institution of higher education works through its teaching, research, and service to seek reform and to help the vulnerable. However, structural change in political and economic systems is also urgently needed. This fact was underscored when two young, African American men were killed during police encounters in the St. Louis region. Citizens protested in Ferguson, Missouri and elsewhere in the region after Michael Brown was shot in August 2014, and after VonDerrit Meyers, Jr., son of SLU employee VonDerrit Meyers, Sr., was shot in October 2014. Protesters, including SLU students, entered SLU's campus, and camped near the Lipic Clock Tower. A set of commitments called the Clock Tower Accords was signed, ending the encampment.

Dr. Jonathan Smith, Vice President for Diversity and Community Engagement, notes: "During the week of the occupation, our campus seemed profoundly different, while remaining much the same as it had been. Faculty taught and students went to classes. The midterm exam period was in full swing and students were spending long and late hours in the library. At the same time, activists and students from such places as Arizona, California, and New York who came to St. Louis to protest the death of Mike Brown, were camping out at our Clock Tower with our students, neighbors, and local activists. They held teach-ins, engaged in provocative protesting, dialogued among themselves and with our faculty, students, and staff. Some of the conversations were thoughtful. Others were loud and tense. Faculty invited activists into classes. Student veterans debated local activists. For that week, SLU felt like a community in full contact with the world. People around the Clock Tower did not always agree with each other, but they regularly broke bread together in that space. And in what now seems even more of an anomaly, all of this happened nonviolently and without arrests or intervention by Public Safety. Over the course of that week, through these formal conversations and informal arguments, the Accords came into being. And that is historic. I still believe, however, that the way in which we lived community that week was not only historic, but miraculous."

For its mission-driven approach to the protesters, SLU was heralded by the Interfaith Partnership of Greater St. Louis and by U.S. Attorney General Eric Holder, Jr.

A Ticking Clock
Dr. Norman A. White

The Clock Tower Accords represented a turning point for our campus. As a community that professes a commitment to social justice, some of us had insulated ourselves for too long. The clock tower occupation blurred those artificial lines and opened the door to conversations that had needed to take place. For a moment during that fateful week, those conversations began to take place in earnest. Protesters and campus administration sat at a table and responded to each other as partners for a change. The conversations were respectful and represented the best of the Jesuit principles that call for us to treat all people with dignity and respect.

We reflected our better selves during those days. We have a long way to go in standing up and living out the Accords.[38] However, we made a start that allows us to know what we are capable of, and what best represents the SLU way. We represent a moral center in this town. We are truly capable of being the men and women for others that we seek to be when we live out this calling and fulfill this commitment to our neighbors. They need us, but more importantly, we need them.

Dr. Norman White is professor of criminal justice at SLU's College for Public Health and Social Justice.

As it reaches its bicentennial milestone, and aware of its role as a partner for change (see sidebar at left), Saint Louis University has many bold plans as of this writing. SLU has added two new residence halls, created an Academic Technology Commons at Pius XII Memorial Library, and formed a redevelopment corporation to promote new investment in the Midtown St. Louis region.[37] This endeavor will impact the area encompassing both the north and south campuses.

In 2017, construction began on a new hospital and ambulatory care facility, in partnership with SSM Health. The new complex is slated to open in 2020. Yet, even as the field of healthcare is changing rapidly, the School of Medicine continues its historic role of care for those who are most vulnerable, aiming to alleviate human suffering through the best possible clinical care, innovative education of health care practitioners, and patient-in-spired research. Dr. Kevin Behrns, M.D., vice president and dean of the School of Medicine, observes: "The three tenets of academic medicine—research, patient care, and education—are areas where SLU will continue to practice and teach medicine in a distinctive way." Behrns is focused on inter-professional education, in order to achieve collaborative, patient-centered care across all healing professions. SLUCare Physician Group's expanded partnership with SSM Health, and the university's plans to double its research budget, will foster large projects that cut across multiple disciplines and connect scientists with clinicians. Dr. Kenneth Olliff, vice president of research, has set an ambitious goal of doubling research grants in five years, from $50 million to $100 million. Olliff seeks to move SLU research to the marketplace more quickly, and to collaborate on geospatial, food and water, health informatics, and urban engagement initiatives.

SLU's newest residence hall is Grand Hall, which opened in Fall 2017.

SLU can provide grant incentives within the region that is indicated with dotted lines, and goes from 39th Street, Spring Avenue, Vandeventer Avenue on the west, to Compton Avenue on the east, and from Laclede Avenue and Interstate 64 on the north to Park Avenue and Interstate 44 on the south.

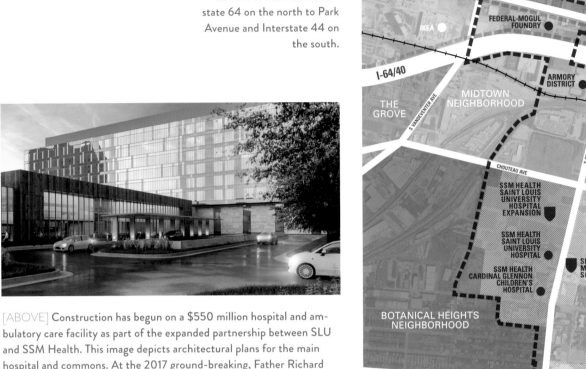

[ABOVE] Construction has begun on a $550 million hospital and ambulatory care facility as part of the expanded partnership between SLU and SSM Health. This image depicts architectural plans for the main hospital and commons. At the 2017 ground-breaking, Father Richard Buhler, S.J. blessed the site, saying: "We stand at a sacred intersection where science and technology meet grace and humanity."

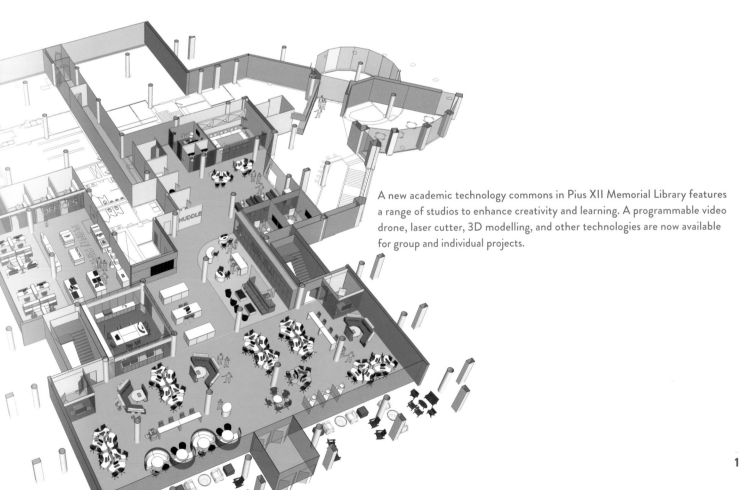

A new academic technology commons in Pius XII Memorial Library features a range of studios to enhance creativity and learning. A programmable video drone, laser cutter, 3D modelling, and other technologies are now available for group and individual projects.

"FROM A SCHOOL FOUNDED ON THE FRONTIER, IT HAS BY THE GIFTS OF SO MANY EXPANDED FRONTIERS IN VIRTUALLY ALL ASPECTS OF OUR INTELLECTUAL LIFE, AND THOSE ENDEAVORS CONTINUE UNABATED."

FATHER RONALD MERCIER, S.J.,
PROVINCIAL OF THE CENTRAL AND SOUTHERN
PROVINCE OF THE SOCIETY OF JESUS, 2017

"We are small but mighty in service to society," avers Dr. Molly Schaller, in describing the School of Education of which she is interim dean. This proud claim would resonate with the founders of the university. The ability to seek and share knowledge and to teach others is an incredible privilege. At SLU, this noble task is understood as an integral part of a shared humanity.

As SLU faces its collective future, it draws upon many inspiring examples from its own history and from modern times. In 2013, the Argentine Jesuit, Jorge Bergoglio, was elected as Pope. He was the first Jesuit so honored. He chose the name Francis, and soon issued a call for a Jubilee Year of Mercy. His positions on justice and stewardship of the environment provide important examples for those in Catholic higher education. In 2016, the 36th General Congregation of the Society of Jesus convened, and called upon its members to take on the ministries of reconciliation.

Dr. Pestello observed at SLU's Bicentennial Mass, "Each person has helped to shape the trajectory of SLU. In 1823, Father Van Quickenborne wrote to Bishop DuBourg, saying it would 'require a miracle' for the college to exist. If that's the case, it seems that we are living a miracle every day."

As research and knowledge expand, dazzling visions of the future may seem to leap past all confines and borders. At the same time, it is relationships: across the university and with the people of the city of St. Louis, which will be a compelling theme in this story, into the next two hundred years and beyond.

Saint Louis University began its year of bicentennial celebrations with a Mass on the banks of the Mississippi River, on the grounds of the Gateway Arch. Over six thousand people took part in it. The Mass was celebrated near the point where the pioneer Jesuits first set foot in St. Louis.

THE PRESIDENTS OF SAINT LOUIS UNIVERSITY

Early leaders of DuBourg's college were François Niel and Edmund Saulnier (see Chapter 1, pages 8-9, 22-3) A leader for the college once the Jesuits took over was Charles Van Quickenborne, S.J. (see Chapter 2, pages 23-5).

Peter Verhaegen, S.J.
(1829-36)

John A. Elet, S.J.
1836-40

James O. Van de Velde, S.J.
1840-43

George A. Carrell, S.J.
1843-47

John B. Druyts, S.J.
1847-54

John S. Verdin, S.J.
1854-59

Ferdinand Coosemans, S.J.
1859-62

Thomas O'Neil, S.J.
1862-68

Francis F. Stuntebeck, S.J.
1868-71

Joseph G. Zealand, S.J.
1871-74

Leopold Bushart, S.J.
1874-77

Joseph E. Keller, S.J.
1877-81

Rudolph J. Meyer, S.J.
1881-85

Henry Moeller, S.J.
1885-89

Edward J. Gleeson, S.J.
1889-90

Joseph Grimmelsman, S.J.
1890-98

James F. X. Hoeffer, S.J.
1898-1900

Williams Banks Rogers, S.J.
1900-08

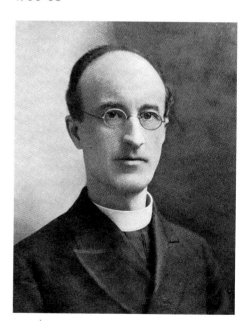

John Pierre Frieden, S.J.
1908-11

Alexander J. Burrowes, S.J.
1911-13

Bernard J. Otting, S.J.
1913-20

William F. Robison, S.J.
1920-24

Charles Cloud, S.J.
1924-30

Robert S. Johnston, S.J.
1930-36

Harry B. Crimmins, S.J.
1936-42

Patrick J. Holloran, S.J.
1943-48

Paul C. Reinert, S.J.
1949-74

Daniel C. O'Connell, S.J.
1974-78

Edward Drummond, S.J.
1978-79

Thomas R. Fitzgerald, S.J.
1979-87

Lawrence Biondi, S.J.
1987- 2013

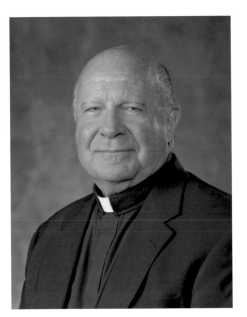

William R. Kauffman
2013-14

Fred P. Pestello, Ph.D.
2014-

HONORARY DEGREES
AND COMMENCEMENT SPEAKERS

FEBRUARY 29, 1844

Howard Watts
Doctor of Science

John H. Polin
Doctor of Science

MARCH 3, 1845

Richard E. Lacy
Doctor of Science

I. Lawrence Page
Doctor of Science

MARCH 3, 1846

Edmund B. O'Callahan
Doctor of Science

JUNE 29, 1865

**Alexander J. P. Garesche,
A.B., A.M., LL.D.***
Doctor of Laws

Moses L. Linton, A.M., M.D.
Doctor of Laws

JUNE 25, 1868

Andrew J. Kennedy, A.M., LL.B.*

JUNE 25, 1873

**Alexander J.P. Garesche,
A.B., A.M., LL.D.***
St. Louis Attorney

JUNE 24, 1874

Michael Courtney, A.B.
Teacher of Penmanship
Doctor of Humanities

H.J. Spaunhorst, LL.D.*

JUNE 30, 1875

William Walsh, S.J., Ph.D.*

JUNE 26, 1876

F.P. Garesche, S.J., Ph.D.*
Professor of Elocution,
Saint Louis University

JUNE 27, 1877

Walter H. Hill, S.J., Ph.D.*
Secretary, Board of Trustees,
Saint Louis University

JUNE 26, 1878

Walter H. Hill, S.J., Ph.D.*
Secretary, Board of Trustees,
Saint Louis University

JUNE 25, 1879

**Jeremiah S. B. Alleyne, A.B.,
A.M., M.D.**
Doctor of Laws

Robert A. Bakewell, A.M., LL.D.
Doctor of Laws

J. Richard Barrett, A.B., A.M., LL.D.
Doctor of Laws

Jerome K. Bauduy, M.D.
Doctor of Laws

Louis C. Boisliniere, M.D.
Doctor of Laws

Henry A. Clover, LL.D.
Doctor of Laws

**Emile Doumeing,
A.B., A.M., M.D.**
Doctor of Laws

**Edward T. Farish,
A.B., A.M., LL.D.**
Doctor of Laws

Augustus H. Garland, LL.D.
United States Senator from Arkansas
Doctor of Laws

Elisha H. Gregory, M.D.*
Doctor of Laws

James Halligan, LL.D.
Doctor of Laws

**Henry B. Kelly,
A.B., A.M., LL.D.**
Doctor of Laws

Timothy L. Papin, M.D.
Doctor of Laws

Thomas C. Reynolds, LL.D.
Doctor of Laws

Ellsworth F. Smith, A.M., M.D.
Doctor of Laws

MARCH 5, 1880

J.T. Hodges, M.D.*

APRIL 14, 1880

**Alexander J. P. Garesche,
A.B., A.M., LL.D.***
St. Louis Attorney

JUNE 28, 1880

Robert A. Bakewell, LL.D.*

Montrose A. Pallen, A.M., M.D.
Doctor of Laws

JUNE 27, 1881

Timothy L. Papin, M.D., LL.D.*

JUNE 28, 1882

Rudolph J. Meyer, S.J., Ph.D.*
President, Saint Louis University

JUNE 25, 1884

Paul G. Robinson, M.D.
Doctor of Laws

JUNE 24, 1885

Conde Benoist Pallen, A.M., Ph.D.*

JUNE 30, 1886

Rudolph J. Meyer, S.J., Ph.D.*
President, Saint Louis University

Martin W. Willis, A.M., Ph.D., LL.D.
Doctor of Laws

JUNE 29, 1887

Daniel Dillon, LL.D.*
Judge, Circuit Court

JUNE 27, 1888

M.J. McLoughlin, A.M., Ph.D.*

JUNE 26, 1889

Robert A. Bakewell, LL.D.*

JUNE 24, 1891

Leslie E. Keeley, M.D.
Doctor of Laws

JUNE 28, 1899

John J. Kain, D.D.*
Archbishop of St. Louis

JUNE 27, 1900

H. M. Calmer, S.J.*

APRIL 25, 1903

Thomas H. Carter*
Former United States Senator
from Montana
Chairman, National World's
Fair Committee

Howard J. Rogers*
President, World's Fair Educational
Departments

JUNE 22, 1903

Alonzo C. Church*

APRIL 30, 1904

Shepard Barclay*
Former Chief Justice,
Supreme Court of Missouri

OCTOBER 18, 1904

Paul Bakewell, LL.D.
President, Saint Louis University
Alumni Association,
Doctor of Laws

Shepard Barclay, LL.D.
Former Justice,
Missouri Supreme Court
Doctor of Laws

Young H. Bond, M.D.
Dean, Saint Louis University
School of Medicine
Doctor of Laws

Paul Capdeville, LL.D.
Mayor of New Orleans
Doctor of Laws

David R. Francis, LL.D.
President,
Louisiana Purchase Exposition
Doctor of Laws

Constantius M. Graham,
F.S.C., Ph.D.
President, Christian Brothers College
Doctor of Divinity

Charles W. Knapp
Publisher/Editor, *St. Louis Republic*
Doctor of Laws

Isaac S. Taylor
Architect and Director of Works,
Louisiana Purchase Exposition,
Doctor of Laws

Julius S. Walsh
President, Mississippi Valley
Trust Company
Doctor of Laws

Edward Douglas White, LL.D.
Justice of the U.S. Supreme Court
Doctor of Laws

MAY 8, 1905

John M. Dodson, LL.D.*
Dean of the School of Law,
University of Chicago

JUNE 28, 1905

Holdridge Ozro Collins,
A.B., A.M., LL.D.
Doctor of Laws

MAY 19, 1906

C. M. Jackson, Ph.D.*
Professor, University of Missouri

JUNE 21, 1906

John Joseph Glennon*
Archbishop of St. Louis

MAY 18, 1907

Professor George Neil Stewart*
University of Chicago

Elias Potter Lyon, A.M., Ph.D.*
Dean, Saint Louis University
School of Medicine

MAY 22, 1908

Elias Potter Lyon, A.M., Ph.D.*
Dean, Saint Louis University
School of Medicine

JUNE 24, 1908

John Joseph Glennon*
Archbishop of St. Louis

Henry Thomas Stein, A.M.
Principal, Keystone State
Normal School
Doctor of Humanities

MAY 22, 1909

John B. Deaver, M.D.*
Philadelphia, Pennsylvania

JUNE 1909

Michael P. Dowling, S.J., Ph.D.*
Creighton University

Francis L. Steuver
Doctor of Laws

JUNE 16, 1910

John W. Noble, LL.D.
Doctor of Laws

O'Neill Ryan, LL.D.*
Dean, Saint Louis University
School of Law
Doctor of Laws

JUNE 7, 1911

Albert Chauncey Eycleshymer,
B.S., Ph.D., M.D.
Professor of Anatomy and
Director of the Anatomy Department,
Saint Louis University
Doctor of Science

Elias Potter Lyon, A.B., Ph.D., M.D.
Dean, Saint Louis University
School of Medicine
Doctor of Science

Conde Benoist Pallen, LL.D.*
New York

MAY 31, 1912

S.J. Meltzer, M.D., LL.D.*
Rockefeller Institute for
Medical Research

JUNE 1, 1912

John Hugo Grimm, Ph.B., LL.B.
Doctor of Laws

Virgil McClure Harris, LL.B.
Doctor of Laws

Elbert B. Owen, D.D.S.*
President, Saint Louis University
Dental College, Alumni Association

JUNE 21, 1912

Alexander J. Burrowes, S.J., Ph.D.*
President, Saint Louis University

John Hugo Grimm, Ph.B., LL.B., LL.D.*

JANUARY 30, 1913

Martin Fischer, Ph.D.*
Professor of Physiology,
University of Cincinnati

JUNE 11, 1913

Festus J. Wade*

JANUARY 31, 1914

Ralph L. Thompson, M.D.*
Professor and Head of the Department
of Pathology, Saint Louis University

JUNE 3, 1914

Melville L. Wilkinson*

JUNE 18, 1914

O'Neill Ryan, LL.D.*
Dean, Saint Louis University
School of Law

JUNE 10, 1915

William F. Robison, S.J., Ph.D.*
Professor of Dogmatic Theology,
Saint Louis University

JUNE 1, 1916

Isaac H. Lionberger*

JUNE 3, 1916

M.P. Ravenel, M.D.*
Professor of Preventive Medicine and
Hygiene, University of Missouri

JUNE 7, 1916

Frank O. Watts*

JUNE 21, 1916

Reverend Monsignor
John J. Tannrath*

MIDYEAR 1916

Augustus G. Pohlman, M.D.*

JUNE 9, 1917

Sterling Edwin Edmunds
Doctor of Laws

David I. Walsh*
Former Governor of Massachusetts

JULY 30, 1917

Simon A. Blackmore, A.B., A.M.
Doctor of Letters

JUNE 3, 1918

John Rourke Kenny
Doctor of Laws

Constantine J. Smyth, LL.D.*
Chief Justice,
Court of Appeals, D.C.

JUNE 5, 1919

Leonard Wood*

OCTOBER 2, 1919

Don Roscoe Joseph, M.S., M.D.*
Vice Dean and Professor of Physiology, Saint
Louis University School of Medicine

OCTOBER 24, 1919

Desire Cardinal Mercier
Archbishop of Malines, France
Doctor of Divinity

JUNE 7, 1920

Elias Potter Lyon, A.B., Ph.D., M.D.*
Dean of the Medical School
University of Minnesota; Former Dean, Saint
Louis University
School of Medicine
Doctor of Laws

JUNE 4, 1921

Marshal Ferdinand Foch
Generalissimo of the Allied Armies
Doctor of Laws

Walter George Smith,
A.M., LL.D., K.S.G.*
Former President,
American Bar Association

FEBRUARY 1, 1922

M.J. O'Connor, S.J., Ph.D.*
President, Saint Louis University

MAY 31, 1922

William Shepherd Benson*
United States Shipping Board,
Doctor of Laws

Hanau Wolf Loeb, A.M., M.D.
Dean, Saint Louis University
School of Medicine
Doctor of Laws

Joseph F. Smith, V.G.
Doctor of Laws

FEBRUARY 1, 1923

William F. Robison, S.J., Ph.D.*
President, Saint Louis University

MAY 9, 1923

Michael Cardinal von Faulhaber
Archbishop of Munich, Germany
Doctor of Divinity

JUNE 5, 1923

Albert C. Fox, S.J., Ph.D.*
President, Marquette University

The 1871 graduates of Saint Louis University's "Commercial Course"

Joseph Bernard Kammerer, A.B., A.M.
Belize, British Honduras
Doctor of Laws

JUNE 7, 1924

Stratton Duluth Brooks
Doctor of Laws

William F. Robison, S.J., Ph.D.*
President, Saint Louis University

FEBRUARY 2, 1925

Hanau Wolf Loeb, A.M., M.D., LL.D.*
Dean, Saint Louis University
School of Medicine

JUNE 4, 1925

Joseph L. Davis, S.J., Ph.D.*
Regent of the School of Commerce and
Finance, Saint Louis University

JUNE 7, 1926

**Charles Phillips Emerson,
A.B., M.D.***
Dean of the School of Medicine,
Indiana University

JUNE 6, 1927

**Daniel W. O'Donoghue,
A.M., LL.M., Ph.D., LL.D.***
Professor of Common Law Pleading,
Georgetown University

JUNE 5, 1928

Patrick Joseph McCormick, S.T.L., Ph.D.*
Professor of Education/
Dean, Catholic Sisters College,
The Catholic University of America

JUNE 4, 1929

George Frederick Zook, Ph.D.*
President, University of Akron (Ohio),
Former Chief of the Division of Higher
Education, United States
Bureau of Education

JUNE 3, 1930

Michael Williams, Litt.D.*
Editor, The Commonwealth

JUNE 5, 1930

*Raphael C. McCarthy, S.J., Ph.D.**
University Council of Regents and Deans,
Saint Louis University

Alphonse McMahon, A.B., M.D.*
Senior Instructor in Internal Medicine,
Saint Louis University

A crowd exits the West Pine Gym after the 1934 commencement ceremony.

JUNE 2, 1931

Alphonse M. Schwitalla, S.J., A.M., Ph.D.*
Dean, Saint Louis University
School of Medicine

MAY 20, 1932

Albert Munsch, S.J., Ph.D.*
Professor of Anthropology,
Saint Louis University

JUNE 7, 1932

William J. McGucken, S.J., A.M., Ph.D.*
Professor of Education and Director
of the Department; Regent of the School of
Education and of the
Junior Corporate Colleges of
Saint Louis University

JUNE 6, 1933

**Edward Augustus Fitzpatrick,
B.S., A.M., Ph.D., LL.D.**
President, St. Mary's
College for Women
Doctor of Literature

Joseph Dolive Elliff, A.B., A.M.
University of Missouri
Doctor of Laws

Samuel K. Wilson, S.J., Ph.D.*
Graduate School Dean,
Loyola University, Chicago

JUNE 5, 1934

John Joseph Glennon, D.D.*
Archbishop of St. Louis

JUNE 4, 1935

William F. Robison, S.J., Ph.D.*
Former President of
Saint Louis University

JUNE 2, 1936

Leo T. Crowley, K.S.G.*
Director, Federal Deposit Insurance
Corporation

OCTOBER 31, 1936

Eugenio Cardinal Pacelli
(Pope Pius XII)
Papal Secretary of State
Doctor of Science

JUNE 1, 1937

Aloysius J. Hogan, S.J., A.B., A.M., Ph.D.*
Former President, Fordham University
Graduate School Dean,
Georgetown University

JUNE 7, 1938

**James Fitzgerald, A.B., A.M.,
LL.B., LL.D.***
Professor of Economics,
University of Detroit

JUNE 6, 1939

Irvin Abel, A.M., M.D.*
Professor of Surgery,
University of Louisville
Former President,
American Medical Association

JUNE 4, 1940

Jacob Mark Lashly, A.M., LL.B.*
President-Elect of the
American Bar Association

JUNE 3, 1941

Francis Xavier Swietlik, A.B., M.A., LL.B.*
Dean, Marquette
University Law School

George W. Wilson
Doctor of Laws

JUNE 2, 1942

John P. Delaney, S.J., M.A., Ph.D., S.T.L.*
Director, Institute of Social Order

MAY 19, 1943

Zacheus J. Maher, S.J.*
American Assistant
to the General, Society of Jesus

NOVEMBER 19, 1943

**Thomas Parran, A.M., Ph.D., LL.D., Sc.D.,
D.P.H.***
U.S. Public Health Service

MAY 17, 1944

**Timothy L. Bouscaren,
S.J., A.B., M.A., LL.B., S.T.L.***
Professor of Canon Law
and Liturgy,
West Baden University

SEPT. 21, 1944

Ross T. McIntire, M.D.*
Surgeon General,
United States Navy

MAY 16, 1945

Phil M. Donnelly, LL.B.*
Governor of Missouri
Doctor of Laws

JUNE 14, 1945

Norman T. Kirk, M.D.*
Surgeon General,
United States Army

FEBRUARY 28, 1946

Harry B. Crimmins, S.J., A.M., Ph.D.*
Chaplain, 70th General Hospital

MAY 15, 1946

John F. Hurley, S.J., Ph.D.*
Superior General, Philippine Missions,
Society of Jesus

Oliver L. Parks, K.S.G.
President, Parks College
Doctor of Science

NOVEMBER 23, 1946

Thomas M. Knapp, S.J.*
President, Rockhurst College

JUNE 3, 1947

Mark K. Carroll, D.D., LL.D.*
Bishop of Wichita
Doctor of Laws

JUNE 1, 1948

George W. Strake, B.S.
Doctor of Science

Kurt von Schuschnigg, J.U.D.*
Former Chancellor of Austria

FEBRUARY 5, 1949

Arthur L. Rayhawk, A.M., Ph.D*.
Associate Professor of Marketing,
Saint Louis University

JUNE 7, 1949

Clarence Francis, B.S.*
Chairman of the Board,
General Foods Corporation

FEBRUARY 4, 1950

Niels Christian Beck, A.B.*
Dean, Parks College of
Saint Louis University

Gustave K. Klausner
Professor of Accounting,
Saint Louis University
Doctor of Laws

JUNE 6, 1950

Louis S. St. Laurent, K.C., LL.D.*
Prime Minister of Canada
Doctor of Laws

FEBRUARY 3, 1951

Thomas Patrick Neill, Ph.D.*
Associate Professor of History,
Saint Louis University

APRIL 15, 1951

**Bernard W. Dempsey, S.J.,
A.M., S.T.L., Ph.D.**
Board of Trustees,
Saint Louis University
Doctor of Laws

JUNE 5, 1951

Maurice J. Tobin*
Secretary of Labor
Doctor of Laws

JUNE 3, 1952

**Ralph J. Bunche, A.M., Ph.D.,
D.H.L., D.Litt., LL.D.***
Director, Department of Trusteeship
United Nations Delegate and
Nobel Laureate
Doctor of Laws

FEBRUARY 1, 1953

Ralph Kinsella Sr., A.M., M.D.*
Professor of Internal Medicine
and Director of the Department,
Saint Louis University

JUNE 2, 1953

**Oliver Cromwell Carmichael,
A.B., B.Sc., A.M., LL.D., Litt.D.***
President, Carnegie Foundation for the
Advancement of Learning

JANUARY 31, 1954

Walter F. Gast, M.S.*
Professor of Management/Departmental
Director,
Saint Louis University

JUNE 1, 1954

Joseph E. Ritter, S.T.D.
Archbishop of St. Louis
Doctor of Laws

**George W. Strake,
B.S., D.Sc., LL.D.***
Houston, Texas

FEBRUARY 6, 1955

James E. Higgins, LL.B.*
Professor of Law,
Saint Louis University

JUNE 7, 1955

Edward A. Doisy, Sr., M.S., Ph.D., D.Sc.
Distinguished Service Professor
of Biochemistry and Director,
Saint Louis University
Doctor of Laws

**Thomas E. Murray, B.S., K.S.G.,
K.M., LL.D.***
Commissioner, Atomic Energy Commission
Doctor of Laws

NOVEMBER 15, 1955

**Robert I. Gannon, S.J., A.M., M.A., S.T.D.,
Litt.D., L.H.D., LL.D.**
Rector, Loyola Academy
and Regis High School
Pastor, St. Ignatius Church,
New York City
Doctor of Laws

Eugene J. McCarthy, A.M.
U.S. House of Representatives (Minnesota)
Doctor of Laws

**Reverend John Courtney Murray, S.J., A.M.,
S.T.L., S.T.D., LL.D.**
Woodstock College
Doctor of Laws

Thomas F. O'Neil, A.B.
President, Mutual Broadcasting System and
General Teleradio, Inc.
Doctor of Laws

NOVEMBER 16, 1955

Herold C. Hunt, A.M., Ed.D., LL.D.
Under Secretary of Health,
Education and Welfare
Doctor of Laws

**Henry R. Luce, A.M., LL.D., Litt.D., L.H.D.,
H.H.D.**
Editor-in-Chief, TIME Inc.
Doctor of Laws

Ethan Allen H. Shepley, A.B., LL.B.
Chancellor,
Washington University
Doctor of Laws

Raymond R. Tucker, A.B., B.S.
Mayor, City of St. Louis
Doctor of Laws

John J. Wright, A.B., S.T.L., S.T.D.
Bishop of Worcester, Massachusetts
Doctor of Laws

FEBRUARY 5, 1956

James W. Colbert Jr., M.D.*
Dean, Saint Louis University
School of Medicine

JUNE 2, 1956

John Burke, B.S.
Cathedral House,
New Delhi, India
Doctor of Laws

**Raymond Roche Tucker,
A.B., B.S., LL.D.***
Mayor, City of St. Louis

FEBRUARY 3, 1957

Walter LaRoy Wilkins, A.M., Ph.D.*
Department of Psychology,
Saint Louis University

JUNE 4, 1957

Lucius D. Clay, B.S.*
Chairman of the Board,
Continental Can Company
Doctor of Laws

NOVEMBER 14, 1957

**Henry Stuart Mackenzie Burns,
B.S., M.A., LL.D.**
President and Director,
Shell Oil Company
National Chairman,
American Red Cross
Doctor of Science

NOVEMBER 17, 1957

Mary Concordia, S.S.M., D.Sc.
Superior General of the
Sisters of St. Mary
Doctor of Laws

F. G. Hochwalt, A.M., Ph.D.
Executive Secretary,
National Catholic
Education Association
Doctor of Laws

FEBRUARY 2, 1958

**Keyes D. Metcalf, A.B., Litt.D., L.H.D.,
LL.D.***
Librarian Emeritus,
Harvard University

JUNE 3, 1958

Wernher von Braun, B.S., Ph.D.*
Technical Director,
Army Ballistic Missile Agency
Doctor of Science

NOVEMBER 16, 1958

John J. Butler
President,
Catholic Charities of St. Louis
Doctor of Laws

**Arthur Sherwood Flemming,
A.M., LL.B., LL.D.**
Secretary, Department of Health,
Education and Welfare
Doctor of Laws

Luke E. Hart, LL.B., LL.D.
Supreme Knight, Knights of
Columbus-Connecticut
Doctor of Letters

FEBRUARY 1, 1959

Walter J. Ong., S.J., Ph.D.*
Department of English,
Saint Louis University

JUNE 6, 1959

**Ethan A. H. Shepley, A.B.,
LL.B., LL.D.***
Chancellor, Washington University

NOVEMBER 22, 1959

Anselm Albareda,
O.S.B., Prefetto
Bibliotica Apostolica Vaticana,
Rome, Italy
Doctor of Laws

**Nathan M. Pusey,
A.B., A.M., Ph.D.**
President, Harvard University
Doctor of Laws

Egidio Vagnozzi
Apostolic Delegate
to the United States
Doctor of Laws

NOVEMBER 23, 1959

**Keyes DeWitt Metcalf, A.B., Litt.D., L.H.D.,
LL.D.**
Librarian Emeritus,
Harvard University
Doctor of Laws

FEBRUARY 7, 1960

Albert R. Zuroweste, D.D.*
Bishop of Belleville, Illinois

MAY 15, 1960

Dominique Pire, O.P.
Nobel Laureate
Doctor of Laws

JUNE 4, 1960

Ernest Joseph Burrus, S.J.
Jesuit Historical Institute, Rome
Visiting Professor,
Saint Louis University
Doctor of Letters

**John T. Ryan Jr.,
B.S., M.B.A., D.Sc.***
President of Mine Safety Appliance Co.
and President of Allegheny Conference
for Community Development, Pittsburgh,
Pennsylvania

NOVEMBER 13, 1960

Edward Teller
Professor of Physics,
University of California
Doctor of Science

FEBRUARY 5, 1961

Glennon P. Flavin, D.D.*
Auxiliary Bishop of St. Louis

JUNE 3, 1961

Edward C. Kenney, M.D., D.Sc.*
Surgeon General,
United States Navy

FEBRUARY 4, 1962

**Robert F. McDermott,
USAF, B.A., M.B.A.***
Dean of the Faculty,
U.S. Air Force Academy
Doctor of Laws

JUNE 2, 1962

**R. Sargent Shriver,
A.B., LL.B., LL.D.***
Director, Peace Corps
Doctor of Laws

FEBRUARY 3, 1963

**Merrimon Cuninggim,
B.D., Ph.D., Litt.D.***
Executive Director,
The Danforth Foundation

APRIL 19, 1963

Hans Küng
Dean-elect of the
Catholic Theological Faculty
University of Münster
Doctor of Laws

APRIL 20, 1963

Tom C. Clark, A.B., LL.B., LL.D.
Associate Justice,
United States Supreme Court
Doctor of Laws

JUNE 1, 1963

O. Meredith Wilson, A.B., Ph.D.*
President, University of Minnesota

FEBRUARY 9, 1964

Carroll A. Hochwalt, B.S., D.Sc.*
Vice President,
Monsanto Chemical Company
Doctor of Science

MAY 8, 1964

Eugene Cardinal Tisserant
Dean, College of Cardinals
Doctor of Letters

JUNE 6, 1964

Oscar V. Batson, M.D.
University of Pennsylvania,
Graduate School of Medicine
Doctor of Law

**William Kurtz Wimsatt Jr.,
B.A., M.A., Ph.D.***
Professor of English,
Yale University
Doctor of Laws

FEBRUARY 7, 1965

**John Jay Corson,
B.S., M.S., Ph.D.***
Professor of Public and
International Affairs
Princeton University

Edgar Monsanto Queeny
Former Chairman of the Board,
Monsanto Company
Doctor of Letters

Charles H. Sommer
President, Monsanto Company
Doctor of Science

Charles Allen Thomas
Chairman of the Board,
Monsanto Company
Doctor of Science

JUNE 5, 1965

John T. Connor, A.B., LL.B.*
Secretary of Commerce
Doctor of Laws

OCTOBER 1965

Adolph Butenandt
President, Max Planck Society
Director of the Institute at
Munich, West Germany
Doctor of Science

Carl F. Cori, Ph.D.
Chairman,
Department of Chemistry,
Washington University
Doctor of Science

Henrik Dam, Ph.D.
Polytechnic Institute,
Copenhagen, Denmark
Nobel Laureate
Doctor of Science

A. Baird Hastings, Ph.D.
Scripps Clinic and
Research Foundation
Doctor of Science

Vincent du Vigneaud, Ph.D.
Department of Biochemistry,
Cornell University
Doctor of Science

A 1961 graduate and his family

FEBRUARY 6, 1966

John Joseph O'Brien, A.M., Ph.D.*
Professor of Education,
Saint Louis University

JUNE 4, 1966

Elmer Ellis, Ph.D.
President, University of Missouri
Doctor of Letters

John C. Weaver, A.M., Ph.D.*
Vice President of Dean and
Faculties and President-Elect, University of
Missouri

FEBRUARY 5, 1967

Everett McKinley Dirksen, LL.D.*
United States Senator from Illinois
Doctor of Laws

JUNE 3, 1967

Daniel Lyons Schlafly, A.B.*
Chairman, Board of Trustees,
Saint Louis University

JULY 1967

Christopher C. Kraft Jr., Ph.D.
Flight Director,
American Manned Space Flights
Doctor of Science

OCTOBER 12, 1967

Robert McAfee Brown
Professor of Religion,
Stanford University
Doctor of Laws

Karl Rahner, S.J.
Professor of Dogmatic Theology
and the History of Dogma,
University of Münster
Doctor of Laws

NOVEMBER 30, 1967

Edward Schillebeeckx, O.P.
Professor of Dogmatic Theology
and History of Theology,
Catholic University
Doctor of Laws

FEBRUARY 4, 1968

George L. Cadigan, D.D.*
Bishop, Episcopal Diocese
of Missouri

JUNE 1, 1968

James P. Hickok
Chairman of the Board,
First National Bank in St. Louis
Doctor of Laws

Grace Bumbry Jaeckel
Opera Singer
Doctor of Humanities

Scene from the 1965 commencement

Theodore David McNeal
United States Senator from Missouri
Doctor of Laws

Daniel Patrick Moynihan, B.A., M.A., Ph.D.*
Director, Joint Center
for Urban Studies of Massachusetts Institute
of Theology and
Harvard University
Doctor of Laws

Harold R. Perry
Bishop of Mons in Mauretania,
Auxiliary Bishop of New Orleans
Doctor of Laws

John A. Shocklee
Pastor, St. Bridget of Erin, St. Louis
Doctor of Laws

OCTOBER 16, 1968

Eugene Carson Blake
General Secretary of the
World Council of Churches
Doctor of Letters

OCTOBER 17, 1968

John G. M. Willebrands
Secretary, Vatican Secretariat
for Christian Unity
Doctor of Letters

OCTOBER 25, 1968

Cleanth Brooks
Author, Cultural Attaché
to U.S. Embassy in London
Doctor of Letters

Harold Howe II
U.S. Commissioner of Education
Doctor of Laws

Clark Kerr
Chairman, Commission on
the Future of Higher Education
of the Carnegie Foundation
Doctor of Laws

Sol Spiegelman, Ph.D.
Professor of Microbiology,
University of Illinois
Doctor of Science

FEBRUARY 2, 1969

August A. Busch Jr.
President/Chairman
of the Board,
Anheuser-Busch
Doctor of Laws

Frederick Seitz, Ph.D.*
President, National Academy
of Science
Doctor of Science

MAY 31, 1969

Dom Helder Pessoa Camara
Archbishop of Olinda and Recife, Brazil
Doctor of Letters

Thomas Hopkinson Eliot, Ph.D.
Chancellor, Washington University
Doctor of Humanities

Luc Gillon
General Administrator
of Lovanium University
Kinshasa, Democratic
Republic of the Congo
Doctor of Laws

David Dodds Henry, Ph.D.
President, University of Illinois
Doctor of Laws

Theodore Martin Hesburgh, C.S.C., Ph.D., S.T.D.*
President, University of Notre Dame
Doctor of Humanities

Henri de Lubac, S.J.
Professor Emeritus,
Institut Catholique of Lyons
Doctor of Letters

FEBRUARY 1, 1970

James Hadley Billington, B.A., D.Phil.*
Professor of History,
Princeton University

JUNE 6, 1970

H. I. Romnes, B.S., LL.D., D.Eng.*

FEBRUARY 7, 1971

John Anthony Brown, M.A., LL.D., L.H.D., Litt.D.*
President, The Lindenwood Colleges

JUNE 5, 1971

Marc H. Tanenbaum, B.S., M.H.L., D.H.Lit.,D.R.E.*
National Director
of Interreligious Affairs,
The American Jewish Committee
Doctor of Letters

AUGUST 23, 1971

Dr. Gerhard Ebeling
Institute of Hermeneutics
and Professor of Theology,
University of Zurich
Doctor of Letters

Erwin Iserloh
Director, Catholic
Ecumenical Institute
Professor of Ecumenial Theology and
of Medieval and Modern Church History,
University of Münster
Doctor of Letters

MAY 13, 1972

John Anthony Brown, M.A., LL.D., L.H.D., Litt.D.
President, Lindenwood Colleges
Doctor of Laws

Joseph Parker Cosand, A.M., L.H.D.*
U.S. Deputy Commissioner
for Higher Education
Doctor of Laws

MAY 12, 1973

Thomas Eagleton, LL.D.
United States Senator
from Missouri
Doctor of Laws

Leonor K. Sullivan*
Member of Congress,
Third District, Missouri
Doctor of Laws

Stuart Symington, LL.D.
United States Senator
from Missouri
Doctor of Laws

OCTOBER 1973

John M. Olin
Honorary Chairman of the Board, Olin
Doctor of Laws

MAY 11, 1974

David Barrett*
Premier, Province of British Columbia
Doctor of Laws

Garret FitzGerald
Foreign Minister of the
Republic of Ireland
Doctor of Laws

APRIL 8, 1975

Edward W. Stimpson*
President, General Aviation Manufacturers
Association

MAY 10, 1975

Robert Hanna Felix, M.D.
Dean Emeritus,
Saint Louis University
School of Medicine
Doctor of Laws

JULY 29, 1975

Daniel James Jr., USAF*
Vice Commander,
Military Airlift Command

DECEMBER 8, 1975

Ardeshir Zahedi
Iranian Ambassador
to the United States
Doctor of Laws

DECEMBER 16, 1975

Grant L. Hansen*
Vice President/General Manager,
Convair Division
General Dynamics Corporation

APRIL 13, 1976

Edwin G. Eigel Jr., B.S., Ph.D.*
Academic Vice President,
Saint Louis University

MAY 8, 1976

Daniel James Jr., USAF
Commander, North American Air
Defense Command
Doctor of Laws

Jacques Kosciusko-Morizet
French Ambassador
to the United States
Doctor of Humanities

AUGUST 2, 1976

Gerald P. Carr, USMC, B.S., M.E., B.S.A.E., M.S.A.E.*
National Aeronautics and
Space Administration,
Lyndon B. Johnson Space Center
Doctor of Science

DECEMBER 20, 1976

Jerome J. Marchetti, S.J., Ph.D.*
Chairman, Administrative Board
of Parks College
Secretary-Treasurer,
Saint Louis University

APRIL 12, 1977

Knut Hagrup*
President, Scandinavian
Airline System

AUGUST 1, 1977

David Sloan Lewis Jr., B.S.A.E.*
Chairman of the Board,
General Dynamics
Doctor of Laws

DECEMBER 19, 1977

Rene H. Miller*
Head, Department of Aeronautics and
Astronautics, The Massachusetts Institute of
Technology

APRIL 10, 1978

Eugene F. Kranz*
Deputy Director of Flight Operations
Lyndon B. Johnson Space Center

MAY 13, 1978

Sarah Caldwell
Operatic Producer and Conductor
Doctor of Humane Letters

JULY 31, 1978

Brockman Adams, B.A., J.D.*
Secretary of Transportation
Doctor of Laws

DECEMBER 18, 1978

Thomas W. Gillespie Jr., B.S.*
Senior Vice President,
Piper Aircraft Corporation

APRIL 9, 1979

Robin H. H. Wilson, B.S., M.B.A.*
Senior President-Operations,
Trans World Airlines

MAY 12, 1979

John Joseph Cardinal Carberry
Archbishop of St. Louis
Doctor of Laws

Dolores DeFina Hope
Doctor of Humane Letters

Leslie Townes "Bob" Hope
Entertainer
Doctor of Humane Letters

Leo F. Weber, S.J.
Provincial of the Missouri Province
Doctor of Laws

JULY 30, 1979

Leon H. Toups, B.S., M.S., E.A.A.*
President and Chief Operating Officer,
Chromalloy American Corporation

DECEMBER 17, 1979

James C. Waugh, B.S.*
Senior Vice President-
Maintenance and Engineering,
Pan American World Airways, Inc.

APRIL 18, 1980

William R. Smanko, S.S.*
Vice President-Defense
and Electronics Systems Center
and General Manager-System Development
Division,
Westinghouse Electric Corporation

JULY 28, 1980

William J. Hogan
Former Executive Vice President
of Finance and Chairman,
Finance Committee,
American Airlines
Doctor of Laws

OCTOBER 18, 1980

Lord Patrick Arthur Devlin
Baron, Life Peer-retired
Doctor of Laws

MAY 16, 1981

John T. Noonan Jr., LL.D.
Professor of Law,
University of California,
Berkeley School of Law
Doctor of Laws

JULY 29, 1981

Leon Zee Seltzer,
Ph.C., B.S.E., Ae.E.*
Dean, Parks College

DECEMBER 16, 1981

James R. Allen, USAF, B.S., M.S.*
Commander in Chief,
Military Airlift Command

APRIL 7, 1982

Thomas Patrick Melady, B.A., M.A., Ph.D.*
Assistant Secretary of Postsecondary Educa-
tion, United States
Department of Education
Doctor of Laws

MAY 15, 1982

William H. Danforth
Chancellor, Washington University
Doctor of Laws

William Evans Douthit
President,
Urban League of St. Louis
Doctor of Humane Letters

James Garber Galbraith, M.D.
Professor of Neurosurgery
Department of Surgery/
Divison of Neurosurgery,
University of Alabama Birmingham
Doctor of Science

Peter H. Raven, Ph.D.*
Director,
Missouri Botanical Gardens
Doctor of Science

John P. Raynor, S.J.
President, Marquette University
Doctor of Laws

JULY 27, 1982

John Nicholas Wurm, Ph.D.*
Bishop of Belleville, Illinois

DECEMBER 15, 1982

Thomas R. Fitzgerald, S.J., Ph.D.*
President, Saint Louis University

APRIL 8, 1983

William H. Rehnquist, LL.D.
United States Supreme Court
Doctor of Laws

APRIL 11, 1983

Thomas R. Fitzgerald, S.J., Ph.D.*
President, Saint Louis University

MAY 12, 1983

Art Buchwald
Author
Doctor of Humane Letters

MAY 14, 1983

John L. May
Archbishop of St. Louis
Doctor of Laws

John H. Poelker
Former Mayor, City of St. Louis
Doctor of Public Service

Leonard Slatkin
Music Director,
Saint Louis Symphony
Doctor of Humane Letters

Leon R. Strauss
Architect and Builder
Doctor of Laws

AUGUST 1, 1983

John F. Yardley, M.S.*
President, McDonnell-Douglas Astronautics
Company and
Corporate Vice President,
McDonnell-Douglas Corporation

DECEMBER 14, 1983

Curtis M. Graves, LL.D.*
Deputy Director of Public Affairs for Aca-
demic Services, National Aeronautics and
Space Administration (NASA)

MARCH 11, 1984

Joseph Cardinal Bernardin
Archbishop of Chicago
Doctor of Humane Letters

APRIL 10, 1984

Edward J. Crane, B.S.*
President, Ozark Air Lines

MAY 10, 1984

William A. Nolen, M.D.
Physician and Author
Doctor of Humane Letters

MAY 12, 1984

James D. Collins, Ph.D.
Professor of Philosophy,
Saint Louis University
Doctor of Humane Letters

John C. Danforth, LL.D.*
United States Senator
from Missouri
Doctor of Legal Laws

Walter J. Ong, S.J., Ph.D.
University Professor of Humanities; William
E. Haren Professor of English;
Professor of Humanities in Psychiatry,
Saint Louis University
Doctor of Humane Letters

JULY 31, 1984

John H. Winant, B.S.*
President and Chief Operating Officer,
National Business Aircraft
Association, Inc.

DECEMBER 17, 1984

Burl W. McLaughlin*
President, Mississippi Valley
Air Lines

APRIL 12, 1985

Allen E. Paulson*
Chairman and President,
Gulfstream Aerospace Corporation

MAY 11, 1985

Richard A. Gephardt, LL.D.*
United States Representative
from Missouri
Doctor of Public Service

Robert M. Heyssel, M.D
President,
The Johns Hopkins Hospital
Doctor of Science

Peter Sutherland
Commissioner of the Commission of the
European Economic Communities
Doctor of Legal Laws

JULY 30, 1985

James P. Keleher, D.D.*
Bishop of Belleville, Illinois

Harold S. Wood, Ph.D.
Professor Emeritus of
Aeronautical Administration,
Parks College of Saint Louis University
Doctor of Legal Laws

DECEMBER 16, 1985

Richard D. Pearson, M.B.A.*
President, Trans World Airlines

APRIL 9, 1986

Umberto Nordio, Ph.D.*
Chairman of the Board and
Chief Executive Officer
of Alitalia Airlines
Doctor of Legal Laws

MAY 16, 1986

William H. Oldendorf, M.D.
Professor of Neurology and Psychiatry,
University of California at Los Angeles
Doctor of Science

MAY 17, 1986

C. Rollins Hanlon, M.D.
Director of the American
College of Surgeons
Doctor of Science

Sanford N. McDonnell
President and Chief
Executive officer,
McDonnell-Douglas Corporation
Doctor of Science

Vincent C. Schoemehl Jr.*
Mayor, City of St. Louis
Doctor of Public Service

Nathan B. Young, LL.D.
Retired Attorney and Judge
Doctor of Legal Laws

JULY 29, 1986

James C. Carter, S.J., Ph.D.*
President, Loyola University,
New Orleans

DECEMBER 16, 1986

Walter J. Boyne, M.B.A.*
Former Director,
National Air and Space Museum Smithsonian
Institute

APRIL 9, 1987

George E. Day, USAF, J.D.*
Attorney at Law,
Fort Walton Beach, Florida

MAY 16, 1987

George H.W. Bush*
Vice President of the United States
Doctor of Legal Laws

Robert F. Hyland
Regional Vice President,
CBS Radio Division
Doctor of Public Service

Harvey A. Itano, Ph.D., M.D.
Professor of Pathology,
University of California
Doctor of Science

JULY 28, 1987

Mervin K. Strickler Jr., Ed.D.*
Aviation Education Consultant

DECEMBER 17, 1987

T. Allan McArtor, M.S.E.*
Administrator,
Federal Aviation Administration

APRIL 8, 1988

Fausto Cereti*
President and Chief
Operating Officer, Alenia
Doctor of Legal Laws

MAY 19, 1988

Robert G. Petersdorf, M.D.
President and Chief Executive Officer,
Association of American
Medical Colleges
Doctor of Science

Procession at Parks College Graduation, July 30, 1969

MAY 21, 1988

Lawrence Biondi, S.J., Ph.D.*
President, Saint Louis University

Henry E. Hampton
President, Blackside, Inc.
Doctor of Humane Letters

Renilda Hilkemeyer, B.S., R.N.
Retired Nursing Educator
Doctor of Public Service

David Merrick
Theatrical Producer
Doctor of Humane Letters

AUGUST 1, 1988

Donald W. Bennett, USAF, B.S.M.E.*
Director of Airports,
Lambert-St. Louis
International Airport

DECEMBER 15, 1988

Paul A. Whelan, Ph.D.*
Vice President for Parks College

APRIL 11, 1989

Jeffrey H. Erickson, M.S.*
President and Chief
Operating Officer,
Midway Airlines

MAY 20, 1989

Clarence C. Barksdale
Vice Chairman,
Boatmen's Bancshares, Inc.
Doctor of Public Service

George E. Ganss, S.J., Ph.D.
Director, Institute of Jesuit Sources
Doctor of Laws

Ambassador Loret Miller Ruppe*
Director, Peace Corps;
Ambassador to Norway
Doctor of Public Service

Gustavo Villapolos Salas, Ph.D.
President, La Universidad Complutense
Doctor of Laws

Adelaide Mahaffey Schlafly
Doctor of Public Service

Daniel L. Schlafly
Doctor of Public Service

JULY 31, 1989

Robert C. Donahue*
Director of Airports,
Federal Aviation
Administration

DECEMBER 14, 1989

Alice Bourke Hayes, Ph.D.*
Provost and Executive Vice President,
Saint Louis University

APRIL 9, 1990

Leonard L. Griggs Jr., M.S.*
Assistant Administrator for Airports, Federal
Aviation Administration

MAY 19, 1990

Barbara Pierce Bush*
First Lady of the United States
Doctor of Humanities

Clyde S. Cahill, LL.D.
Circuit Judge, City of St. Louis
Doctor of Laws

Leighton E. Cluff, M.D.
President, Robert Wood
Johnston Foundation
Doctor of Science

Henry Givens Jr., Ph.D.
President, Harris-Stowe State College
Doctor of Humanities

Ellen Robinson Grass, LL.D., D.Sc.
President, Grass Foundation
Doctor of Science

Charles H. Hoessle
Director, Saint Louis Zoo
Doctor of Laws

FEBRUARY 25, 1991

Jon Sobrino, S.J., Ph.D.
Professor of Theology,
University of Central America
in San Salvador
Doctor of Humanities

MAY 18, 1991

Charles Blakey Blackmar, LL.D.
Missouri Chief Justice
Doctor of Laws

Andrew M. Greeley, Ph.D.
Sociologist, Educator and Writer
Doctor of Humanities

Edward J. (Ted) Koppel*
Anchor for ABC's Nightline
Doctor of Humane Letters

Kathryn E. Nelson
Program Director for
Danforth Foundation
Doctor of Humanities

Paul H. Poberezny
Chairman of the Board, Experimental
Aircraft Assoc.
Doctor of Science

MAY 16, 1992

Mary Ann Eckhoff, S.S.N.D., Ph.D.
Superintendent of Education,
St. Louis Archdiocese
Doctor of Humanities

Joseph Garagiola*
Co-host of NBC's Today
Doctor of Humane Letters

Theodore McMillian, LL.D.
Circuit Judge, U.S. Court of Appeals
for the Eighth Circuit
Doctor of Laws

OCTOBER 14, 1992

Kenneth D. Kaunda
Former President of Zambia
Doctor of Laws

OCTOBER 23, 1992

Gregorio Peces-Barba, Ph.D.
Rector de la Universidad
Carlos III de Madrid
Doctor of Humanities

Rosa Chacel
Author
Doctor of Letters

D. Javier Gurpide
Vice Presidente del
Banco Bilbao Vizcaya
Doctor of Laws

MAY 15, 1993

Ian T. Jackson, M.D.,
Director of the Institute for Craniofacial and
Reconstructive Surgery
Doctor of Science

Sisters Mary Joel Kolmer,
Shirley Kolmer, Ph.D.,
Kathleen McGuire, Ph.D., Agnes Mueller and
Barbara Ann Muttra (posthumously)
Accepting in Their Honor:
Sister Mildred Gross
Provincial of the Adorers
of the Blood of Christ
Doctor of Humanities

Jacob Neusner, Ph.D.
Distinguished Research Professor,
University of South Florida
Doctor of Humane Letters

May 2014

John W. Padberg, S.J., Ph.D.*
Director, Institute of
Jesuit Sources

MAY 14, 1994

Mildred L. Jamison, R.N.
Founder of Faith House
Doctor of Humanities

John W. O'Malley, S.J., Ph.D.
Professor of Church History,
Weston School of Theology
Doctor of Humane Letters

Hays H. Rockwell, D.H.*
Episcopal Bishop of the
Diocese of Missouri
Doctor of Humanities

Donald M. Suggs, D.D.S.
President and Publisher,
St. Louis American
Doctor of Laws

JANUARY 31, 1995

Andrew Young
U.S. Representative
to the United Nations
Civil and Human Rights Leader
Doctor of Laws

MAY 20, 1995

Jack Buck*
Sports Director,
KMOX/CBS Radio
Doctor of Humanities

John E. Connelly
Chairman and
Chief Executive Officer,
JEC Enterprises, Ltd.
Doctor of Humanities

Justin Rigali
Archbishop of St. Louis
Doctor of Humane Letters

MAY 18, 1996

Daniel T. Barry, Ph.D., M.D.
Astronaut, National
Aeronautics and
Space Administration
Doctor of Science

Alfred Fleishman
Co-Founder,
Fleishman-Hillard, Inc.
Doctor of Humane Letters

Ada Sue Hinshaw, Ph.D., R.N.
Dean and Professor,
University of Michigan
School of Nursing
Former Director, the
National Institutes of Health
Center of Nursing Research
Doctor of Science

Michael Novack, M.A.*
George Fredrick Jewett Chair
in Religion and Public Policy
at the American Enterprise Institute, Washington, D.C. Theologian, Author and former
U.S. Ambassador
Doctor of Humanities

Harry Wu, Ph.D.
Human Rights Activist
Doctor of Humanities

MAY 17, 1997

Anne Keefe, M.A.*
Journalist, KETC-Channel 9
Doctor of Humane Letters

Ira Herskowitz, Ph.D.
Professor of Biochemistry
and Biophysics
University of California-San Francisco
Doctor of Science

Richard J. Mark, M.S.
President and CEO,
St. Mary's Hospital
of East St. Louis, Ill.
Doctor of Public Service

Mary Ross
Retiring Alderwoman-
Fifth Ward City of St. Louis
Board of Alderman
Doctor of Public Service

Janet D. Rowley, M.D., D.Sc.
Professor of Medicine, Molecular Genetics
and Cell Biology,
University of Chicago
Doctor of Science

MAY 16, 1998

Tim Russert, J.D.*
Moderator, NBC's Meet the Press
Doctor of Public Service

**Judith Spector Aronson, Ph.D.,
and Adam Aronson, B.S.**
Art Patrons
Doctor of Fine Arts

Frankie Muse Freeman, J.D.
Civil Rights Leader
Doctor of Laws

**Judith Pearce Jones
and Dennis M. Jones**
Founders, Jones Medical Industries Inc.
Doctor of Humanities

Otto Felix Schwarz, Ph.D.
President and CEO, IMMUNO
Doctor of Science

MAY 15, 1999

Archbishop Joseph Pittau, S.J., Ph.D.
Secretary, Congregation
for Catholic Education
Doctor of Laws

Cokie Roberts, B.A.*
Journalist, This Week
with Sam Donaldson
and Cokie Roberts
Doctor of Public Service

Steven V. Roberts, B.A.*
Shapiro Professor of Media
and Public Affairs,
George Washington University
Doctor of Public Service

Hon. Ronnie L. White, J.D.
Judge, Missouri Supreme Court
Doctor of Laws

MAY 20, 2000

August A. Busch III*
Chairman of the Board and President,
Anheuser-Busch Companies Inc.
Doctor of Laws

Mary Adele Bruemmer, M.A.
University Volunteer
Doctor of Humanities

Marilyn Fox
Community Volunteer
Doctor of Public Service

Sam Fox, B.S.
Chairman and Chief Executive Officer,
Harbour Group Ltd.
Doctor of Public Service

Bishop Wilton D. Gregory, Ph.D.
Bishop of Belleville, Illinois
Doctor of Humanities

MAY 19, 2001

Richard Baron, J.D.
President, McCormack Baron
& Associates
Doctor of Fine Arts

Margaret A. Farley, R.S.M., Ph.D.
Gilbert L. Stark Professor
of Theological Ethics
Yale University Divinity School
Doctor of Humanities

Elizabeth and Raymond Kalinowski
Community Volunteers
Doctor of Humanities

Arnold L. Mitchem, Ph.D.*
President, Council for Opportunity
in Education
Doctor of Humanities

MAY 18, 2002

Alice Bourke Hayes, Ph.D.*
President, University of San Diego
Doctor of Laws

Bishop Joseph Lee Han-taek, S.J., M.S.
Auxiliary Bishop of Seoul Korea
Doctor of Laws

Mary Ann Barrett Shanahan
Community Volunteer
Doctor of Humanities

Michael F. Shanahan Sr., B.S.
Chairman of the Board and CEO,
Engineered Support Systems Inc.
Doctor of Laws

MAY 17, 2003

Martin L. Mathews
President, CEO & Co-founder
Mathews-Dickey
Boys' and Girls' Club
Doctor of Humanities

Bill McClellan*
Columnist,
St. Louis Post-Dispatch

Emily Rauh Pulitzer, M.A.
Founder and President
Pulitzer Foundation for the Arts
Doctor of Fine Arts

Very Rev. Frank Reale, S.J., M.A.
Provincial, Jesuits of the
Missouri Province
Doctor of Humanities

MAY 15, 2004

Wolf Blitzer, M.A.*
CNN Anchor
Doctor of Public Service

Clara L. Adams-Ender, M.S.N., M.M.A.S.
Brigadier General and Nurse,
U.S. Army
Doctor of Science

Kathleen Hummel, M.S.W.
and Scott Hummel, M.S.W.
Founders, Our Little Haven
Doctor of Humanities

Bishop Robert J. Shaheen
Bishop, Eparchy of
Our Lady of Lebanon
Doctor of Humanities

MAY 14, 2005

Houston A. Baker Jr., Ph.D.*
Professor, Duke University
Doctor of Humane Letters

Joe Edwards, B.A.
St. Louis-area Developer
Doctor of Fine Arts

Bernadine Healy, M.D.
Cardiologist and Health Administrator
Doctor of Science

Floyd D. Loop, M.D.
Cardiologist, The Cleveland Clinic
Doctor of Science

MAY 20, 2006

Chris Lowney, M.A.*
Author, *Heroic Leadership*
Doctor of Laws

Maurice B. McNamee, S.J., Ph.D.
Professor Emeritus, SLU
Doctor of Fine Arts

Ruth Stoble, B.S.
and Frank Stroble, M.B.A.
Supporters of Catholic Education
Doctor of Humanities

Parks College graduates have a tradition of tossing paper airplanes when their class is announced.

This scene is from May 2017.

JUNE 30, 2006

Nasrallah Peter Cardinal Sfeir
Patriarch of Antioch and All the East
Doctor of Laws

MAY 19, 2007

Lawrence P. "Yogi" Berra*
Baseball Hall of Famer and Author
Doctor of Laws

Benjamin Carson
Neurosurgeon and Author
Doctor of Science

Chang-Soo Huh
Chairman and CEO,
GS Holdings Group
Doctor of Laws

Joseph and Rosemary Shaughnessy
Philanthropists and
Community Supporters
Doctor of Laws

MAY 17, 2008

Joe Buck*
Broadcaster, Fox Sports
Doctor of Humanities

Maxine Clark
Founder, Chairman and
Chief Executive Bear,
Build-A-Bear Workshop
Doctor of Laws

Charles and Shirley Drury
Hoteliers and Philanthropists
Doctor of Humanities

MAY 16, 2009

Greg Mortenson*
Humanitarian and Author
Doctor of Humanities

William H.T. "Bucky" Bush
Co-founder and Chairman,
Bush O'Donnell
Capital Partners LLC
Doctor of Law

Nancy and Al Siwak
Business Owners
and Community Volunteers
Doctor of Humanities

MAY 15, 2010

Most Rev. Pietro Sambi*
Archbishop and Apostolic Nuncio
to the United States
Doctor of Laws

Father Valentine Peter, J.C.D., S.T.D.
Former Executive Director,
Boys Town
Doctor of Humanities

Sister Mary Antona Ebo, F.S.M.
Civil Rights Pioneer
Doctor of Humanities

MAY 21, 2011

Anthony R. Tersigni*
President and CEO
of Ascension Health Inc.
Doctor of Public Service

Brother Mel Meyer, S.M.
Artist
Doctor of Fine Arts

Harlene E. and Marvin S. Wool
Entrepreneurs and Philanthropists
Doctor of Humanities

MAY 19, 2012

James Martin, S.J.*
Author
Doctor of Humane Letters

Doug and Ann Brown
Philanthropists
Doctor of Humanities

His Beatitude Bechara Peter Rai
Patriarch of the Maronite
Catholic Church
Doctor of Humanities

Paul A. Young
Professor of Anatomy
and Neurobiology
Doctor of Science

MAY 18, 2013

Metee Auapinyakul
Executive Director,
Banpu Public Company Limited
*Doctor of Business,
Engineering and Technology*

John Foppe*
Author and Executive Director,
Society of St. Vincent de Paul
*Doctor of Humanities
and Public Service*

Joe and Loretta Scott
Entrepreneurs and Philanthropists
Doctor of Humanities

Chanin Vongkusolkit
Chief Executive Officer,
President and Director,
Banpu Public Company Limited
Doctor of Business,
Engineering and Technology

MAY 17, 2014

Hon. Jimmie Edwards*
Judge, 22nd Judicial
Court of St. Louis
Founder, Innovative
Concept Academy
Doctor of Laws

Peggy Ritter
Philanthropist
Doctor of Humanities

David and Thelma Steward
Entrepreneurs and Philanthropists
Doctor of Humanities

Joseph Tetlow, S.J.
Spiritual Director and Author
Doctor of Humane Letters

MAY 16, 2015

Anita Lyons Bond
Educator and Civil Rights Champion
Doctor of Humanities

Garry Kasparov*
Chess Grandmaster and Founder of the
United Civil Front Movement
Doctor of Laws

Gene Kranz
Former Director of NASA's Mission Control
Doctor of Science

MAY 14, 2016

Kevin F. O'Malley, J.D.*
U.S. Ambassador to Ireland
Doctor of Science

Mary Jean Ryan, F.S.M.
Former CEO, SSM Health
Doctor of Public Service

MAY 20, 2017

Diana Natalico, Ph.D.*
President of the University of Texas at El Paso
Doctor of Science

Richard H. McClure
retired president of UniGroup
co-chair of the Ferguson Commission
Managing Director, Spero Advisors
Doctor of Public Service

John W. Padberg, S.J.
Professor of History at Saint Louis University,
former administrator including as president
of Weston Jesuit School of Theology
Doctor of Divinity

Reverend Starsky D. Wilson
President and CEO of Deaconess
Foundation, Pastor of Saint John's
United Church of Christ,
co-chair of the Ferguson Commission
Doctor of Public Service

NOTES

INTRODUCTION, pages 3-5

1. "Fifty oldest St. Louis-founded firms and institutions," *St. Louis Business Journal* (April 20-26, 1987): 16B.

2. DuBourg to Rosati, May 1826, (ASLA).

3. Claude H. Heithaus, S.J., *The Truth about St. Louis University* (St. Louis: Saint Louis University, 1940), 8.

4. Society of Jesus, General Congregation 34, Decree 17 http://www.sjweb.info/documents/education/CG34_D17_ENG.pdf.

CHAPTER 1, pages 6-29

1. The Panic of 1819 was a "traumatic awakening to the capitalist reality of boom-and-bust," which "plunged Americans into their first experience of general and devastating economic prostration." Charles Sellers, *The Market Revolution: Jacksonian America 1815-1846* (New York and Oxford: Oxford University Press, 1991), 136-37.

2. Steven Mintz, *Huck's Raft* (Cambridge: Belknap Press of Harvard University Press, 2004), 197-98.

3. Francis W. Nichols, "Theology at Saint Louis University 1818-2013" [unpublished, 2014], 12.

4. John T. Scharf, *History of Saint Louis City and County* (Philadelphia: Louis H. Everts & Co., 1883), 148. See also Charles Peterson, *Colonial St. Louis: Building a Creole Capital* (Tucson: Patrice Press, 1993).

5. Frederick Louis Billon, *Annals of St. Louis in its Early Days Under the French and Spanish Dominations* (St. Louis: F.L. Billon, 1886), 1:420; the "trustee" system of fund-raising in the early American church included schools.

6. Rich Roberts, "Notes for Saint Louis University History" [unpublished]. See also Nichols.

7. L.U. Reavis, *Saint Louis, the future great city of the world* (St. Louis: St. Louis County court, 1870 and 1875), 36.

8. In 1814, DuBourg appealed to Fr. John Anthony Grassi, Superior of the Maryland Jesuits, for men: Gilbert Garraghan, S.J., *The Jesuits of the Middle United States* (New York: America Press, 1938), 1:40; Thomas Hughes, S.J., *History of the Society of Jesus in North America, Colonial and Federal* (New York, Bombay and Calcutta: Longmans, Green, and Co., 1910), 2:1008: "writing to him from New Orleans, 26 Mar., 1814 (Md.-N.Y. Archives, under date)."

9. Annabelle M. Melville, *Louis William DuBourg: Bishop of Louisiana and the Floridas, Bishop of Montauban, and Archbishop of Besançon, 1766-1833* (Chicago: Loyola University Press, 1986), 341-42.

10. W.J. Howlett, *Life of Rev. Charles Nerinckx: Pioneer Missionary of Kentucky and Founder of the Sisters of Loretto at the Foot of the Cross* (Techny, IL: Mission Press S.V.D., 1915), 190-208; Martin John Spalding, *Sketches of the Early Catholic Missions of Kentucky* (Louisville: B.J.Webb & Brother; Baltimore: J. Murphy, 1844).

11. Ann Hunt to J.B.C. Lucas, January 4-5, 1818 (MHSA).

12. T.Wilson to J.B.C. Lucas, July 12, 1817 (MHSA).

13. Garraghan, 1:101.

14. Extensive scholarship exists on the pre-Suppression Jesuits in North America. A key resource is Reuben Gold Thwaites, editor: *The Jesuit Relations and Allied Documents; Travels and Explorations of the Jesuit Missionaries in New France, 1610-1791* (Cleveland: Burrows Brothers Company, 1896-1901).

15. Billon, 12.

16. All of the Jesuits in North America except Meurin were expelled when the 1763 suppression by France was violently carried out. He died in Illinois, but his remains were later moved to the cemetery at Florissant, and are now in Calvary.

17. Michael Dickey, *The People of the River's Mouth: In Search of the Missouria Indians* (Columbia: University of Missouri Press, 2011).

18. Peterson, 17-23.

19. Robert L. Ramsay, *Our Storehouse of Missouri Place Names* (Columbia: University of Missouri Press, 1952), 47; John Francis McDermott, "*Paincourt* and Poverty," *Mid-America* 5 (1933): 10-12.

20. Scharf, 1:823.

21. Patricia Cleary, *The World, the Flesh, and the Devil: A History of Colonial St. Louis* (Columbia and London: University of Missouri Press, 2011), 225, 236-37.

22. Reavis, 35.

23. *Missouri, a Guide to the "Show me" state.* Compiled by workers of the Writers' Program of the Work Projects Administration in the State of Missouri (Lawrence: University Press of Kansas, 1986), 117.

24. Willard Rollings, *Unaffected by the Gospel* (Albuquerque: University of New Mexico Press, 2004).

25. On this topic, many excellent sources exist, including Ira Berlin, *Generations of Captivity* (Cambridge and London: Harvard University Press, 2003); on African Muslims in colonial and antebellum America, see Kambiz GhaneaBassiri, *A History of Islam in America* (Cambridge: Cambridge University Press, 2010).

26. Father Van De Velde describing boat passage in 1817, cited in Garraghan, 1:14.

27. Many accounts of the Maryland Province at this time exist. Relating to slavery, see: R. Emmett Curran, S.J., "'Splendid Poverty': Jesuit Slaveholding in Maryland, 1805-1838," 125-146 in Randall M. Miller and Jon L. Wakelyn, editors, *Catholics in the Old South* (Macon: Mercer University Press, 1983), 131; Edward F. Beckett, S.J., "Listening to our History: Inculturation and Jesuit Slaveholding," *Studies in the Spirituality of Jesuits* 28:5 (November 1996): 5; Garraghan, 1:Chapter 1 in entirety.

28. Father Verreydt memoirs (JACSUS).

29. *Ibid.*; New evidence regarding the sur-names of the enslaved persons has come to light during summer 2017 thanks to work by Kelly Schmidt, see forthcoming report by SLU and Society of Jesus Province of the Central United States.

30. Judocus Van Assche begins his memoirs with these words, 1874 letter to Walter Hill, S.J. (SLUA).

31. "Letter from St. Louis" [no author], *Woodstock Letters* 1 (October 19, 1871): 54.

32. Walter Hill, S.J. "Notes for a History of St. Louis University" (SLUA); Brother Peter De Meyer "Reminiscences of Pioneer Life" (JACSUS).

33. De Meyer memoirs (JACSUS).

34. Roberts, Ch. 1, 17; Garraghan, 1: 272-73, 282-83.

35. Robert Costello, S.J., "My Dreams, Our Dreams," in *Ourselves, Our Church, Our Dreams: The Missouri Province Convocation* (St. Louis: Missouri Province Planning, 1986), 41-2.

36. Kohl's 1858 work: *Reisen im Nordwesten der Vereinigten Staaten* (*Travels in the Northwestern Parts of the United States*) includes a section on SLU that was translated as part of Laurence Kenny papers (SLUA); The full, complex story of the land is in Garraghan, 1:276-78, fn. 14. In 1772, the Spanish government granted a strip of land to Gabriel Dodier, who sold it in 1793 for $80 to Esther, a mulatto woman freed by her owner, Jacques Clamorgan. She transferred the property to Clamorgan and it was sold at a public auction to meet a debt; see Garraghan for subsequent transfers. DuBourg seems to have paid $200 for the land.

37. Garraghan, 1:275.

38. John F. Darby, *Personal Recollections of John F. Darby* (St. Louis: G.I. Jones and Company, 1880), 163.

39. Garraghan, 1:272-73, fn. 8.

40. *Ibid.*, 291.

41. William Fanning, S.J., *Bulletin of the St. Louis University: A Historical Sketch* 4:5 (December 1908): 15.

42. Lowrie J. Daly, S.J., "A Day in the Life of the Old School," *Saint Louis University Magazine* 45:1 (January-February 1972): 23.

43. Peter Kenney, S.J. "Memorial, 1832" (SLUA).

44. Garraghan, 1:322 describing St. Louis College.

45. Thomas Hughes, S.J. to Charles Cloud, S.J. from Italy 1928 (SLUA).

46. For a full discussion, see Garraghan, 1, Ch. 10 in entirety.

47. Garraghan, 1:325; William McGucken, S.J., *The Jesuits and Education* (New York: Bruce, 1932), 75.

48. Claude Heithaus, S.J., 8.

Caption on page 13: George Catlin, *Letters and Notes*, 2:32 (1841, reprint 1973).

SIDEBAR by Christy Finsel:

1. Felix and Margaret Diskin, and Ron and Rose Brogan. "Osage Mission Museum, Saint Paul." *Kansas Sampler Foundation*, 2007. Retrieved August 3, 2016 from http://www.kansassampler.org/8wonders/historyresults.php?id=286. Prior to his death in 2008, Father Carl Starkloff, S.J. translated one of the House Histories from Latin to English, detailing Osage Mission activities from 1854-1862. (JACSUS). Christy Finsel translated two additional House Histories from Latin to English (1869), and another from July 1873 to July 1874 (JACSUS).

2. Ron and Rose Brogan, "The Stage is Set." *A Catholic Mission.* Retrieved August 3, 2016 at http://www.acatholicmission.org/1-the-stage-is-set.html.

3. Garraghan, "The Osage Mission," in 1:177.

4. Scott McCullough, "American Indian Sites Throughout Missouri Reflect Missouri's Early History. Learn About the Original Americans and Find Out How Missouri Indians Lived." *Vacation in Missouri and It's Your Show*. Retrieved August 3, 2016 at https://www.visitmo.com/missouri-travel/missouris-indian-heritage.aspx.

5. Diskin, et al., and Garraghan, 1:177.

6. *Ibid.*, 178-179.

7. *Ibid.*, 493.

8. Velma Nieberding, "Catholic Education Among the Osage," *Chronicles of Oklahoma* 32:3 (1954): 291-92. See also Garraghan, "The Osage Mission," 1:51.

9. Garraghan, 1:269, 291, 332.

10. *Ibid.*, 1:166, 291.

11. Diskin, et al., 2.

12. Eddy Red Eagle, Jr. Personal interview by Christy Finsel. August 3, 2016.

13. Louis Burns, *Osage Mission Baptisms, Marriages and Internment 1820-1886.* (Fallbrook, CA: Ciga Press, 1996). See also Garraghan, 2:502.

14. Diskin, et al. 28; In the Diskins' unpublished manuscript, they noted the following material from Father Paul Mary Ponziglione's unpublished manuscript: "In 1871 the Osage abandoned their villages in Kansas when they left on their fall bison hunt. When they returned from the hunt in early 1872, they settled on their new reservation."

15. Dennis [Last name unknown], "Osage Tribe." *Access Genealogy*, 2011. Retrieved August 3, 2016 at https://www.access-genealogy.com/native/osage-tribe.htm. Also, former Osage Chief Gray, who spoke at a Lewis and Clark Commemoration event at the Missouri History Museum, mentioned this statistic.

16. Nieberding, 294.

17. Eddy Red Eagle, Jr.

18. Diskin, personal communication, July 26 2016.

19. Burns, 427.

20. Prior to his death in 2008, Reverend Carl Starkloff, S.J. translated a letter written by Father Ponziglione on December 31, 1885, to Pope Leo XII, on behalf of Osage, requesting canonization of Kateri Tekakwitha. (JACSUS)

21. Eddy Red Eagle, Jr.

22. Jason Zaun. E-mail to the author. August 3, 2016. Mr. Zaun is Chief of Staff of the Osage Nation.

SIDEBAR on slavery:

1. Saidiya Hartman, *Lose Your Mother* (New York: Farrar, Straus and Girous, 2007).

2. Dickey, 71; Walter Johnson, *Soul by Soul: Life Inside the Antebellum Slave Market* (Cambridge and London: Harvard University Press, 1999).

3. Berlin, 163.

4. *Ibid.*, 213.

CHAPTER 2, pages 30-55

1. Garraghan, 3:Ch. 30, 90.

2. Roberts, notes for Chapter 5.

3. Sources differ on the date: early 1825 or March 1826 are given.

4. Papers of Peter Verhaegen, S.J. at JACSUS and SLUA. Also, his: "Discourse on Man," 397 and 418 (JACSUS).

5. Mary Anne Pernoud, "The First Week of the University," *Saint Louis University Magazine* 46:2 (January 1973): 28-9.

6. John W. Padberg, S.J., "Development of the *Ratio Studiorum*," in Vincent J. Duminuco, S.J., ed., *The Jesuit* Ratio Studiorum: *Four Hundredth Anniversary Perspectives* (New York: Fordham University Press, 2000), 97.

7. Daly, 21-3.

8. William Carr Lane to his son Victor, January 28, 1845 (MHSA).

9. Garraghan, 3:Ch. 34, 251.

10. Gabriel Codina, S.J., "The 'Modus Parisiensis,'" in Duminuco, 28-49.

11. Victor Lane to Mary Lane, June 11, 1844 (MHSA).

12. "Alumni Interview: Oldest Graduate Recalls Stories of Early U. Days," *Varsity Breeze* 1:5 (December 15, 1921): 7.

13. Garraghan provides extensive descriptions of the campus, 3:Ch. 34, 220+.

14. Lewis Foulk Thomas, editor. *The valley of the Mississippi illustrated in a series of views.* Painted and lithographed by J.C. Wild; St. Louis, 1841-42 (St. Louis: J. Garnier, 1948), 33.

15. *Ibid.*, 34.

16. Garraghan, 3:Ch. 34, 248.

17. Nichols, 24.

18. Garraghan, 3:Ch. 34, 205.

19. Laurence Kenny, S.J.'s translation of Kohl (SLUA).

20. Saint Louis University Board of Trustees minutes, October 4, 1836, 19 (SLUA).

21. Richard Barret, "Law Department of the St. Louis University" handwritten, unpublished account (SLUA).

22. John T. McGreevy, *American Jesuits and the World* (Princeton and Oxford: Princeton University Press, 2016), 77, 85.

23. Martha Bray, *Joseph Nicollet and his Map* (Philadelphia: American Philosophical Society, 1980), 141.

24. Dr. M.L. Linton lecture, November 4, 1845 and Dr. A. Litton lecture, Feb 28, 1851 (BAWU).

25. McGreevy, 85, see fn. 108, 257.

26. Dr. Charles Alexander Pope correspondence, April 17, 1855 (SLUA).

27. Garraghan, 3:Ch. 34, 204, fn. 2.

28. Quote from Isidore Boudreaux, S.J. who was master of novices for over 23 years at Florissant, in Garraghan, 1:557, citing an 1860 letter to Peter Jan Beckx, S.J.

29. Rothensteiner, John E., *History of the Archdiocese of St. Louis: In its Various Stages of Development from A.D. 1673 to A.D. 1928* (St. Louis: Blackwell Wielandy, 1928), 1:337.

30. Raymond A. Schroth, S.J., *The American Jesuits: A History* (New York: New York University Press, 2007), 62.

31. Verhaegen to Vespre, 1840 (JACSUS).

32. Personal communication, Father John W. Padberg, S.J.

33. Verhaegen to Chouteau, December 33, 1842 (MHSA).

34. Adam Arenson, *The Great Heart of the Republic: St. Louis and the Cultural Civil War* (Cambridge and London: Harvard University Press, 2011), 235-36.

35. Many useful sources on this period: Arenson; Berlin, 224; Garraghan, Ch. 22; McGreevy, Ch. 3. For information about the 1819 protest in St. Louis see Judge Nathan B. Young's "Number One City in Civil Rights History," *St. Louis American* 35:42 (September 22, 1964): 1. This protest was curated in a 2017 exhibit at the Museum of History in St. Louis, Missouri.

36. Harriet Frazier, *Runaway and Freed Missouri Slaves and Those Who Helped Them: 1763-1865* (North Carolina and London: McFarland and Company Press, Inc., 2004), 10.

37. Cyprian Clamorgan, *The Colored Aristocracy of St. Louis.* Edited and with an introduction by Julie Winch [originally published 1858] (Columbia: University of Missouri Press, 1999).

38. Garraghan 1:273 fn. 8.

39. *Ibid.*, 3:560+ and 1:606.

40. Michael Fellman, *Inside War: The Guerilla Conflict in Missouri During the American Civil War* (NY and Oxford: Oxford University Press, 1989), 74. See also: Walter Hill, S.J., *Historical Sketch of the St. Louis University* (Patrick Fox Publisher: St. Louis, 1879); Garraghan; and William B. Faherty, S.J. *Better the Dream: Saint Louis: University and Community,* (St. Louis: Saint Louis University, 1968) for details on the university and province during the Civil War.

41. Garraghan, 1:156.

42. Schroth, 80.

43. Roy Basler, editor., *The Collected Works of Abraham Lincoln* (New Brunswick: Rutgers University Press, 1953), 500.

44. De Smet to Beckx October 20, 1861, cited in Garraghan, 2:158.

45. Garraghan, 1:167.

46. 1867 BOT minutes, 21 (SLUA).

SIDEBAR on Nicollet:

1. Bray, 228.

Caption page 34: Faherty, 300.

Caption page 35: Robert Carriker, *Father Peter John De Smet: Jesuit in the West* (Norman: University of Oklahoma Press, 1995), 161.

Caption page 38: Ronald Crown lecture: "History of SLU Library," presented at SLU in 2009.

Caption on page 43: A rosewood surgical case used by Dr. Matthias Adolph E. Borck, M.D., Professor of Surgery at Marion Sims College 1893-St. Louis University 1904, presented by his widow, Dr. Henrietta Stoffregen-Borck, to the university in 1931. The medicine case belonged to Missouri doctor, Dr. W.B. Lucas.

Caption page 44: Translation and reference from Father Claude Pavur, S.J., personal communication.

Map on pages 48-49: an adaptation of "United states. (to accompany)" p. 60 in *A Comprehensive Atlas, Geographical, Historical & Commercial.* By T.G. Bradford. William D. Ticknor, Boston. Wiley& Long, New York, 1835. List Number 2643.067 in the David Rumsey collection.

Sites referenced in the map on pages 48-9:

Seminaries:

1. St. Stanislaus Seminary, Florissant, Missouri, 1823

2. St. Mary of the Lake Seminary, Mundelein, Illinois, 1921

3. St. Mary's (theologate), St. Marys, Kansas, 1931

Missions:

1. Missouri Mission (later Vice Province and Province), Florissant, Missouri, 1823

2. Kickapoo Mission, Fort Leavenworth, Kansas, 1836

3. Potawatomi Mission, Sugar Creek, Kansas, 1839 (moved to St. Marys, Kansas in 1847)

4. Potawatomi Mission, Council Bluffs, Iowa

5. Rocky Mountain Mission 1840+ included:

   a. St. Paul's among the Metis, near the Columbia - Coulee Dam, Washington

   b. St. Mary's Mission among the Flatheads near present day Stevensville and Missoula, Montana

c. Sacred Heart Mission among the Coeur d'Alene in Cataldo, Idaho

d. St. Francis Xavier Mission on the Willamette River near present day Oregon City, Oregon

e. St. Ignatius Mission among the Kalispels in Ignatius, Montana

f. St. Francis Regis Mission at Colville, Washington

g. St. Peter's Mission near Cascade, Montana

6. Westport Mission (now Kansas City, Missouri) among Shawnee, 1841

7. St. Francis Hieronymo, Osage Mission in Neosha, Kansas 1846-7

8. St. Stephen's mission assigned to Society of Jesus, Fremont County, Wyoming, 1882

9. St. Francis and Holy Rosary, Rosebud Reservation, South Dakota, 1886

CHAPTER 3, pages 56-85

1. John Waide, "Jesuits and Baseball: 19th Century SLU Prefect Diaries Online," SLU Special Collections "Currents" (February 11, 2014) http://pius7.slu.edu/special_collections/?p=2280

2. Saint Louis University 1868 *Course Catalog*, 19 (SLUA).

3. Allan P. Farrell, S.J., *The Jesuit Code of Liberal Education* (Milwaukee: Bruce, 1938), 38-9, 41-2.

4. Hill, 176-77, 180.

5. Faherty, 175-80; Nichols, 41.

6. Philip Gleason, *Contending with Modernity* (New York and Oxford: Oxford University Press, 1995), 5, 21-38, 52.

7. David P. Miros, *Rudolph J. Meyer and Saint Louis University: A Study of the Society of Jesus' Theological and Educational Enterprise at the Turn of the Century 1885-1915* (UMI, dissertation, 2005); Garraghan, 3:506. See also Rudolph Meyer, *The World in Which We Live* (St. Louis, Missouri and Freiburg: B. Herder, 1908).

8. Edward J. Power, *Catholic higher education in America* (New York: Appleton-Century-Crofts, 1972), 245; Garraghan, 3:505-510. See also Matthew Garrett, "The Identity of American Catholic Higher Education: A Historical Overview," *Catholic Education: A Journal of Inquiry and Practice* 10:2 (July 2013): 233.

9. McGreevy, 13, 18.

10. Thomas Hughes, S.J., "Notes from the West (Letter from Fr. Hughes) St. Louis, MO," *Woodstock Letters* 19:3 (1890): 294.

11. Sellers, 152.

12. Howard Gray, S.J., "The Experience of Ignatius Loyola: Background to Jesuit Education," in Vincent J. Duminuco, S.J., ed. *The Jesuit Ratio Studiorum: 400th Anniversary Perspectives*. New York: Fordham University Press, 2000, 14-15.

13. Kenny correspondence (SLUA).

14. Miros (citing a 1908 SLU course catalog), 13-4.

15. Tens of thousands of African American males were caught up in a system that some argue was even more brutal than slavery, because the men were "leased" for their labor, and not owned, and were thus utterly disposable in the logic of the owners of lumber camps, quarries, farms, factories and mines across eleven states. This system, masked by the concept of "peonage" and tolerated by the federal government, was allowed to persist until the 1950s. But only one case of post-Civil War involuntary servitude was reported in Missouri: six men were convicted for enslaving forty individuals in 1906, according to Jonathan Klusmeyer, *Slavery Continued: Peonage in Missouri*. M.A. thesis for Department of History, (University of Central Missouri, November 2013); see also Douglas Blackmon, *Slavery by Another Name* (New York: Doubleday, 2008).

16. Gail Missa Grant, *At the Elbows of My Elders: Our Family's Journey Toward Civil Rights* (St. Louis: University of Missouri Press, 2008). Relates the birth of her father at home in 1903, and other conditions of the time.

17. Colin Gordon, *Mapping Decline* (Philadelphia: University of Pennsylvania Press, 2008) argues that, as a racialized geography developed through restrictive deeds and the practices of realtors, a "white noose" encircled the city, extracting its wealth. The 2015 *Forward through Ferguson* report identifies ongoing problems due to multiple municipalities. See: http://forwardthroughferguson.org/report/executive-summary/.

18. Dolan, Jay, *The American Catholic Experience* (Garden City, NY: Doubleday & Company, Inc., 1985), 359-60.

19. *Ibid*.

20. Scharf, 2:1664.

21. In 1880, Panken invited the Oblate Sisters of Providence to St. Louis to take charge of the school, and Mother Louise Noel, head of the order, also came to serve. See Mary Seematter, "Overcoming Obstacles: Serving Black Catholics in St. Louis, 1873-1993," *Gateway Heritage* 20:4 (Spring 2000): 16-29. St. Elizabeth's parish moved to Mill Creek Valley in 1912.

22. Rothensteiner, 492-93.

23. Jeffrey R. Dorr, S.J., "Race in St. Louis's Catholic Church: Discourse, Structures, and Segregation 1873-1941." M.A. thesis, 2015, Saint Louis University, 16-18.

24. Rothensteiner, 490; "Officially, the Jesuits had universal jurisdiction over black Catholics in St. Louis," writes Donald J. Kemper, "Catholic Integration in St. Louis, 1935-1947," *Missouri Historical Review* 73 (October 1978): 5.

25. Dorr, 368.

26. 1911 BOT minutes, 369 (SLUA).

27. Dolan, 370.

28. *Globe*, June 9, 1884 in 1888 Scrapbook, 30-1 (SLUA).

29. Faherty, 185.

30. Nichols, 61.

31. From a biography prepared and sent in 1938 to James White & Co. publishers, author not given (JACSUS). The original framing is attributed to Caesar Augustus, emperor of Rome from 27 B.C. to 14 A.D.

32. Charles J. Mehok, S.J., *William Banks Rogers, S.J.: eighteenth president of Saint Louis University, 1900-1908* [unpublished M.A. dissertation] 1945, 7.

33. J.W. Buel, *The Magic City* (St. Louis and Philadelphia: Historical Publishing, 1894), 3139-41.

34. James Bernard Macelwane, S.J., *Jesuit Seismological Association 1925-1950* (Central Station: Saint Louis University, 1950), 139.

35. Faherty, 249-250.

36. Mark Neilson, "Preliminary Draft: A History of the Saint Louis University School of Law" St. Louis, 1994 [unpublished], 21.

37. Alphonse M. Schwitalla, S.J. "St. Louis University School of Medicine." Historical summary; Lyon in 1911 report, Frieden file (all in SLUA).

38. Copy of undated, unsigned letter in medical school files, referring to 1909 data and to the author as "medical school regent" (SLUA).

39. Faherty, 244-5; Course catalog (1909): 90-100.

40. Abraham Flexner, *Medical Education in the United States and Canada: A Report to Carnegie Foundation for the Advancement of Teaching*. Bulletin Number four (New York: Carnegie, 1910), 80. In making this assessment, Flexner placed Saint Louis University in a category with New York

University, Syracuse University, North-western University, Jefferson Medical College (Philadelphia), Tulane University (New Orleans), and the University of Texas as being "handicapped ... in one respect or another by resources inadequate to the ambition and competency of their faculties," 39.

41. Report of the Dean (Lyon), p. 81 in the 1910-1921 Minutes of the Executive Committee Meetings, (SLUA).

SIDEBAR on Meyer:

Opening quote: Meyer, 346.

Caption on page 64:: F.J.K., S.J., "The Badge of Loyola," *Woodstock Letters* 29:1 (1900): 1-5.

CHAPTER 4, pages 86-115

1. Faherty, 287.

2. *Ibid.,* 268.

3. *The University News* (March 6, 1936): 8 and (December 6, 1940): 4, respectively.

4. Medical School trustee minutes, 1915, 226 (SLUA).

5. Laurence Kenny notes (SLUA).

6. Emphasis in original: Festus J. Wade and Bernard Otting, S.J. correspondence, December 24, 1917 (SLUA).

7. William P. Leahy, *Adapting to America: Catholics, Jesuits, and Higher Education in the Twentieth Century* (Washington: Georgetown University, 1991), 83; see also Faherty, 266-280.

8. Helen Dicroce, "Heritage of Saint Louis University School of Nursing 1928-2000," http://www.slu.edu/colleges/NR/heritage/index.html. See also "Sourcebook" by Alphonse, Schwitalla, S.J. (Christmas 1943), 105 (SSMA).

9. William J. McGucken, S.J., "Editorial Survey: Should We Have Coeducation in Catholic Colleges and Universities?" *Thought* 13:51 (December 1938): 537-40.

10. Leahy, 85. For more background, see Paul A. Fitzgerald, S.J., *The Governance of Jesuit Colleges in the United States: 1920-1970* (Notre Dame, Indiana: University of Notre Dame Press, 1984), 69.

11. Schroth, 60.

12. Walter Ong, Book Review of *A History of Esthetics,* in *The Modern Schoolman,* 17:3 (March 1940): 57.

13. *The University News* (November 6, 1931): 1; Faherty, 297.

14. Thomas Gavin, S.J., *Champion of Youth: A Dynamic Story of a Dynamic Man, Father Daniel A. Lord, S.J.* (Boston: The Daughters of St. Paul, 1977).

15. William Markoe, S.J., unpublished memoirs, 122-124 (JACSUS). In the Markoe memoirs edited by Feit and Nolan, this quote is on pages 116-117.

16. Stephen Werner, *Prophet of the Christian Social Manifesto: Joseph Husslein, S.J.: His Life, Work and Social Thought* (Milwaukee: Marquette University Press, 2001), 24.

17. Markoe, 297.

18. Gladys W. Gruenberg, *Labor Peacemaker: The Life and Works of Father Leo Brown, S.J.* (St. Louis: Institute of Jesuit Sources, 1981), 47.

19. D. Stephen Long, "Bernard Dempsey's Theological Economics: Usury, Profit, and Human Fulfillment," *Theological Studies* 57 (1996): 694; see also Perry J. Roets, "Bernard W. Dempsey, S.J." *Review of Social Economy* 49:4 (1991): 546-58.

20. *The University News* (May 10, 1935): 1; (October 15, 1937): 4; (November 27, 1946): 10.

21. Robert Schulman, "High Priest of Medicine," *Postgraduate Medicine* 3:1 (1948): 54-59.

22. *Ibid.*

23. Markoe, 120.

24. Sister Margaret Mary Jarvis, S.S.M. cited in Sister Agnes Clare Frenay, *The Reverend Alphonse M. Schwitalla, S.J.: 1882-1965* [unpublished] (St. Louis University School of Nursing and Allied Health Professions, 1977), 16 (SSMA).

25. *Ibid.,* 3; see also Schwitalla: Sourcebook (1943), 10-11.

26. Markoe memoirs, edited by Feit and Nolan, 5.

27. 1911 BOT minutes, 369 (SLUA).

28. 1921 Medical school minutes, 22 (SLUA).

29. Clarence Lang, *Grassroots at the Gateway* (Ann Arbor: University of Michigan Press, 2009), 64. Another good source on the period and events is Florence Shinkle's "Go Write Your Little Letters," *St. Louis Post-Dispatch* (June 22, 1997): Everyday Magazine, 1C. Gleason writes that despite its problems, SLU "was far ahead of other institutions in the city or region," 238. Father George Dunne, S.J.'s "The Sin of Segregation" in *Commonweal* (September 21, 1945): 542-45, demonstrated support for Heithaus, and was considered a milestone. See also Dunne's 1990 book *The King's Pawn.*

30. Markoe, 430.

31. Schroth, 81.

32. William M. Shea, "Jesuits and Scholarship," in William Shea and Daniel Van Slyke, editors, *Trying Times* (Atlanta: Scholars Press, 1999), 200-204; See also, Schroth, 122.

33. Faherty, 314.

34. Reinert in transcript of interviews conducted in 1994 for *Seasons of Change* between Father Paul Reinert, S.J. and Dr. Paul Shore, (SLUA), 50.

35. Bob Jackson, "Schools of the University: Parks." *The University News* (February 6, 1953): 7.

36. J.C. Snyder, "Typhus Fever in the Second World War," *California Medicine* 6:1 (January 1947): 3-10.

37. Marilyn Nickels, "Showered with Stones," *U.S. Catholic Historian* 3:4 (Spring 1984): 273-78.

38. Faherty, 323.

39. Father Claude Heithaus, S.J.'s sermon at College Church in 1944 is reproduced in full at *The University News* (February 11, 1944): 1.

40. Patricia L. Adams, "Fighting for Democracy in St. Louis: Civil Rights During World War II," *Missouri Historical Review* 80 (October 1985): 71.

41. Interview Peter and Michael Heithaus with author (April 2016).

42. Faherty, "The Museum of the Western Jesuit Missions," *Gateway Heritage: The Quarterly Magazine of the Missouri Historical Society,* 20:1 (Winter, 1999-2000): 20-31.

43. C.P.G. '14, "John P. Markoe 1914" West Point Association of Graduates, Memorials, Cullum 5292.

Caption on page 95: Schwitalla, *Sourcebook* 1943, 13.

Caption on page 103: A "rare" integrated dance was sponsored by the *Interracial Review* in SLU's gymnasium on February 24, 1933. William Howland Kenney, *Jazz on the River* (Chicago: University of Chicago Press, 2005), 105.

Caption on page 114: John Conner, "Well done, sir," in *Colliers* (June 10, 1950): 18.

CHAPTER 5, pages 116-145

1. Robert Henle, S.J., "Objectives of the Catholic Liberal Arts College," August 1955 [unpublished] (SLUA).

2. Extensive scholarship on this theme exists across disciplines; see also materials on critical accounting as a sub-field.

3. David J. O'Brien, "The Land O' Lakes Statement" *Boston College Magazine* (Winter 1998): 3. Reproduced by Boston College Office of University Mission and Ministry.

4. James T. Fisher, *Dr. America* (Amherst: University of Massachusetts Press, 1997), 218, refers to: "the powerful institutional machinery of the Church that reached its peak in the 1950s."

5. Clyde Cahill, Jr., "Letter from a Negro Student," *The University News* (October 20, 1950): 5; see also Gene Bogan, "Discrimination against Negro students found at local restaurants," *The University News* (October 15, 1950): 1; and 2017 interview with Dr. Ronald Hoffman conducted by Jennifer Sherer (SLUA). "Students Crack the Color Line," *America* (November 11, 1950): 152. Also excerpted in "Students Crack Color Line," *The University News* (November 10, 1950): 4.

6. Vernon Bourke, "Philosophy at St. Louis University, Thirties to the Sixties." [unpublished] November 21, 1975, 36 (SLUA).

7. Fitzgerald, 120.

8. Garrett, 238. Fitzgerald terms 1964 a "watershed year" in Jesuit higher education. See: 150, 188, 201, 212; see also Gleason, 317.

9. John W. Padberg, S.J., Martin D. O'Keefe, S.J. and John L. McCarthy, S.J., *For Matters of Greater Moment: The First Thirty Jesuit General Congregations* (St. Louis: Institute of Jesuit Sources, 1994), 62.

10. John W. Padberg, S.J., *Together as a Companionship: a History of the Thirty-First, Thirty-Second, and Thirty-Third General Congregations of the Society of Jesus* (St Louis: Institute of Jesuit Sources, 1994), 50. For more on this period, see: Raymond A. Schroth, S.J. "How we got here; a history" in *Conversations* 41 (September 2012): 2-4; Patrick Howell, S.J., "The 'New' Jesuits: The Response of the Society of Jesus to Vatican II, 1962-2012: some alacrity, some resistance," *Conversations* 42 (Fall 2012): 7-11; and John W. O'Malley, S.J. "The Council's Spirit: Vatican II: A time for reconciliation." *Conversations* 42 (Fall 2012), 2-6.

11. Metropolitan College catalog (SLUA). For more on Reinert's thoughts about race relations as he established Metropolitan College, see Paul Reinert, S.J. and Dr. Paul Shore, *Seasons of Change* (Bronx: Saint Louis University Press and Fordham University Press, 1997): 24.

12. Joseph Simeone, email to Eileen Searls "Comments and notes on 'final draft'", dated June 11, 2011 (SLU Law School archives).

13. Neilson, 10.

14. Neilson, 96 quoting Eileen Searls' letter to Immel, circulated by Immel to the faculty in fall 1963.

15. Fitzgerald, 158.

16. *Universitas* 44:4 (Nov-Dec 1971), 16.

17. Joel C. Eissenberg, Ph.D. and Enrico Di Cera, MD, "*In vitro veritas:* 90 years of Biochemistry at Saint Louis University," *Missouri Medicine* 110:4 (July-August 2013): 297-301.

18. Interview with Constance Wagner, as well as materials submitted as tributes to Eileen Searls (SLUA).

19. Patricia Kay Nance, "The Vatican Film Library at Saint Louis University: 1950 – 1990." April 1991 (M.S. thesis, unpublished), 26, 42-3.

20. Maurice B. McNamee, S.J., *Recollections in Tranquility* (St. Louis: St. Louis University Press, 2001), 311-12.

21. Hans Küng, "The Church and Freedom," *Commonweal* 78 (June 21, 1963): 343-53.

22. Mark J. Curran, *Coming of Age with the Jesuits* (Bloomington: Trafford Publishing, 2012), 133. Curran's interesting memories of the graduate school during his studies of Latin American history at SLU emphasize the excellence and passion of his professors.

23. Walter Ong, reference letters in papers (SLUA).

24. *The University News*, September 26, 2002; Additional information from interviews and correspondence with former students in the program.

25. "Research programs get boost from access to new computer," *Chalk Talk* 11:8 (May 1969): 3 (SLUA); "Yalem IBM lucky in cards, love," *The University News* (November 30, 1962): 5.

26. Ong, "The Jinnee in the Well-Wrought Urn," in *An Ong Reader: Challenges for Further Inquiry.* Thomas J. Farrell and Paul A. Soukup, editors. (Cresskill, N.J.: Hampton Press, 2002), 201.

27. Ong, "Ramus and the Transit to the Modern Mind," in *An Ong Reader,* 237.

28. "Each of those acquisitions was the subject of an article by Ong, as was Milton's *Art of Logic* – further proof, if any were needed, that acquiring books and acquiring understanding were to him one and the same." Jennifer Lowe, paper presented at South Central Renaissance Conference March 24, 2016.

29. Paul Reinert, S.J., *The Urban Catholic University* (New York: Sheed and Ward, 1970), 78.

30. I.H. Lionberger, "Depreciation caused by unstable growth," in Saint Louis (Mo.) City Plan Commission. *The Zone Plan. City plan commission, St. Louis, Missouri. Harland Bartholomew, engineer.* (St. Louis, MO: Nixon-Jones printing co., 1919), 60-1.

31. Lorenzo J. Greene, Gary R. Kremer and Antonio F. Holland, *Missouri's Black Heritage* (Columbia and London: University of Missouri Press, 1980), 163-65.

32. See Clarence Lang, 139; and Joseph Heathcott and Máire Agnes Murphy, "Corridors of Flight, Zones of Renewal: Industry, Planning, and Policy in the Making of Metropolitan St. Louis, 1940-1980," *Journal of Urban History* 31 (2005): 159-60.

33. Florence Shinkle, "Grand Father; for almost half a century, Father Paul Reinert has been teaching the joy of giving," *St. Louis Post-Dispatch* (January 22, 1995): Everyday Magazine, 1C.

34. Joseph Knapp, S.J., *The Presence of the Past: The Beginnings of the Civil War in St. Louis: The History of Hazelwood-Fordyce House from Camp Jackson and General Frost to St. Louis University and Harriet Frost Fordyce* (St. Louis: St. Louis University Press, 1979).

35. Heathcott and Murphy, 167-71.

36. Henry J. Schmandt, George D. Wendel, and E. Allan Tomey, *Federal Aid to St. Louis* (Washington, DC: The Brookings Institution, 1983), 50-1.

37. Reinert 1970, 120-44.

38. Reinert in transcript of interviews conducted in 1994, 8-9.

39. *Ibid.,* 3.

40. Edward Drummond, S.J. citing Weber in *"The State of the University,"* October 29, 1978 address to Civic Dinner guests (SLU Marketing & Communications).

41. Board of trustees minutes, October 15 1957, 2 (SLUA).

42. Richard Roberts, "Two Hours with the New President," *Universitas* 47:4 (July 1974): 5.

43. Nichols, 99-213.

CHAPTER 6, pages 146-179

The title of this chapter is taken from a quote attributed to an "unnamed Jesuit" cited by Edward Wakin, "'Ratio Studiorum' on the Mississippi" in *The Catholic Campus* (NY: Macmillan, 1963), 73.

1. John Kavanaugh, S.J. quoted in Laura Geiser, "Life, hope and homilies," *Universitas* 35:1 (Fall 2008): 14.

2. Peter Hernon, "The big questions remain the same through the ages," *St. Louis Globe-Democrat* (October 8, 1978): 9.

3. Jane Priwer, "Daniel L. Schlafly: Our 'man for the decade,'" *Universitas* 4:3 (Winter 1979): 8-9.

4. Nichols, 217-226.

5. Dr. Ken Parker, interview with the author, 2016.

6. Dr. Eleonore Stump, *Wandering in Darkness: Narrative and the Problem of Suffering* (Oxford University Press, 2010), 149; John Kavanaugh, *Following Christ in a Consumer Society* (Maryknoll, NY: Orbis Books, 2006 (25th edition)), 117.

7. Faherty, 183; also discussed in James Jerome Conn, S.J., *Catholic Universities in the United States and Ecclesiastical Authority* (Rome: Editrice Pontificia Università Gregoriana, 1991), 158.

8. Gleason, 174.

9. Faherty, 302-305.

10. Henle, 4. Also quoted in Fitzgerald, 159-160.

11. Henle, 1969 address on graduate schools (SLUA).

12. Gleason, 221.

13. Shea, 197-199.

14. Gleason, 322.

15. Jack Rice, "Literary Requiem for a Jesuit," *St. Louis Post-Dispatch* (July 15, 1976): 2D reviewing *For the Sake of Argument* by James F. Meara, S.J. For more on the history of the department of philosophy, see also Vernon Bourke history (1975); James Meara, S.J., *For the Sake of Argument* (St. Louis: Jesuit Community, 1976); and department self-study, 2016 (SLUA).

16. Program Review and Self-Study, Saint Louis University Department of Philosophy, 2016; interview with Father Theodore Vitali, C.P., 2017.

17. McNamee, 76-7.

18. "The Scrapbook: Fitzgerald Era to End at Close of School Year," *Universitas* 12:3 (Autumn 1986): 4.

19. Peter Salsich, interview with the author, May 22, 2017.

20. Mary Flick, "And eighty for those who are strong" *Universitas* 15:4 (Summer 1990): 23.

21. From the 1971 Archive, quoted also in 1976 *Archive* (SLUA).

22. See for example Paul Reinert, S.J., "In El Salvador," *The Roundtable: Voices from Central America* (Summer 1983): 3-6.

23. Lawrence Biondi, S.J., c.v. 2016 (SLUA). Other sources include: Jeannette Cooperman, "The Complex Legacy of Lawrence Biondi," *St. Louis Magazine* (October 2013): 116+; Laura Geiser, "Farewell, Father Biondi," *Universitas* (Fall 2013): 9-15; Robert Lowes, "The P.R. Prez," *St. Louis Magazine* (October 1991): 47+.

24. BOT minutes, July 16, 1966 (SLUA).

25. "Economic Impact Report" *Universitas* 39:2 (Spring 2013): 9-20.

26. Dr. Paul Vita, interview with the author, 2016; additional information from Viki Villareal, 2017.

27. Jeff Daniel, "McLuhan's Two Messengers," *St Louis Post-Dispatch* (August 10, 1997): 4C.

28. Terry Demsey, S.J., interview with author, 2017.

29. James Kimmey, M.D., interview with author, 2017.

30. Neilson, 110-11.

31. John Ammann, interview with the author, 2017.

32. Patricia Lee, interview with the author, 2017.

33. Roger Goldman, interview with the author, 2017.

34. Jaye Shyken, M.D., in "Crisis Response: SLUCare OB expands care for moms-to-be hooked on opioids." https://www.slu.edu/news/2016/october/wish-center-opens.php.

35. Dr. Michelle Sabick, interview with the author, 2017.

36. James Kimmey, M.D., "Strategic Plan Development 2014-15: Process Description and Critique," internal document.

37. "A Grand Plan," *Universitas* 43:1 (Spring 2017): 12.

38. For more information about the Clock Tower Accords, see https://www.slu.edu/about/catholic-jesuit-identity/diversity/clock-towers-accords.php.

Caption on page 167: Katy Gurley, "Goronwy Broun: 81 Years a 'Doc'," *Globe Democrat* (August 11 1976): 12A.

SOURCES CONSULTED

ARCHIVAL COLLECTIONS

ASLA: Archdiocese of St. Louis Archives, St. Louis, Missouri

BAWU: Becker Library/Medical School Archives at Washington University in St. Louis, Missouri

JACSUS: Jesuit Archives of the Central and Southern United States, St. Louis, Missouri

MHSA: Missouri Historical Society Archives, St. Louis, Missouri

SLUA: Saint Louis University including North Campus Archives, Law School Archives, and Medical School Archives, St. Louis, Missouri

SSMA: SSM Health Archives, St. Louis, Missouri

OTHER MATERIALS

Adams, Patricia L. "Fighting for Democracy in St. Louis: Civil Rights During World War II." *Missouri Historical Review* 80 (October 1985): 58-75.

Adams, Rita, William C. Einspanier and B.T. Lukaszewski, S.J. *Saint Louis University: 150 Years.* St. Louis: Saint Louis University, 1968.

Arenson, Adam. *The Great Heart of the Republic: St. Louis and the Cultural Civil War.* Cambridge and London: Harvard University Press, 2011.

Barret, Richard Aylett. *Law Department of the St. Louis University.* 1902. Handwritten notes (SLUA).

Basler, Roy, editor. *The Collected Works of Abraham Lincoln.* Volume VI. New Brunswick: Rutgers University Press, 1953.

Beckett, Edward F., S.J. "Listening to our History: Inculturation and Jesuit Slaveholding." *Studies in the Spirituality of Jesuits* 28:5 (November 1996): 1-48.

Berlin, Ira. *Generations of Captivity.* Cambridge and London: Harvard University Press, 2003.

Billon, Frederick Louis. *Annals of St. Louis in its Early Days Under the French and Spanish Dominations.* St. Louis: F.L. Billon, 1886.

Blackmon, Douglas A. *Slavery by Another Name.* New York: Doubleday, 2008.

Bourke, Vernon. "Philosophy at St. Louis University, Thirties to the Sixties." [unpublished] November 21, 1975 (SLUA).

Bray, Martha. *Joseph Nicollet and his Map.* Philadelphia: American Philosophical Society, 1980.

Brosnahan, Timothy, S.J. "Courses Leading to the baccalaureate in Harvard College and Boston College." Woodstock: College Press, 1900.

Brownson, Henry F. *Orestes A. Brownson's Latter Life: From 1856 to 1876.* Detroit: H.F. Brownson, Publishers, 1900.

Buel, J.W. *The magic city: a massive portfolio of original photographic views of the great world's fair and its treasures of art, including a vivid representation of the famous Midway Plaisance.* St. Louis and Philadelphia: Historical Publishing, 1894.

Carriker, Robert C. *Father Peter John De Smet: Jesuit in the West.* Norman: University of Oklahoma Press, 1995.

Clamorgan, Cyprian. *The Colored Aristocracy of St. Louis.* [originally published 1858] Edited and with an introduction by Julie Winch. Columbia: University of Missouri Press, 1999.

Cleary, Patricia. *The World, the Flesh, and the Devil: A History of Colonial St. Louis.* Columbia and London: University of Missouri Press, 2011.

Codina, Gabriel, S.J. "The 'Modus Parisiensis,'" 28-49 in Duminuco, Vincent, J., S.J. *The Jesuit Ratio Studiorum: 400th Anniversary Perspectives.* New York: Fordham University Press, 2000.

Conner, John. "Well done, sir." *Colliers* (June 10, 1950): 18+.

Coon, James Jerome, S.J. *Catholic Universities in the United States and Ecclesiastical Authority.* Rome: Editrice Pontificia Università Gregoriana, 1991.

Cooperman, Jeannette. "The Complex Legacy of Lawrence Biondi." *St. Louis Magazine* (October 2013): 116+.

Costello, Robert, S.J. "My Dreams, Our Dreams," 39-45 in *Ourselves, Our Church, Our Dreams: The Missouri Province Convocation.* St. Louis: Missouri Province Planning, 1986.

Curran, Mark J. *Coming of Age with the Jesuits.* Bloomington: Trafford Publishing, 2012.

Curran, R. Emmett, S.J. "'Splendid Poverty': Jesuit Slaveholding in Maryland, 1805-1838," 125-146 in *Catholics in the Old South.* Randall M. Miller and Jon L. Wakelyn, editors. Macon: Mercer University Press, 1983.

Daly, Lowrie J, S.J. "A Day in the Life of the Old School." *Saint Louis University Magazine* 45:1 (January-February 1972):21-23.

Daniel, Jeff. "McLuhan's Two Messengers." *St. Louis Post-Dispatch* (August 10, 1997): 4C.

Darby, John F. *Personal Recollections of John F. Darby.* St. Louis: G.I. Jones and Company, 1880.

Dickey, Michael. *The People of the River's Mouth: In Search of the Missouria Indians.* Columbia: University of Missouri Press, 2011.

DiCroce, Helen. "Heritage of Saint Louis University School of Nursing 1928-2000," http://www.slu.edu/colleges/NR/heri-tage/index.html.

Dolan, Jay. *The American Catholic Experience.* Garden City, NY: Doubleday & Company, Inc., 1985.

Donnelly, Francis P., S.J. *Principles of Jesuit Education in Practice.* New York: P.J. Kennedy & Sons, 1934.

Dorr, Jeffrey R., S.J. "Race in St. Louis's Catholic Church: Discourse, Structures, and Segregation 1873-1941." Saint Louis University M.A. thesis, 2015.

Duminuco, Vincent, J., S.J., editor. *The Jesuit Ratio Studiorum: 400th Anniversary Perspectives.* New York: Fordham University Press, 2000.

Dunne, George H., S.J. "The Sin of Segregation." *Commonweal* (September 21, 1945): 542-45.

Efford, Alison Clark. *German Immigrants, Race, and Citizenship in the Civil War Era.* German Historical Institute. Washington, DC and Cambridge: Cambridge University Press, 2013.

Eissenberg, Joel C., Ph.D. and Enrico Di Cera, MD, "In vitro veritas: 90 years of Biochemistry at Saint Louis University." *Missouri Medicine* 110:4 (July August 2013): 297-301.

Faherty, William B., S.J. *Better the Dream: Saint Louis: University and Community.* St. Louis: Saint Louis University, 1968.

Faherty, William B., S.J. "The Museum of the Western Jesuit Missions." *Gateway Heritage: The Quarterly Magazine of the Missouri Historical Society* 20:1 (Winter, 1999-2000): 20-31.

Fanning, William, S.J. *Bulletin of the St. Louis University: A Historical Sketch* 4:5 (December 1908).

Farrell, Allan P., S.J. *The Jesuit Code of Liberal Education.* Milwaukee: Bruce, 1938.

Feit, Kenneth P. and Thomas M. Nolan, editors. *Memoirs of Father William Markoe, S.J.* [unpublished] 1972 (SLUA).

Fellman, Michael. *Inside War: The Guerilla Conflict in Missouri During the American Civil War.* NY and Oxford: Oxford University Press, 1989.

Ferguson Commission. *"Forward Through Ferguson: A Path Toward Racial Equity."* October, 2015. Available at: http://3680or2khmk-3bzkp33juiea1.wpengine.netdna-cdn.com/wp-content/uploads/2015/09/101415_FergusonCommissionReport.pdf.

Fisher, James T. *Dr. America.* Amherst: University of Massachusetts Press, 1997.

Fitzgerald, Paul A. S.J. *The Governance of Jesuit Colleges in the United States: 1920-1970.* Notre Dame, Indiana: University of Notre Dame Press, 1984.

Flexner, Abraham. *Medical Education in the United States and Canada: A Report to Carnegie Foundation for the Advancement of Teaching.* Bulletin Number four. New York: Carnegie, 1910.

Flick, Mary, C.S.J. "And eighty for those who are strong." *Universitas* 15:4 (Summer 1990): 23.

Frazier, Harriet. *Runaway and Freed Missouri Slaves and Those Who Helped Them: 1763-1865.* Jefferson, North Carolina and London: McFarland and Company, Inc. Press, 2004.

Frenay, Agnes Claire, S.S.M. *The Reverend Alphonse M. Schwitalla, S.J.: 1882-1965.* [unpublished] St. Louis University School of Nursing and Allied Health Professions, 1977 (SSMA).

Gallay, Alan. *Indian Slavery in Colonial America.* Lincoln and London: University of Nebraska Press, 2009.

Ganss, George E., S.J. *The Jesuit Educational Tradition and Saint Louis University: Some Bearings for the University's Sesquicentennial 1818-1968.* St. Louis: The Sesquicentennial Committee of Saint Louis University, 1969.

Ganss, George E., S.J. *Saint Ignatius' Idea of a Jesuit University.* Milwaukee: The Marquette University Press, 1954.

Garanzini, Michael, S.J. "A New Turning Point." *Conversations* 48 (Fall 2015): 10-11.

Garraghan, Gilbert J., S.J. *The Jesuits of the Middle United States.* New York: America Press, 1938.

Garrett, Matthew. "The Identity of American Catholic Higher Education: A Historical Overview." *Catholic Education: A Journal of Inquiry and Practice* 10:2 (July 2013): 229-47.

Gavin, Thomas F., S.J. *Champion of Youth: A Dynamic Story of a Dynamic Man, Father Daniel A. Lord, S.J.* Boston: The Daughters of St. Paul, 1977.

Geiser, Laura. "Life, hope and homilies." *Universitas* 35:1 (Fall 2008): 12-15.

Geiser, Laura. "Farewell, Father Biondi." *Universitas* 39:3 (Fall 2013): 9-15.

GhaneaBassiri, Kambiz. *A History of Islam in America.* Cambridge: Cambridge University Press, 2010.

Gilson, Étienne. *The Philosopher and Theology.* New York: Random House, 1962.

Gleason, Philip. *Contending with Modernity.* New York and Oxford: Oxford University Press, 1995.

Gordon, Colin. *Mapping Decline.* Philadelphia: University of Pennsylvania Press, 2008.

Grant, Gail Milissa. *At the Elbows of My Elders: Our Family's Journey Toward Civil Rights.* St. Louis: University of Missouri Press, 2008.

Gray, Howard, S.J. "The Experience of Ignatius Loyola: Background to Jesuit Education," 1-21 in Vincent J. Duminuco, S.J., ed. *The Jesuit Ratio Studiorum: 400th Anniversary Perspectives.* New York: Fordham University Press, 2000.

Greene, Lorenzo J., Gary R. Kremer and Antonio F. Holland. *Missouri's Black Heritage.* Columbia and London: University of Missouri Press, 1980.

Gruenberg, Gladys W. *Labor Peacemaker: The Life and Works of Father Leo C. Brown, S.J.* St. Louis: Institute of Jesuit Sources, 1981.

Hartman, Saidiya V. *Lose Your Mother.* New York: Farrar, Straus and Giroux, 2007.

Heathcott, Joseph and Máire Agnes Murphy. "Corridors of Flight, Zones of Renewal: Industry, Planning, and Policy in the Making of Metropolitan St. Louis, 1940-1980." *Journal of Urban History* 31 (2005): 151-189.

Heithaus, Claude H., S.J. *The Truth about St. Louis University.* St. Louis: Saint Louis University, 1940.

Henle, Robert, S.J. "Objectives of the Catholic Liberal Arts College." August 1955 [unpublished] (SLUA).

Herron, Peter. "The big questions remain the same through the ages." *St. Louis Globe-Democrat* (October 8, 1978): 9.

Hill, Walter, S.J. *Historical Sketch of the St. Louis University.* St Louis: Patrick Fox Publisher, 1879.

Howell, Patrick, S.J. "The 'New' Jesuits: The Response of the Society of Jesus to Vatican II, 1962-2012: some alacrity, some resistance." *Conversations* 42 (Fall 2012): 7-11.

Howlett, W. J. *Life of Rev. Charles Nerinckx: Pioneer Missionary of Kentucky and Founder of the Sisters of Loretto at the Foot of the Cross.* Techny, IL: Mission Press S.V.D., 1915.

Hughes, Thomas, S.J. *History of the Society of Jesus in North America, Colonial and Federal.* New York, Bombay and Calcutta: Longmans, Green, and Company, 1910.

Hughes, Thomas, S.J. "Notes from the West (Letter from Fr. Hughes) St. Louis, MO." *Woodstock Letters* 19:3 (1890): 291-301.

Ignatius of Loyola. *The Constitutions of the Society of Jesus.* St. Louis: The Institute of Jesuit Sources, 1970. Translated by George E. Ganss, S.J.

Johnson, Walter. *Soul by Soul: Life Inside the Antebellum Slave Market.* Cambridge and London: Harvard University Press, 1999.

Kavanaugh, John, S.J. *Following Christ in a Consumer Society: The Spirituality of Cultural Resistance.* Maryknoll, NY: Orbis Books, 2006 (25th edition).

Kemper, Donald J. "Catholic Integration in St. Louis, 1935-1947." *Missouri Historical Review* 73 (October 1978): 1-22.

Kenney, Peter, S.J. *Memorial.* May 1832. Handwritten document (SLUA).

Kenney, William Howland. *Jazz on the River.* Chicago: University of Chicago Press, 2005.

Klusmeyer, Jonathan. *Slavery Continued: Peonage in Missouri.* M.A. thesis for Department of History, University of Central Missouri, November 2013.

Knapp, Joseph, S.J. *The Presence of the Past: The Beginnings of the Civil War in St. Louis: The History of Hazelwood-Fordyce House from Camp Jackson and General Frost to St. Louis University and Harriet Frost Fordyce.* St. Louis: St. Louis University Press, 1979.

Krauthamer, Barbara. *Black Slaves, Indian Masters.* Chapel Hill: University of North Carolina Press, 2013.

Küng, Hans. "The Church and Freedom." *Commonweal* 78 (June 21, 1963): 343-353.

Lang, Clarence. *Grassroots at the Gateway.* Ann Arbor: University of Michigan Press, 2009.

Leahy, William P., S.J. *Adapting to America: Catholics, Jesuits, and Higher Education in the Twentieth Century.* Washington, DC: Georgetown University Press, 1991.

Lionberger, I. H. "Depreciation caused by unstable growth." 60-61 in Saint Louis (Mo.) City Plan Commission. *The Zone Plan. City plan commission, St. Louis, Missouri. Harland Bartholomew, engineer.* St. Louis, MO: Nixon-Jones printing co., 1919.

Long, D. Stephen. "Bernard Dempsey's Theological Economics: Usury, Profit, and Human Fulfillment." *Theological Studies* 57 (1996): 690- 706.

Lowes, Robert. "The P.R. Prez." *St. Louis Magazine* (October 1991): 47+.

Macelwane, James Bernard, S.J. *Jesuit Seismological Association 1925-1950.* Central Station: Saint Louis University, 1950.

Markoe, William, S.J. Memoirs. [unpublished] (JACSUS).

McDermott, John Francis. "Paincourt and Poverty." *Mid-America* 5 (1933): 10-12.

McGreevy, John T. *American Jesuits and the World.* Princeton and Oxford: Princeton University Press, 2016.

McGucken, William J., S.J. *The Jesuits and Education: The Society's Teaching Principles and Practice, Especially in Secondary Education in the United States.* New York: Bruce, 1932.

McGucken, William J., S.J. "Editorial Survey: Should We Have Coeducation in Catholic Colleges and Universities?" *Thought* 13:51 (December 1938): 537-540.

McNamee, Maurice, S.J. *Recollections in Tranquility.* St. Louis: Saint Louis University Press, 2001.

Meara, James, S.J. *For the Sake of Argument.* St. Louis: Jesuit Community, 1976.

Mehok, Charles J., S.J. *William Banks Rogers, S.J.: eighteenth president of Saint Louis University, 1900-1908.* Saint Louis University M.A. dissertation, 1945.

Melville, Annabelle M. *Louis William DuBourg: Bishop of Louisiana and the Floridas, Bishop of Montauban, and Archbishop of Besançon, 1766-1833.* Chicago: Loyola University Press, 1986.

Meyer, Rudolph, S.J. *The World in Which We Live.* St. Louis, Missouri and Freiburg: B. Herder, 1908.

Miller, Randall M. and Jon L. Wakelyn, editors. *Catholics in the Old South.* Macon: Mercer University Press, 1983.

Mintz, Steven. *Huck's Raft.* Cambridge: Belknap Press of Harvard University Press, 2004.

Miros, David P. *Rudolf J. Meyer and Saint Louis University: A Study of the Society of Jesus' Theological and Educational Enterprise at the Turn of the Century, 1885-1915.* Saint Louis University Dissertation. Ann Arbor: UMI, 2005.

Missouri, a Guide to the "Show me" state. Compiled by workers of the Writers' Program of the Work Projects Administration in the State of Missouri. Lawrence: University Press of Kansas, 1986.

Nance, Patricia Kay. "The Vatican Film Library at Saint Louis University: 1950–1990." April 1991 [M.S. thesis, unpublished] (SLUA).

Neilson, Mark. "Preliminary Draft: A History of the Saint Louis University School of Law." St. Louis, 1994. [unpublished] (SLUA).

Nichols, Francis W. "Theology at Saint Louis University 1818-2013." 2014 [unpublished] (SLUA).

Nickels, Marilyn. "Showered with Stones." *U.S. Catholic Historian* 3:4 (Spring 1984): 273-78.

Nicollet, Joseph N. *Report intended to illustrate a map of the hydrographical basin of the upper Mississippi River.* Senate document no. 237. Washington: Blair and Rives, printers, 1843.

O'Brien, David J. "The Land O' Lakes Statement." *Boston College Magazine* (Winter 1998): 3. Reproduced by Boston College Office of University Mission and Ministry.

O'Malley, John W., S.J. *The First Jesuits.* Cambridge and London: Harvard University Press, 1993.

O'Malley, John W., S.J. "The Council's Spirit: Vatican II: A time for reconciliation." *Conversations* 42 (Fall 2012): 2-6.

Ong, Walter, S.J. *An Ong Reader: Challenges for Further Inquiry.* Thomas J. Farrell and Paul A. Soukup, editors. Cresskill, N.J.: Hampton Press, 2002.

Ong, Walter, S.J. Book Review of *A History of Esthetics, The Modern Schoolman,* 17:3 (March 1940): 57.

Padberg, John W., S.J. "Development of the *Ratio Studiorum,*" 80-100 in Vincent J. Duminuco, S.J., ed., *The Jesuit* Ratio Studiorum: *Four Hundredth Anniversary Perspectives.* New York: Fordham University Press, 2000.

Padberg, John W., S.J. *Together as a Companionship: a History of the Thirty-First, Thirty-Second, and Thirty-Third General Congregations of the Society of Jesus.* St Louis: Institute of Jesuit Sources, 1994.

Padberg, John W., S.J., Martin D. O'Keefe, S.J. and John L. McCarthy, S.J. *For Matters of Greater Moment: The First Thirty Jesuit General Congregations.* St. Louis: Institute of Jesuit Sources, 1994.

Pernoud, Mary Anne. "The First Week of the University." *Saint Louis University Magazine* 46:2 (January, 1973): 28-29.

Peterson, Charles. *Colonial St. Louis: Building a Creole Capital.* Tucson: Patrice Press, 1993.

Power, Edward J. *Catholic higher education in America.* New York: Appleton-Century-Crofts, 1972.

Jane Priwer, "Daniel L. Schlafly: Our 'man for the decade,'" *Universitas* 4:3 (Winter 1979): 8-9.

Ramsay, Robert L. *Our Storehouse of Missouri Place Names.* Columbia: University of Missouri Press, 1952.

Reavis, L.U. *Saint Louis, the future great city of the world.* St. Louis: St. Louis County court, 1870 and 1875.

Reinert, Paul, S.J. *The Urban Catholic University.* New York: Sheed and Ward, 1970.

Reinert, Paul, S.J. *To turn the tide.* New York: Random House, 1972.

Reinert, Paul, S.J. and Paul Shore. *Seasons of Change.* Bronx: Saint Louis University Press and Fordham University Press, 1997.

Reinert, Paul, S.J. "In El Salvador" *The Roundtable: Voices from Central America* (Summer 1983): 3-6.

Ribadeneira, Pedro de, S.J. *Life of Ignatius.* Translated by Claude Pavur, S.J. St. Louis: Institute of Jesuit Sources, 2014.

Rice, Jack. "Literary Requiem for a Jesuit." *St. Louis Post-Dispatch* (July 15 1976): 2D.

Roberts, Richard. "Notes for Saint Louis University History." [unpublished] (SLUA).

Roberts, Richard. "Two Hours with the New President." *Saint Louis University Magazine* 47:4 (July 1974): 5-8.

Roets, Perry, S.J. "Bernard W. Dempsey, S.J." *Review of Social Economy* 49:4 (1991): 546-558.

Rollings, Willard. *Unaffected by the Gospel.* Albuquerque: University of New Mexico Press, 2004.

Rothensteiner, John E. *History of the Archdiocese of St. Louis: In its Various Stages of Development from A.D. 1673 to A.D. 1928.* St. Louis: Blackwell Wielandy, 1928.

Scharf, J. Thomas. *History of Saint Louis City and County.* Philadelphia: Louis H. Everts & Co., 1883.

Schmandt, Henry J., George D. Wendel, and E. Allan Tomey. *Federal Aid to St. Louis.* Washington, DC: The Brookings Institution, 1983.

Schroth, Raymond A., S.J. *The American Jesuits: A History.* New York: New York University Press, 2007.

Schroth, Raymond A., S.J. "How we got here: a history." *Conversations* 41 (September 2012): 2-4.

Schulman, Robert. "High Priest of Medicine." *Postgraduate Medicine* 3:1 (1948): 54-59.

Schwitalla, Alphonse, S.J. "St. Louis University School of Medicine." Historical summary. [unpublished] (SLUA).

Schwitalla, Alphonse, S.J. "Sourcebook: On the Relationship between the Sisters of St. Mary, St. Louis, Missouri and St. Louis University. With Historical Notes 1903-1943." [unpublished] 1943 (SSMA).

Seematter, Mary. "Overcoming Obstacles: Serving Black Catholics in St. Louis, 1873-1993." *Gateway Heritage* 20: 4 (Spring 2000): 16-29.

Sellers, Charles. *The Market Revolution: Jacksonian America 1815-1846.* New York and Oxford: Oxford University Press, 1991.

Shea, William M. "Jesuits and Scholarship" 194-213 in *Trying Times,* William Shea and Daniel Van Slyke, editors. Atlanta: Scholars Press, 1999.

Shinkle, Florence. "Go Write Your Little Letters," *St. Louis Post-Dispatch* (June 22, 1997): Everyday Magazine, 1C.

Shinkle, Florence. "Grand Father; for almost half a century, Father Paul Reinert has been teaching the joy of giving." *St. Louis Post-Dispatch* (January 22, 1995): Everyday Magazine, 1C.

Skrainka, Philip. *St. Louis: Its History and Ideals.* St. Louis: Lambert-Deacon-Hull Printing, 1910.

Snyder, J.C. "Typhus Fever in the Second World War." *California Medicine* 6:1 (January 1947): 3-10.

Spalding, Martin John. *Sketches of the Early Catholic Missions of Kentucky.* Louisville: B.J.Webb & Brother; Baltimore: J. Murphy, 1844.

Stump, Eleonore. *Wandering in Darkness: Narrative and the Problem of Suffering.* Oxford University Press, 2010.

Thomas, Lewis Foulk, editor. *The valley of the Mississippi illustrated in a series of views.* Painted and lithographed by J.C. Wild; St. Louis, 1841-42. St. Louis: J. Garnier, 1948.

Thwaites, Reuben Gold, editor. *The Jesuit Relations and Allied Documents; Travels and Explorations of the Jesuit Missionaries in New France, 1610-1791.* Cleveland: Burrows Brothers Company, 1896-1901.

Waide, John. "Jesuits and Baseball: 19th Century SLU Prefect Diaries Online." SLU Special Collections "Currents" (February 11, 2014) http://pius7.slu.edu/special_collections/?p=2280.

Wakin, Edward. " 'Ratio Studiorum' on the Mississippi," 69-95 in *The Catholic Campus.* NY: Macmillan, 1963.

Werner, Stephen. *Prophet of the Christian Social Manifesto: Joseph Husslein, S.J.: His life, work and social thought.* Milwaukee: Marquette University Press, 2001.

ACKNOWLEDGEMENTS

In 2015, a small group of people at Saint Louis University met to discuss the ambitious project of creating an illustrated book about the two hundred year history of the institution. That group was comprised of: Joseph Adorjan, Mary Bruemmer, Father Chris Collins, S.J., Laura Geiser, Dr. Ellen Harshman, Ann Knezetic, Father John W. Padberg, S.J., John Waide, and Father Daniel White. This core group was instrumental throughout the process of research, writing and editing, image-collection, and production of this book. Archivist Alicia Detelich of Pius XII Library (now at Yale) was essential to the project. The creative gifts and skill of Dana Hinterleitner make this book visually compelling, and were well-supported by Steve Dolan and Jim Holzer. The expert staff at Pius XII Library were of great help, including: Debbie Cribbs, Charles Croissant, Susan Ganey, Drew Kupsky, Jennifer Lowe, and Jess Touchette. Advice, information, and insights were generously provided at key stages by: Dr. Philip Alderson, John Ammann, Dr. Heidi Ardizzone, Dr. Gregory Beabout, Father Lawrence Biondi, S.J., Jay Bryant, Mary Flick, C.S.J., Roger Goldman, Peter and Michael Heithaus, Elizabeth Holzer, Dr. James Kimmey, Patricia Lee, Cynthia McKenna, Dr. Teri Murray, William Rehg, S.J., Dr. Michelle Sabick, Peter Salsich, Dr. John Slosar, Irma Sommer, Dr. Katrina Thompson, Dr. Sara Van Den Berg, Viki Villareal at SLU Madrid, Father Theodore Vitali, C.P., and Dr. Stephen Werner. At the Jesuit Archives of the Central and Southern United States Province: David Miros, Mary McDonald, Alexandra Bisio, Cass Sunstein, and Ann Rosentreter assisted with expertise and alacrity, as did Sandy Ashby at the Franciscan Sisters of Mary; Charles Brown at UMSL; Sister Eleanor Craig of the Loretto Heritage Center in Kentucky; Scott Grimwood of SSM Archives; Father Claude Pavur, S.J. of the Institute of Jesuit Sources in Boston; Emily Sanders and Rena Schergen at the St. Louis Archdiocese Archives; Chris Peimann at the Sheldon Art Gallery; Ashley Howdeshell of Loyola University Chicago; Mike Meiners at the *St. Louis Post-Dispatch*, and Richard Sorensen at the Smithsonian Institution. Mark Haenchen generously shared wonderful photographs of the Doisy Center, and Haroon Iqbal provided brilliant technical assistance at the perfect moment. SLU's deans, directors, and other top administrators, as well as the Jesuit Community, have provided tremendous support for this book.

Many people across the SLU community and beyond helped with planning, support, and production, including: Jittaun Allen, Anne-Marie Apollo Noël, Amelia Arnold, Kate Bax, David Brinker, Judi Buncher, Blythe Burkhardt, Dave Cassens, Jessica Ciccone, Erika Cohn, Ronald Crown, Lisa DeLorenzo, Bill Devers, Jeffrey Dorr, S.J., Corie Dugas, Mark Evans, Jeff Fowler, Katie Gortz, James Greathouse, Lynn Hartke, Ronald Hoffman, Jeff Hovey, Jamie Klopmeyer, Matt Krob, Danielle Lacey, Petruta Lipan, Patrick McCarthy, Brian Merlo, Tony Minor, Father J.J. Mueller, S.J., Donna Neely, Robert Palank, Drs. Frances and Fred Pestello, Sean Polley, Jake Prange, Sue Ratz, Connor Richardson, Margo Riley, Amy Russell, Barb Sapienza, Marie Sarson, Kelly Schmidt, Eileen Searls, Jennifer Sherer, Alice Smith, Maria Tsikalas, Ruth Vilches, Paul Vita, Joanne Vogel, Constance Wagner, Adam Westrich, and Melanie Whittington. Guest essayists: Christy Finsel of the Osage Nation; Gregory Pass, Ph.D., Assistant Dean for Special Collections at SLU; and Maureen Wangard, have been thoughtful, erudite colleagues. Collections at the Missouri Museum of History and at Becker Archives at Washington University were useful. To members of the bicentennial steering and advisory committees, individuals and groups across all of SLU's campuses, friends, family, and dozens of complete strangers: thank you for listening to me rave about this inspiring and remarkable university. More than any person, John Waide has been a steady, genial, and incredibly knowledgeable colleague throughout.

Dolores Byrnes
October 2017

PHOTOGRAPH AND IMAGE CREDITS

Most of the images reproduced in this book are of or from materials owned by the Saint Louis University Pius XII Library Special Collections or by the Marketing and Communications Department. They are either already available as digitized images, or were photographed by Steve Dolan. All images which are exceptions to this are listed below, by source. We thank these generous people and organizations for their assistance. These images appear, courtesy of:

Archives of the Archdiocese of St. Louis (Concordat, pages 18-19)

Archives of SSM Health in St. Louis (Letter, page 95; Nursing students, page 96; Desloge aerial, page 107)

Archives of the Society of Jesus: Central and Southern United States Province (pages 32-3, 35, 46, 68-9, 102, 115); photographed by Jim Holzer (pages 21, 70, 75, 78, 108)

Justin Barr, dust cover image

David Carson of *St. Louis Post-Dispatch* (page 177)

Colliers, October 1950 (page 114).

St. Louis Globe Democrat, Katy Gurley August 11 1976, "Goronwy Broun: 81 Years a 'Doc'" p. 12A. (page 167)

Pictorial History of St. Louis by Richard Compton and Camille Dry, (in the public domain) with assistance from Jeremy Munro, Collections Information Coordinator Crystal Bridges Museum of American Art (page 27, 54-5)

Franciscan Sisters of Mary, Bridgeton, Missouri: SMI Clinic Lantern Slide, SSM Mother Seraphia (Schloctermeyer), seated (1900s), SSM Mother Aloysia Schruefer (1920) (page 85)

Mark Haenchen of SLU for images of the Doisy building (page 159)

Cody Hammer, Osage Nation Communications Department (page 12)

Danielle Lacey (dust jacket, author head shot)

Architect: Lawrence Group; Associate Architect: HGA Architects and Engineers (SSM image on page 179)

Life Magazine, October 1954 issue (page 138)

Loretto Heritage Center Archives and Museum, Nerinx, Kentucky (pamphlet on page 10-11)

Loyola University Chicago Archives and Special Collections (Father Hoeffer, S.J., page 184)

Father "JJ" Mueller, S.J. (pages 4 and 41 (crown))

Ratio, Inc (ATC image page 178)

David Rumsey Map Collection, www.davidrumsey.com. "United states. (to accompany)" from page 60 in *A Comprehensive Atlas, Geographical, Historical & Commercial.* By T.G. Bradford. William D. Ticknor, Boston. Wiley & Long, New York, 1835. List Number 2643.067 in the David Rumsey collection. (For map used on pages 48-9) and image of St. Louis 1844 map (pages 46-7)

Saint Louis University Casa de Salud (page 166)

Saint Louis University Earthquake Center, Department of Earth and Atmospheric Sciences in Ritter Hall (page 82)

Saint Louis University Madrid communications department (page 137)

Saint Louis University Museum of Contemporary Religious Art (page 163)

Sheldon Concert Hall and Art Galleries, Red Window (page 162)

Smithsonian Institution: George Catlin painting (page 13)

St. Louis Mercantile Library at the University of Missouri-St. Louis, Norbury Wayman Collection (map of Paincourt, pages 14-15)

THE **ADMINISTRATION** OF SAINT LOUIS UNIVERSITY

EXECUTIVE STAFF: 2017-2018

Kevin Behrns, M.D., Vice President for Medical Affairs, Dean, SOM

Nancy Brickhouse, Ph.D., Provost

Chris Collins, S.J., Special Assistant for Mission and Identity

Justin Daffron, S.J., Special Assistant to the President

Jeff Fowler, Vice President for Marketing and Communications

Jay Goff, Vice President for Enrollment and Retention

David Hakanson, Vice President for ITS, Chief Information Officer

David Heimburger, Vice President for Business and Finance, CFO

William Kauffman, J.D., Vice President, General Counsel, Secretary of the University, and Chief of Staff

Michael Lucido, Vice President for Facilities Services

Mickey Luna, J.D., Vice President for Human Resources Management

Sheila Manion, Vice President for Development

Chris May, Athletics Director

Ken Olliff, Ph.D., Vice President, Research

Fred P. Pestello, Ph.D., President

Kent Porterfield, Ed.D., Vice President for Student Development

Jonathan Smith, Ph.D., Vice President for Diversity and Community Engagement

Paul Vita, Ph.D., Vice President/Rector of Madrid Campus

DEANS AND DIRECTORS

College of Arts and Sciences
Dean Christopher Duncan, Ph.D.

College of Philosophy and Letters
Dean William Rehg, S.J.

College for Public Health and Social Justice
Interim Dean Thomas Burroughs, Ph.D.

Doisy College of Health Sciences
Dean Mardell Wilson, Ed.D., RD, LDN

John Cook School of Business
Dean Mark Higgins, Ph.D.

Libraries
Dean David Cassens, M.A., M.L.I.S.

Madrid, Spain Campus
Dean and Director Paul Vita, Ph.D.

Parks College of Engineering, Aviation and Technology
Dean Michelle Sabick, Ph.D.

School of Education
Interim Dean Molly Schaller, Ph.D.

School of Law
Dean William Johnson, J.D.

School of Medicine
Dean/VP Kevin Behrns, M.D.

School of Nursing
Dean Teri Murray, Ph.D.

School of Professional Studies
Dean Tracy Chapman, Ph.D.

Directors of Degree Granting Centers

Center for Advanced Dental Education
Executive Director John Hatton, D.M.D.

Center for Health Outcomes Research (SLUCOR)
Deputy Director Leslie Hinyard, Ph.D.

INDEX

70th General Hospital Unit, 113

Academy for young Gentlemen, 8

Adorjan, Joseph, 159

Aelen, S.J., Herman, 12

African Americans, 16, 18, 21, 23, 25, 52-4, 68-9, 86, 104-9, 122-3, 126-7, 140-4, 177

Alexander, Felicia Stevens, 104, 109

Alexandrian Society, 149

Allied Health Professions, School of, see: Doisy College of Health Sciences.

Alpha Sigma Nu, 122, 169

Alvarez, Eugenie, 8

America, 100, 104, 123

Ammann, John, 165

Anderledy, S.J., Anton, 63

Anduzi, Aristides, 9

Anglum (Missouri), 68

Annan, Robert, 163

anti-Catholic, anti-Jesuit sentiment/riots, 45, 52-4

Aquinas, St. Thomas, 115, 132, 149-51

Archive (yearbook), 88, 113, 117

Archivum Romanum Societatis Iesu (ARSA, Archives of the House of the Superior General), 132

Arrupe, S.J., Pedro, 126

Art history, 162

Arts and Sciences, College of, 89, 95, 109, 111, 117, 147-151, 176

Ashe, S.L., Edwarda, 109

Association of American Colleges, 125

Association of Black Collegians, 143

Association of Jesuit Colleges and Universities, 124

athletics, 41, 57, 60, 76-7, 118-9, 123

aviation engineering, 86, 112. See also Parks College of Engineering, Aviation and Technology

Badin, Stephen, 11

Bannon, S.J., John, 117, 136

Barclay, Shepard, 41

Barret, Richard Aylett, 44

Barret, Richard Farril, 44

baseball, 41, 60

Baselmans, S.J., Henry, 52

basketball, 118, 123

Bates, Edward (Missouri senator), 29, 44

Beabout, Gregory, 156, 169

Beckx, S.J., Peter Jan, 50, 52-4, 57

Behrns, Kevin, 178

Belgium, 11, 17

Belize, 70, 136

Belshe, Robert, 156, 166

Beman, Millie Matfeldt, 170

Bender, John, 76-7

Berger, Mary Odilia, 94

Berlin, Ira, 21

Berry, Lola, 174

Biblioteca Apostolica Vaticana, 132-3

Biddle, Thomas, 25

Billiken(s), 76, 119, 123

biochemical sciences/biochemistry, 110, 129, 138

Biondi, S.J., Lawrence, 147, 152, 154, 156-9, 163, 166-7, 175

Black Alumni Association, 172

Blackmon, Douglas, 21

Blow, (Henry) Taylor, 127

Blum, S.J., Victor, 113

Bolton, Herbert Eugene, 136

Bond, Young H., 84

Bork, S.J., Austin, 108

Boston College, 124

Bouchard, S.J., James, 68

Boudreaux, S.J., Isidore, 49

Bourke, S.J., Vernon, 122, 151

Brady, Kathleen, 160

Brady, Matthew, 33

Brennan, Donald, 151, 156

Brethren of the Common Life, 37

Breuning, Bertha, 83

Brickhouse, Nancy, 176

Brochau, Augustus Van Liew, 78

Brockhaus, Robert, 155

Bronsgeest, S.J., Henry, 87

Brooks, S.J., Peter, 109

Brosnahan, S.J., Timothy, 64

Broun, Jr., Goronwy O., 110

Broun, Sr., Goronwy O., 110, 167

Brown, Charles, 127

Brown, S.J., Leo, 103-5, 127

Brown, Michael, 177

Bruemmer, Mary, 94, 96-7, 117, 175, end sheet caption

Brzozowski, S.J., Thaddeus, 11

Buckholz, Richard, 148

Buckner, Richard Aylett, 44

Buel, James, 66

Buffalo Mission of the Society of Jesus, 49, 63, 110

Buhler, S.J., Richard, 179

Burke, S.J., John, 79, 84-5, 107

Burrowes, S.J., Alexander, 57, 63, 64, 94, 108

Burrus, S.J., Ernest, 132

Busch, August, 117

Busch Student Center, 158

Bush, William, 157

Business school: See Commerce and Finance, School of; and John Cook School of Business.

Byrne, Leo C., 134

Cahokia, Illinois, 12, 112, 168

Cahill, Jr., Clyde, 122-3

Callahan, S.J., Michael, 52

Calmer, S.J., Henry, 67

Calvary Cemetery (St. Louis), 68, 127

Camp Jackson, 41, 52-3, 142

Campbell, James, 89

Campion College of the Sacred Heart, 49

Cancer center, 167

Caray, Harry, 123

Carnegie Commission on Higher Education, 147

Carnegie Foundation for the Advancement of Teaching, 84-5

Carroll, Catherine J., 115

Carroll College, 77

Carter, Jimmy, 123

Casa de Salud, 159, 167

Catherine II (the Great), 11

Catholic Economic Association, 105

Catholic Legal Assistance Ministry, 165

Catholic University, 134

Catlin, George, 13

Cavallo, Cheryl, 169

Center for Advanced Dental Education (CADE), 144, 158, 167

Center for Health Outcomes Research (SLU COR), 147, 174

Center for Health Services Education and Research, 164

Center for Liturgy, 149

Center for Vaccine Development, 166

Chaifetz, Richard, 156

Chaifetz Arena, 156, 158

Chambers, Charles Bosseron, 24

Chambers, Thomas, 166

Chaney, Rick, 161

Chapman, Tracy, 174

Charropin, S.J., Charles, 58-60, 70-1, 172

Childress, Richard, 127

cholera epidemics in St. Louis, 41

Choppesky, S.J., Jonathan, 138

Chouteau, Auguste, 10, 13, 15, 16, 37, 40

Chouteau, Marie-Thérèse Bourgeois, 13

Chouteau, Pierre, 13, 52

Cicero, 61, 64, 74, 89

Civic Progress, 141

civil rights movement, 114, 126-7

Civil War, 21, 32-33, 41, 52-4, 68, 142

Clamorgan, Cyprian, 66

Clark, S.J., Charles 'Dismas,' 103

Clark, Jean, 120

Clarke, Powhatan Hughes, 92-3

Claver, Peter, 108, 172

Cleary, S.J., Frank, 148

Clemens Hall, 91, 123, 153

Clock Tower Accords, 177-8

Cloud, S.J., Charles, 27, 108, 110

Cochems, Eddie, 77

Code Noir (Black Code), 52

Codina, S.J., Gabriel, 37

coeducation, 83, 86, 94-7

Coeur d'Alene Mission of the Sacred Heart of Jesus, 32-3, 46, 48-9, 206

Cold War, 136

Collège de Guyenne, 10-1

Collège de la Madeleine, 10-1

College Hill (or College Farm), 40, 58, 60, 62, 78, 83

Colleton, S.J., Philip, 52

Collins, S.J., Chris, 175

Collins, James, 151

Commerce and Finance (School of), 57, 89, 91, 105, 109, 114, 147, 152. See also John Cook School of Business.

Commonweal, 134

Compton, Arthur Holly, 154

Concordat (between Society of Jesus and Bishop DuBourg), 18-9, 26, 49

"Connor's Addition,"24-5

Control Data Institute, 138

Conway, S.J., James, 83

Cook, John, School of Business, 155, 158, 168. See also Commerce and Finance (School of).

Cook, Lucy, 155

"corporate colleges," 95

Correctional Center, Bonne Terre, Missouri, 148

Cortex Innovation Community, 158

Costello, S.J., Robert, 24

Creighton College/University, 48-9, 63, 64, 97, 108, 115

Crimmins, S.J., Harry, 48, 113

Crowley, Francis, 94

Crowley, Raymond, 109

crowning traditions, 41, 120

Cupples House, 143, 162-3

Cupples, Samuel, 163

Curran, Mark, 136

Curriculum, 8, 25, 27, 29, 36-9, 61-3, 74, 89, 148, 150-51; core, 148; reform, 57, 64, 111, 151

Dacus, Joseph, 66

Daly, Leo A., Company, 134

Daly, S.J., Lowrie, 36, 132-3

Dam, Henryk, 129

Damen, S.J., Arnold, 27, 33, 49, 68

Darby, John, 25, 39

Davis, S.J., Joseph, 83, 114

Day, Dorothy, 105, 134

De Andreis, Felix, 9, 16

De Coen, S.J., Francis Xavier, 12

De La Croix, Charles, 12

De Leyba, Fernando, 16

De Maillet, Francis, 20

De Meyer, Peter, 20, 22

De Neckère, C.M., Raymond, 9

De Saint-Ange de Bellerive, Captain Louis Groston, 13

De Sedella, Antonio, 13

De Smet bridge (at World's Fair), 80

De Smet Hall, 73, 88, 139

De Smet, S.J., Peter John, 10, 17, 20, 25, 32-3, 35, 40, 46-7, 49, 54, 66, 68, 87, 142, 158, 163

Deglman, S.J., George, 94

Demling, Mark, 119

Dempsey, S.J., Bernard, 100, 103, 105, 109

Dempsey, 'Boots', 112

Dempsey, S.J., Terrence, 163

Dentistry (School), 57, 84-5, 88, 89, 90, 109, 110, 144, 150. See also Center for Advanced Dental Education.

"Departments" first listed, 74

Depression (economic), 91, 100, 102, 104-5, 138

Desloge, Firmin (person and/or hospital), 85, 106-7, 131

Detroit Mercy College/University, 48-9, 64

Deys, Leon, 9

Dickens, Charles, 39, 79

Dickey, James, 21

discrimination (racial), 68-9, 108-9, 122-3, 140-2, 164-5, 177

Divinity studies/school, 9, 29, 50, 74, 77, 92, 144, 148

Doisy College of Health Sciences, 97, 147, 170, 174

Doisy, Ada Alley, 129

Doisy, Alice Ackert, 129

Doisy, Edward A., 110, 117, 129, 131

Doisy, Edward A., Research Center, 158-9

Doisy, Margaret McCormick, 129

Dombrowski, John, 148

Dorr, S.J., Jeffrey, 69

Dowling, S.J., Edward, 127

Doyle, Adele, 83

Doyle, John, 66

Doyle, John (philosophy department), 169

Drake, Charles, 54

Dreyer, Rob, 162

Drummond, S.J., Edward, 117, 144-5, 148

Druyts, S.J., John, 45

DuBourg Hall, 73, 74-5, 83, 86-8, 90, 106, 108, 131-3, 141, 176

DuBourg, Louis W.V. (Bishop), 3, 5, 7-13, 16-25, 32, 49, 50, 180

Duchesne, R.S.C.J., Rose Philippine, 10, 16

Dueker, Jack, 119

Dufford, Robert, 149

Duncan, Chris, 176

Dunklin, Daniel (Missouri governor), 29

Dunne, S.J., George, 103

Eberhardt, Walter C. "Doc," 119

Eberle, Alphonse George, 111

Eden Seminary, 114

Education (School of), 86, 94-7, 138, 147, 180

Eils, S.J., Henry, 74

El Salvador, 154

Elet, S.J., John Anthony, 17, 20

Eliot, William Greenleaf, 63

endowment (at SLU), 5, 78, 86, 89

Engineering and Earth Sciences (School of), 144

Engler, Bob, 117

enrollment, 5, 22-3, 39, 64, 73, 78, 82-3, 89, 91, 111, 113, 115, 118

Ermatinger, Charles, 132-3

Eslick, Leonard, 151

Ethics across the curriculum, 148

Evans, Alvin, 127

Eycleshymer, Albert, 84

Faherty, S.J., William, 5, 34, 63, 73, 80, 115, 172

Fanning, S.J., William, 77

Federal Communications Commission (FCC), 154

Federation of Colored Catholics (also known as Federated Colored Catholics), 109

Finsel, Christy, 12, 65

Finucane, Daniel, 169

Firmin Desloge Hospital, 85, 106-7, 131

Fitzgerald, S.J., Thomas, 123, 147, 152-3, 161

Fitzgerald, S.J., William, 124

Fitzsimmons, Paul, 127

Flaget, Benedict Joseph, 17

Fletcher, Thomas (Governor), 21, 54

Fleur de Lis (publication), 77, 100

Flexner, Abraham, 84-5

Florissant, Missouri (also called Saint Ferdinand), 10, 12, 13, 17, 21-3, 25. See from: Indian school; St. Regis. See also St. Stanislaus Seminary.

Flying Billikens, 113

Foley, S.J., John, 149

Folin, Otto, 129

Fontbonne University, 95

football, 57, 76-7, 118

Fordham University, 100, 109

Fordyce, Harriet Frost, 142

Forster, Michael, 143

Fortis, S.J., Luigi, 32

forward pass, 77

Founders' Day, 134

"Four Minute Speakers" (WWI), 92

Fox, Maxine, 159

Fox, Robert, 159, 166

Francis, Pope (Jorge Bergoglio), 180

Franciscan Sisters of Mary, 85, 95-7, 107

Franco, Francisco, 137

Frederick II (Emperor), 133

Frieden, S.J., John Pierre, 77, 82-3, 86

Frommelt, S.J., Horace, 108

Frost, Daniel Marsh, 142

Fulbright Program, 136

Fusz Hall, 134, 145, 149, 163

G.I. Bill of Rights, 118

Gamma Pi Epsilon, 122

Garanzini, S.J., Michael, 156, 171

Garesché, S.J., Edward, 102

Garraghan, S.J., Gilbert, 5, 11, 12, 23, 27, 32-3, 38, 54, 63, 172

Garvey, S.J., Arnold, 68

Gathe, Joseph, 123

General Congregation (of the Society of Jesus), 5, 102, 126, 180

Geophysics (Institute of Geophysical Technology), 110-111, 113, 138, 144, 150

George, John, 169

Georgetown College/University, 8, 10, 17, 29, 49, 64, 128

Gilsinan, James, 169

Gilson, Étienne, 100, 150

Gleason, Philip, 64, 151

Glennon, John, 109

Gnägi, Alberto, 159

Goedeker, Brooks, 178

Goesse, S.J., John, 83, 110

Goldman, Gordon, 167

Goldman, Roger, 165

Goldner, Jesse, 164-5

Goldstein, Joel, 169

Gonzaga University, 49, 97

Goodman, Stanley, 154

Gould, Mary, 148

Graduate school (at SLU), 106, 150-51

Graham, Jane, 66

Grand Act of 1903, 78, 80

Grand Hall, 178

Grand and Lindell campus, 30, 38, 54-5, 57, 71-5, 86-91, 140-2

Grandgenett, Duane, 144

Gray, S.J., Howard, 67

Gray, S.J., John, 161

Gregory XVI, Pope, 32

Greiff, Donald, 113

Griesedieck Hall, 145, 153

Grimmelsman, S.J., Joseph, 63

Grosswasser, Nelly, 169

Gruender, S.J., Hubert, 94

Grzeda, Anthony, 168

Guelker, Bob, 119

Guyot, François, 9

Hall, Frederick Alton, 92

Harney, William, 35

Harper, J.P., 84

Harris, Stan, 122

Harshman, Ellen, 155

Hartman, Saidiya, 21

Harvey, Thomas, 165

Hatton, John, 167

Havern, Ann, 11

Hayden, Andrew, 168

Hayden, Tim, 155

Hayes, S.J., James, 52

Health law, 164

Health Resource Center, 167

Health sciences, 138

Hellmann, O.F.M., J.A. Wayne, 148

Heithaus, S.J., Claude, 5, 100, 103, 109, 114-5, 173

Heithaus, Jessie, 173

Henle, S.J., Robert, 118, 128, 149, 150-51

Herron, Ivory Lee, 122-3

Hesburgh, C.S.C., Theodore, 124-5

Higgins, James, 127

Higgins, S.J., John, 138

higher education (changes in), 64, 82, 94, 111, 117-8, 124-5, 150-1, 158-9

Hill, S.J., Walter, 5, 20, 22, 54, 60, 62-3, 172; Historical Sketch of the St. Louis University, 60, 172

Hinyard, Leslie, 174

Hoecken, S.J., Christian, 12

Hoeffer, S.J., James F.X., 63, 78

Hoffman, Ronald, 123

Holder, Jr., Eric, 177

Holloran, S.J., Patrick, 97, 109, 112

Hollos, Aurelia, 83

Holton brothers (Charles, John, Joseph), 93

Horace, 58, 61, 74

Horvath, Frances, 170

Howard University, 119

Howe, Harold, 151

Hrubetz, Joan, 170

Hudlin, Richard, 102

Hughes, S.J., Thomas, 27, 38, 63, 66

Husslein, S.J., Joseph, 67, 103, 104, 109, 164

Hutchison, S.J., William, 171

Ignatius of Loyola (Saint), 3, 30, 61, 64, 111, 174

Ilboudo, Christelle, 171

Immel, Vincent, 127, 164-5, 169

Indian school: see Florissant, Missouri

Institute for Entrepreneurial Studies (later Jefferson-Smurfit Center for Entrepreneurial Studies), 155

Institute of International Business (later Boeing Institute of International Business), 155

Institute of Jesuit Sources, 128

Institute for Molecular Virology, 144, 159

Institute of Social Order, 102, 104

integration (at SLU), 68-9, 86, 102-104, 108-109, 114, 115, 122-3

Interfaith Partnership of Greater St. Louis, 177

International Association of Catholic Universities, 124

International Federation of Catholic Universities (IFCU), 124

Interracial Review, 103

Intramural Law Review, 127

Jackson, Dewey, 103

Jarvis, S.S.M., Margaret Mary, 107

Jefferson, Thomas, 21

Jesuit Educational Association, 97, 124-5, 128

Jewish Law Center, 130

John Carroll University, 49

Johnson, Andrew, 142

Johnson, Lyndon B., 134

Johnson, Sandra, 156

Johnson, William, 164

Johnston, S.J., Robert, 92, 104, 109

Jones, Mary Ann, 109

Joset, S.J., Joseph, 52

Juvenile law, 127, 164-5

KBIL (forerunner to KSLU), 120

KETC, 136, 154

Kalaf, Emily Growney, 168

Katz, Jerry, 155

Katzman, Philip, 129

Kauffman, William, 175, 176

Kavanaugh, S.J., John, 148-9, 169

Keller, S.J., Joseph, 74

Kelly, S.J., Robert M., 113

Kennedy, John F., 118, 126, 136

Kennedy, Leo, 94

Kennedy, Robert, 134

Kenney, S.J., Peter, 26-7, 32, 50

Kenny, S.J., Laurence, 39, 67, 92

Kenrick, Peter, 57, 68

Keough, Harry, 119

Kernaghan, R.S.C.J., Marie, 95

Kickapoo Mission (Fort Leavenworth, Kansas), 48-9, 206

Kim, Seung Hee, 155

Kimmey, James, 164, 176

King, Donald, 127, 164-5

King, Jr., Martin Luther, 21, 144

Kinsella, Ralph, 110

Klausner, Gustav Kadysh, 114

Klubertanz, S.J., George, 151

Knights of Columbus, 132

Knobbe, Jerry, 119

Kohl, Johann Georg, 25, 39

Koning, S.J., William, 52

Korean War, 131, 143

Kuhnmuench, S.J., Otto, 114

Küng, Hans, 134

labor, 67, 104-105

Labre program, 171

LaFarge, S.J., John, 100, 109

Lambert, Albert Bond, 92

Land o' Lakes (conference and statement), 124-5

Lander, David, 164-5

Lane, Belden, 169

Lane, William Carr (Missouri representative), 29, 37

Law clinic (SLU), 127, 164-5

Law college (19th century), 43-4, 50, 147

Law college/school (20th century), 57, 82-3, 89, 98-100, 111, 113, 122, 127, 130, 147, 152-3, 156-7, 164-5

Lay, Henry, 159

Lay, S.J., Thomas, 152

lay advisors and collaboration, 82, 124-5, 164, 175, 178

lay trustees, 117, 124-5

Lazarists, 9

Laclède, Pierre Liguest, 13, 14

Las Vegas College (now Regis University), 48-9

Le Berthon, Ted, 109

Ledochowski, S.J., Wlodimir, 97

Lee, John Fitzgerald, 78

Lee, Patricia Hureston, 165

Legal Aid Society, 127, 164-5

Lionberger, I.H., 140

Leo XIII, Pope, 12, 65, 67, 126

Ley, Willy, 138

Library, 33, 38-9, 74, 131. See also Pius XII Memorial Library.

Lilly, S.J., Linus Augustine, 100, 111

Lincoln, Abraham, 44, 54

Lindbergh, Charles, 112

Linton, Moses, 42, 45, 46-7, 65-6, 68

Littiken, Al, 158-160

Litton, Abram, 45

Loeb, Hanau, 85, 95, 108, 129

Loewenstein, Paul, 159

Lohr, Curtis H., 113

Lord, S.J., Daniel, 102-3

Louisiana Purchase, 10, 21, 57, 78-81

Lowe, Jennifer, 139

Loyola Marymount University in Los Angeles, 128

Loyola College (now University) of Chicago, 33, 48-50, 64

Loyola University New Orleans, 100

Lukaszewski, S.J., Boleslaus, 172

Lukens, C.D., 84

Lyon, Elias Potter, 84-5

Lyon, Nathaniel, 142

Lyons, Anita, 122

Macauley, Ed "Easy," 118

Macelwane, S.J., James, 64, 103, 110-1, 113, 150

Madrid (SLU campus), 5, 117, 136-7, 147, 155, 156, 160-1

Maginnis, Jane, 108

Magis (strategic plan), 176

Maguire, Mary, 83

Maher, S.J., Trafford, 128

Maher, S.J., Zacheus, 97

Manion, Tim, 149

Marchetti, S.J., Jerome, 152

Marchlewski, S.J., Michael, 137

Marguerite Hall, 145, 171

Marion Sims College (later Marion-Sims-Beaumont), 84

Maritain, Jacques, 100, 151

Markoe, S.J., John, 102-3, 108-9, 114-15

Markoe, Mary Prince, 102

Markoe, S.J., William, 68, 102-3, 104, 106, 108-9, 114-15

Marquette, S.J., Jacques, 12, 13

Marquette College/University, 48-9, 63, 64, 78

Marshall, Kenneth, 144

Martin, John, 9

Martín, S.J., Luis García, 63

Martin, S.J., Michael, 67

Maryhurst Normal College, 95

Maryland Province of the Society of Jesus, 17, 21, 49. See also Georgetown College (later University).

Maryville University, 95

Matteson, Bob, 119

May, S.J., Ignatius, 52

May, Morton, 134

Mayden, Richard, 148

McAuliffe, Dan, 118

McCosh, James, 63

McDaniel, Hazel (married name Tebeau), 106

McElroy, S.J., John, 27

McGannon, S.J., Barry, 152

McGucken, S.J., William, 27, 97

McLuhan, Marshall, 111, 138-9, 162

McMillian, Theodore, 122

McNamara, Charles, 77

McNamee, S.J., Maurice, 122, 152, 162-3

Meara, S.J., James, 151

Meachum, John Barry, 52

Medical College of St. Louis University (19th century), 30, 37, 42-3, 45-7, 50, 65, 90

Medical School (School of Medicine 20th century), 57, 78, 84-5, 88, 89, 90, 92, 106-7, 110, 117, 152, 156, 166-7, 168, 171, 174

MEDLaunch, 168

Melville, Annabelle, 10

Mercier, S.J., Ronald, 180

Messina (Italy), 37, 61

Mestrovic, Ivan, 134

meteorology, 40, 82-3

Metropolitan College, 117, 126, 163, 174

Meurin, S.J., Sébastian Louis, 13

Meyer, Avis, 169

Meyer, S.J., Rudolph, 57, 63, 64, 94, 150

Meyers, Jr., VonDerrit, 177

Meyers, Sr., VonDerrit, 177

Micah program, 171

Mill Creek Valley, 140-42

Miller, Douglas, 167

Minteer, Shelley, 148

mission (statement of SLU), 3, 147

Missouri College Union, 78

Missouri Mission (later Vice Province and Province) of the Society of Jesus, 3, 5, 11, 21-7, 32, 48-57, 63, 64, 70, 79, 136, 158, 206

Missouri Valley Thomism, 151

Mitcheff, Monica, 167

Modern Schoolman, The (now Res Philosophica), 100-1

Moeller, S.J., Henry, 63

Monteleone, Patricia, 166-7

Moragues, Vicente, 113

moral education, 36, 61, 76, 144-5, 148, 180

Morrissey Hall, 152-3

Mount Saint Rose Sanitarium, 95

Mueller, S.J., J.J., 148, 172

Mullanphy, John, 36

Mundae, Rusdeep, 168

Murphy, S.J., William Stack, 52

Murphy, S.J., William J., 124

Murray, Teri, 170

museum (19th century campus), 62

Museum of Art (SLUMA), 158, 163, 173

Museum of Contemporary Religious Art (MOCRA), 163

Museum of Western Jesuit Missions, 115, 172-3

National Aeronautics and Space Administration (NASA), 138, 168

National Association for the Advancement of Colored People (NAACP), 126, 141

National Catholic Educational Association (NCEA), 78, 124, 150

National Catholic Press Association, 148

National juvenile law center, 127, 164-5

Native Americans, 7, 10-15, 18, 20-23, 26-7, 32-3, 35, 48-9, 65-6, 68-9, 173 ; Jesuit missions among, 206-7

Nawrocki, Mary Francis, 115

Neale, S.J., Charles, 19

Neale, S.J., Francis, 32

neo-scholasticism, 100, 151

Nerinckx, Charles, 11, 17, 33, 50

Nicholas V (Pope), 132

Nicollet, Joseph, 40, 83

Niel, François 8, 9

Ninth and Washington campus, 24-5, 30-1, 37-9, 56-63, 66, 70-1

Nobel prize, 129

Nobili, S.J., John, 33

Norman, Sandra, 147

Northside Revitalization (St. Louis), 171

Notre Dame, University of, 50, 64, 89, 124-5

Nursing (School), 86, 95-7, 107, 147, 150, 170, 174

O'Boyle, Rose, 83

O'Brien, John, 164-5

O'Connell, S.J., Daniel, 117, 144

O'Connor, Roc, 149

O'Donnell, Edward F., 157

Oblate Sisters, 68

Olliff, Kenneth, 178

Ong, S.J., Walter, 100, 111, 117, 137, 138-9, 149, 156

opioid crisis, 167

Order of Railroad Telegraphers, 162-3

Osage, 10, 12, 16, 65, 173

Otting, S.J., Bernard, 92, 94

"Our Mission Today: The Service of Faith and the Promotion of Justice," 126

Pacem in Terris, 124

Padberg, S.J., John W., 16, 50, 128, 159

Padre Arrupe Hall, 137, 161

Padre Rubio Hall, 137, 161

"Paincourt" (colonial St. Louis), 14-15

Painter, Earl, 77

Palermo, 61

Pallen, Conde, 64

Panken, S.J., Ignatius, 40, 52, 68-9, 108

Parker, Kenneth, 148

Parks College of Aviation (now Parks College of Engineering, Aviation and Technology), 112, 120, 138, 144, 147, 152, 158, 168

Parks, Oliver Lafayette, 112

Pass, Gregory, 132-3

Paul, Rene, 9

Paul III, Pope, 3

Peace Corps, 136

Père Marquette Gallery, 131, 132, 159

Perry, Harold R., 115

Pesch, S.J., Heinrich, 105

Pestello, Ferdinando, 175

Pestello, Frances, 175

Pestello, Fred, 63, 77, 98, 114, 147, 174-8

Pestello, Vitina, 175

Philalethic Literary and Debating Society, 39, 63, 77, 98, 114

philosophy (department), 100-1, 150-1,

Philosophy and Letters (also sometimes called Philosophy and Science), 57, 73-4, 89, 128, 145, 147, 150

Pi Lambda Theta (now Lambda Pi Eta), 145

Pickwicks, The (baseball team), 41

Pillman, Dorothy, 145

Pinkerton, Henry, 113

Pius VII, Pope, 10

Pius IX, Pope, 63

Pius XI, Pope, 95, 97, 104

Pius XII, Pope, 124, 131, 132, 134-5

Pius XII Memorial Library, 133-5, 152, 178-9

Playhouse Club, 115

Polish Law Collection, 130

Pomarède, Leon, 27, 38

Ponziglione, S.J., Paul Mary, 12, 68

Pope, Charles Alexander, 45

Porterfield, Kent, 171, 176

post-graduate lectures, 63, 65, 147, 150

Potawatomi Mission (Council Bluffs, Iowa), 48-9, 206

Potawatomi Mission (Sugar Creek, Kansas, moved to St. Marys, Kansas), 48-9, 206

Potter, Peter, 84

Power, Richard, 127

presidency (of SLU), 63, 78, 124, 175. See also list of presidents, 180-185.

prison degree program, 148

Professional Studies (School of), 147, 174

protests (by students), 143, 177

Public Health, School of, 164

Public Health and Social Justice, College for, 147, 164, 174

Pulitzer, Joseph, 109

pumpkin launch, 168

Puppendahl, S.S.M., Mary Concordia, 95-7, 107

Purcell, John Baptist, 34

Purcell, Thomas, 109, 110

Quadragesimo Anno, 104-105

Queen's Work, The, 102

Quinn, Thomas, 127

Quintanilla, Tawanda, 174

Quonset huts on SLU quad, 122

racial equality, 69, 106, 122-3, 144

Rafalko, Walter, 127

Range, Don, 119

Ratio Studiorum (Plan of Studies), 6, 36-7, 64, 98, 111, 114

Reale, S.J., Frank, 160-1

Reavis, L.U., 66

Rebekah Hospital, 78

rector role in Jesuit universities, 48, 63, 124

Red Eagle, Eddy, 12

Reel, John, 38

Regis University: see Las Vegas College.

Reinert, S.J., Paul, 82, 111-2, 117-8, 121, 124-6, 129, 131, 140-4, 147, 152, 158, 174

Reiselman, Henry, 20

Relay for Life, 180-81

Rerum Novarum ("of revolutionary change," also: "Rights and Duties of Capital and Labor"), 65, 67, 104-105, 126

Reserve Officers' Training Corps (ROTC), 113, 143, 163

Rhodes, Mary, 11

Ring, Nancy McNeir, 97, 169

Ritter, Joseph, 69, 109

Roberts, Richard, 9

Robinson, Bradbury, 77

Robinson, S.J., Charles, 113

Robison, S.J., William, 95

Robyn, Alfred, 83

Rockhurst College/University, 48-9

Rocky Mountain Mission, 48-9, 206-7. See also DeSmet, Native Americans.

Rogers, S.J., William Banks, 50, 57, 63, 64, 78-80, 84-5, 89, 95, 117, 147

Rooney, S.J., Richard, 112

Roosevelt, Theodore, 78, 80

Roothaan, S.J., Jan, 27, 32, 35, 50

Rosati, Joseph, 12, 16, 22, 25, 49, 52

Ross, Anna, 83

Rothensteiner, John, 49

Ruddy, T. Michael, 169

Rueppel, S.J., George, 83, 98-9, 113

Ryan, John, 104

Ryan, F.S.M., Mary Jean, 159

Ryan, O'Neill, 83

SSM Health, 167, 178-9

Sabick, Michelle, 168

Sacred Heart Mission among the Coeur d'Alene (Cataldo, Idaho), 32-3, 46

Saint Louis University: charter, 28-9, 172; high school, 82, 86, 93, 95, 106

Saint Louis University Law Journal, 127

Saker, Julie, 147

San Ignacio Hall, 160

Saulnier, Edmund, 8-9, 22

Schaller, Molly, 180

Scheller, S.J., Aloysius, 164

Schlafly, Daniel, 148

Schloctermeyer, S.S.M., Mary Seraphia, 85

Schmandt, Henry, 109

Schoenmakers, S.J., John, 12

scholarships, 172

scholasticism, 100-101

Schruefer, S.S.M., Mary Aloysia, 85

Schumpeter, Joseph, 105

Schuschnigg, Kurt von, 127

Schwitalla, S.J., Alphonse, 82, 84, 95, 97, 106-7, 110, 150

Scott Hall, 157

Scott, Dred, 127

Scott, Joseph, 157

Scott, Loretta, 157

Searls, Eileen, 130

Sebesta, S.J., James, 168

segregation, 68-9, 108-9, 140-2

seismography, 82, 110-111

Sell, Scott, 168

Servary, John, 22

Seton, Elizabeth Ann, 10

Shaner, Michael, 169

Shannon, S.J., James, 82, 94, 106

Sharp-Shooter, The (student newspaper), 39

Shea, William, 148

Shedenhelm, Murray, 168

Sheldon Gallery, 162

Shelly v. Kraemer (1948), 141

Shepard, Elihu, 9, 22

Sherman, S.J., Thomas, 44

Sherman, William T., 44

Shyken, Jaye, 167

Sibert, Alayna, 170

Simeone, Joseph, 127

Simms, Margaret, 109

Sinclitico, Joseph, 127

Sisters of Charity, 10

Sisters of Loretto at the Foot of the Cross, 11, 12, 109

Sisters of St. Mary, 85, 95-7, 107. Later known as: Franciscan Sisters of Mary.

Sisters of the Sacred Heart, 10, 16, 23

Slavery, 17, 18, 20, 21, 23, 25, 52-4, 68; "neo-slavery," 21, 68

Slosar, John, 164, 169

SLUCare, 167, 178

Sly, William, 148

Smedts, S.J., John Baptist, 17, 20

Smith, Alice, 145

Smith, Clemmie, 109

Smith, James, 175

Smith, Jonathan, 177

Smith, Samuel, 9

Smith, Sylvester, 109

Smith, S.J., Thurber Montgomery, 150

Smurfit Irish Law Center, 130

soccer, 118-119

Social Service (School of), 86, 104, 109, 124, 138, 164

Social Work (School of), 147, 164, 171

Society of Jesus, 3, 5, 10-12, 17- 21, 25-7, 33, 37, 48-50, 57, 63, 65, 67-9, 78, 98, 104, 105, 108, 110, 111, 124-126, 132, 148, 173, 175, 178. See also General Congregations.

Sodality Hall, 94-5

Sodality of Our Lady, 102

Sorin, C.S.C., Edward, 50

South Kinloch (Missouri), 68

Spalding, John Lancaster, 61

St. Elizabeth's (parish and church), 52, 68, 102-103, 106, 108-109

St. Francis Xavier Church (built 1841), 37, 38, 41, 52, 56-7, 68; (built 1884), 41, 67, 73, 86-7, 90, 124, 141, 152, 176

St. Ignatius (later John Carroll University), 48-9

St. John's College (Toledo, Ohio), 48-9

St. John's Hospital, 78

St. Joseph's College, 48-9

St. Louis Archdiocesan Commission on Human Rights, 127

St. Louis (city of), 52-4, 68, 118-9, 123-4, 140-2, 154-5, 164-5, 177, 178; Midtown region, 125, 147, 154-5, 158. See also Pain-court.

St. Louis College (later Saint Louis University), 5, 7-12, 16, 22-5, 29, 48-9. See also individual entries.

St. Louis Conference on Religion and Race, 127

St. Louis Globe Democrat, 61, 63, 78, 122-3, 167 (image of Dr. Broun)

St. Louis Jesuits (music group), 149

St. Louis Medical and Surgical Journal, 42, 46

St. Louis Medical Society of Missouri, 43

St. Louis Post-Dispatch, 158, 109, 177 (image)

St. Louis Red Stockings, 41, 60

St. Louis Republican, 37

St. Louis Review, 148

St. Louis Urban League, 127

St. Malachy's, 108-9

St. Mary of the Lake Seminary (Mundelein, Illinois), 48-9, 206

St. Mary's College (Baltimore, MD), 8, 10

St. Mary's College (St. Marys, Kansas), 48-50, 64, 105, 144, 206

St. Mary's Infirmary, 78, 95, 97, 106-7

St. Regis: see Florissant, Missouri

St. Stanislaus Seminary, 12, 17, 21-3, 32-3, 41, 48-9, 50, 52, 68, 102, 106, 108, 112, 115, 172-3, 206

St. Stephen's Mission (Fremont County, Wyoming), 48-9, 68-9, 206

Stanton, Edwin, 32

Stewart, Bob, 119

Strahan, Charles, 20

Strauss, Leon, 154

Stuart, Christina, 11

Student Bar Association, 127

Stump, Eleonore, 149, 171

Sullivan, Patrick, 9

Sullivant, S.J., Raymond, 117, 137

Summer School of Catholic Action, 102

Taeusch, Carl F., 115

Taft, William Howard, 77

Tams, Ernst, 110

Technology (Institute), 86, 113, 138. See also Parks College of Engineering, Aviation and Technology

Tekakwitha, Kateri, 12

Telegraphy (School), 92

Tenet Healthcare, 167

Thakur, Ratna, 167

Theobald, Stephen, 109

Theology (theological studies), 9, 22, 50, 67, 78, 80, 89, 105, 128, 144, 148-9, 169, 171

Thérèse of Lisieux (Saint), "Little Flower," 98-9

Third Plenary Council of Baltimore, 68-9

Thomas, Lewis Foulk, 38

Thompson, Ralph, 84

Thought, 100

Thro, S.J., Linus, 151

Timmermans, S.J., Peter Joseph, 20

Tongiorgi, S.J., Salvatore, 61

Toro, Enrique, 167

Trost, Tom, 119

Trudeau, Jean Baptiste, 16

Truman, Harry S., 131

Tucker, Raymond, 141

Twomey, S.J., Louis, 100, 103

typhus fever, 113

U.S. Center for Disease Control, 164, 167

Union of Socialist Soviet Republics (USSR), 136

Universidad Pontificia Comillas, 137

"University in Print," 104

University News, The (student newspaper), 88, 91, 94, 100, 104-5, 108, 112, 114-5, 123, 141

University of Alcalá, 37

University of Missouri, 84, 109, 110

University of Notre Dame, 50, 64, 89

University of Paris, 37

usury, 105

Van Assche, S.J., Judocus, 17, 20

Van Buren, Martin, 39

Van de Velde, S.J., James, 17, 27, 52

Van der Heyden, S.J., W.B., 52

Van Quickenborne, S.J., Charles, 12, 13, 20, 22, 25, 49, 180

Van Sweevelt, S.J., Peter Judocus, 40

Varsity Breeze, 38, 89

Varsity Song, 83, 90

Vashon High School, 123

Vatican Film Library, 105, 131-4

Vatican II (Second Ecumenical Vatican Council), 124-5, 128, 149

Vaughn, Arthur, 109

Velazquez, Sergo, 119

Verhaegen Hall, 73

Verhaegen, S.J., Peter, 5, 17, 20, 21, 25, 27, 29, 30, 32, 35, 36, 43, 44, 50, 52, 124, 172

Verhaegen, Thierry, 172

Verreydt, S.J., Felix, 12, 17, 20, 21

Vespre, S.J., Francis, 52

Vietnam, 143

Villalonga, S.J., Joachim, 80

Vincentians, 9

Vining, Robert, 127

Virgil, 61, 89, 132

Vita, Paul, 160-1

Vitali, C.P., Theodore, 151

Voss, Michael-John, 165

Walz, Bruce, 148

WEW (campus radio station), 98, 104, 120

WHO (World Health Organization) 110, 164

WISH (Women and Infant Substance Abuse Help), 167

Wade, Festus, 78, 92

Wade, S.J., William, 151

Waide, John, 60, 119, 172

Walsh, Peter, 22

Wangard, Maureen, 117, 125

Washington University, 45, 92, 129, 154

Waugh, Evelyn, 120

Weathers, Henry Hudson, 109

Weber, S.J., Leo, 144-5

Webster College, 95, 109

Webster, Daniel, 39

Weixlmann, Joseph, 176

Wendel, George, 142

Weninger, S.J., Francis, 27, 54

Wesleyan Cemetery, 127

West Pine Street, 123, 152-3

Weston Jesuit School of Theology, 128

White, Norman, 178

White, Raymond, 164-5

White Marsh: see Maryland Province.

Wilkins, Roy, 126

Williams, Ethel, 109

Williams, Loren, 145

Williams, Walter Dakin, 127

Wilson, Mardell, 170

Witherspoon, Fredda, 109

Wolff, Michael, 164

Wood, Margaret, 83

Woods, William Evans, 98

Woodstock Theological Seminary, 148

Wool, Marvin and Harlene, Center, 158

World War I, 92-3

World War II, 48, 111, 113-15, 119, 127, 136

World's Fair (1904), 57, 66, 78-81

Xavier University, 48-9, 64

Yalem, Charles, 138

Yates, S.J., James, 36

Young Catholic Crusaders, 108

Younge, Walter A., 109

Zehnder, Kenneth, 167

Zuercher, S.J., Joseph, 109

"WE SHALL GO GLADLY."

IGNATIUS OF LOYOLA, 1538